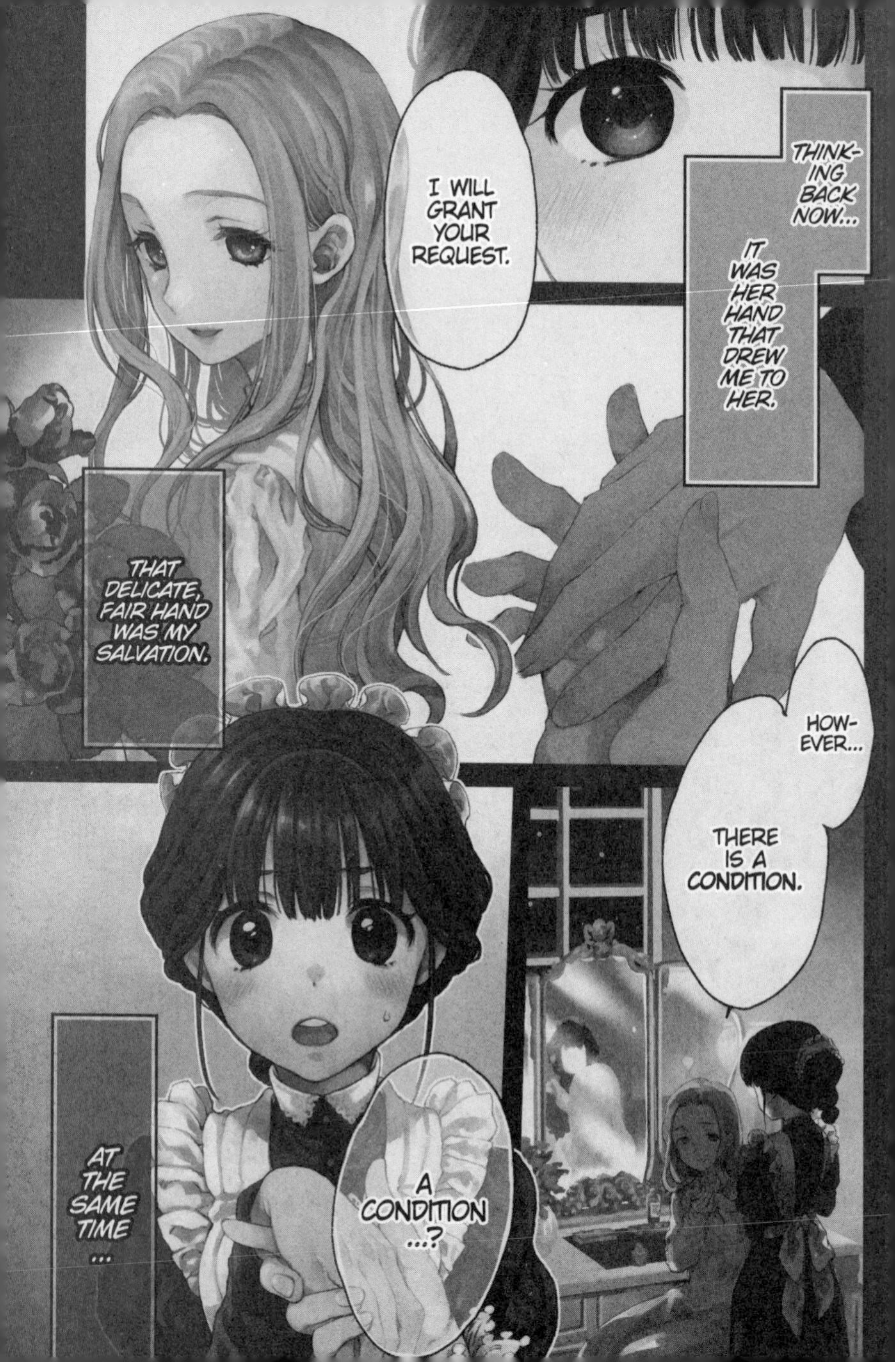
THINKING BACK NOW...
IT WAS HER HAND THAT DREW ME TO HER.
I WILL GRANT YOUR REQUEST.
THAT DELICATE, FAIR HAND WAS MY SALVATION.
HOWEVER...
THERE IS A CONDITION.
A CONDITION ...?
AT THE SAME TIME ...

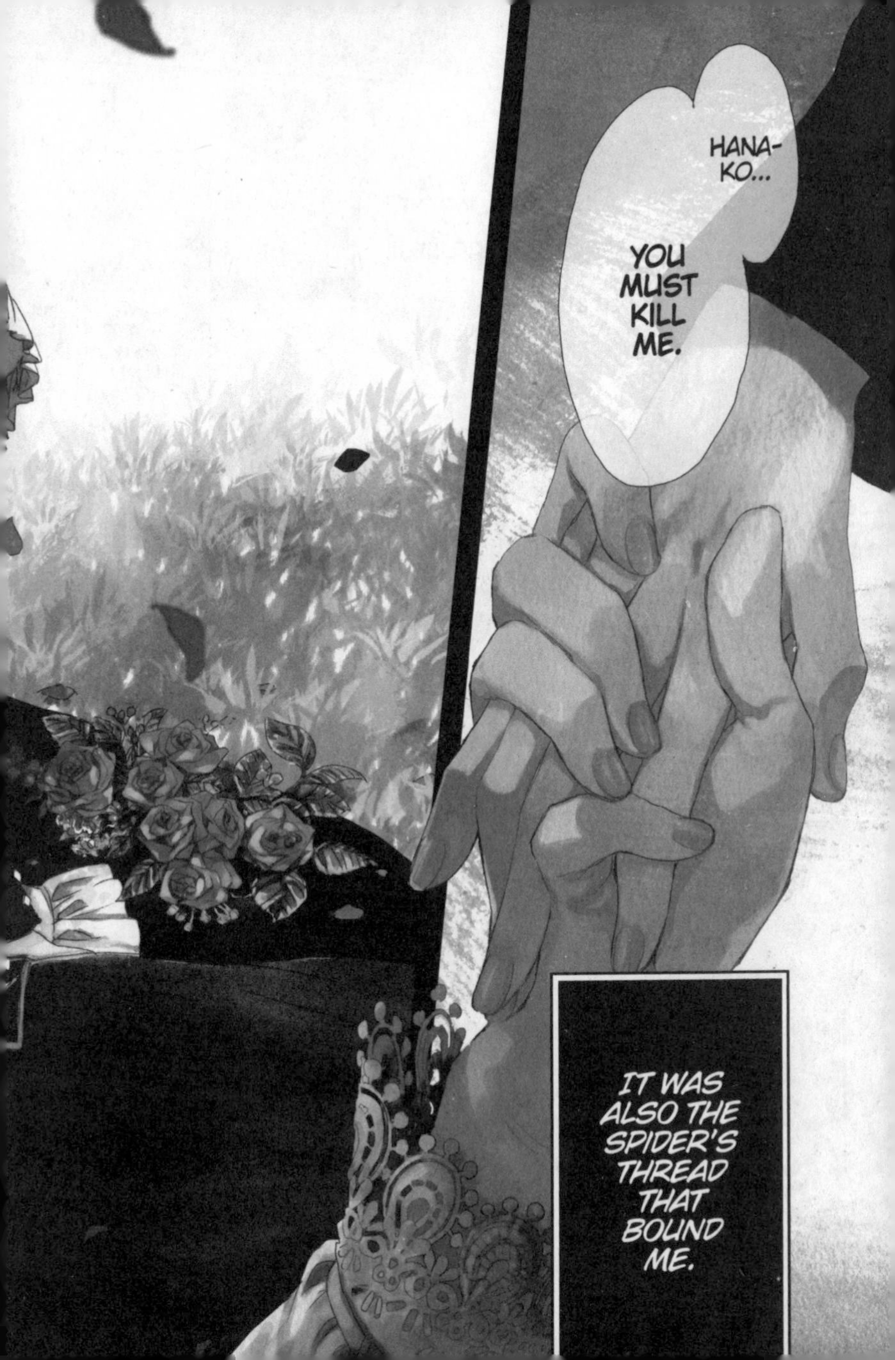
HANA-KO...
YOU MUST KILL ME.
IT WAS ALSO THE SPIDER'S THREAD THAT BOUND ME.

{ Chapter 1 }
The Beginning of Farewell

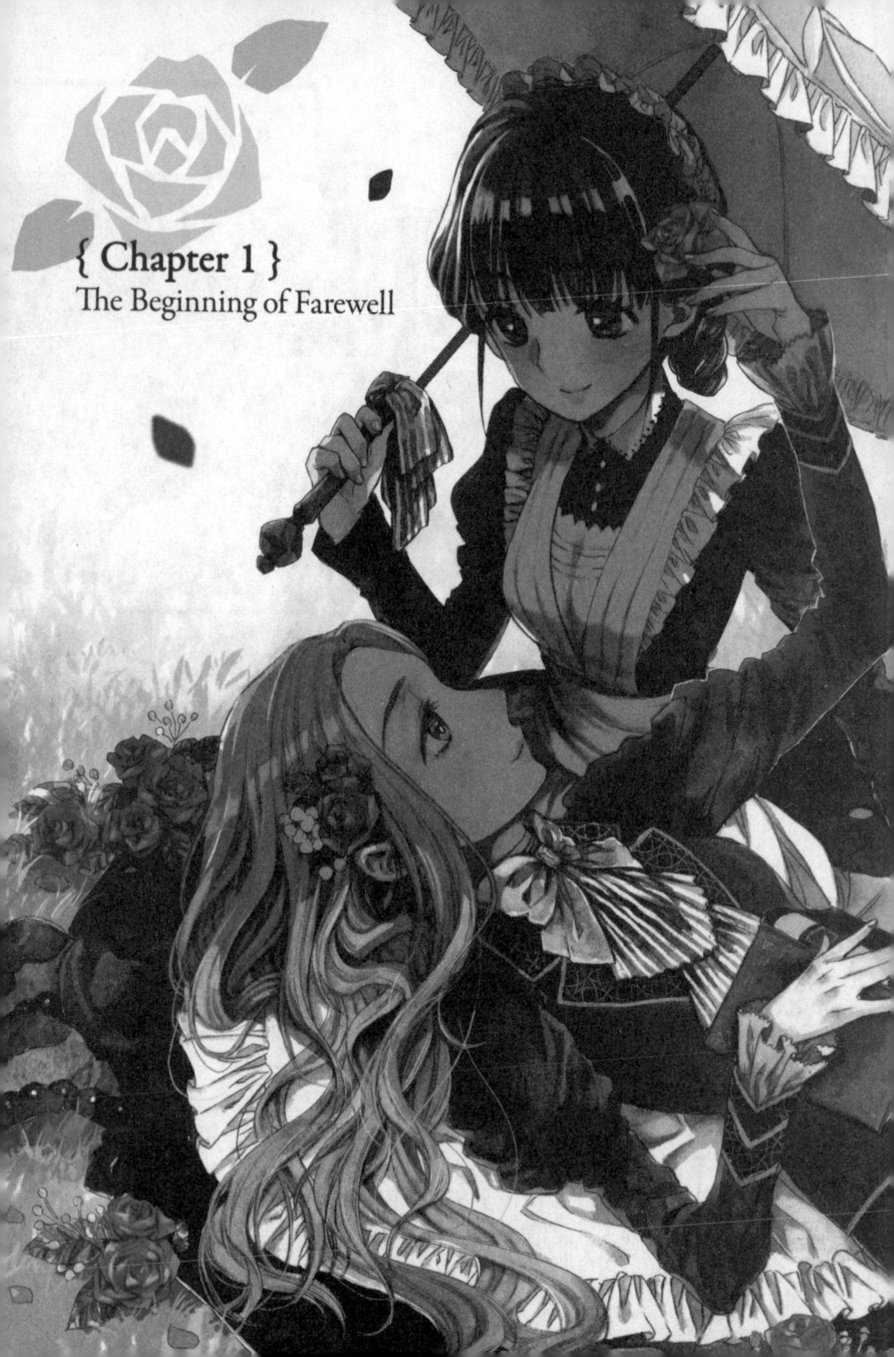

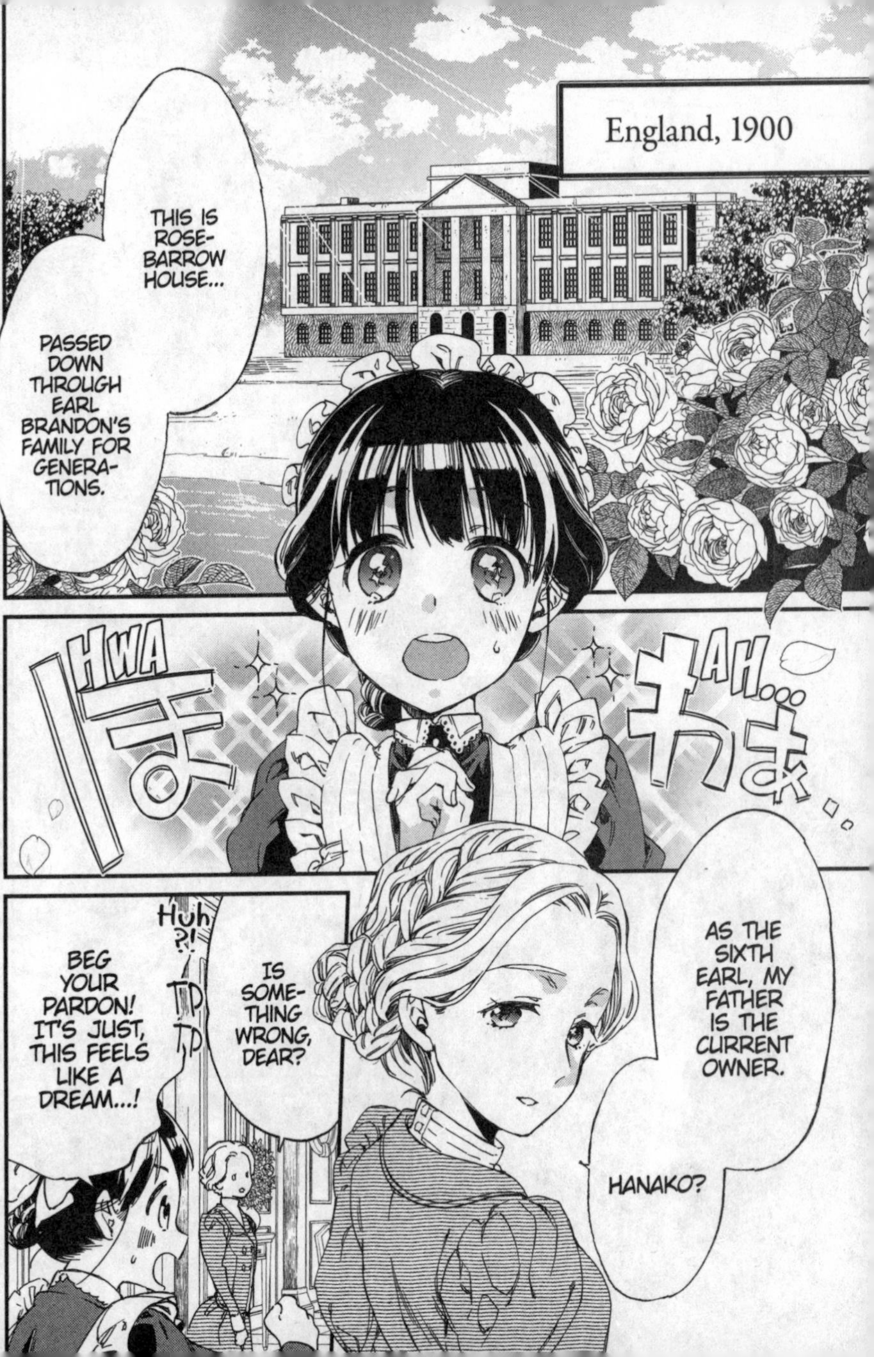
England, 1900
THIS IS ROSE-BARROW HOUSE...
PASSED DOWN THROUGH EARL BRANDON'S FAMILY FOR GENERATIONS.
HWA
AH...
AS THE SIXTH EARL, MY FATHER IS THE CURRENT OWNER.
HANAKO?
IS SOMETHING WRONG, DEAR?
Huh?!
TP TP
BEG YOUR PARDON! IT'S JUST, THIS FEELS LIKE A DREAM...!

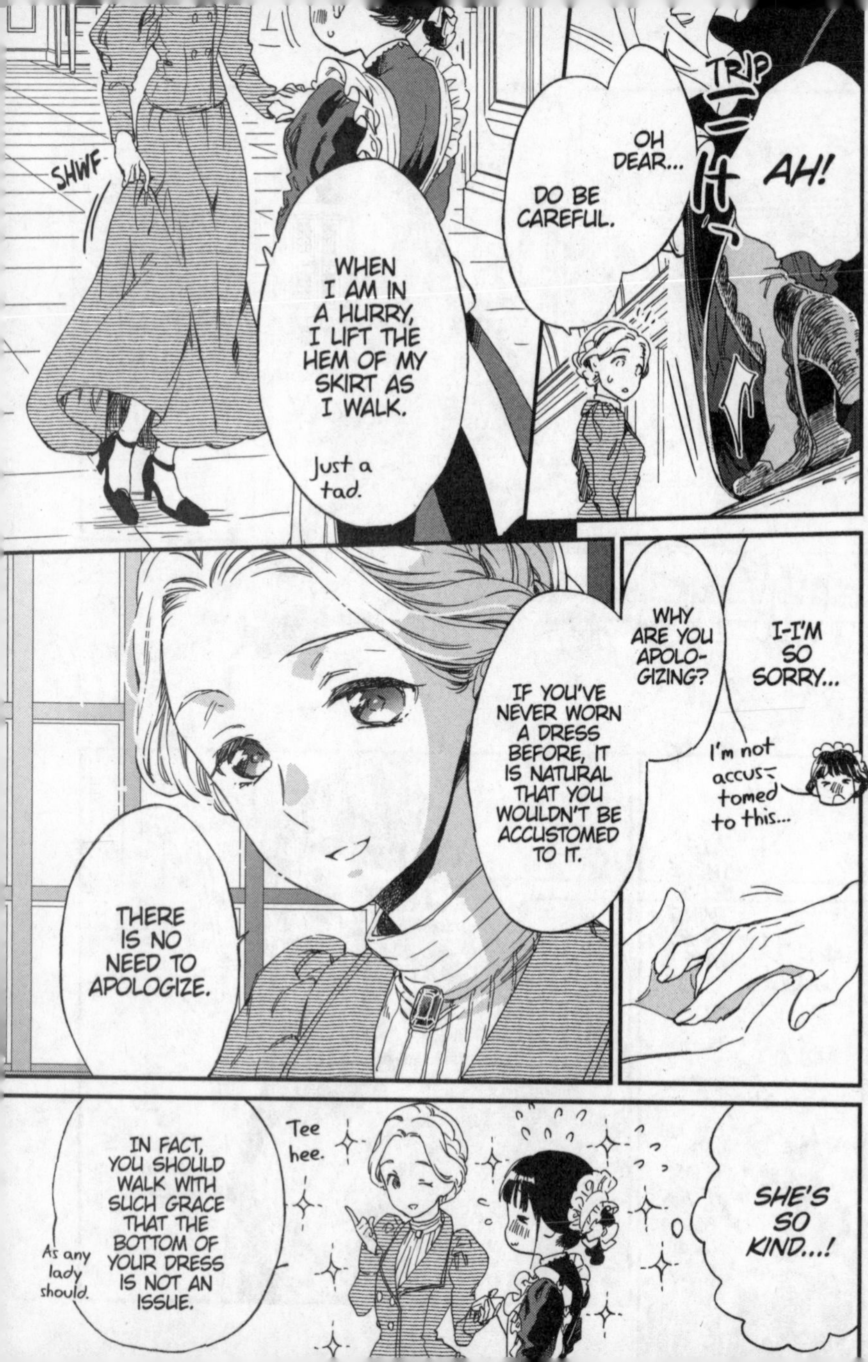
TRIP
AH!
OH DEAR... DO BE CAREFUL.
SHWF
WHEN I AM IN A HURRY, I LIFT THE HEM OF MY SKIRT AS I WALK.
Just a tad.
I-I'M SO SORRY...
I'm not accus-tomed to this...
WHY ARE YOU APOLOGIZING?
IF YOU'VE NEVER WORN A DRESS BEFORE, IT IS NATURAL THAT YOU WOULDN'T BE ACCUSTOMED TO IT.
THERE IS NO NEED TO APOLOGIZE.
SHE'S SO KIND...!
Tee hee.
IN FACT, YOU SHOULD WALK WITH SUCH GRACE THAT THE BOTTOM OF YOUR DRESS IS NOT AN ISSUE.
As any lady should.

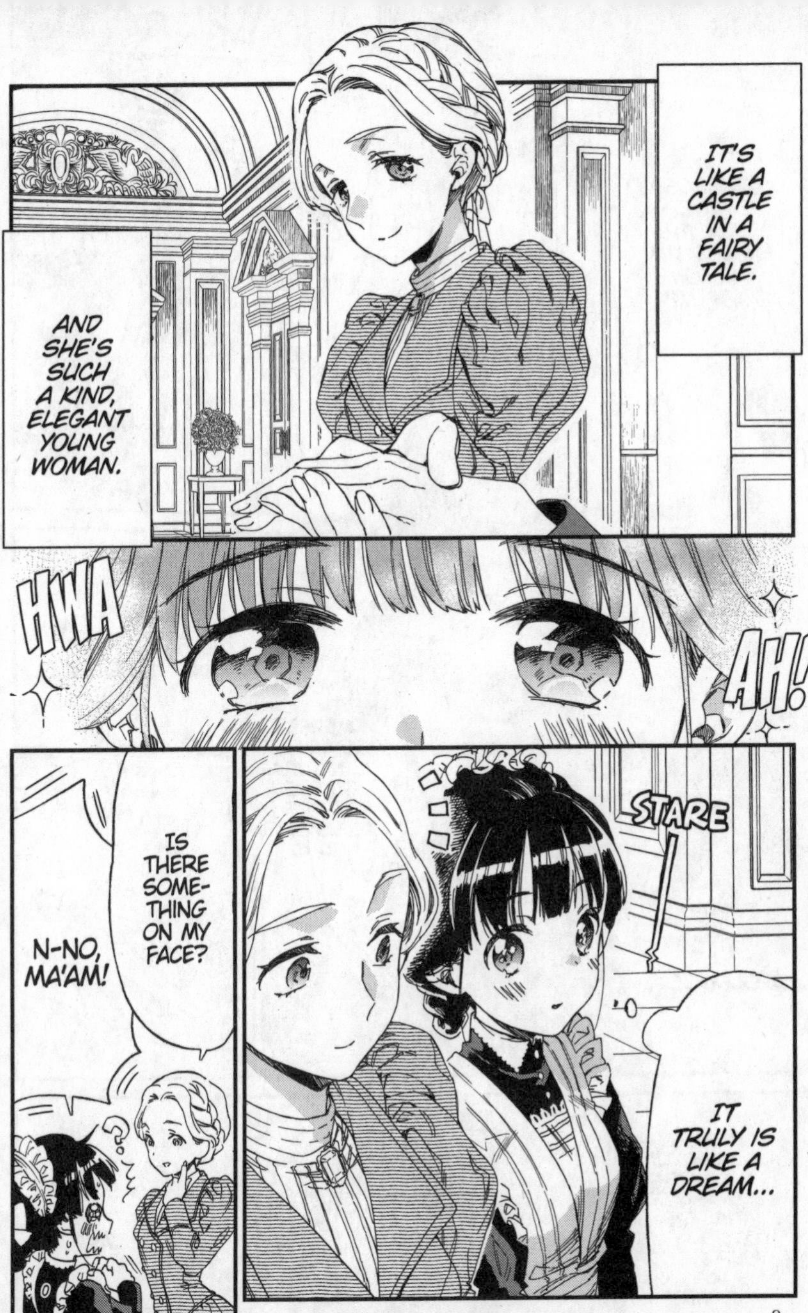
IT'S LIKE A CASTLE IN A FAIRY TALE.
AND SHE'S SUCH A KIND, ELEGANT YOUNG WOMAN.
HWA
AH!
STARE
IT TRULY IS LIKE A DREAM...
IS THERE SOMETHING ON MY FACE?
N-NO, MA'AM!

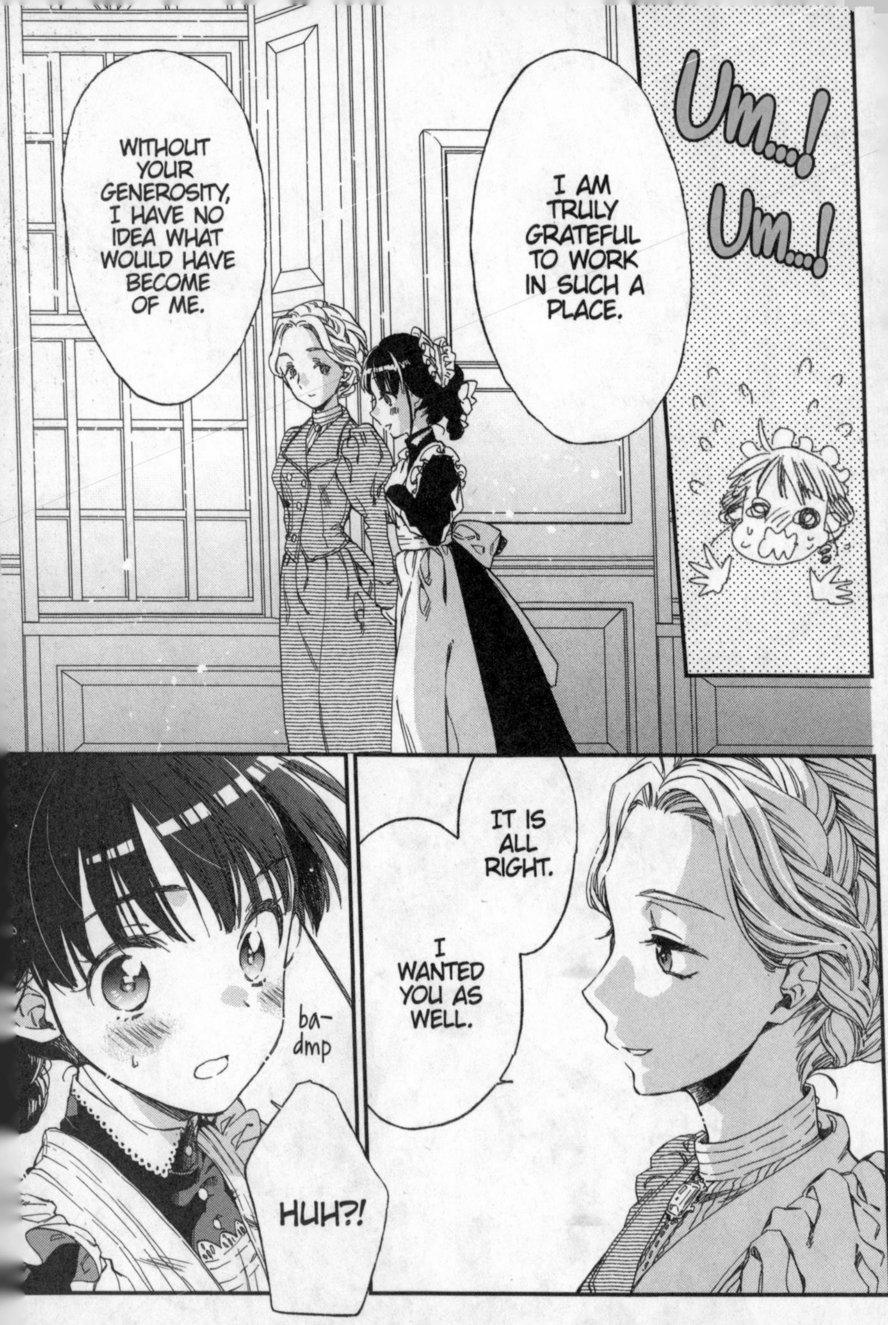
I AM TRULY GRATEFUL TO WORK IN SUCH A PLACE.
WITHOUT YOUR GENEROSITY, I HAVE NO IDEA WHAT WOULD HAVE BECOME OF ME.
Um...! Um...!
IT IS ALL RIGHT.
I WANTED YOU AS WELL.
ba-dmp
HUH?!

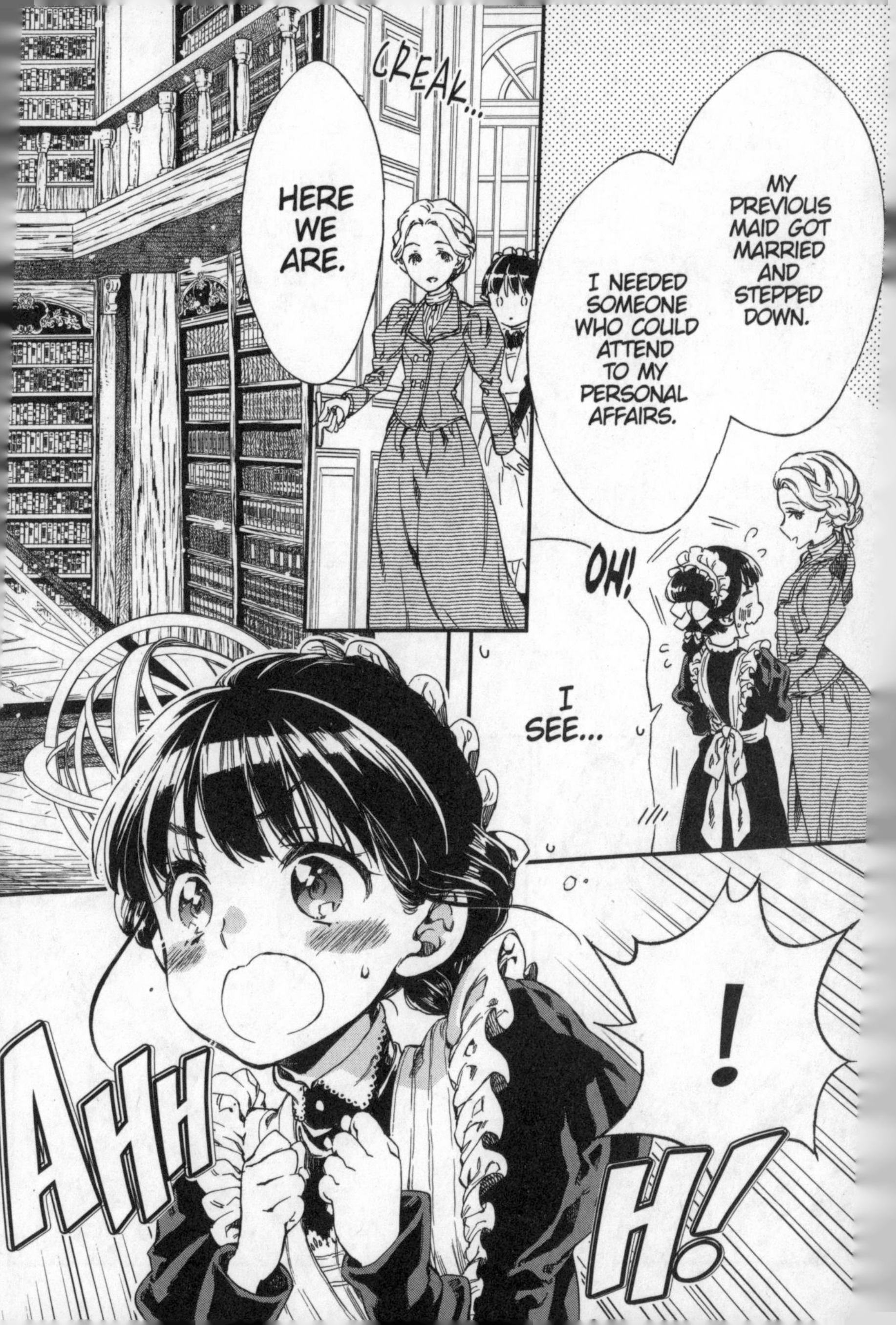
MY PREVIOUS MAID GOT MARRIED AND STEPPED DOWN.
I NEEDED SOMEONE WHO COULD ATTEND TO MY PERSONAL AFFAIRS.
OH!
I SEE...
CREAK...
HERE WE ARE.
!
AHHH!

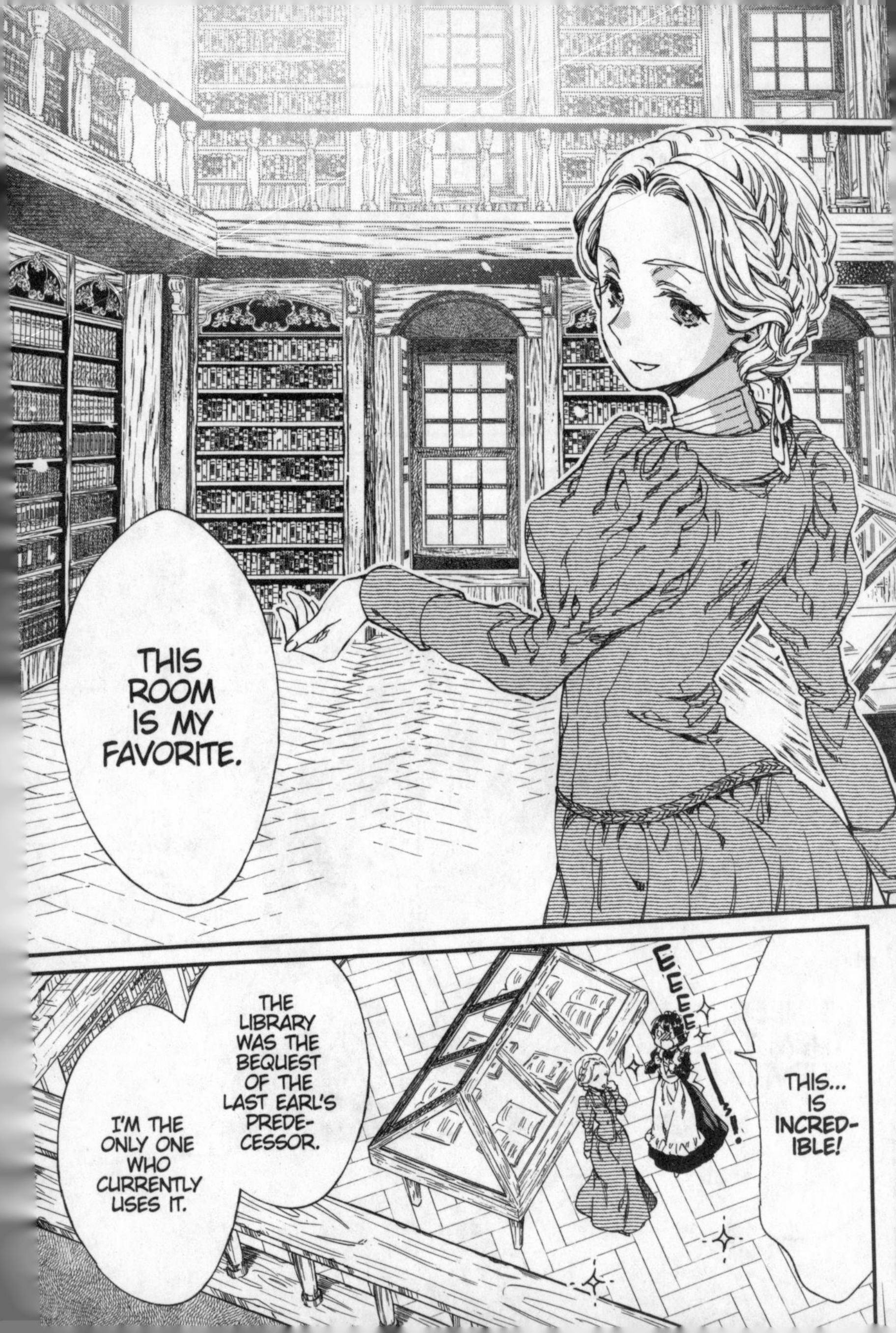
THIS ROOM IS MY FAVORITE.
THIS... IS INCREDIBLE!
EEEEE—!!
THE LIBRARY WAS THE BEQUEST OF THE LAST EARL'S PREDE-CESSOR.
I'M THE ONLY ONE WHO CURRENTLY USES IT.

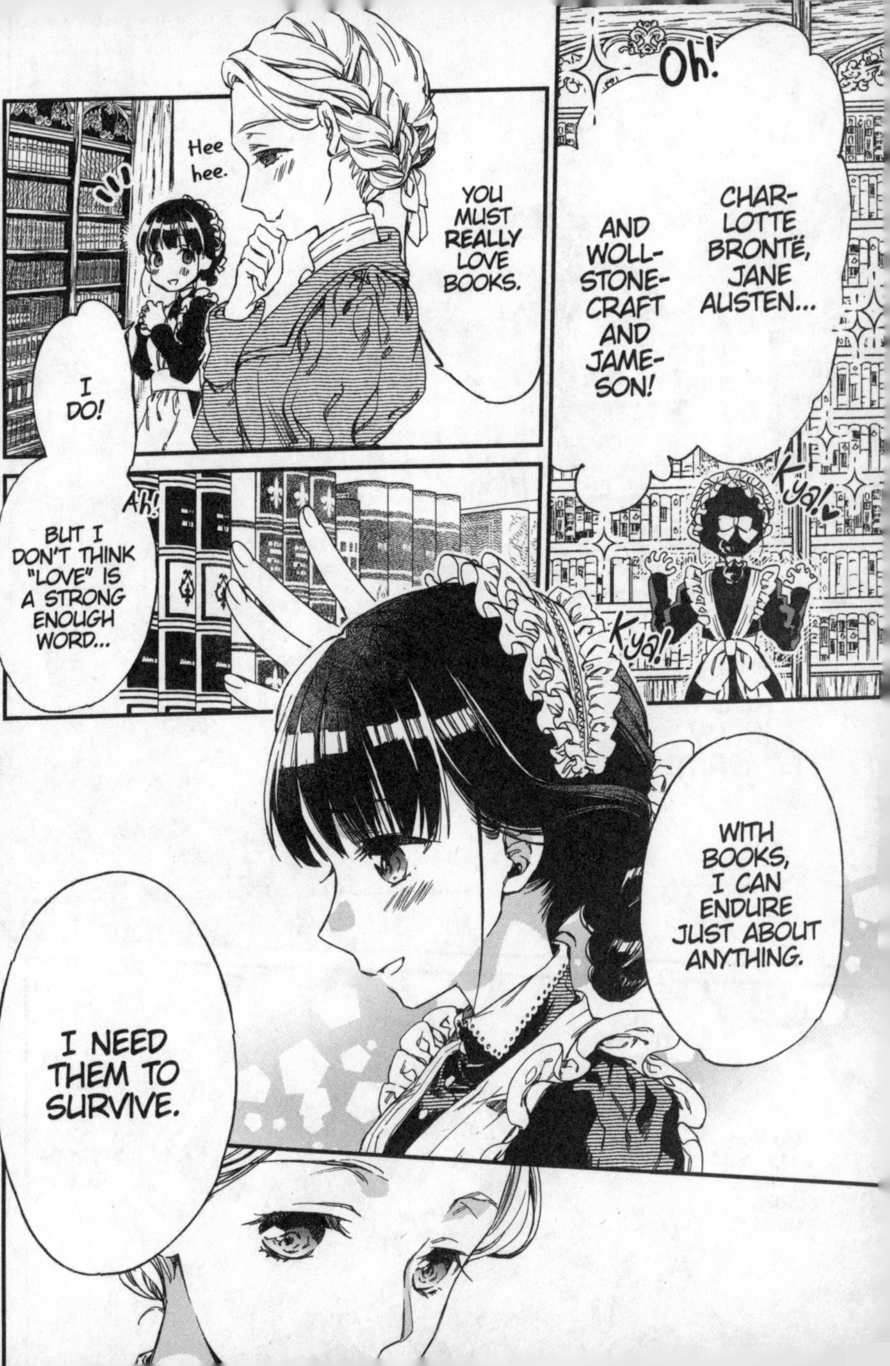
Oh!
CHAR-LOTTE BRONTË, JANE AUSTEN...
AND WOLL-STONE-CRAFT AND JAME-SON!
Kya!
Kya!
Hee hee.
YOU MUST REALLY LOVE BOOKS.
I DO!
Ah!
BUT I DON'T THINK "LOVE" IS A STRONG ENOUGH WORD...
WITH BOOKS, I CAN ENDURE JUST ABOUT ANYTHING.
I NEED THEM TO SURVIVE.

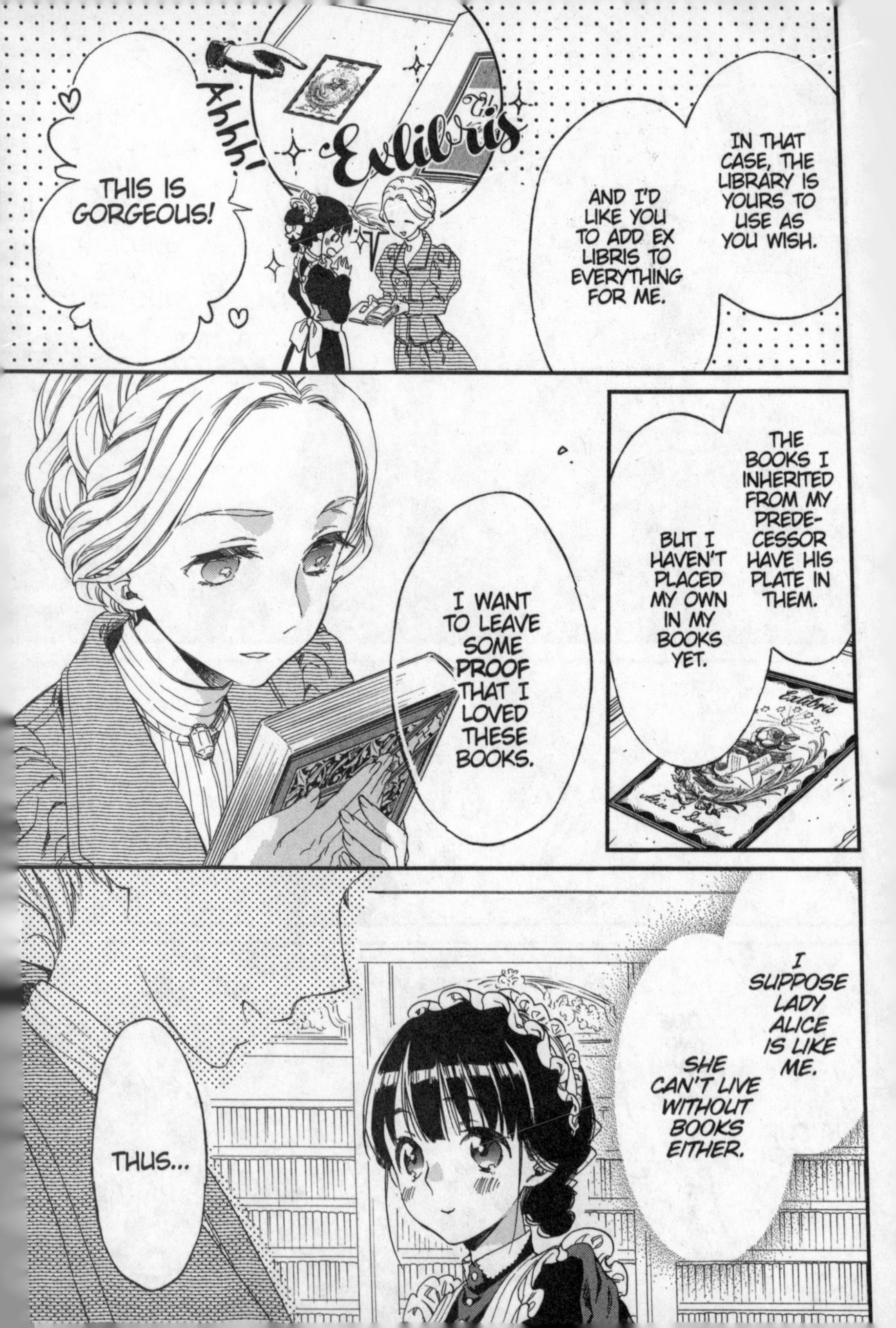
IN THAT CASE, THE LIBRARY IS YOURS TO USE AS YOU WISH.
AND I'D LIKE YOU TO ADD EX LIBRIS TO EVERYTHING FOR ME.
Exlibris
Ahhh!
THIS IS GORGEOUS!
THE BOOKS I INHERITED FROM MY PREDE-CESSOR HAVE HIS PLATE IN THEM.
BUT I HAVEN'T PLACED MY OWN IN MY BOOKS YET.
Exlibris
I WANT TO LEAVE SOME PROOF THAT I LOVED THESE BOOKS.
I SUPPOSE LADY ALICE IS LIKE ME.
SHE CAN'T LIVE WITHOUT BOOKS EITHER.
THUS...

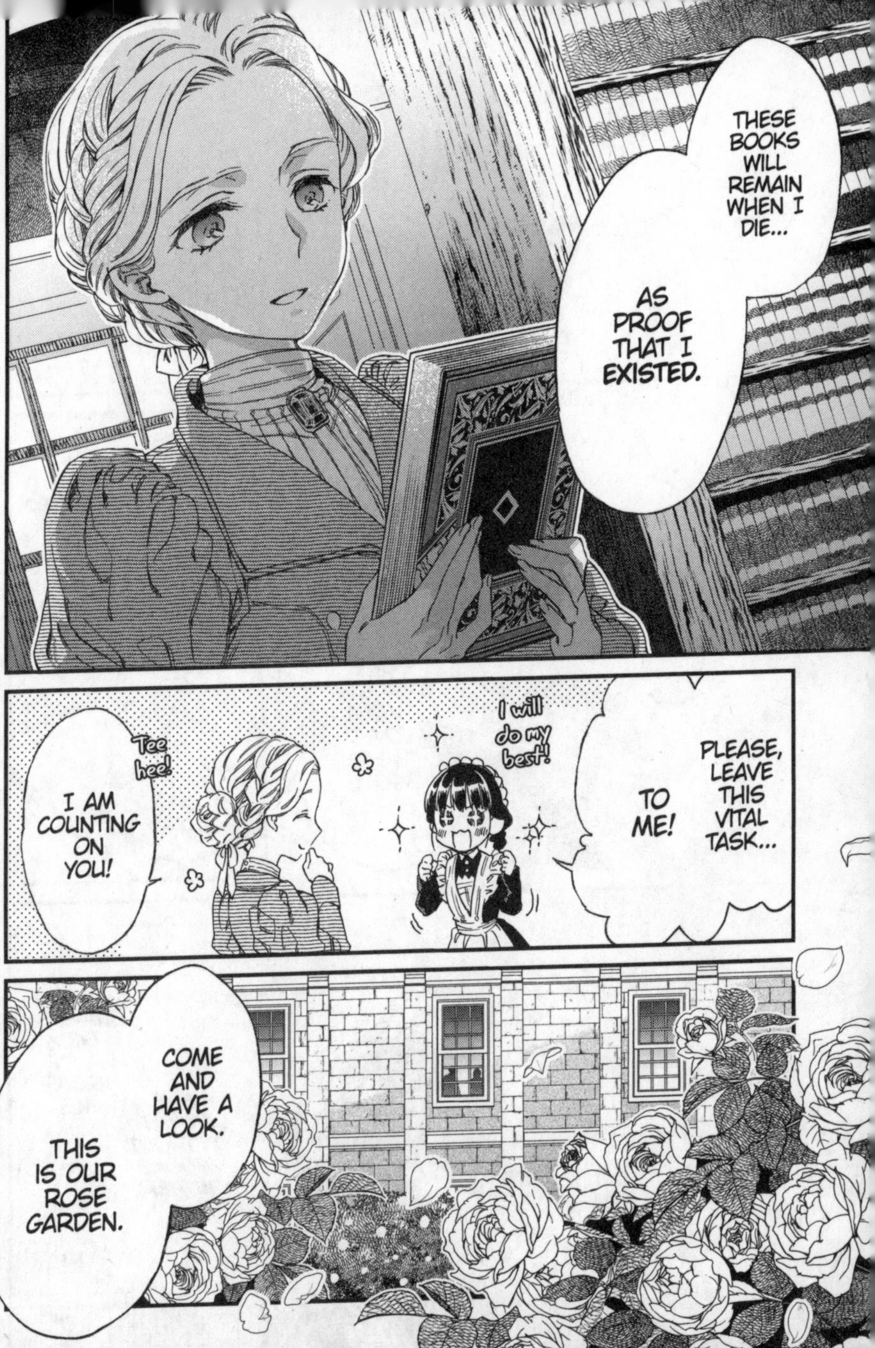
THESE BOOKS WILL REMAIN WHEN I DIE...
AS PROOF THAT I EXISTED.
PLEASE, LEAVE THIS VITAL TASK...
TO ME!
I will do my best!
Tee hee!
I AM COUNTING ON YOU!
COME AND HAVE A LOOK.
THIS IS OUR ROSE GARDEN.

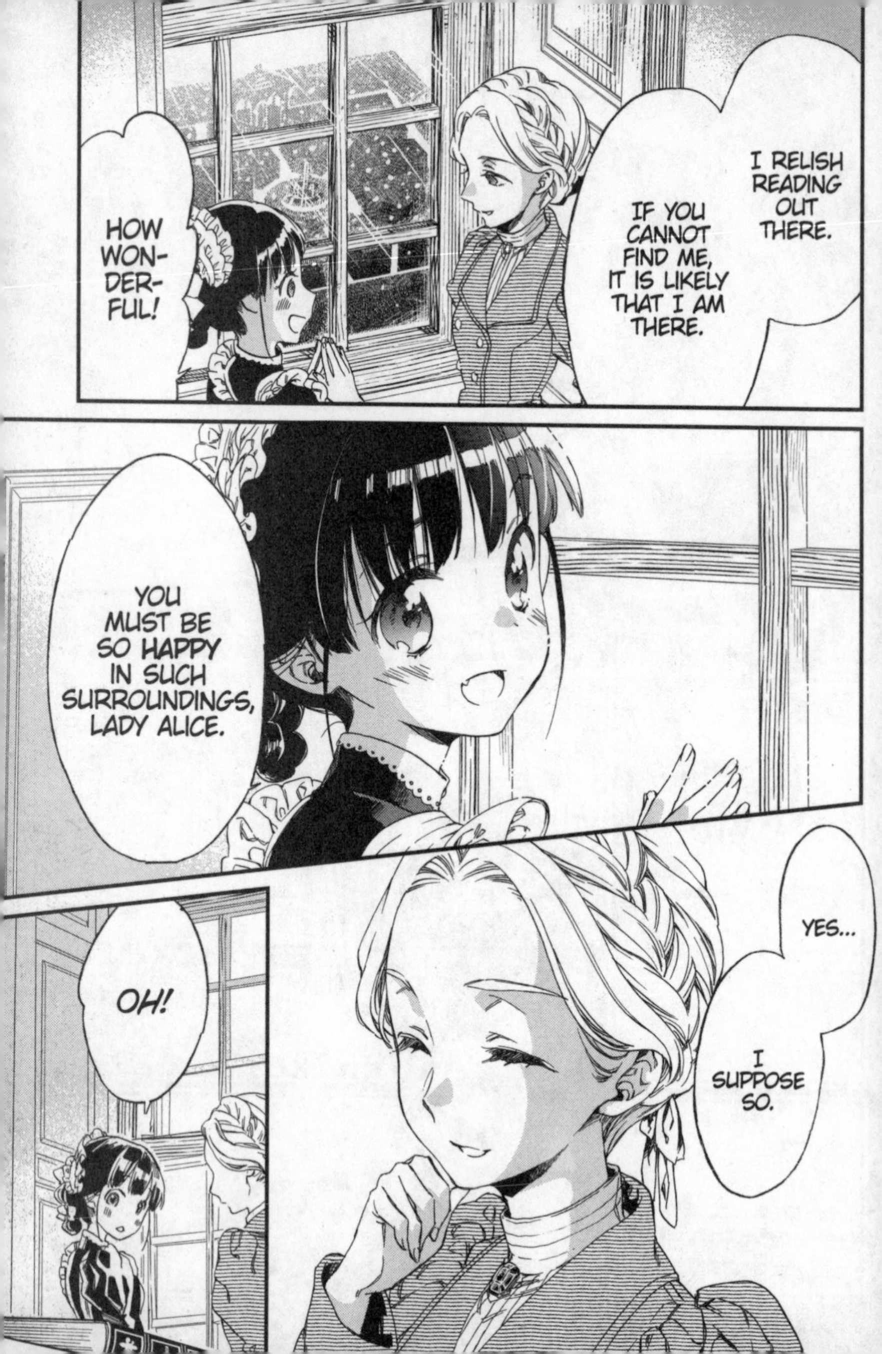
I RELISH READING OUT THERE.
IF YOU CANNOT FIND ME, IT IS LIKELY THAT I AM THERE.
HOW WON-DER-FUL!
YOU MUST BE SO HAPPY IN SUCH SURROUNDINGS, LADY ALICE.
YES...
I SUPPOSE SO.
OH!

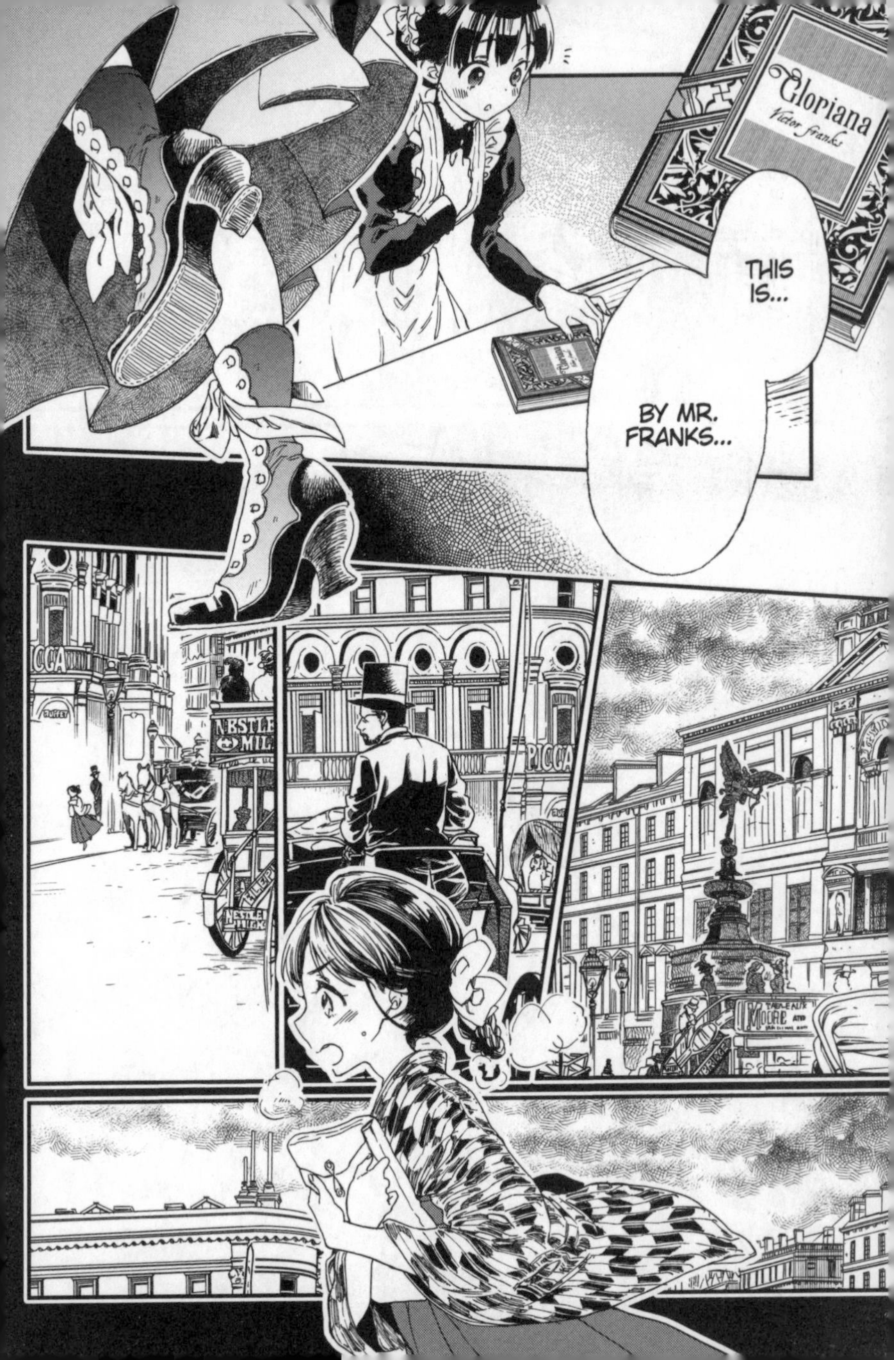
Gloriana
Victor Franks
THIS IS... BY MR. FRANKS...

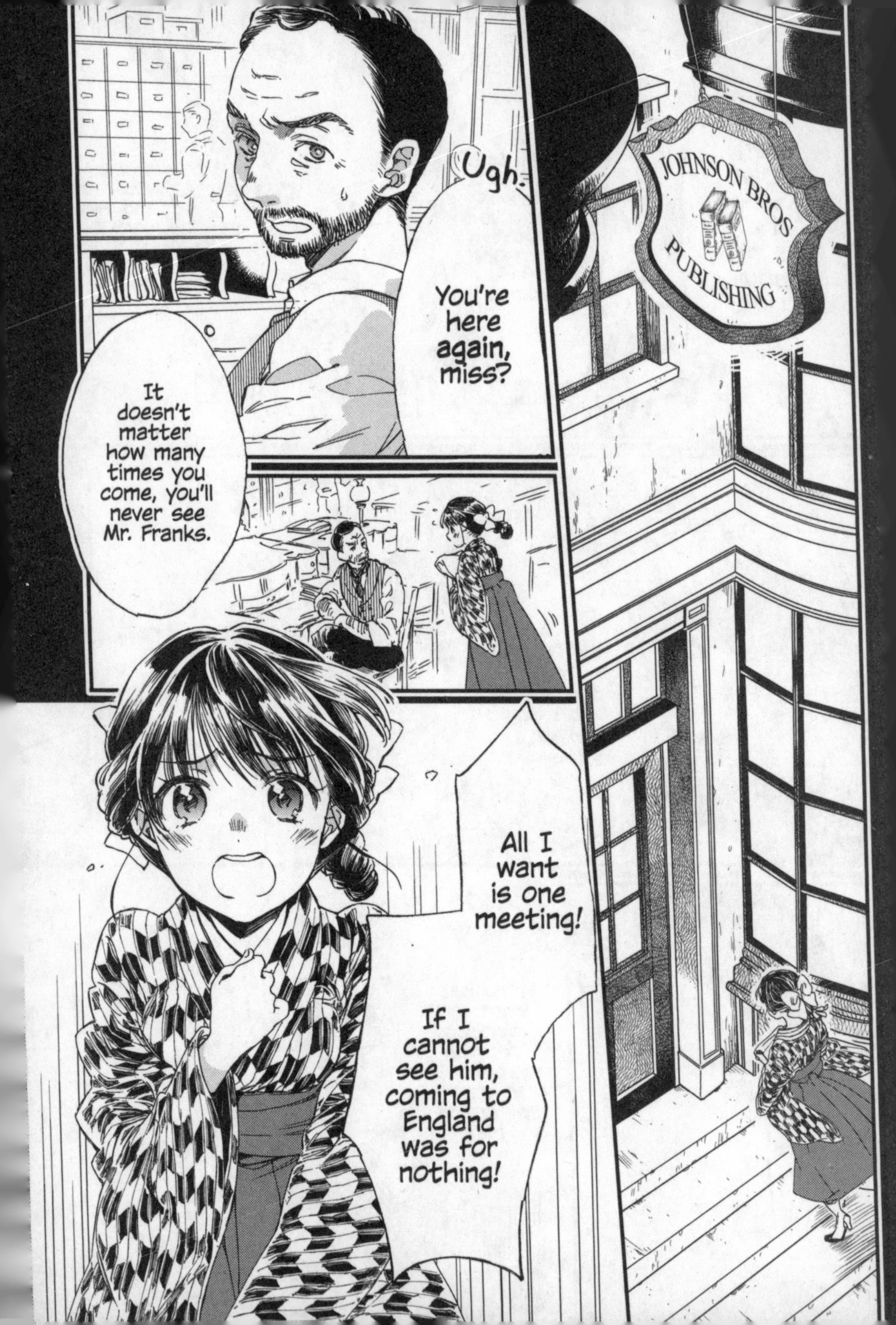
JOHNSON BROS PUBLISHING
Ugh.
You're here again, miss?
It doesn't matter how many times you come, you'll never see Mr. Franks.
All I want is one meeting!
If I cannot see him, coming to England was for nothing!

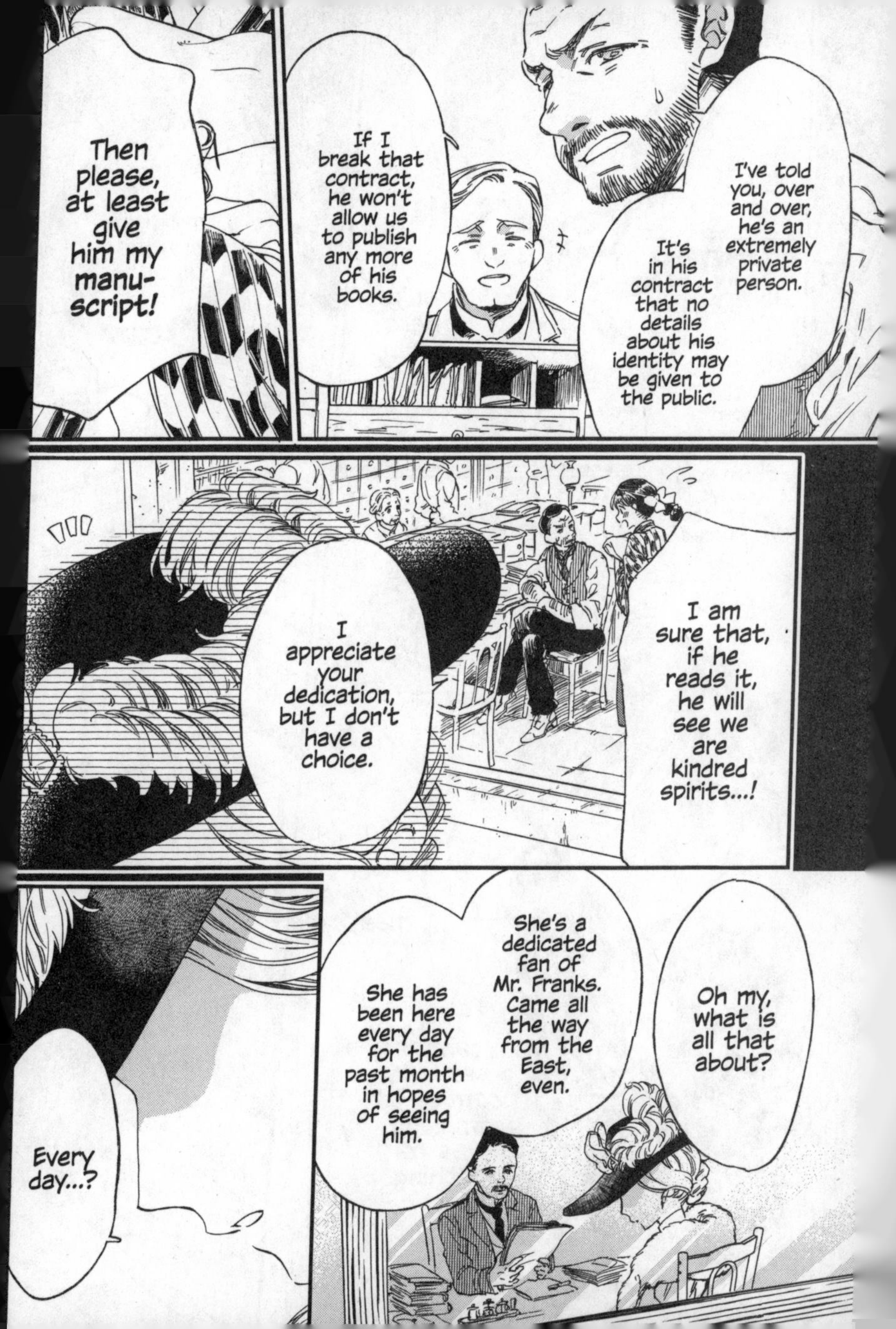
I've told you, over and over, he's an extremely private person.
It's in his contract that no details about his identity may be given to the public.
If I break that contract, he won't allow us to publish any more of his books.
Then please, at least give him my manu-script!
I am sure that, if he reads it, he will see we are kindred spirits...!
I appreciate your dedication, but I don't have a choice.
Oh my, what is all that about?
She's a dedicated fan of Mr. Franks. Came all the way from the East, even.
She has been here every day for the past month in hopes of seeing him.
Every day...?

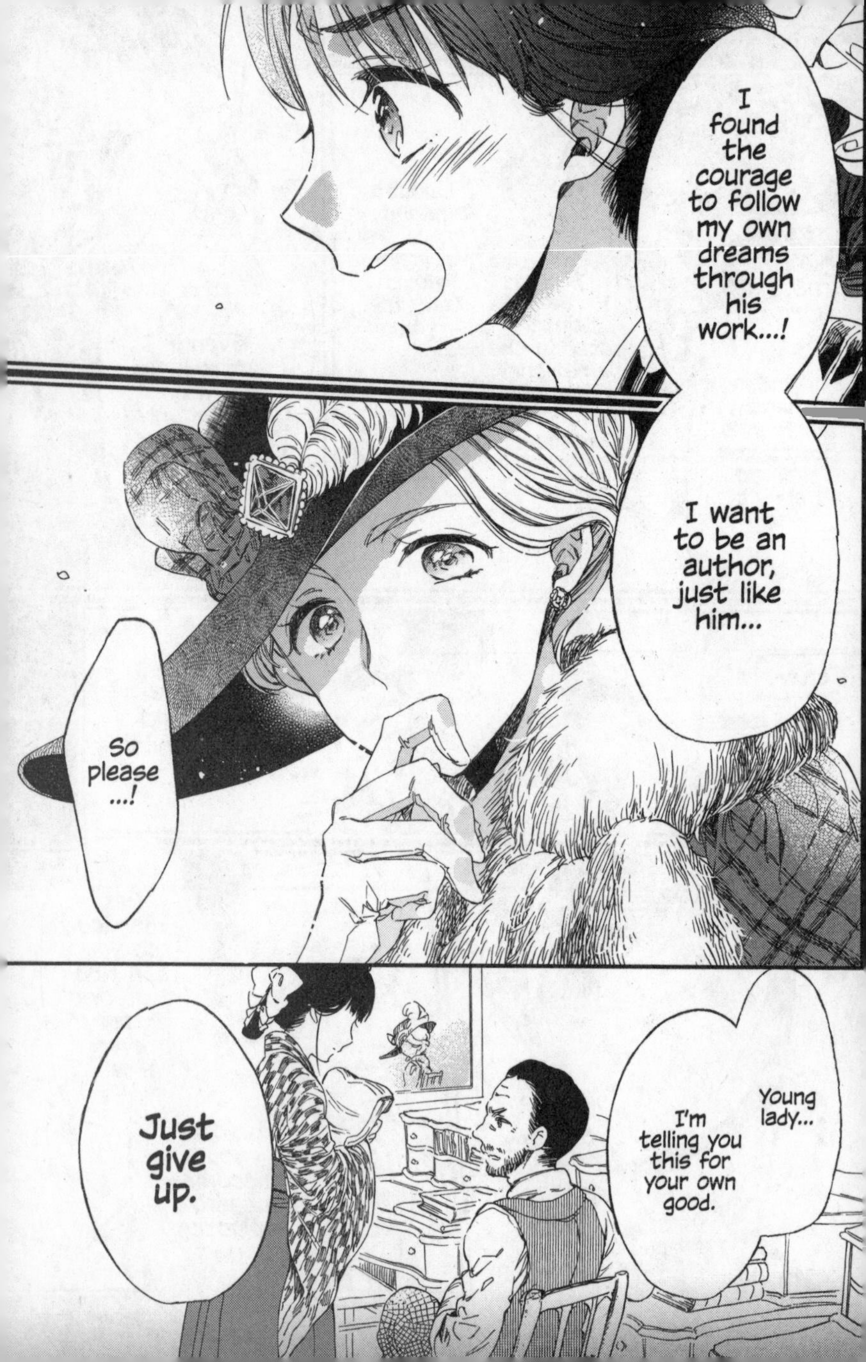
I found the courage to follow my own dreams through his work...!
I want to be an author, just like him...
So please ...!
Young lady...
I'm telling you this for your own good.
Just give up.

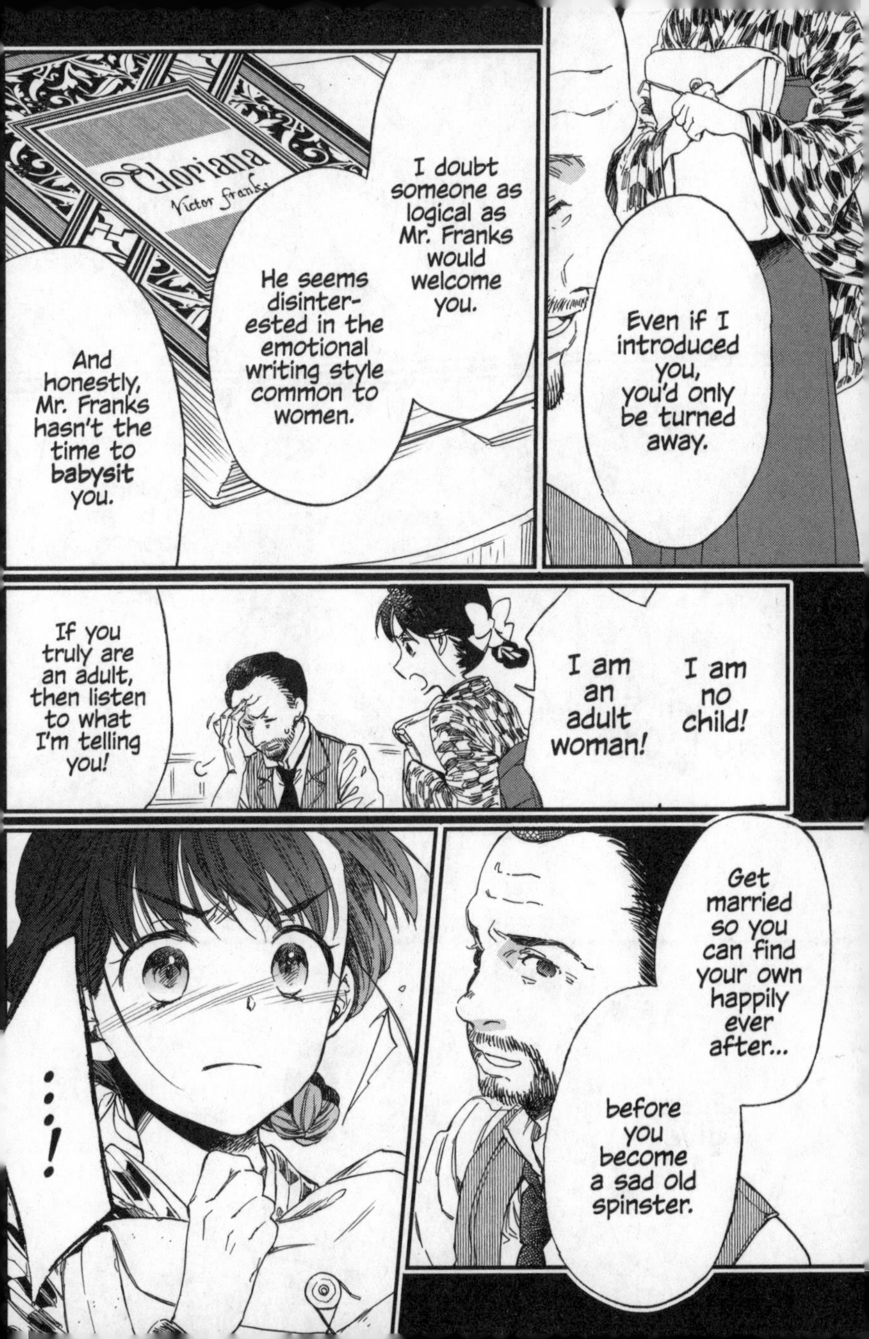
Even if I introduced you, you'd only be turned away.
Gloriana
Victor frank
I doubt someone as logical as Mr. Franks would welcome you.
He seems disinterested in the emotional writing style common to women.
And honestly, Mr. Franks hasn't the time to babysit you.
I am no child!
I am an adult woman!
If you truly are an adult, then listen to what I'm telling you!
Get married so you can find your own happily ever after...
before you become a sad old spinster.
...!

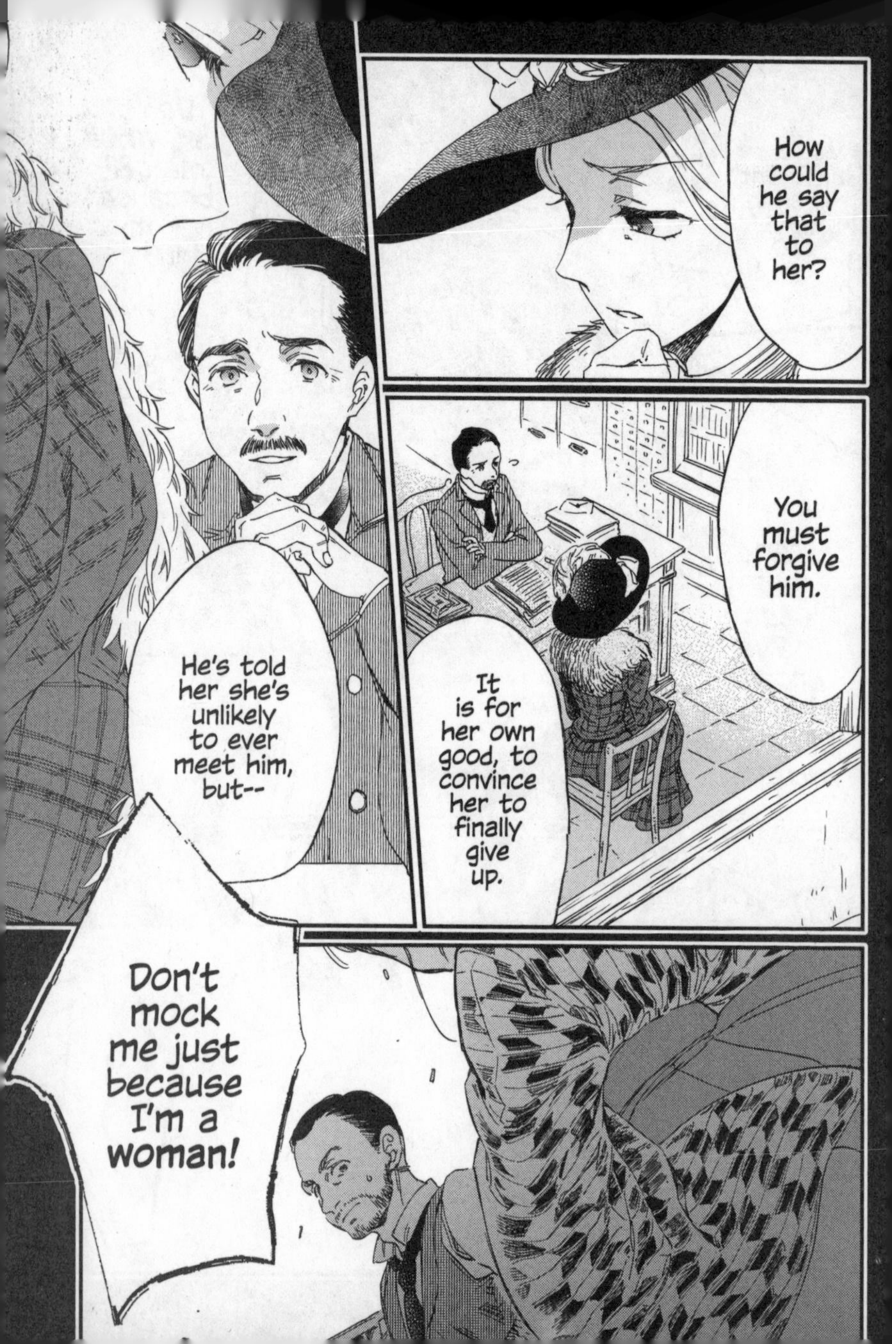
How could he say that to her?
You must forgive him.
It is for her own good, to convince her to finally give up.
He's told her she's unlikely to ever meet him, but--
Don't mock me just because I'm a woman!

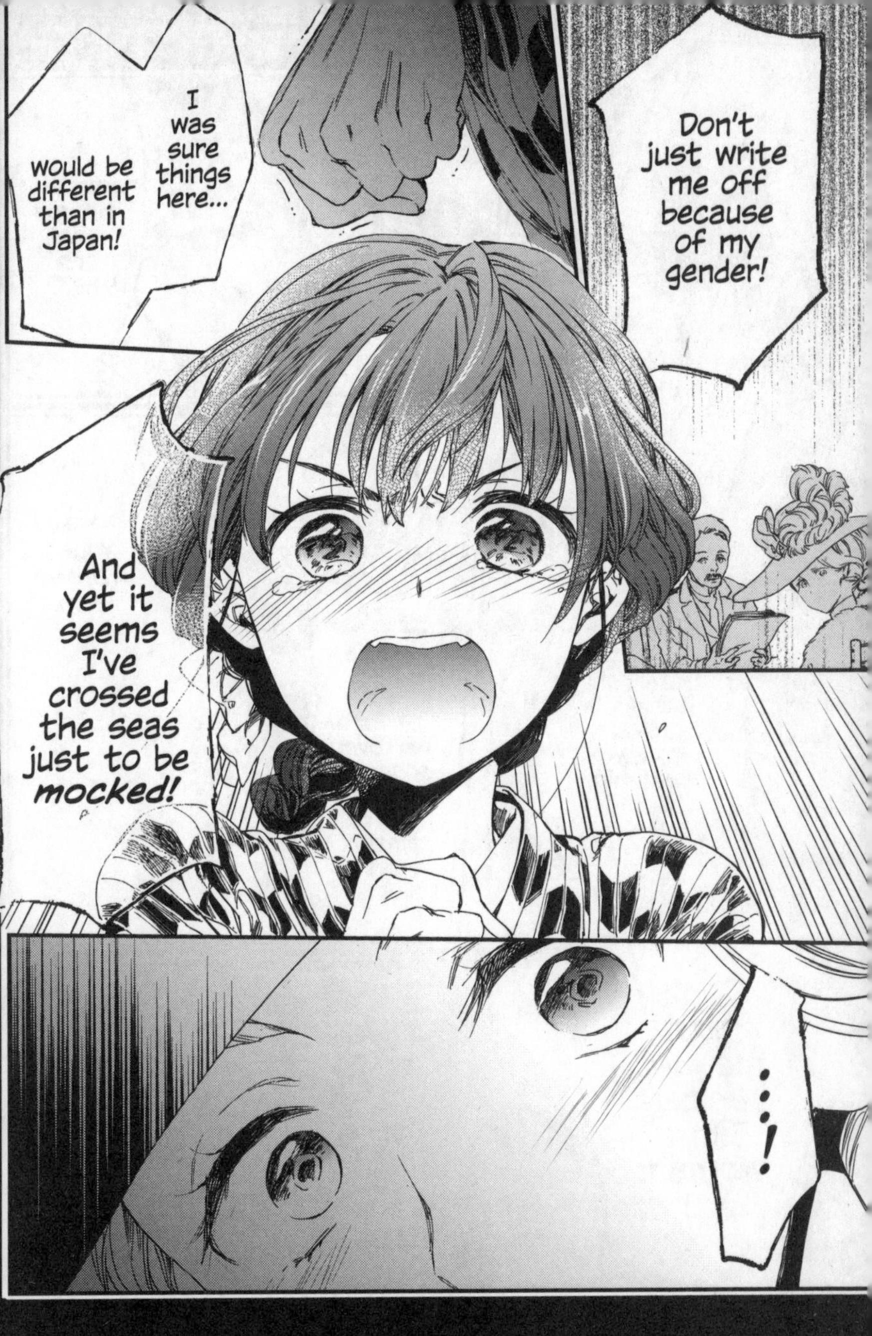
Don't just write me off because of my gender!
I was sure things here...
would be different than in Japan!
And yet it seems I've crossed the seas just to be *mocked!*
...!

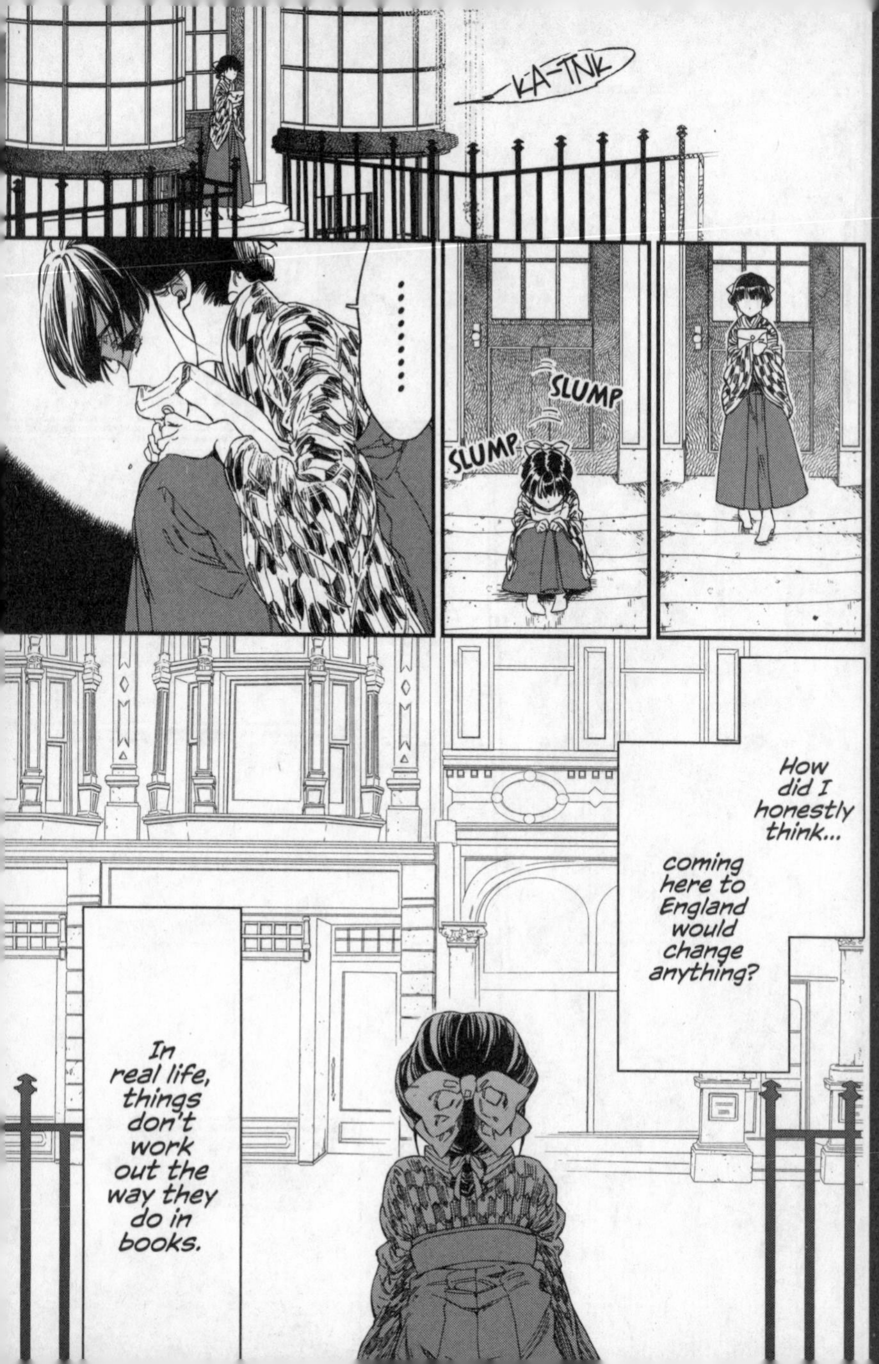
KA-TNK
SLUMP
SLUMP
......
How did I honestly think...
coming here to England would change anything?
In real life, things don't work out the way they do in books.

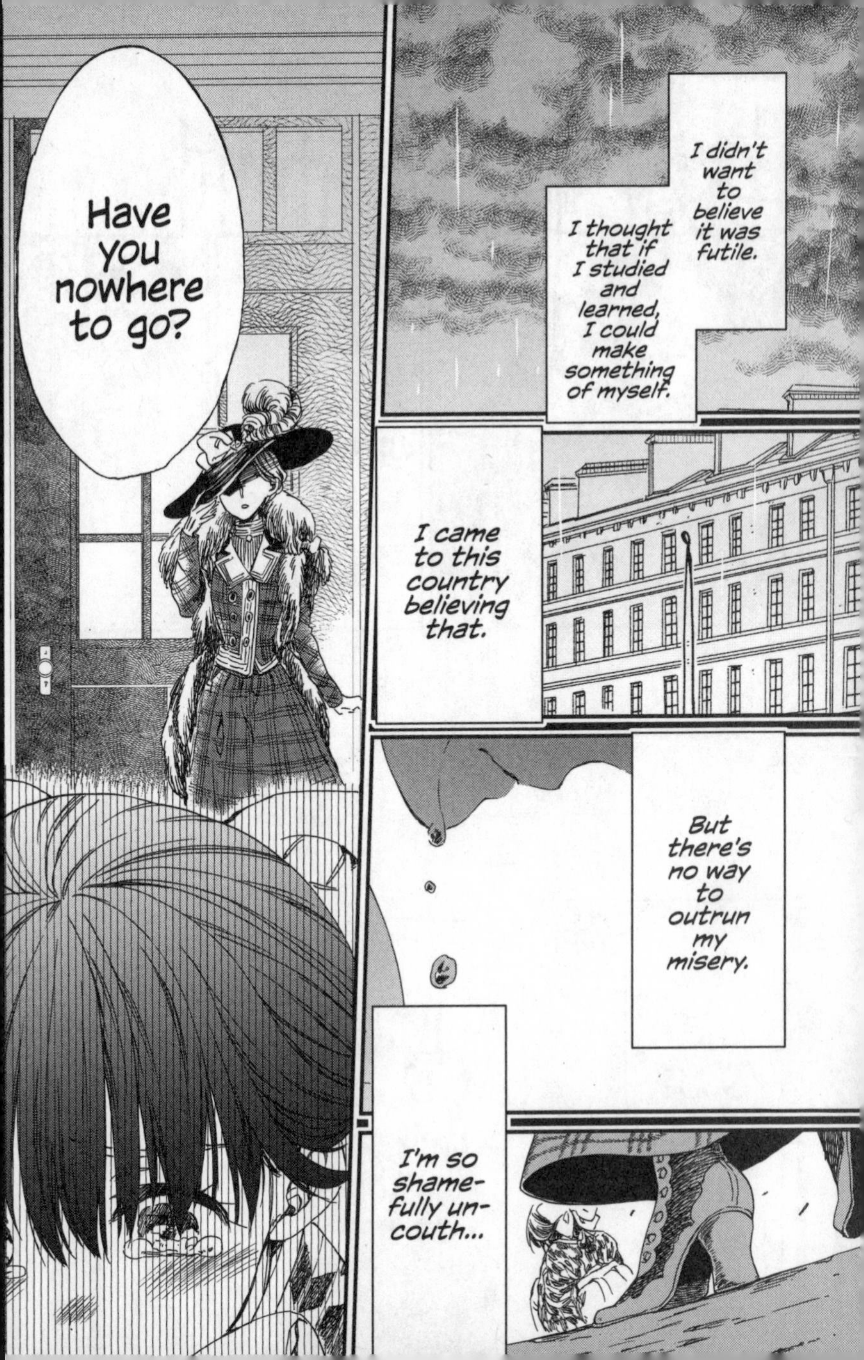
I didn't want to believe it was futile.
I thought that if I studied and learned, I could make something of myself.
I came to this country believing that.
But there's no way to outrun my misery.
I'm so shame-fully un-couth...
Have you nowhere to go?

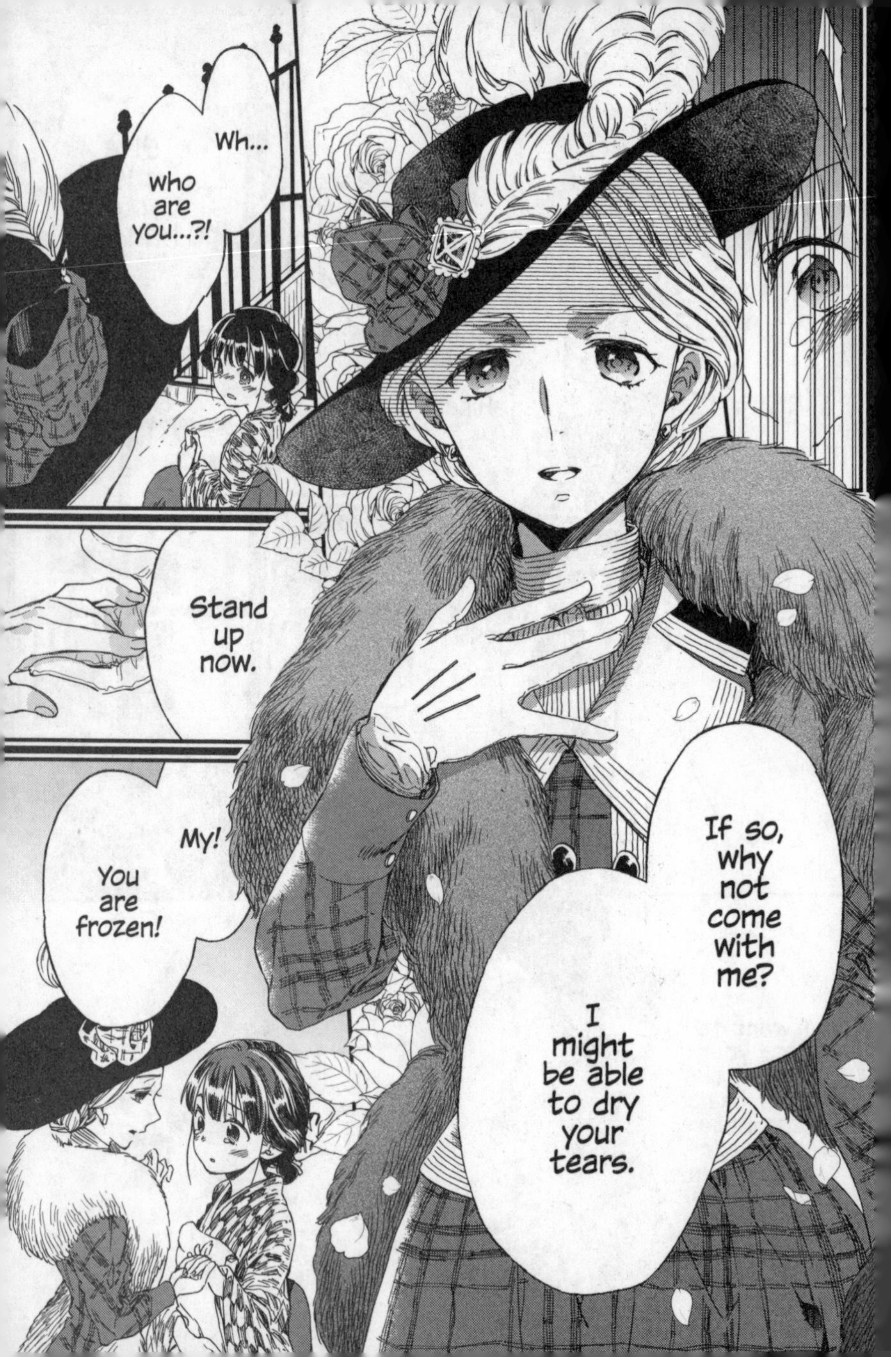
If so, why not come with me?
I might be able to dry your tears.
Wh... who are you...?!
Stand up now.
My! You are frozen!

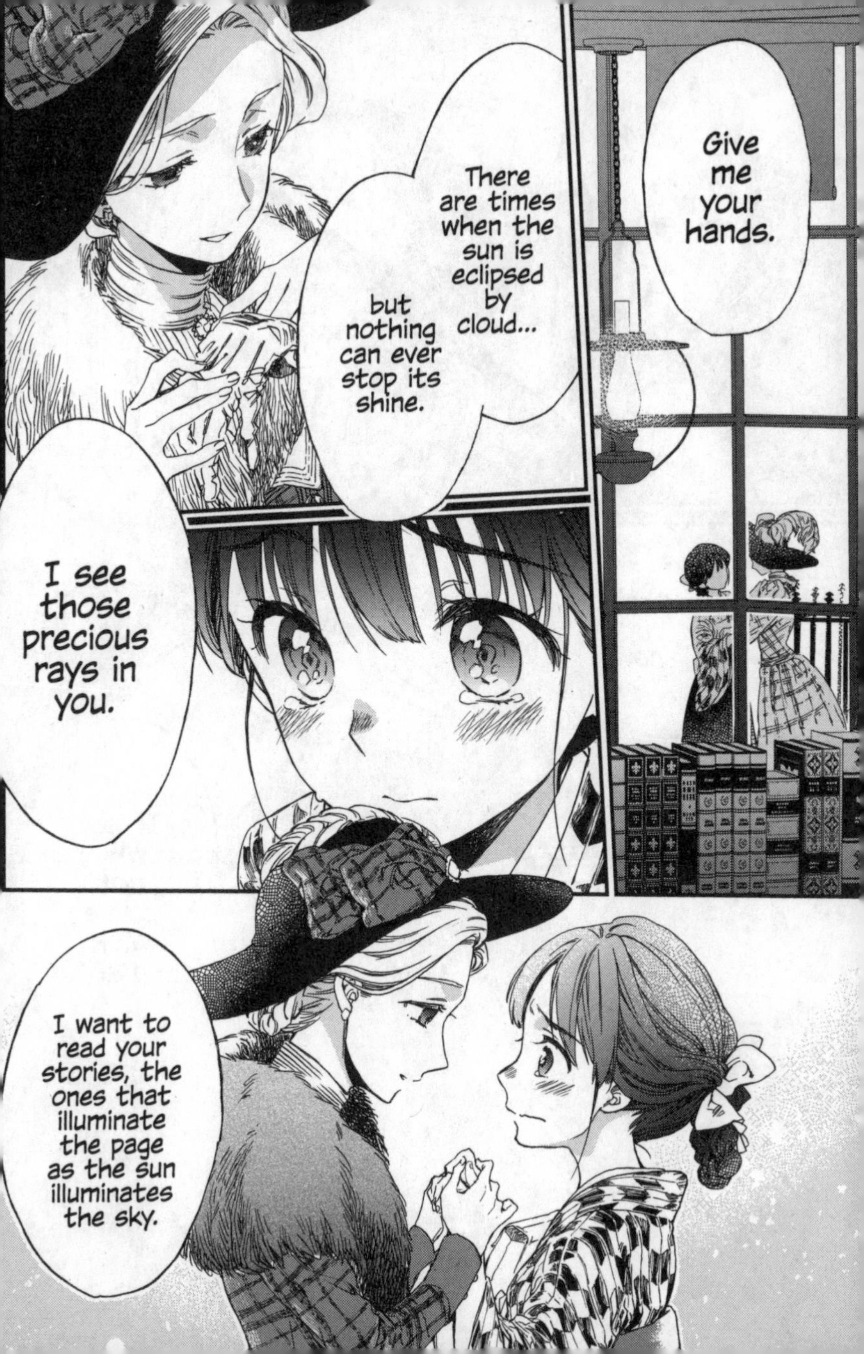
Give me your hands.
There are times when the sun is eclipsed by cloud...
but nothing can ever stop its shine.
I see those precious rays in you.
I want to read your stories, the ones that illuminate the page as the sun illuminates the sky.

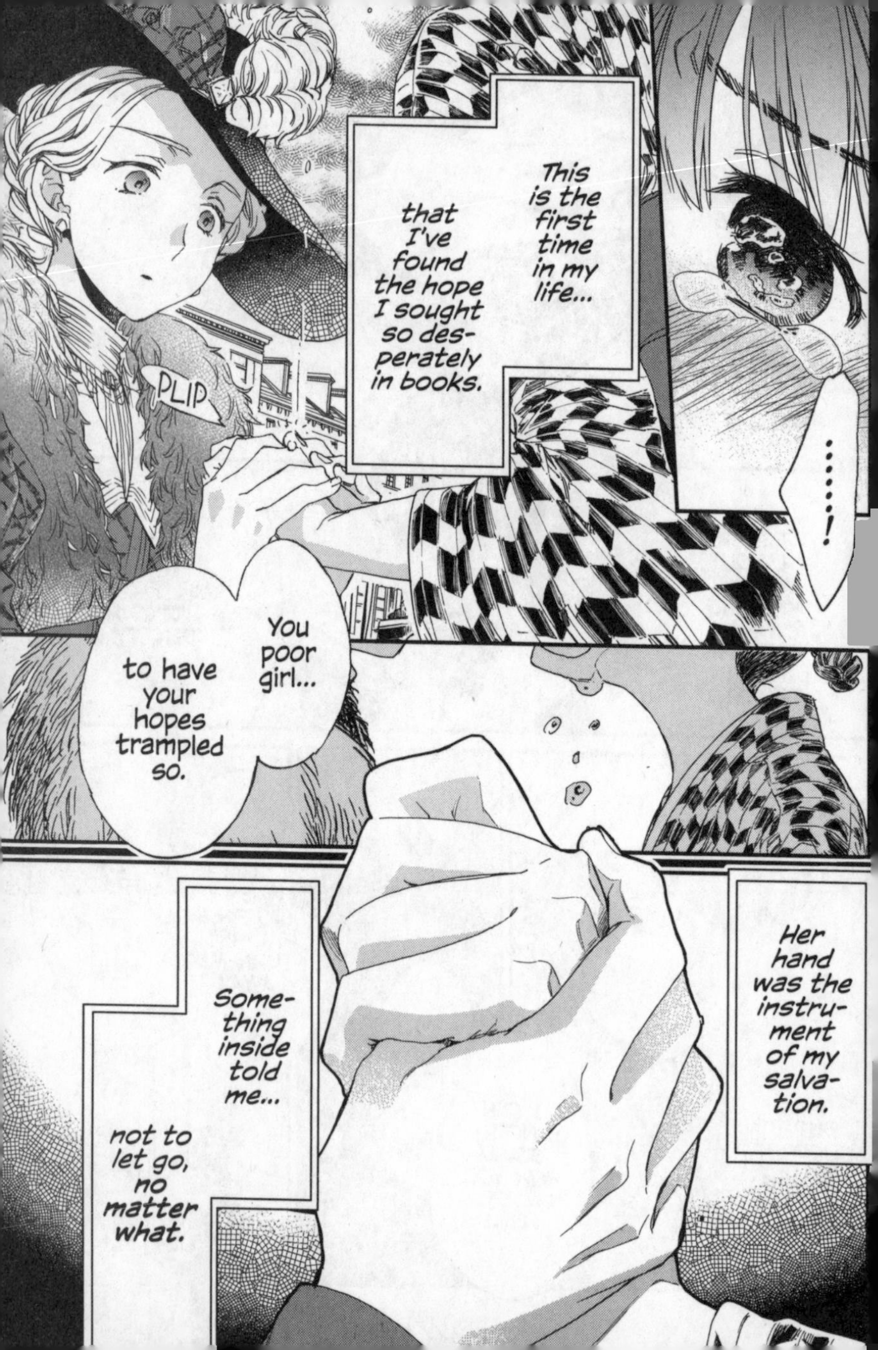
......!
This is the first time in my life...
that I've found the hope I sought so desperately in books.
PLIP
You poor girl...
to have your hopes trampled so.
Her hand was the instrument of my salvation.
Something inside told me...
not to let go, no matter what.

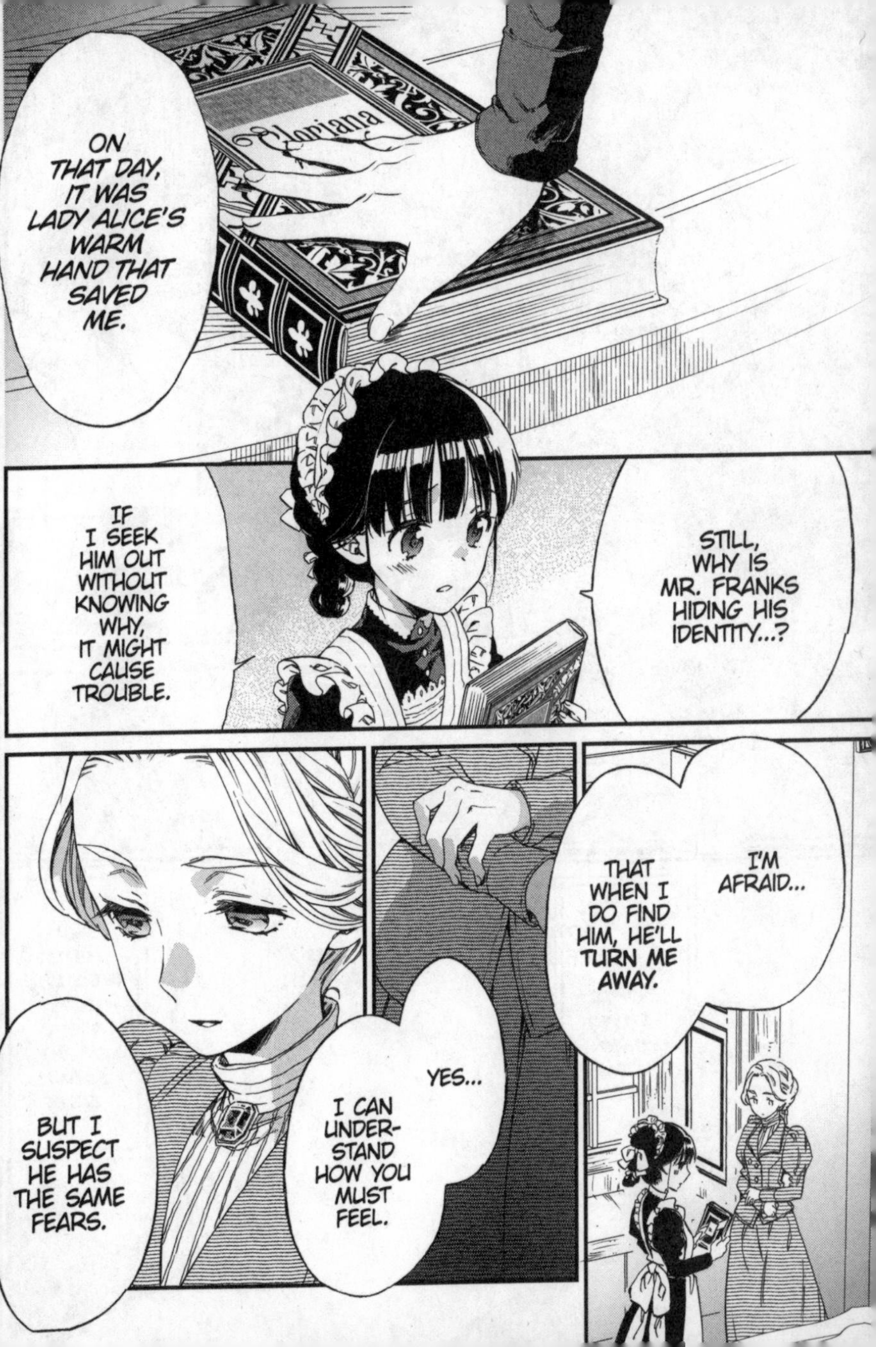
ON THAT DAY, IT WAS LADY ALICE'S WARM HAND THAT SAVED ME.
STILL, WHY IS MR. FRANKS HIDING HIS IDENTITY...?
IF I SEEK HIM OUT WITHOUT KNOWING WHY, IT MIGHT CAUSE TROUBLE.
I'M AFRAID...
THAT WHEN I DO FIND HIM, HE'LL TURN ME AWAY.
YES...
I CAN UNDER-STAND HOW YOU MUST FEEL.
BUT I SUSPECT HE HAS THE SAME FEARS.

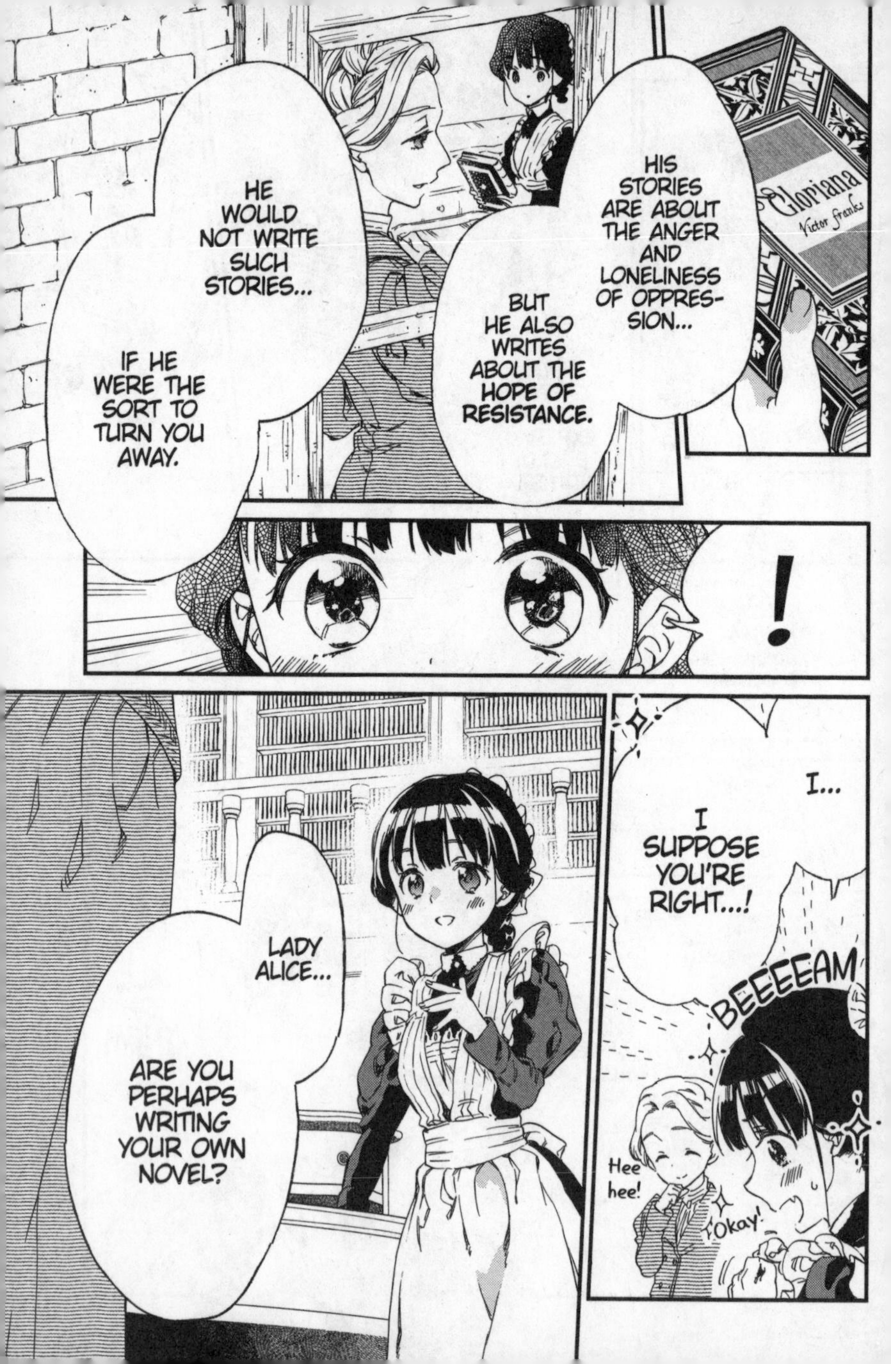
Gloriana
Victor franks
HIS STORIES ARE ABOUT THE ANGER AND LONELINESS OF OPPRES-SION...
BUT HE ALSO WRITES ABOUT THE HOPE OF RESISTANCE.
HE WOULD NOT WRITE SUCH STORIES...
IF HE WERE THE SORT TO TURN YOU AWAY.
!
I...
I SUPPOSE YOU'RE RIGHT...!
BEEEEAM
Okay!
Hee hee!
LADY ALICE...
ARE YOU PERHAPS WRITING YOUR OWN NOVEL?

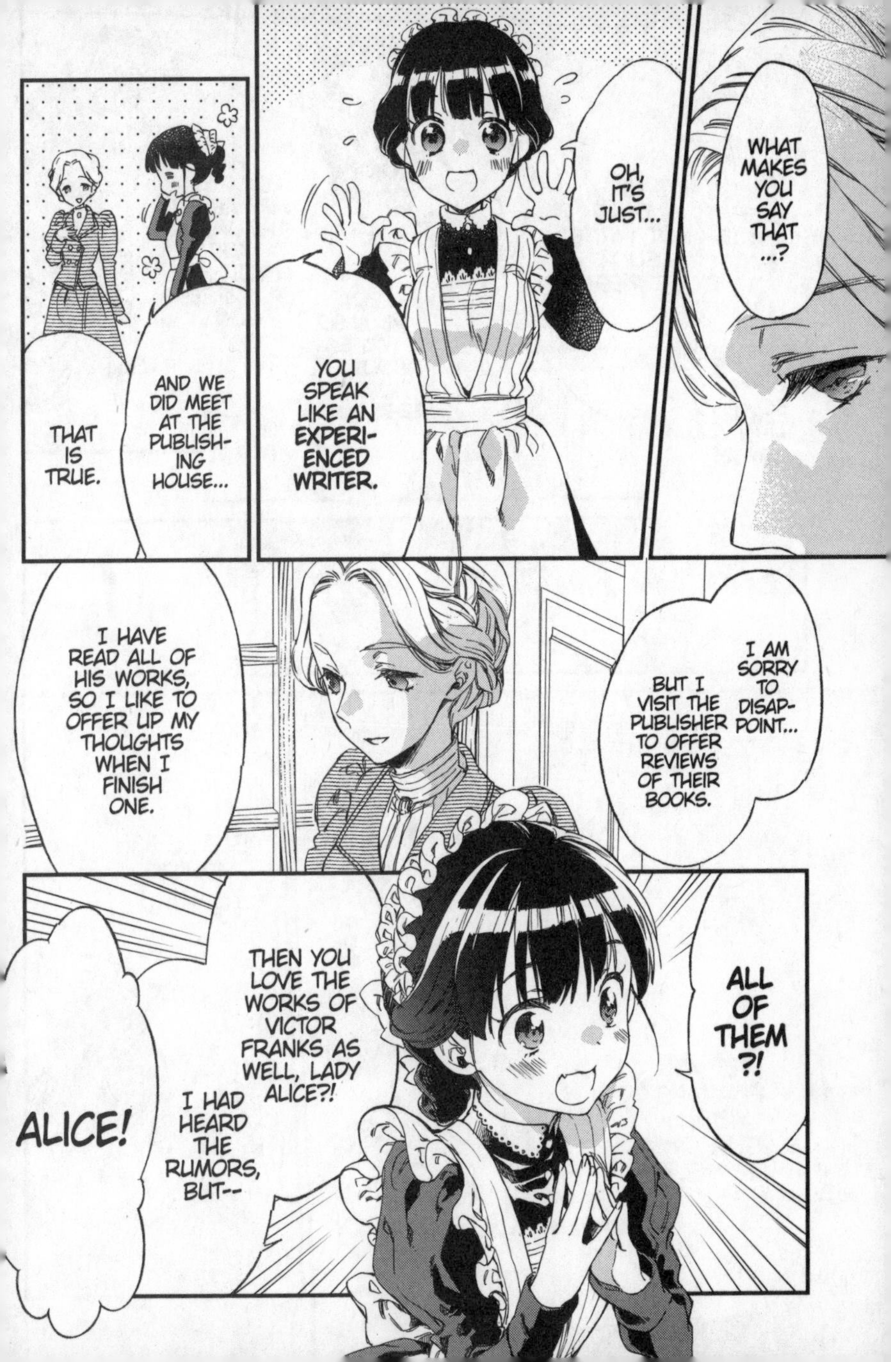
WHAT MAKES YOU SAY THAT ...?
OH, IT'S JUST...
YOU SPEAK LIKE AN EXPERIENCED WRITER.
AND WE DID MEET AT THE PUBLISHING HOUSE...
THAT IS TRUE.
I AM SORRY TO DISAPPOINT...
BUT I VISIT THE PUBLISHER TO OFFER REVIEWS OF THEIR BOOKS.
I HAVE READ ALL OF HIS WORKS, SO I LIKE TO OFFER UP MY THOUGHTS WHEN I FINISH ONE.
ALL OF THEM?!
THEN YOU LOVE THE WORKS OF VICTOR FRANKS AS WELL, LADY ALICE?!
I HAD HEARD THE RUMORS, BUT--
ALICE!

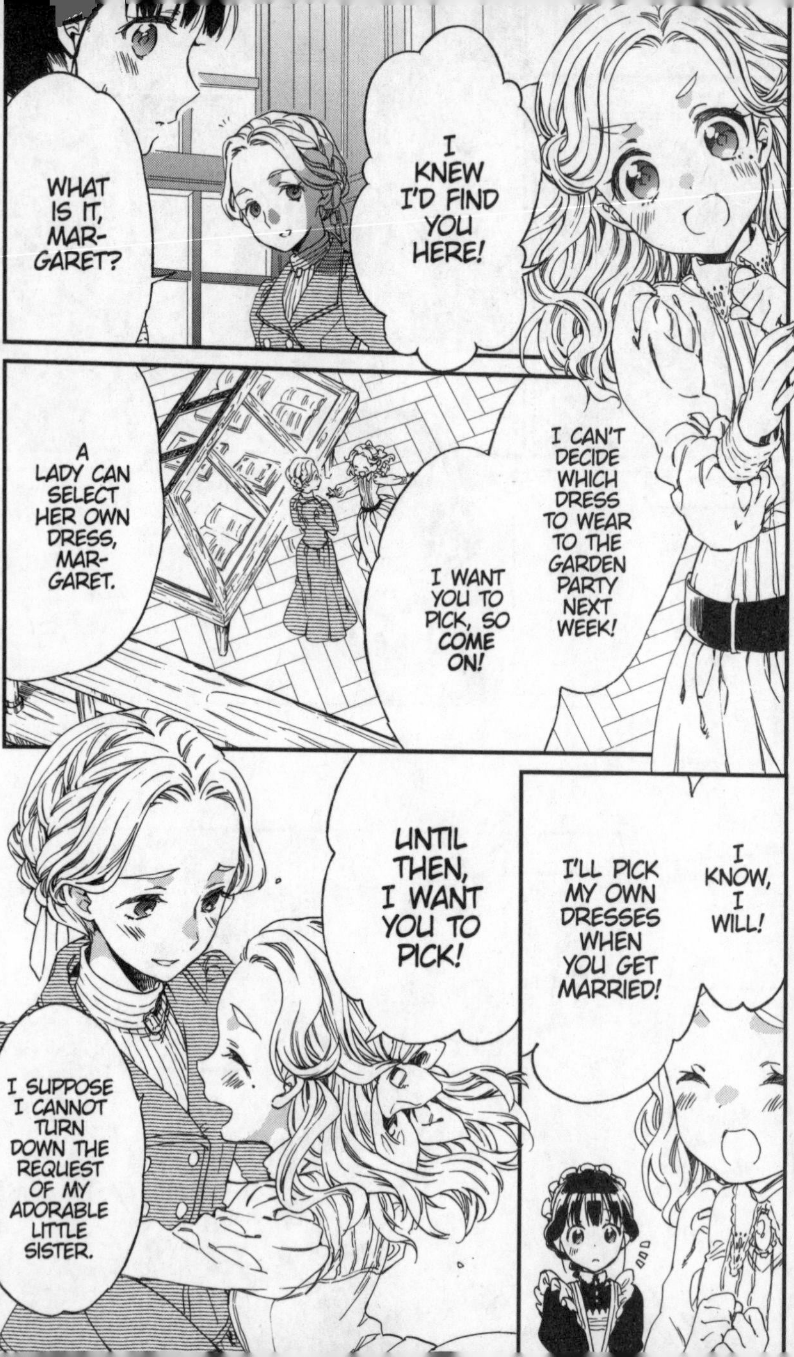
I KNEW I'D FIND YOU HERE!
WHAT IS IT, MAR-GARET?
I CAN'T DECIDE WHICH DRESS TO WEAR TO THE GARDEN PARTY NEXT WEEK!
I WANT YOU TO PICK, SO COME ON!
A LADY CAN SELECT HER OWN DRESS, MAR-GARET.
I KNOW, I WILL!
I'LL PICK MY OWN DRESSES WHEN YOU GET MARRIED!
UNTIL THEN, I WANT YOU TO PICK!
I SUPPOSE I CANNOT TURN DOWN THE REQUEST OF MY ADORABLE LITTLE SISTER.

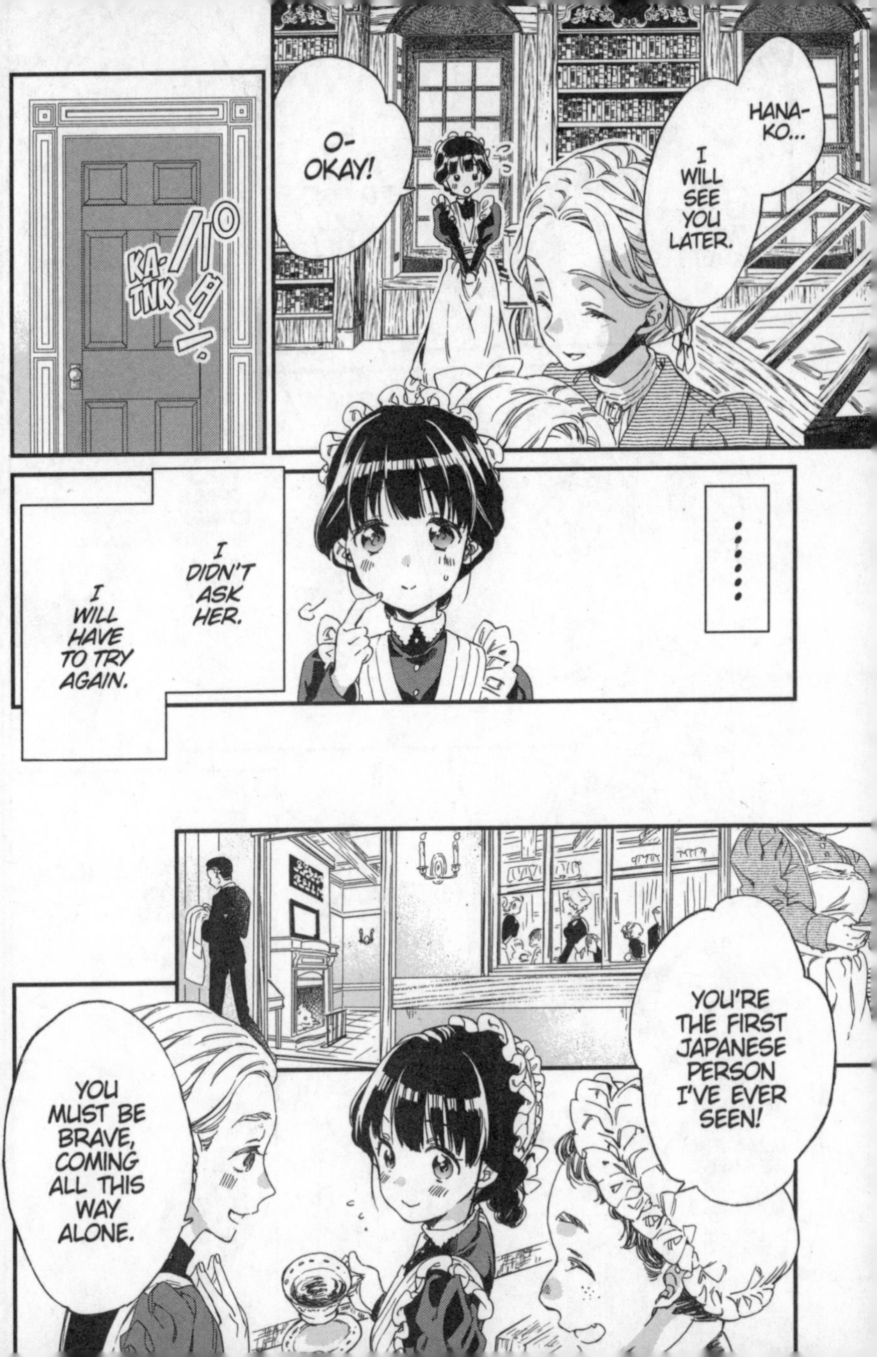
HANA-KO... I WILL SEE YOU LATER.
O-OKAY!
KA-TNK
パタン！
......
I DIDN'T ASK HER.
I WILL HAVE TO TRY AGAIN.
YOU'RE THE FIRST JAPANESE PERSON I'VE EVER SEEN!
YOU MUST BE BRAVE, COMING ALL THIS WAY ALONE.

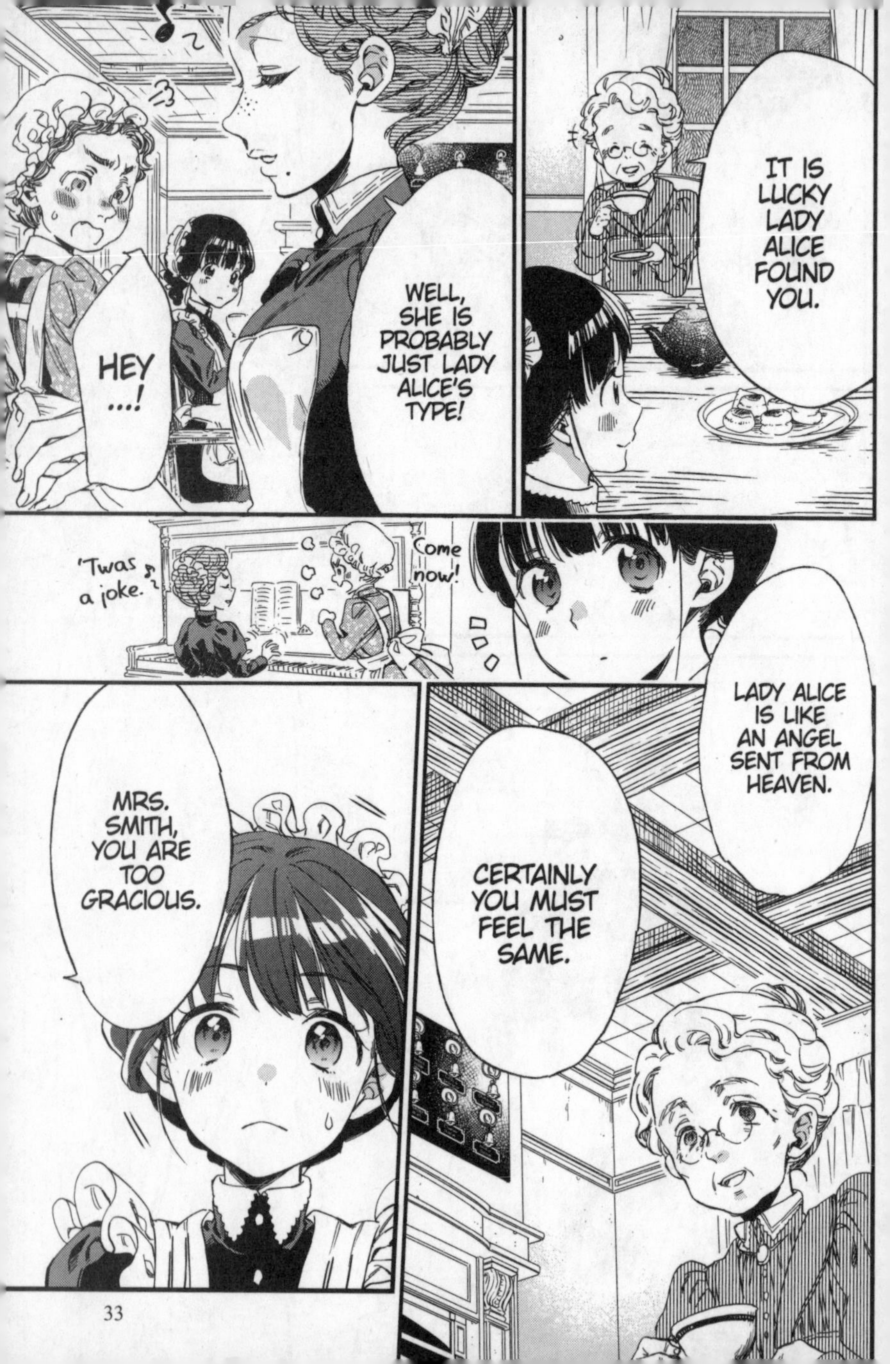
IT IS LUCKY LADY ALICE FOUND YOU.
WELL, SHE IS PROBABLY JUST LADY ALICE'S TYPE!
HEY ...!
Come now!
'Twas a joke.
LADY ALICE IS LIKE AN ANGEL SENT FROM HEAVEN.
CERTAINLY YOU MUST FEEL THE SAME.
MRS. SMITH, YOU ARE TOO GRACIOUS.

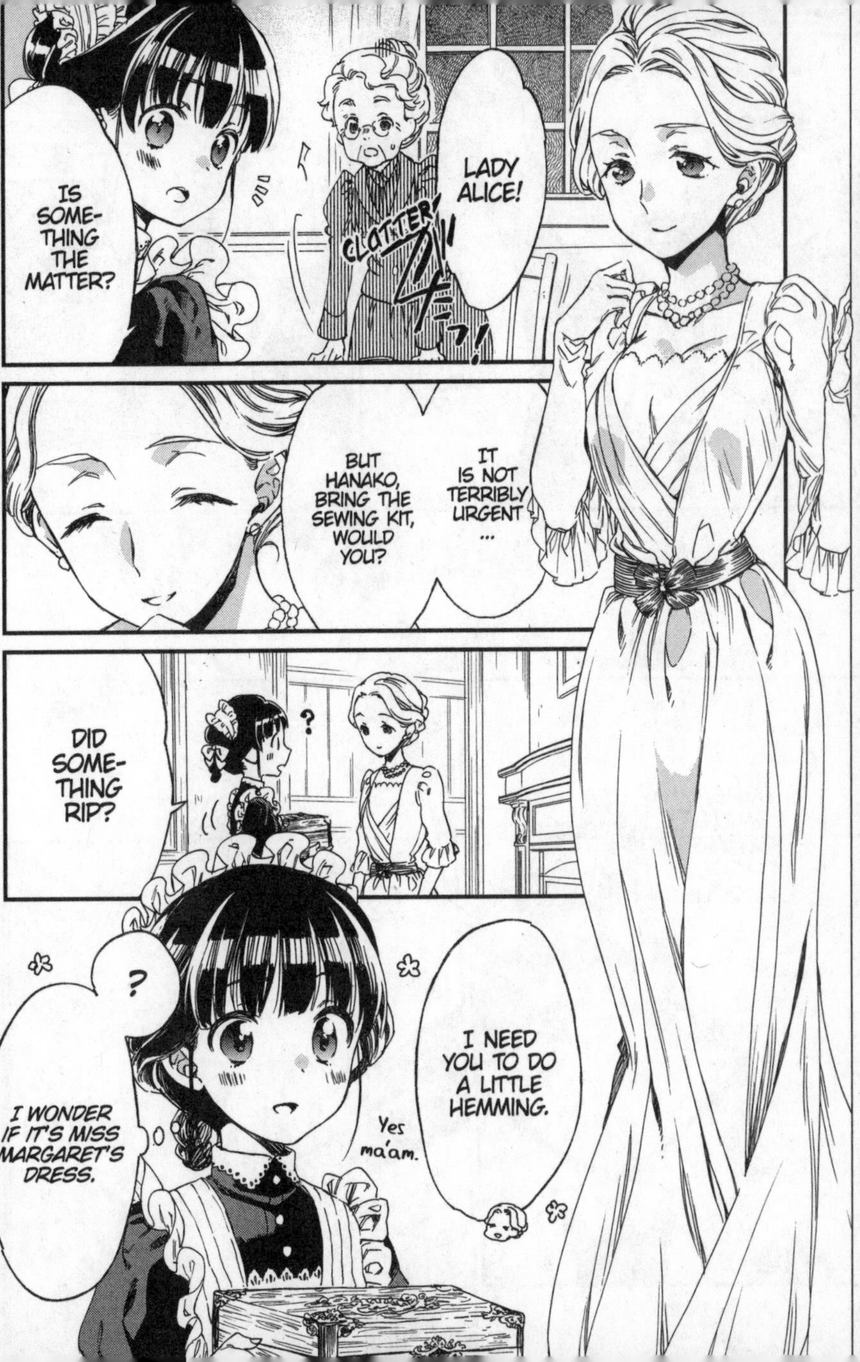
LADY ALICE!
CLATTER
IS SOMETHING THE MATTER?
IT IS NOT TERRIBLY URGENT ...
BUT HANAKO, BRING THE SEWING KIT, WOULD YOU?
DID SOMETHING RIP?
I NEED YOU TO DO A LITTLE HEMMING.
Yes ma'am.
I WONDER IF IT'S MISS MARGARET'S DRESS.

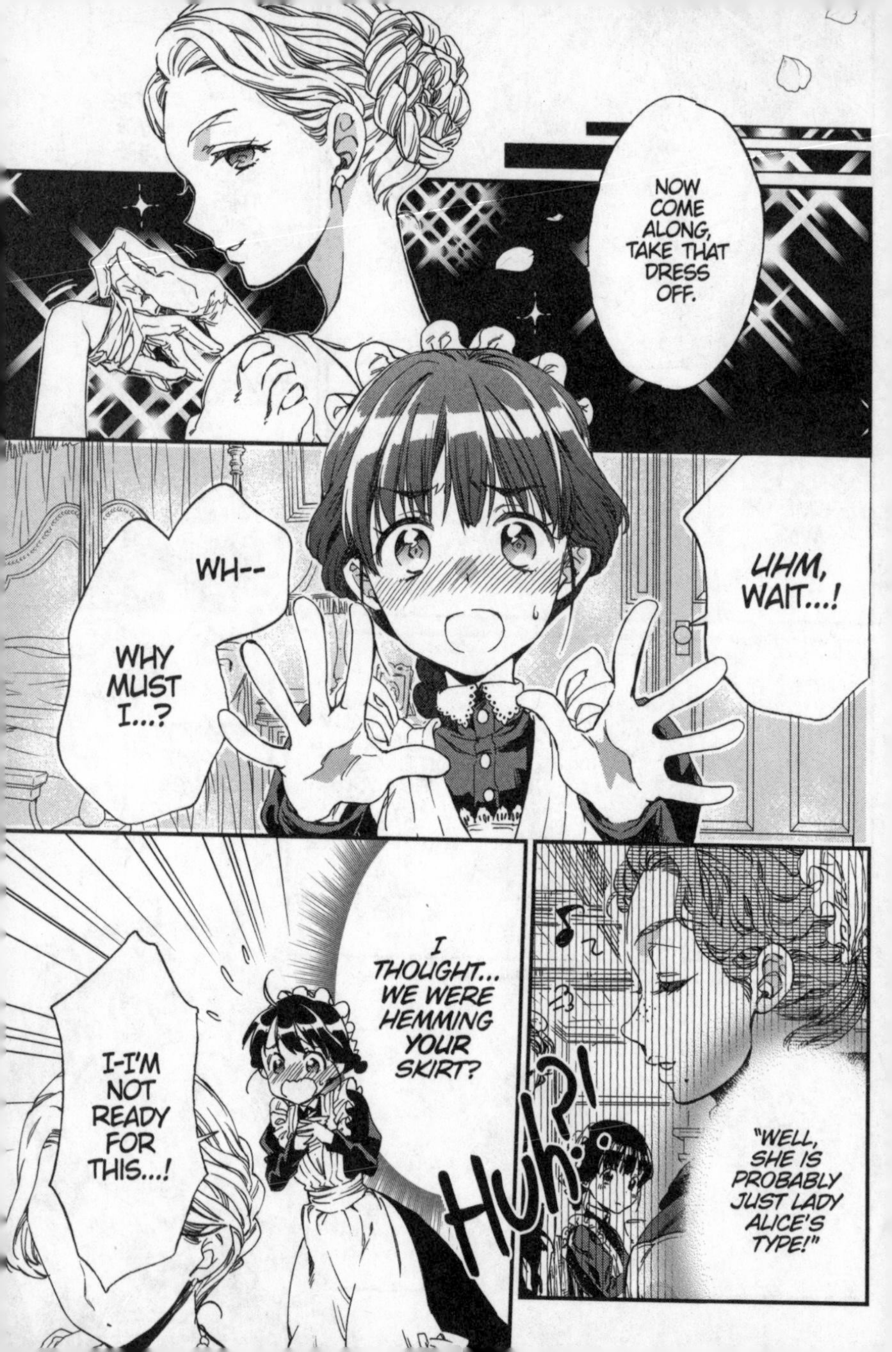
NOW COME ALONG, TAKE THAT DRESS OFF.
UHM, WAIT...!
WH--
WHY MUST I...?
"WELL, SHE IS PROBABLY JUST LADY ALICE'S TYPE!"
HUH?!
I THOUGHT... WE WERE HEMMING YOUR SKIRT?
I-I'M NOT READY FOR THIS...!

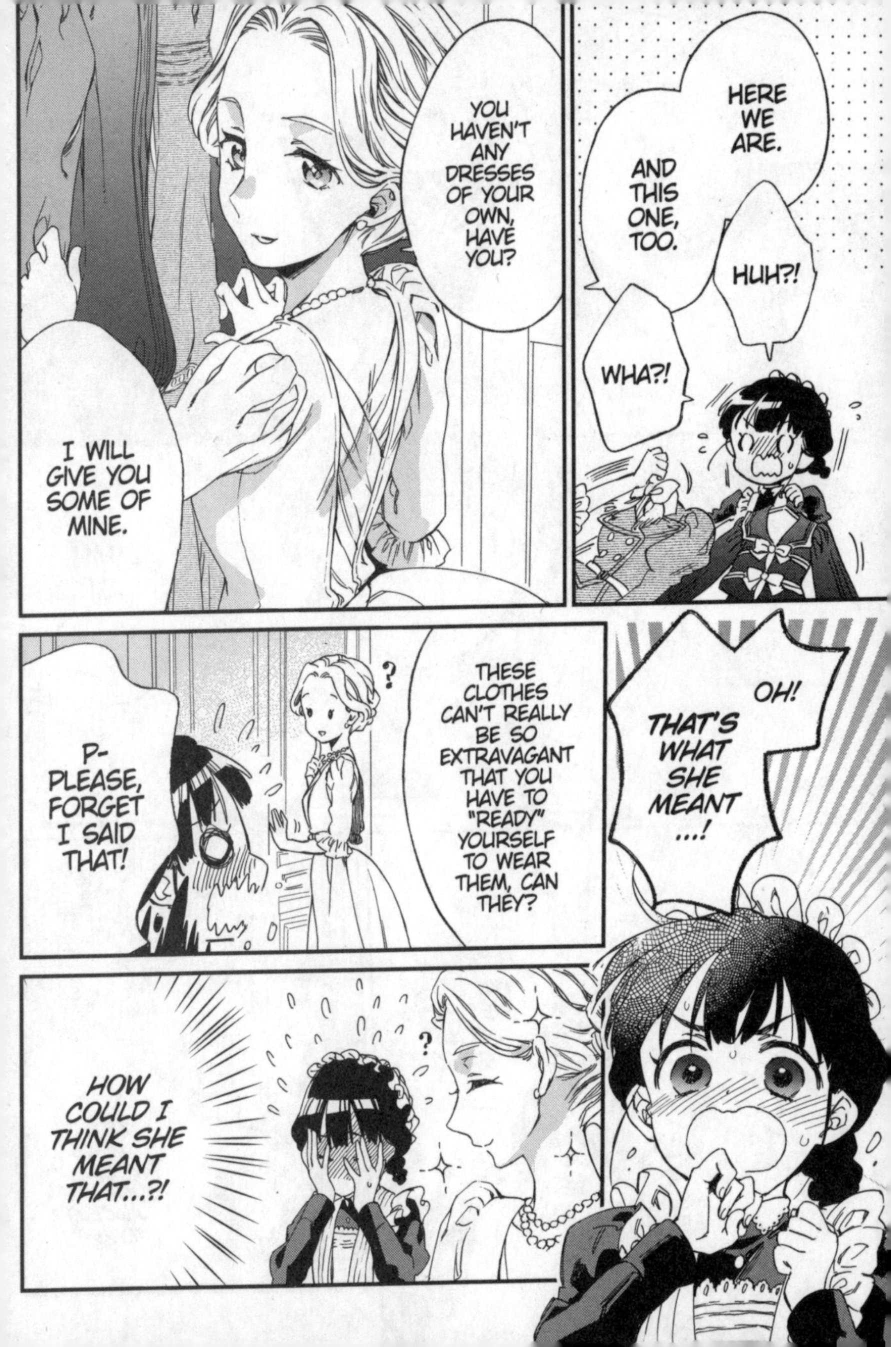
HERE WE ARE.
AND THIS ONE, TOO.
HUH?!
WHA?!
YOU HAVEN'T ANY DRESSES OF YOUR OWN, HAVE YOU?
I WILL GIVE YOU SOME OF MINE.
OH!
THAT'S WHAT SHE MEANT ...!
THESE CLOTHES CAN'T REALLY BE SO EXTRAVAGANT THAT YOU HAVE TO "READY" YOURSELF TO WEAR THEM, CAN THEY?
?
P-PLEASE, FORGET I SAID THAT!
?
HOW COULD I THINK SHE MEANT THAT...?!

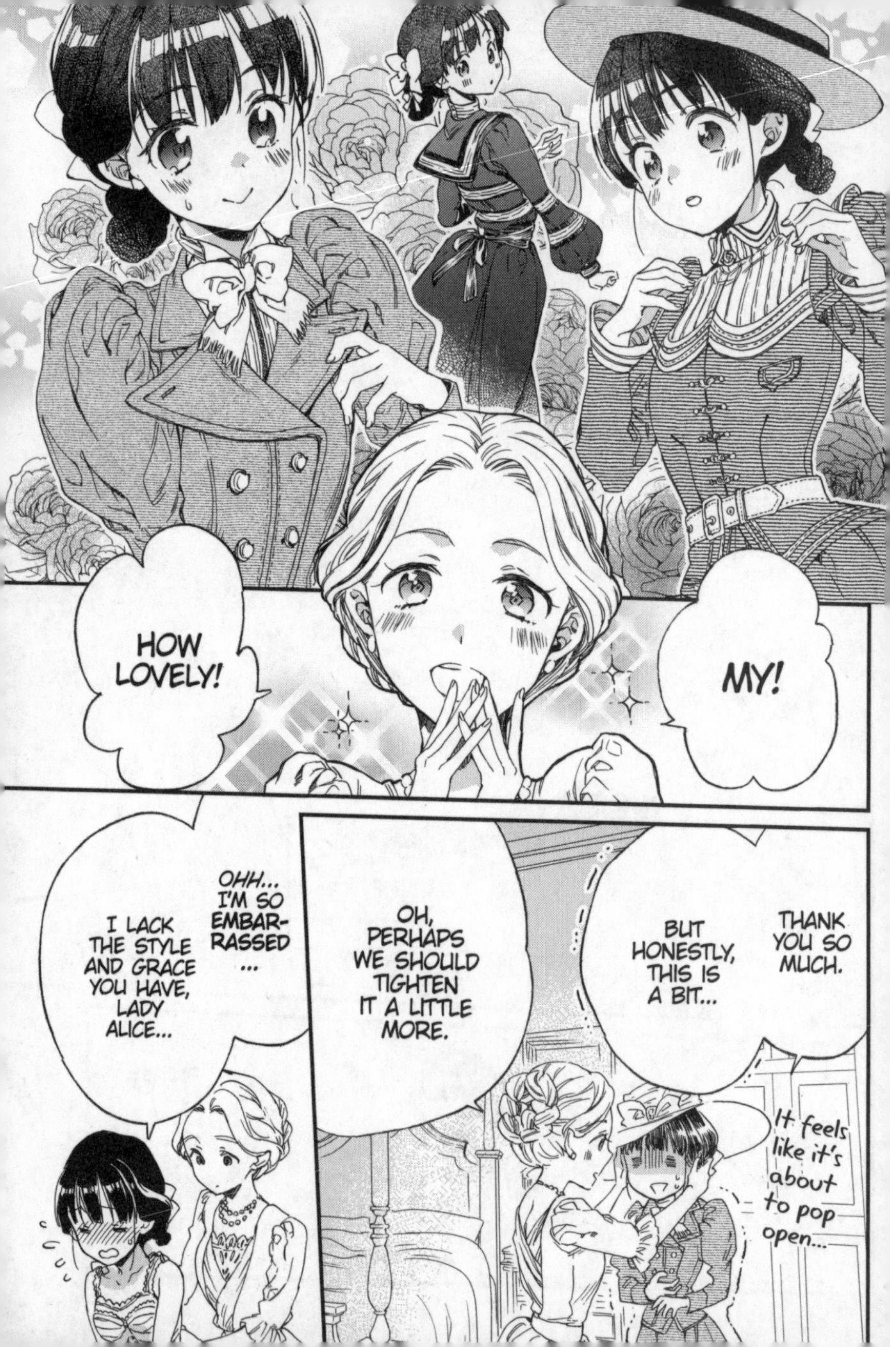
MY!
HOW LOVELY!
THANK YOU SO MUCH.
BUT HONESTLY, THIS IS A BIT...
OH, PERHAPS WE SHOULD TIGHTEN IT A LITTLE MORE.
It feels like it's about to pop open...
OHH... I'M SO EMBARRASSED...
I LACK THE STYLE AND GRACE YOU HAVE, LADY ALICE...

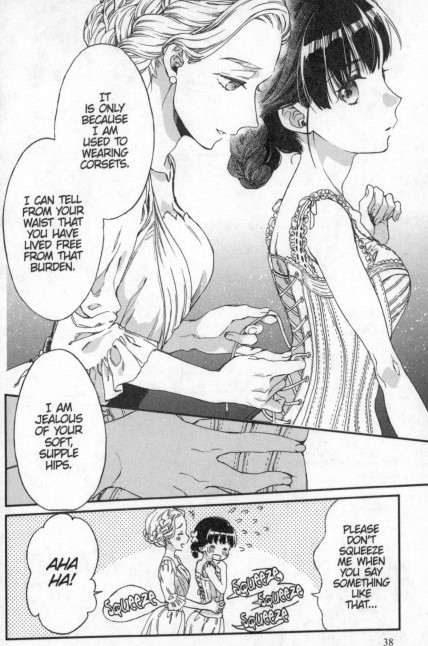

IT IS ONLY BECAUSE I AM USED TO WEARING CORSETS.

I CAN TELL FROM YOUR WAIST THAT YOU HAVE LIVED FREE FROM THAT BURDEN.

I AM JEALOUS OF YOUR SOFT, SUPPLE HIPS.

AHA HA!

SQUEEZE
SQUEEZE SQUEEZE SQUEEZE

PLEASE DON'T SQUEEZE ME WHEN YOU SAY SOMETHING LIKE THAT...

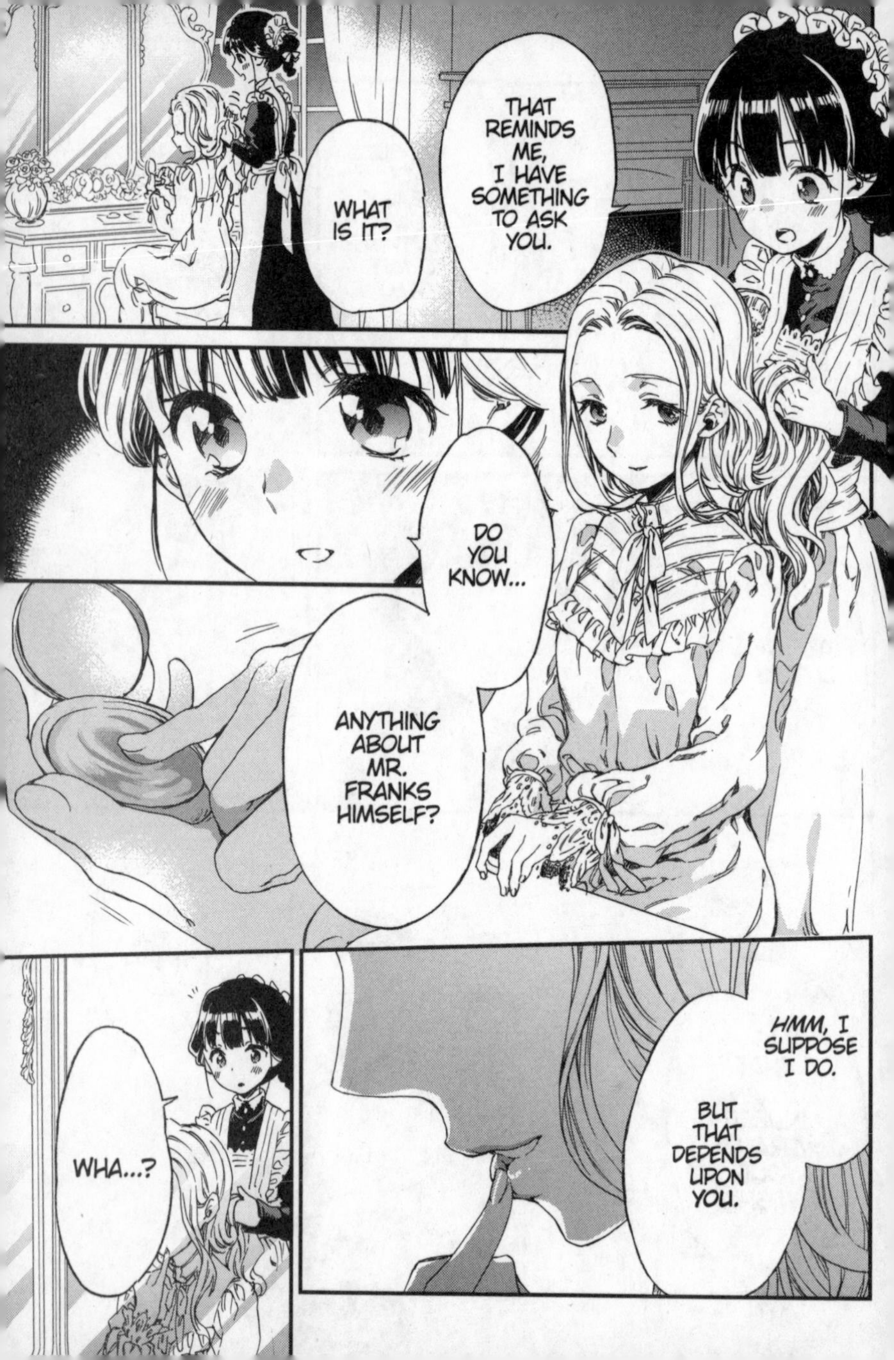
THAT REMINDS ME, I HAVE SOMETHING TO ASK YOU.
WHAT IS IT?
DO YOU KNOW...
ANYTHING ABOUT MR. FRANKS HIMSELF?
HMM, I SUPPOSE I DO.
BUT THAT DEPENDS UPON YOU.
WHA...?

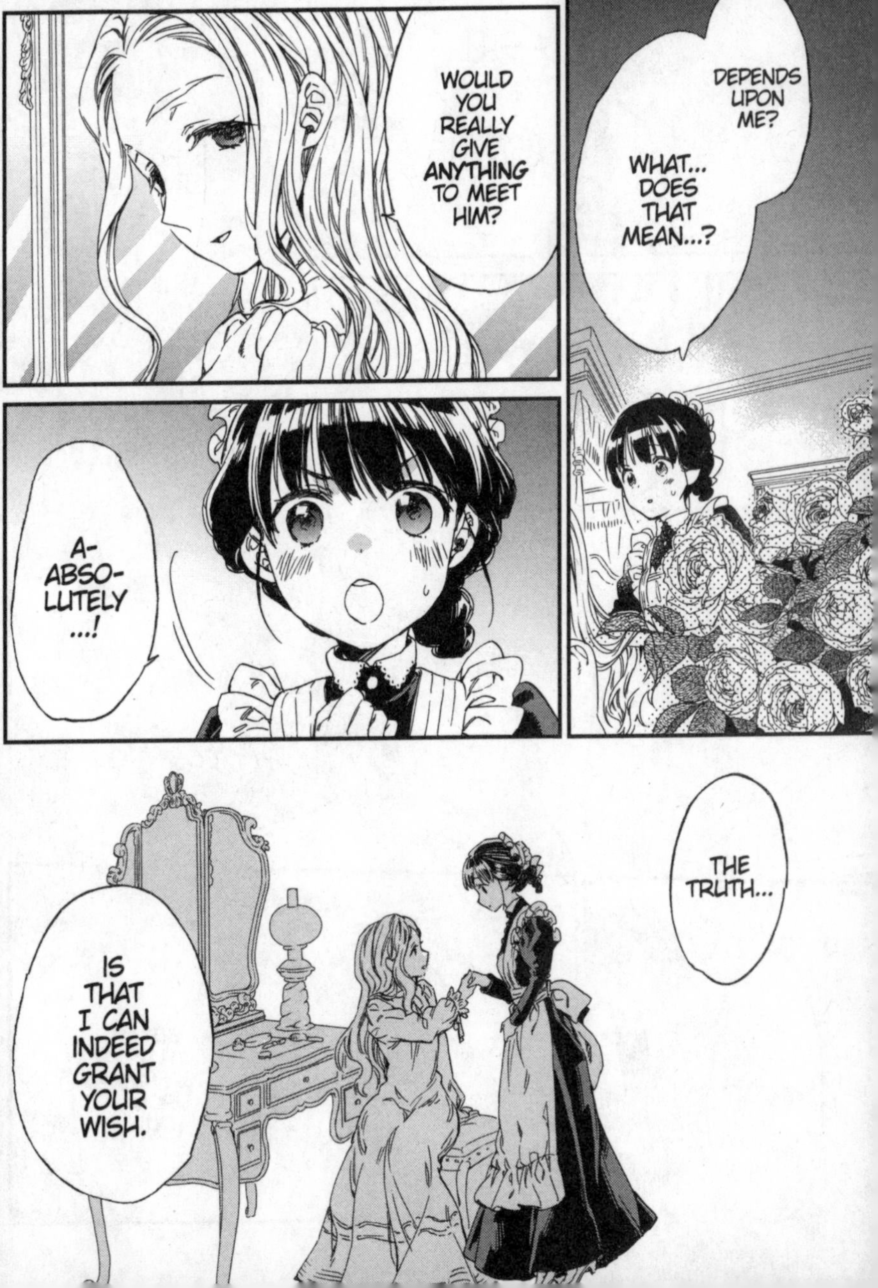
DEPENDS UPON ME?
WHAT... DOES THAT MEAN...?
WOULD YOU REALLY GIVE ANYTHING TO MEET HIM?
A-ABSO-LUTELY...!
THE TRUTH...
IS THAT I CAN INDEED GRANT YOUR WISH.

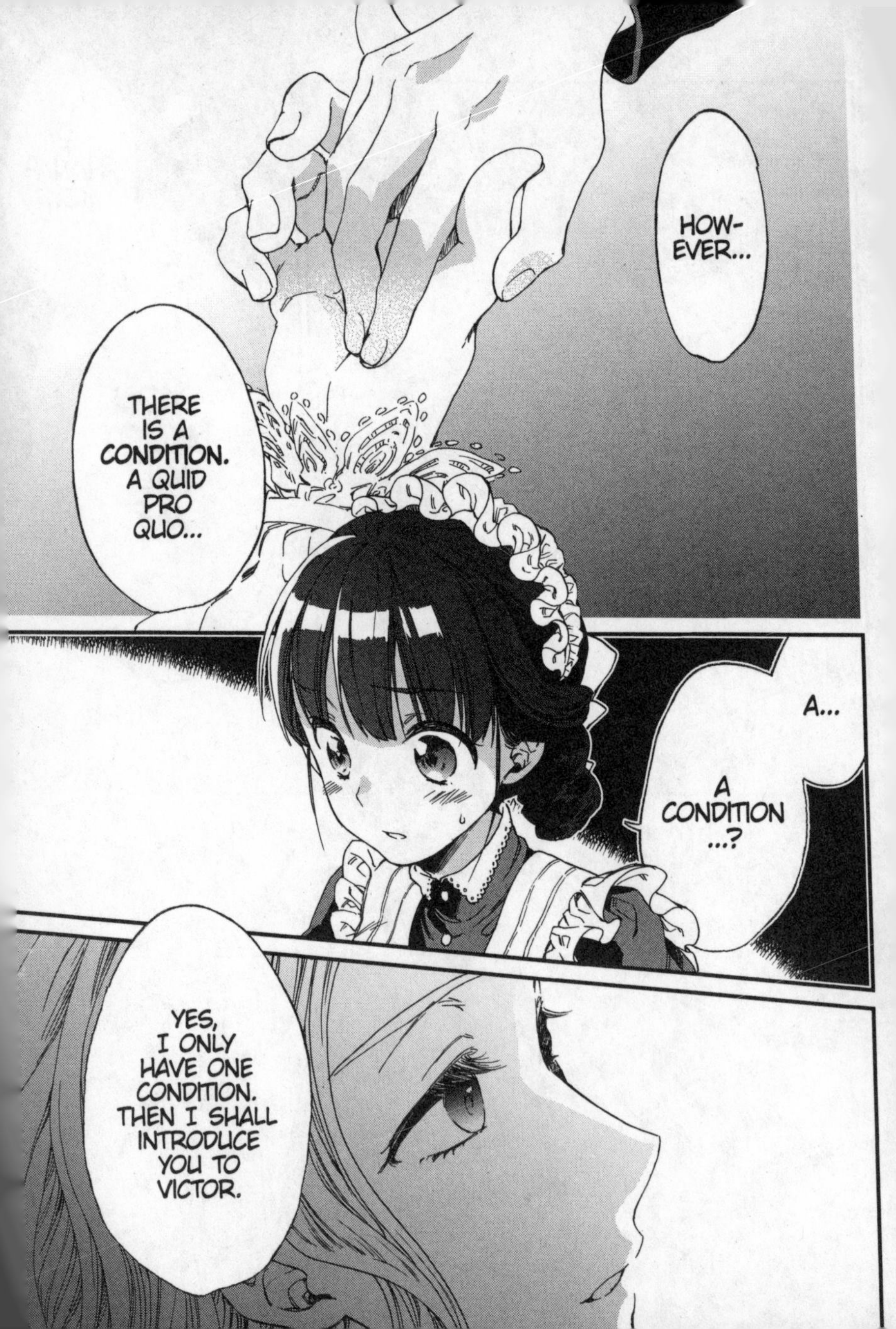
HOW-EVER...
THERE IS A CONDITION. A QUID PRO QUO...
A...
A CONDITION ...?
YES, I ONLY HAVE ONE CONDITION. THEN I SHALL INTRODUCE YOU TO VICTOR.

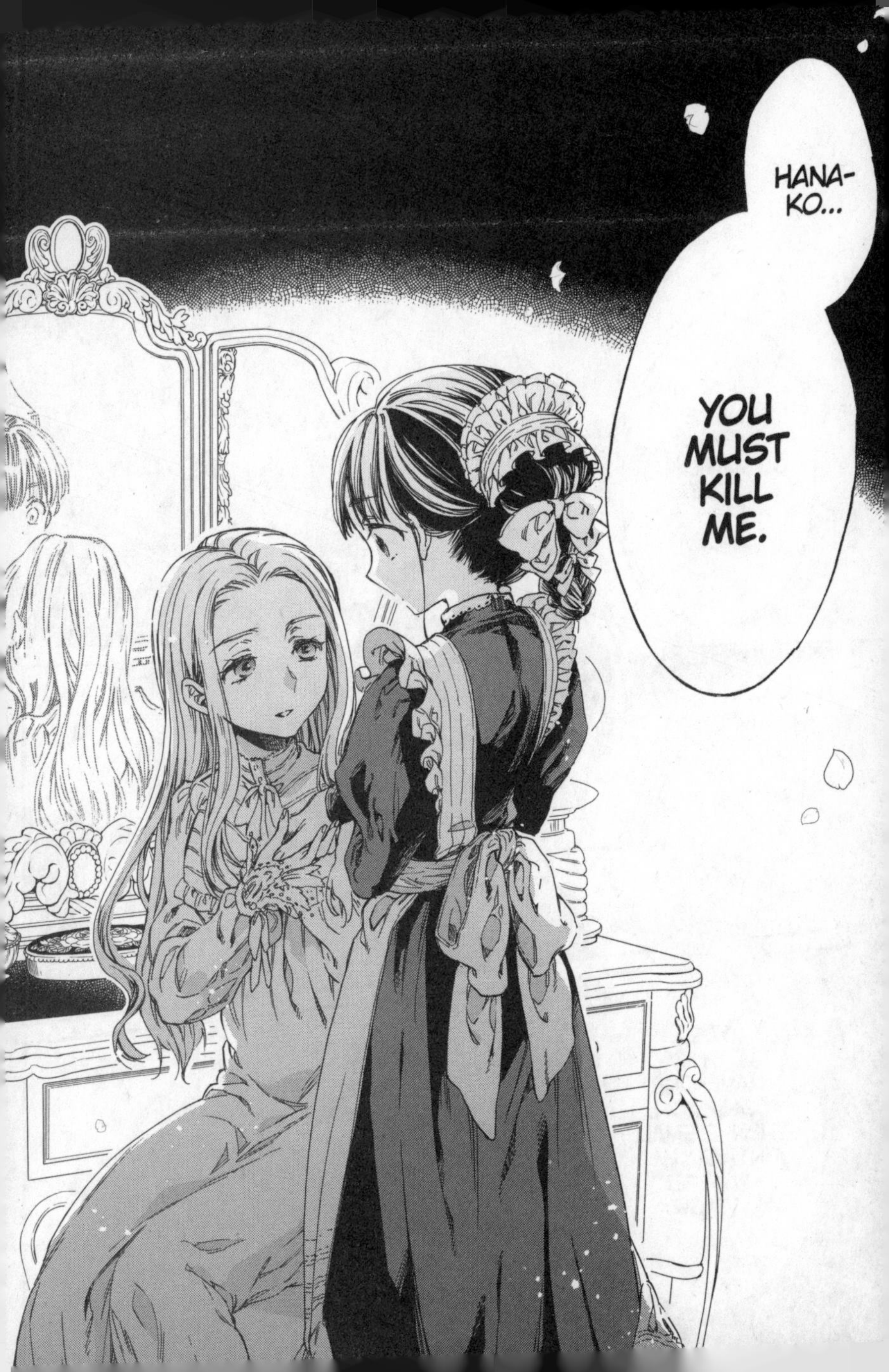
HANA-
KO...
YOU
MUST
KILL
ME.

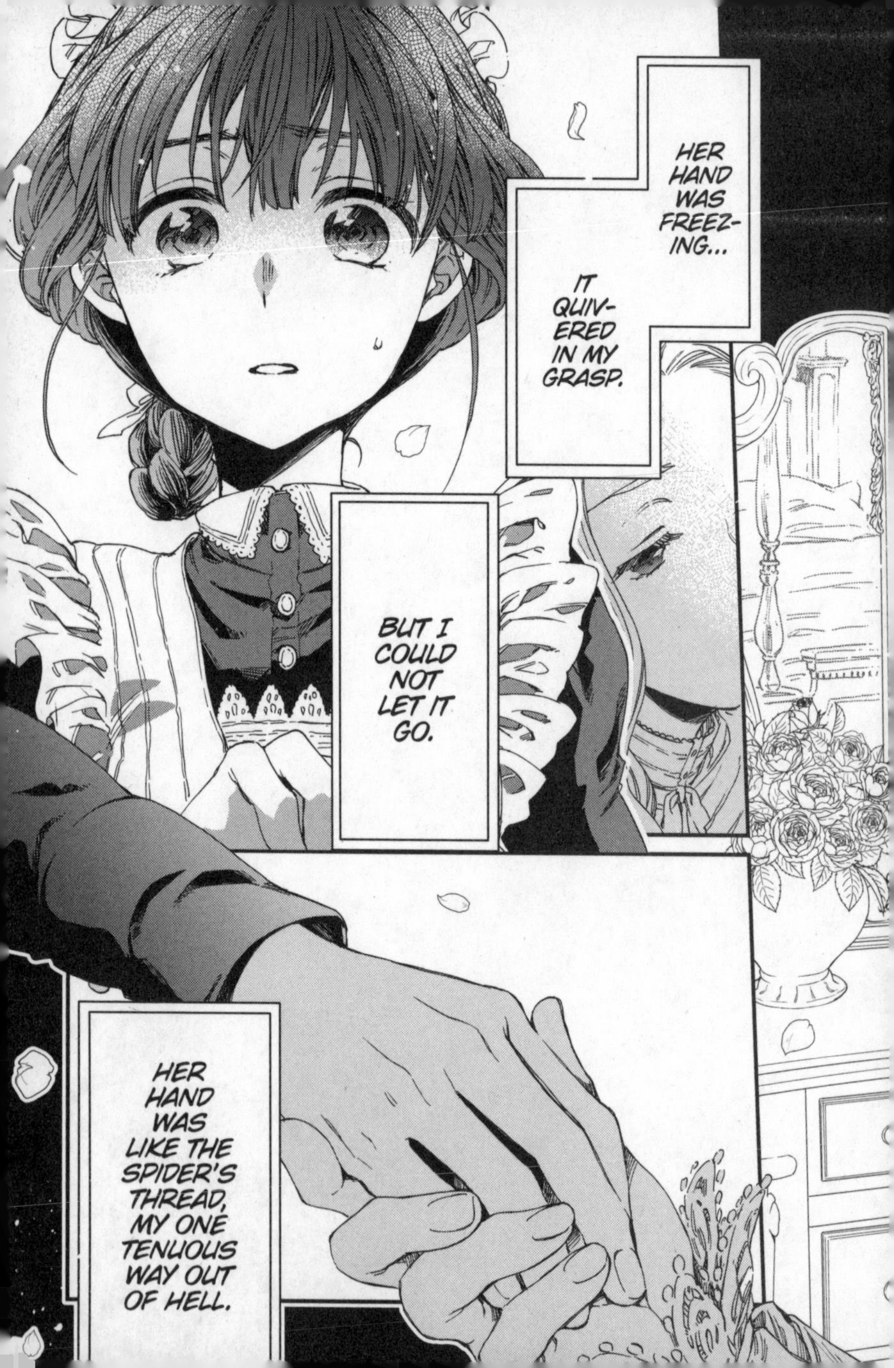
HER HAND WAS FREEZ-ING...
IT QUIV-ERED IN MY GRASP.
BUT I COULD NOT LET IT GO.
HER HAND WAS LIKE THE SPIDER'S THREAD, MY ONE TENUOUS WAY OUT OF HELL.

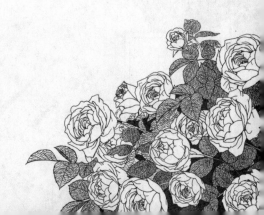

Goodbye,
my Rose Garden

{ Chapter 2 }
The Sun, the Thorns, and the Accomplices

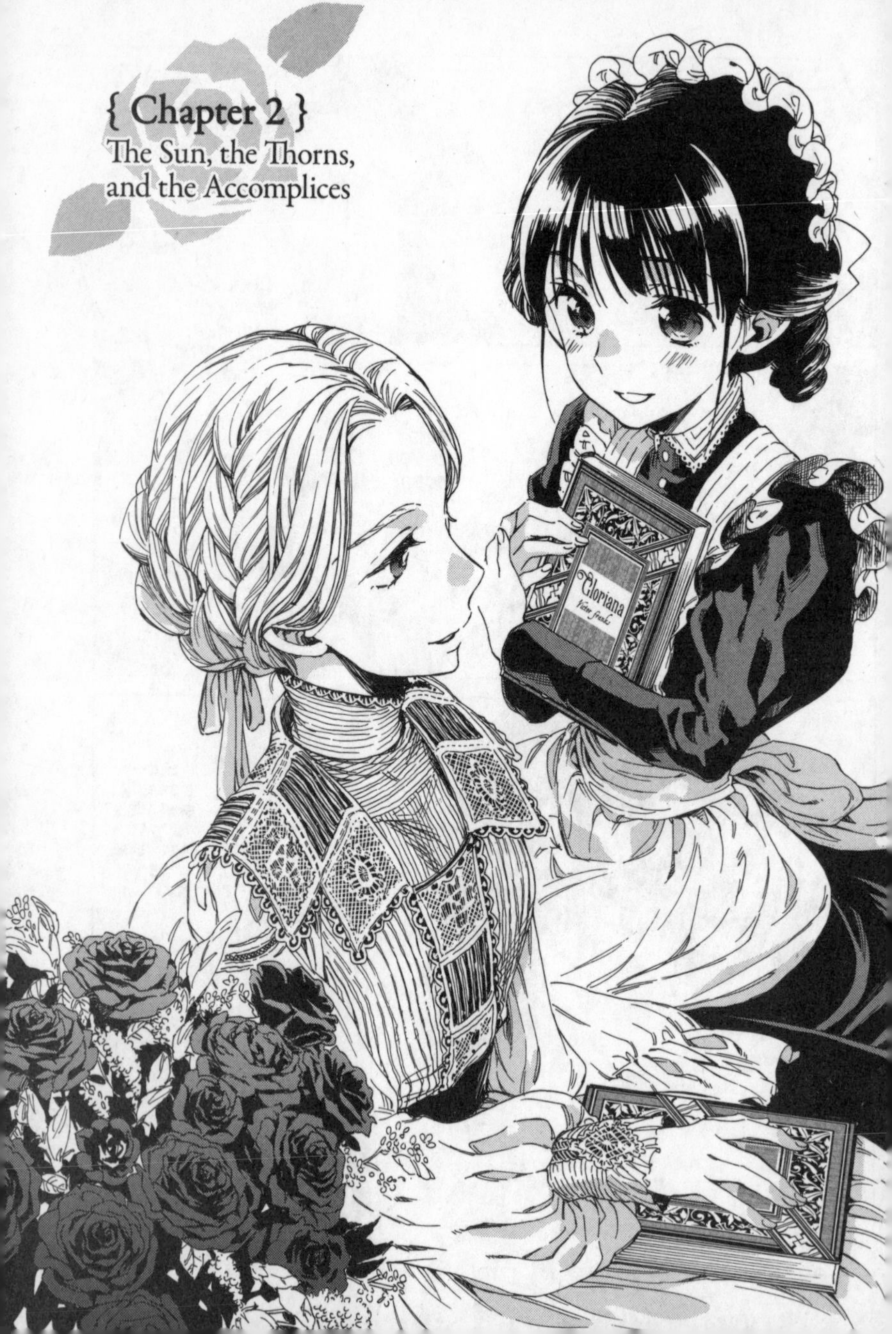
Gloriana
Victor Franks

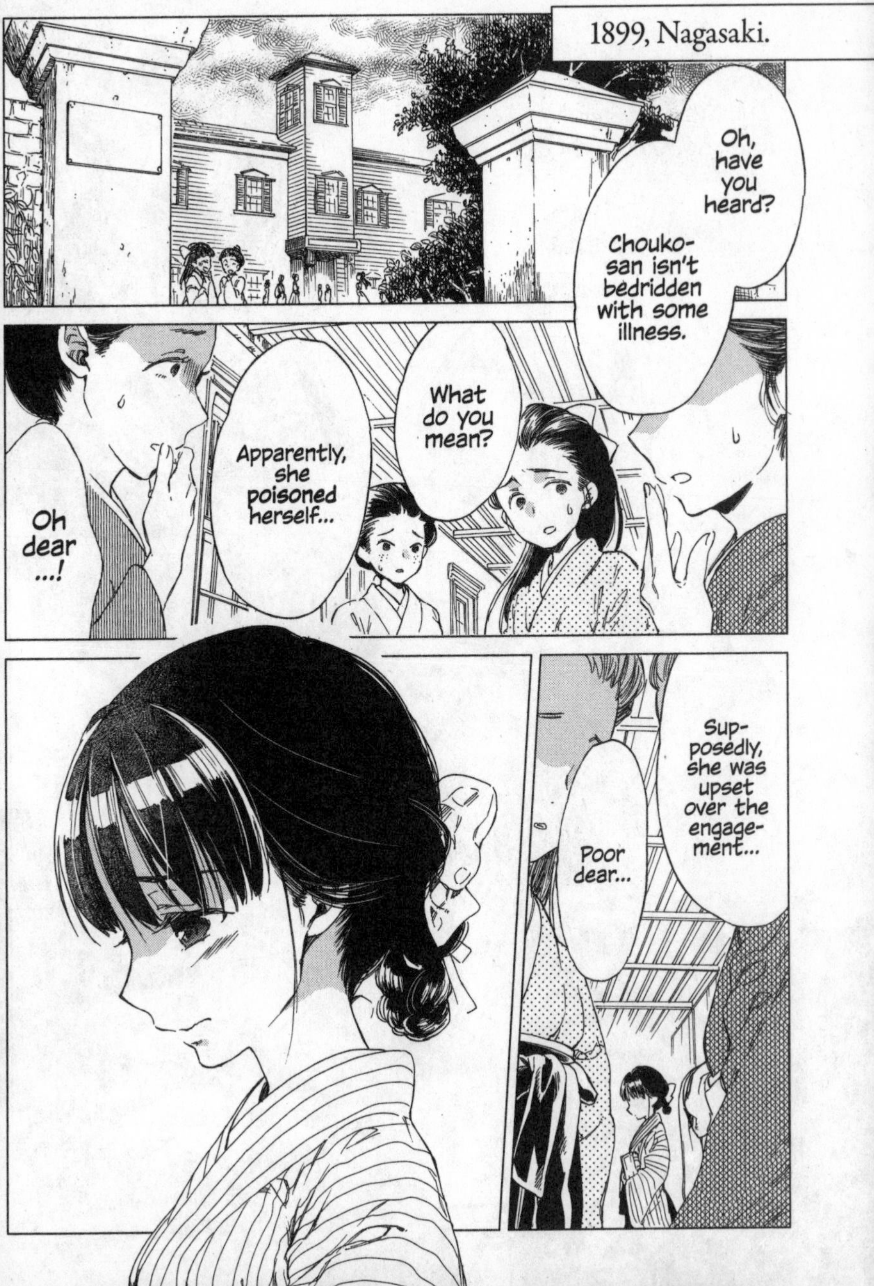
1899, Nagasaki.
Oh, have you heard?
Chouko-san isn't bedridden with some illness.
What do you mean?
Apparently, she poisoned herself...
Oh dear ...!
Supposedly, she was upset over the engagement...
Poor dear...

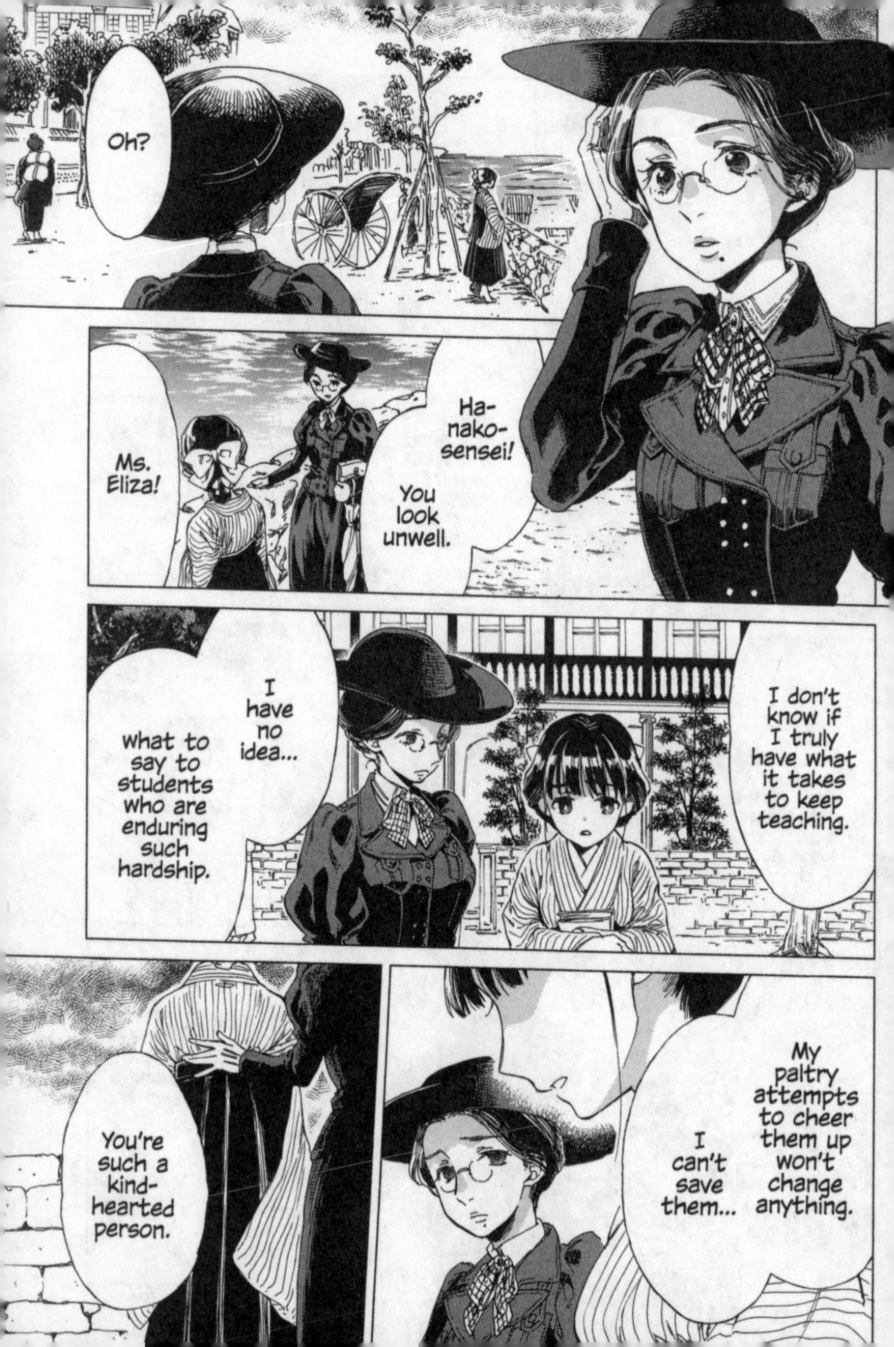
Oh?
Hanako-sensei!
You look unwell.
Ms. Eliza!
I don't know if I truly have what it takes to keep teaching.
I have no idea...
what to say to students who are enduring such hardship.
My paltry attempts to cheer them up won't change anything.
I can't save them...
You're such a kind-hearted person.

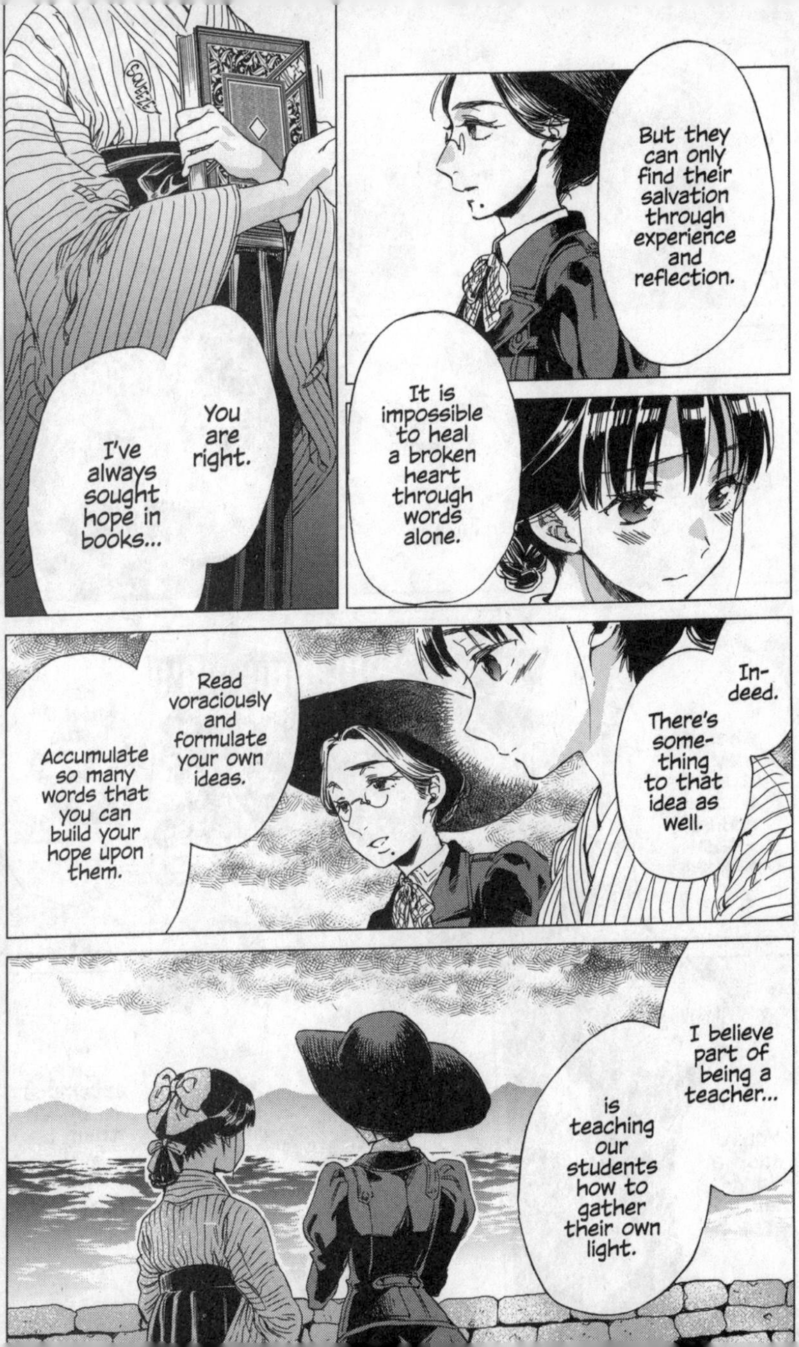
But they can only find their salvation through experience and reflection.
It is impossible to heal a broken heart through words alone.
SQUEEZE
You are right.
I've always sought hope in books...
In-deed.
There's some-thing to that idea as well.
Read voraciously and formulate your own ideas.
Accumulate so many words that you can build your hope upon them.
I believe part of being a teacher...
is teaching our students how to gather their own light.

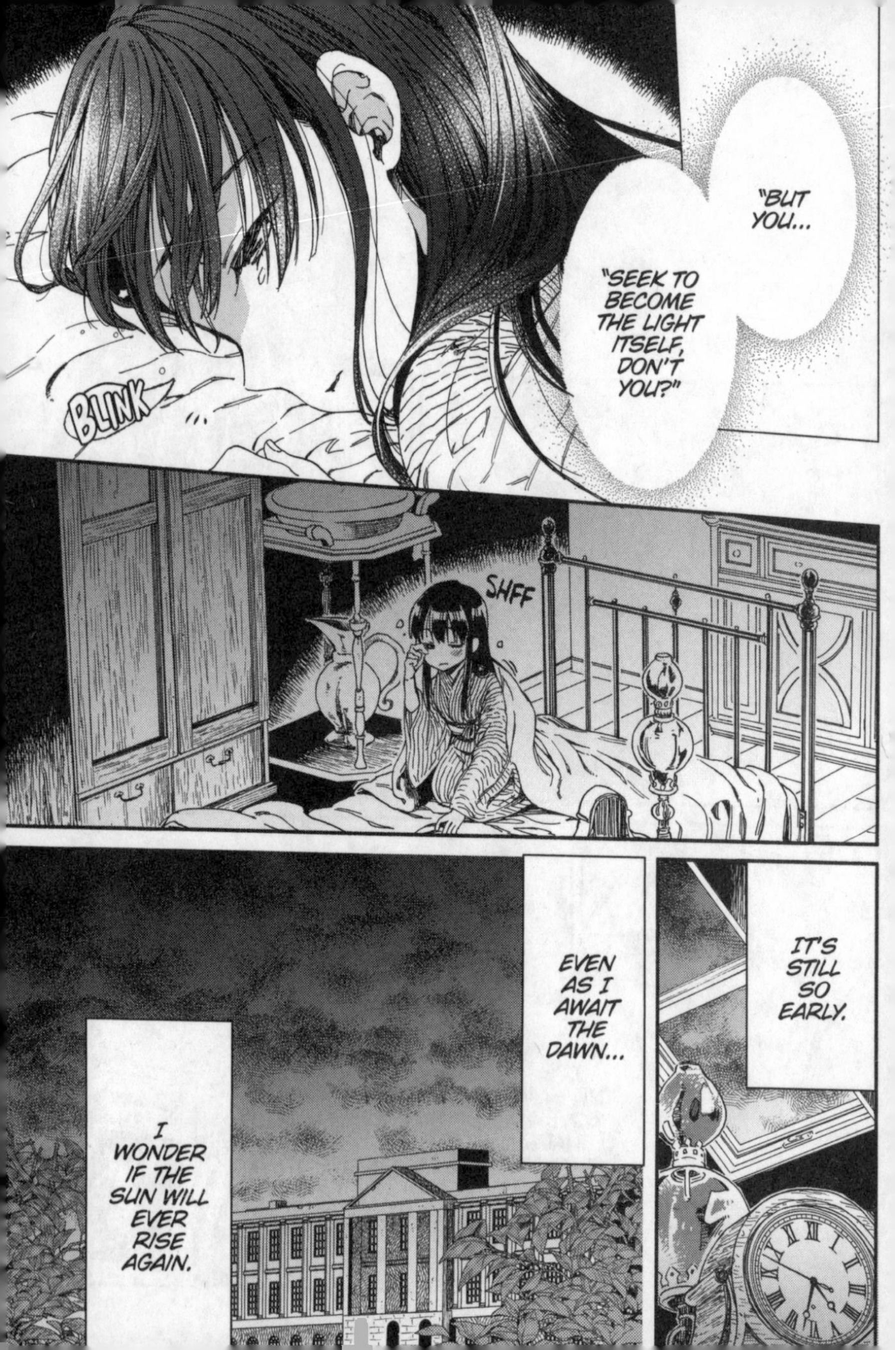
"BUT YOU...
"SEEK TO BECOME THE LIGHT ITSELF, DON'T YOU?"
BLINK
SHFF
IT'S STILL SO EARLY.
EVEN AS I AWAIT THE DAWN...
I WONDER IF THE SUN WILL EVER RISE AGAIN.

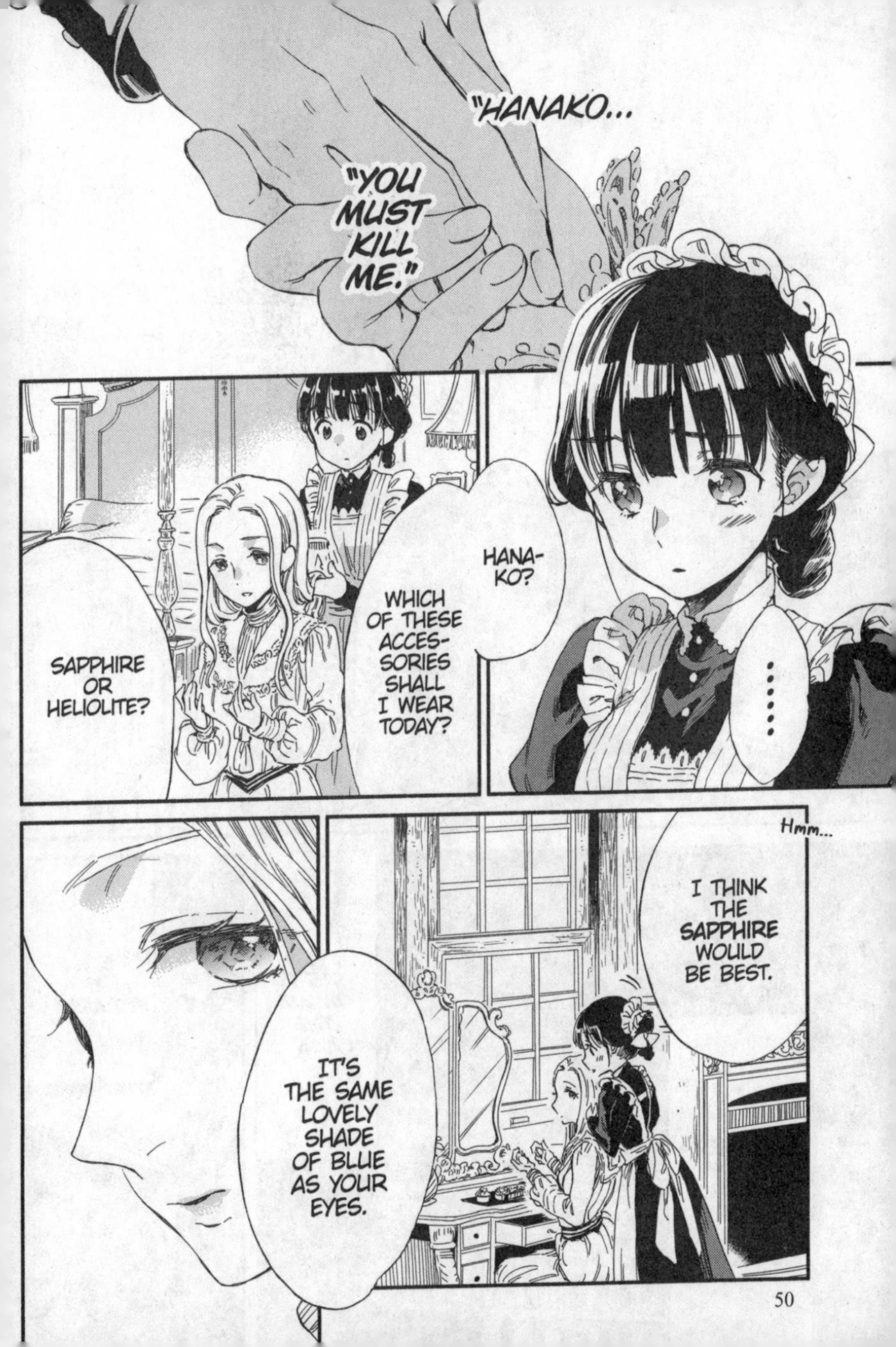
"HANAKO...
"YOU MUST KILL ME."
HANA-KO?
......
WHICH OF THESE ACCES-SORIES SHALL I WEAR TODAY?
SAPPHIRE OR HELIOLITE?
Hmm...
I THINK THE SAPPHIRE WOULD BE BEST.
IT'S THE SAME LOVELY SHADE OF BLUE AS YOUR EYES.

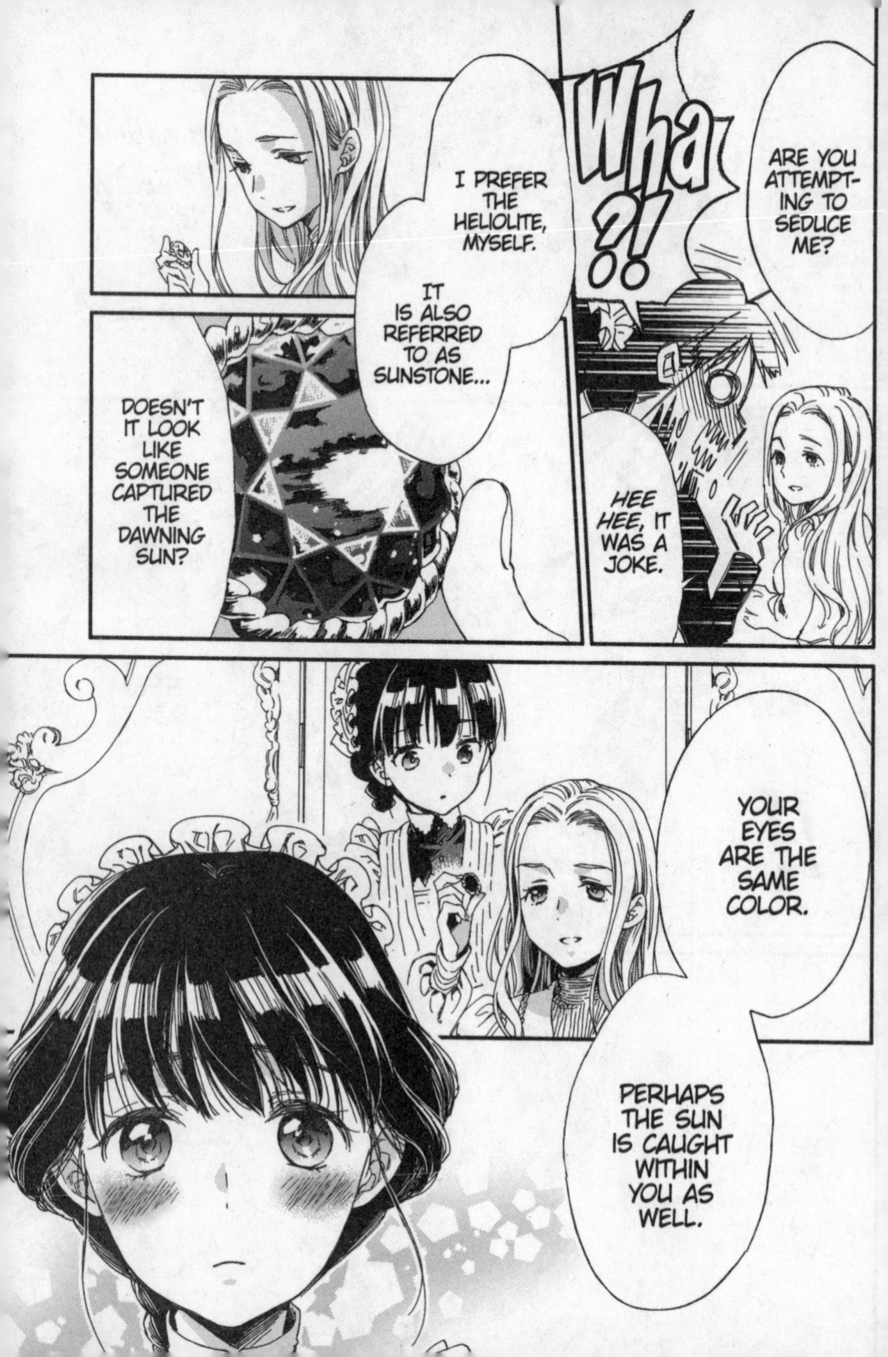
ARE YOU ATTEMPTING TO SEDUCE ME?
Wha?!
HEE HEE, IT WAS A JOKE.
I PREFER THE HELIOLITE, MYSELF.
IT IS ALSO REFERRED TO AS SUNSTONE...
DOESN'T IT LOOK LIKE SOMEONE CAPTURED THE DAWNING SUN?
YOUR EYES ARE THE SAME COLOR.
PERHAPS THE SUN IS CAUGHT WITHIN YOU AS WELL.

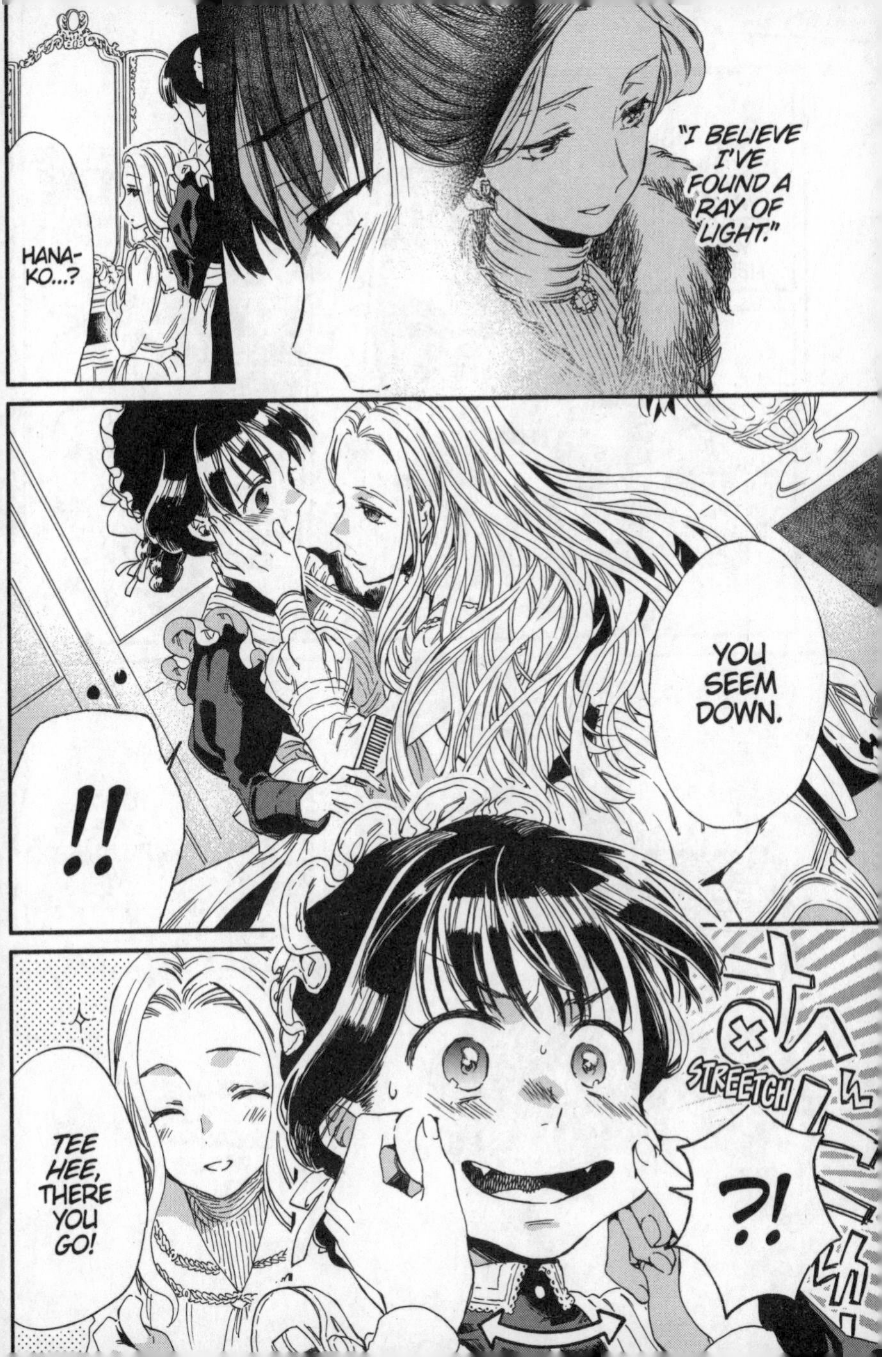
"I BELIEVE I'VE FOUND A RAY OF LIGHT."
HANA-KO...?
YOU SEEM DOWN.
!!
STREETCH
?!
TEE HEE, THERE YOU GO!

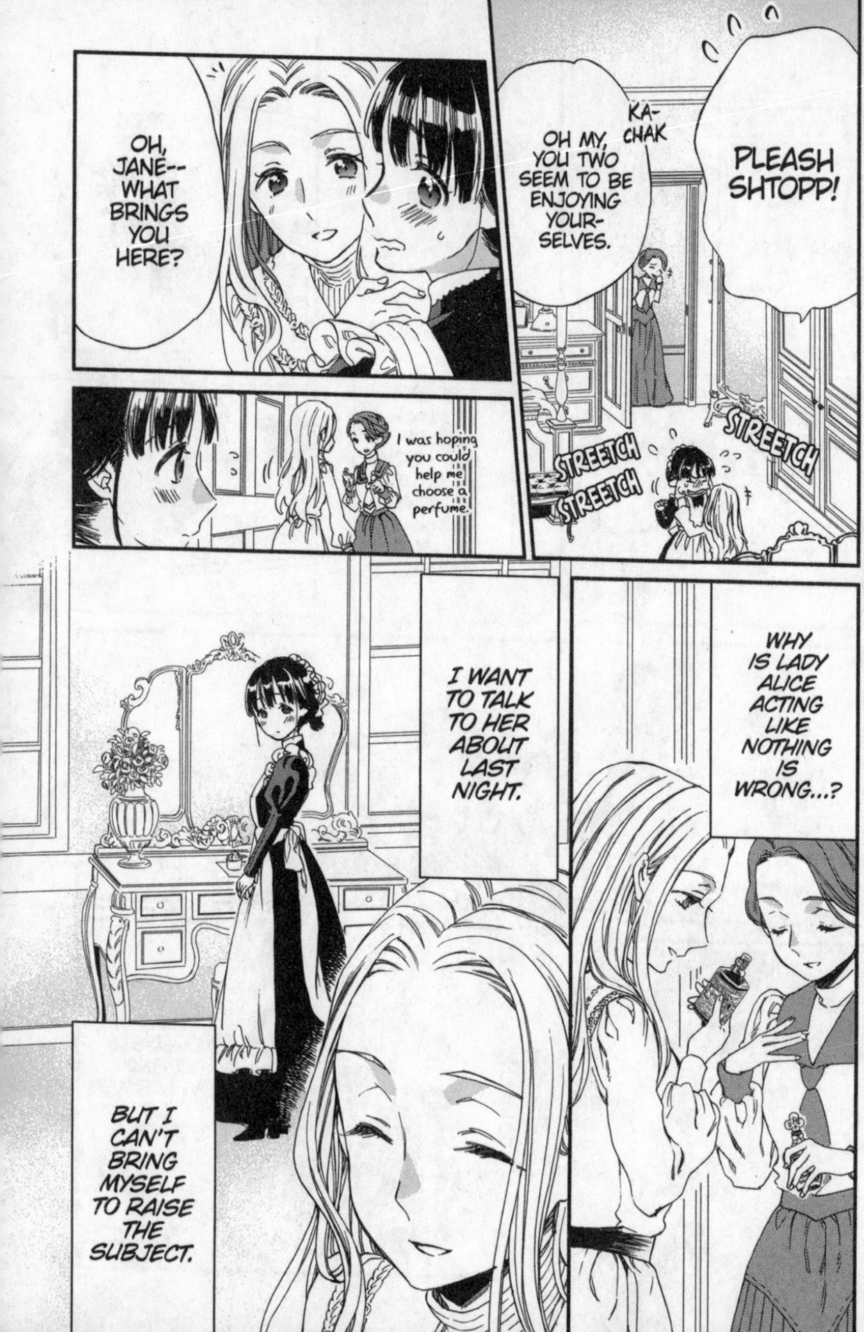
PLEASH SHTOPP!
KA-CHAK
OH MY, YOU TWO SEEM TO BE ENJOYING YOUR-SELVES.
STREETCH
STREETCH
STREETCH
OH, JANE--WHAT BRINGS YOU HERE?
I was hoping you could help me choose a perfume.
WHY IS LADY ALICE ACTING LIKE NOTHING IS WRONG...?
I WANT TO TALK TO HER ABOUT LAST NIGHT.
BUT I CAN'T BRING MYSELF TO RAISE THE SUBJECT.

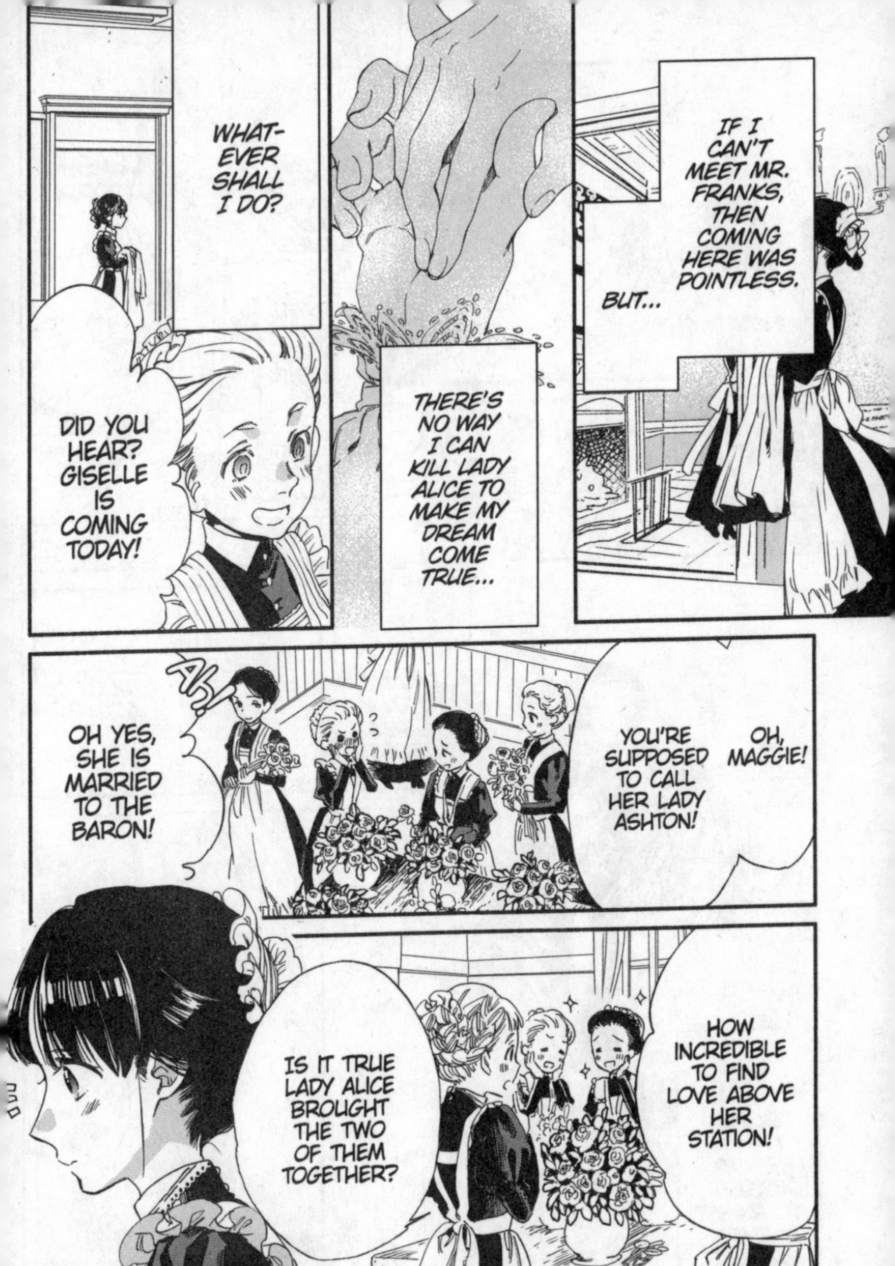
IF I CAN'T MEET MR. FRANKS, THEN COMING HERE WAS POINTLESS.
BUT...
THERE'S NO WAY I CAN KILL LADY ALICE TO MAKE MY DREAM COME TRUE...
WHAT-EVER SHALL I DO?
DID YOU HEAR? GISELLE IS COMING TODAY!
OH, MAGGIE!
YOU'RE SUPPOSED TO CALL HER LADY ASHTON!
AH!
OH YES, SHE IS MARRIED TO THE BARON!
HOW INCREDIBLE TO FIND LOVE ABOVE HER STATION!
IS IT TRUE LADY ALICE BROUGHT THE TWO OF THEM TOGETHER?

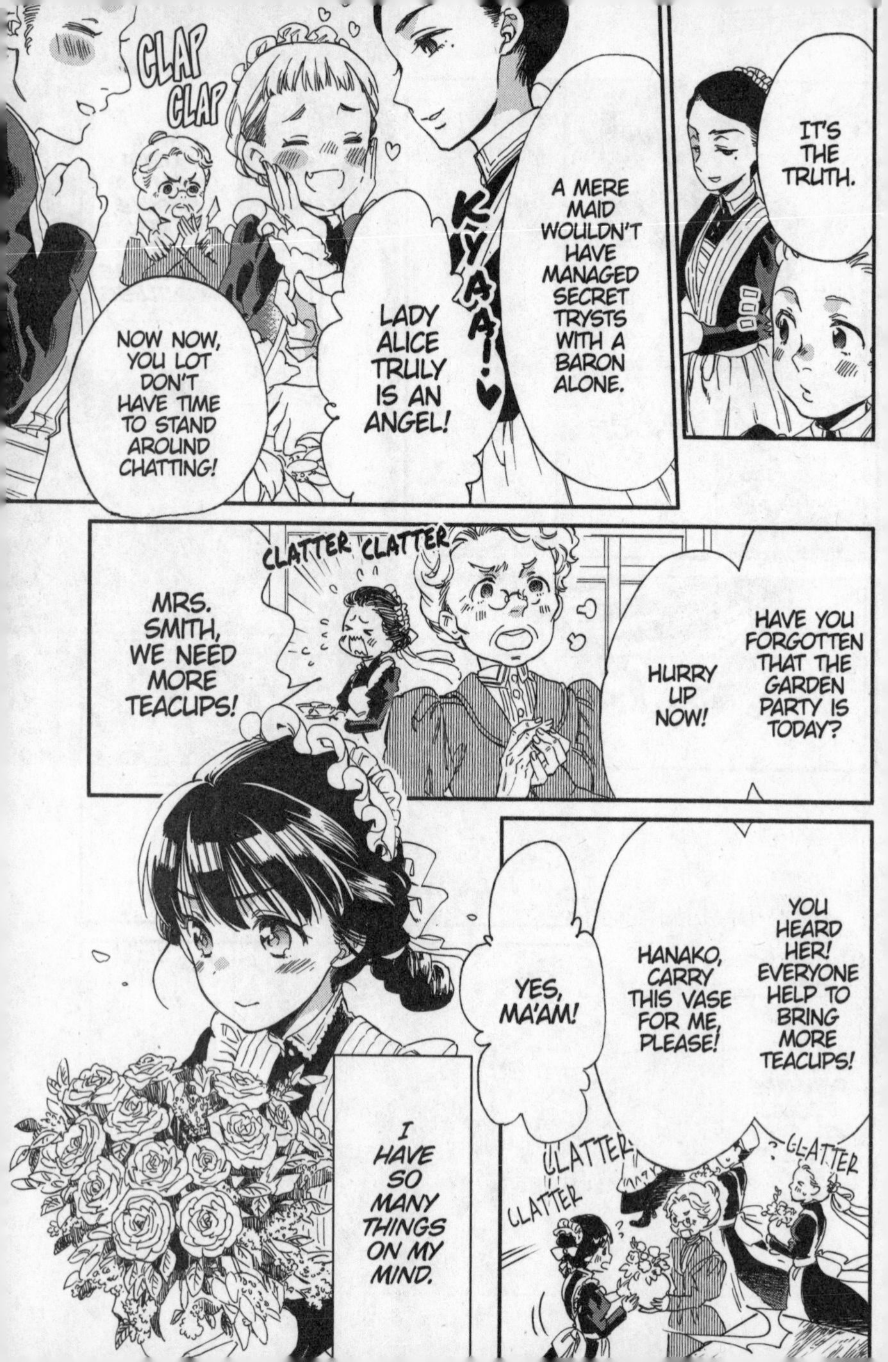
IT'S THE TRUTH.
A MERE MAID WOULDN'T HAVE MANAGED SECRET TRYSTS WITH A BARON ALONE.
KYAA!♥
LADY ALICE TRULY IS AN ANGEL!
CLAP CLAP
NOW NOW, YOU LOT DON'T HAVE TIME TO STAND AROUND CHATTING!
HAVE YOU FORGOTTEN THAT THE GARDEN PARTY IS TODAY?
HURRY UP NOW!
CLATTER CLATTER
MRS. SMITH, WE NEED MORE TEACUPS!
YOU HEARD HER! EVERYONE HELP TO BRING MORE TEACUPS!
HANAKO, CARRY THIS VASE FOR ME, PLEASE!
YES, MA'AM!
CLATTER
CLATTER
CLATTER
I HAVE SO MANY THINGS ON MY MIND.

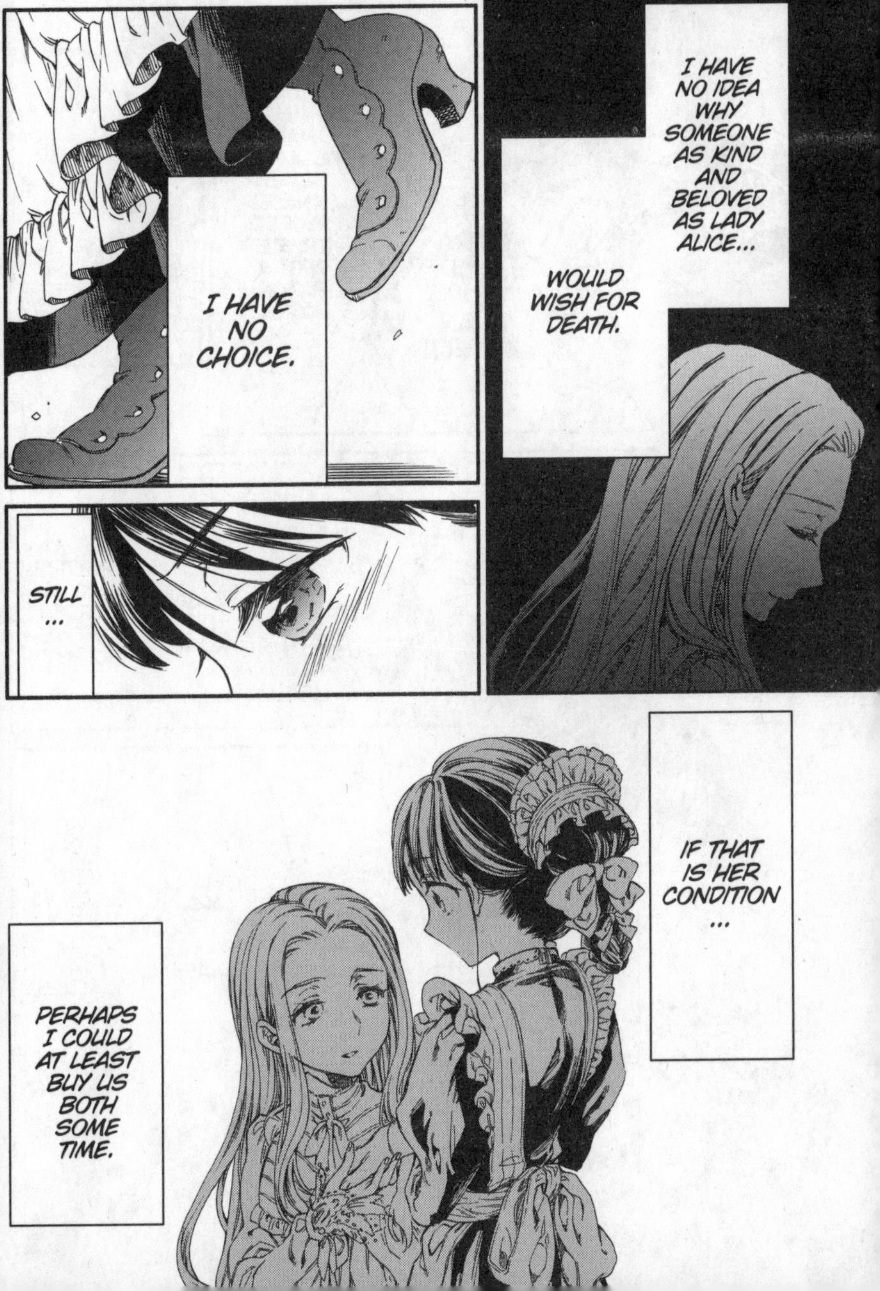
I HAVE NO IDEA WHY SOMEONE AS KIND AND BELOVED AS LADY ALICE...
WOULD WISH FOR DEATH.
I HAVE NO CHOICE.
STILL ...
IF THAT IS HER CONDITION ...
PERHAPS I COULD AT LEAST BUY US BOTH SOME TIME.

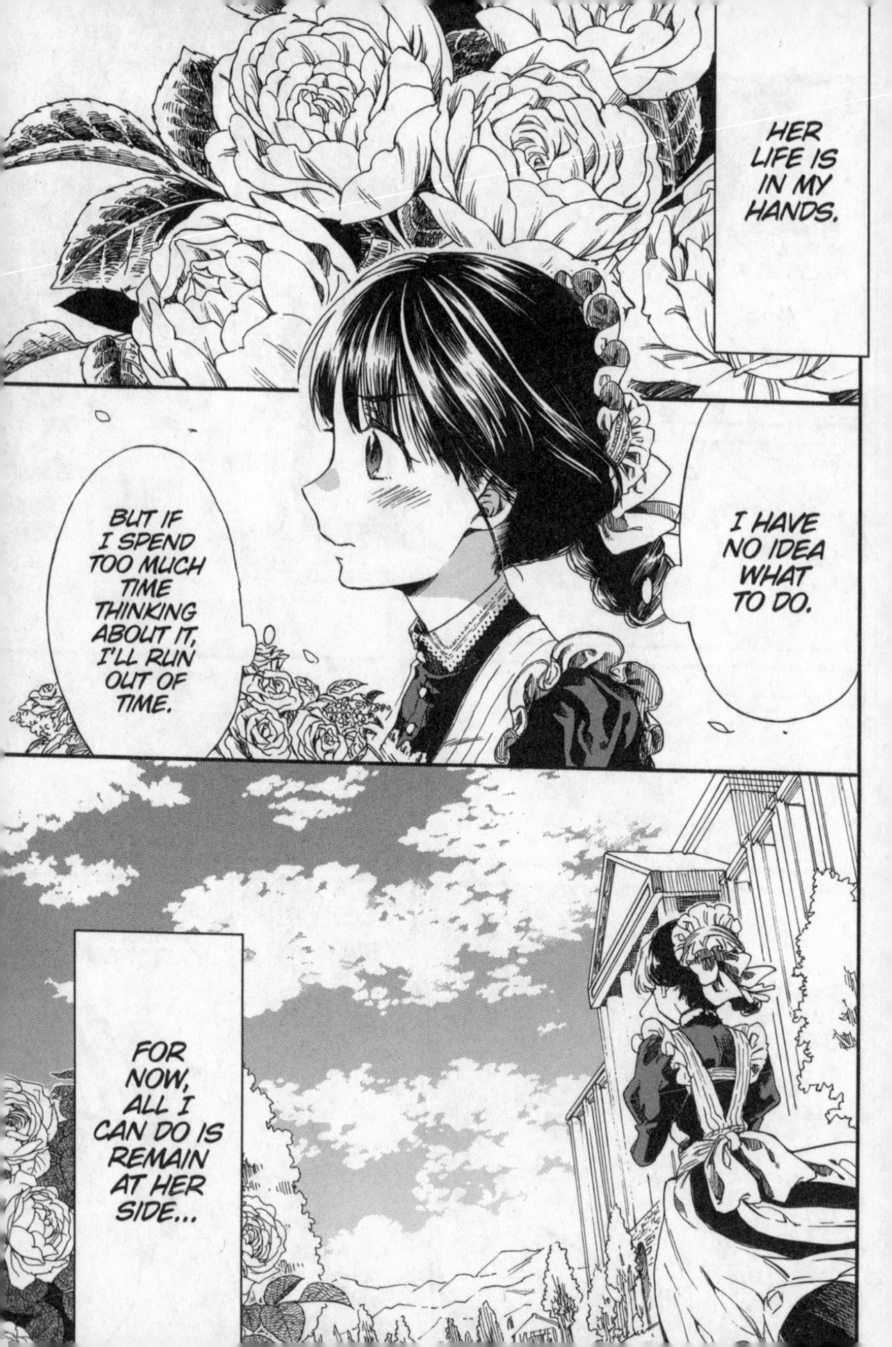
HER LIFE IS IN MY HANDS.
I HAVE NO IDEA WHAT TO DO.
BUT IF I SPEND TOO MUCH TIME THINKING ABOUT IT, I'LL RUN OUT OF TIME.
FOR NOW, ALL I CAN DO IS REMAIN AT HER SIDE...

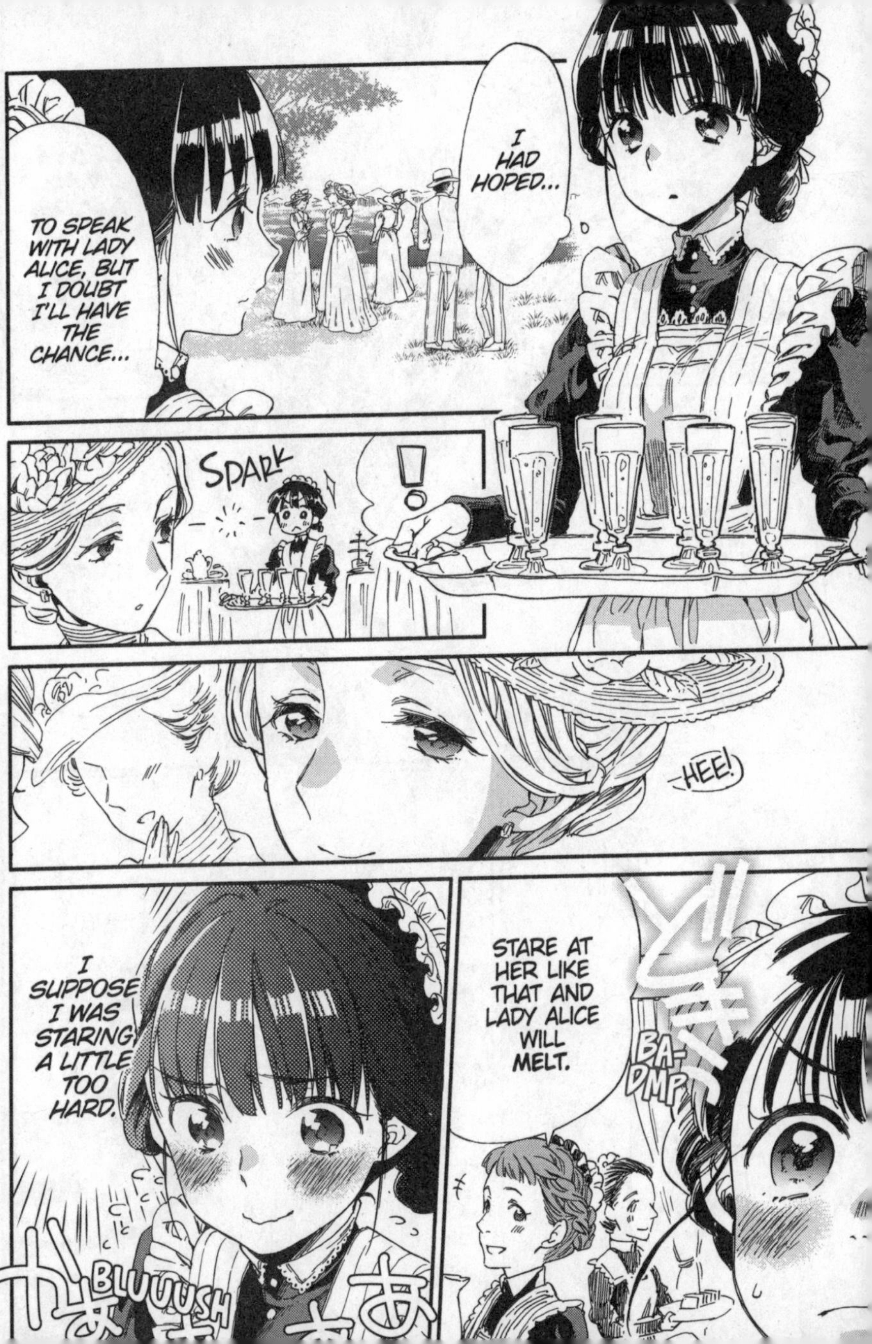

I HAD HOPED...
TO SPEAK WITH LADY ALICE, BUT I DOUBT I'LL HAVE THE CHANCE...
SPARK
!
HEE!
STARE AT HER LIKE THAT AND LADY ALICE WILL MELT.
BA-DMP
I SUPPOSE I WAS STARING A LITTLE TOO HARD.
BLUUUSH

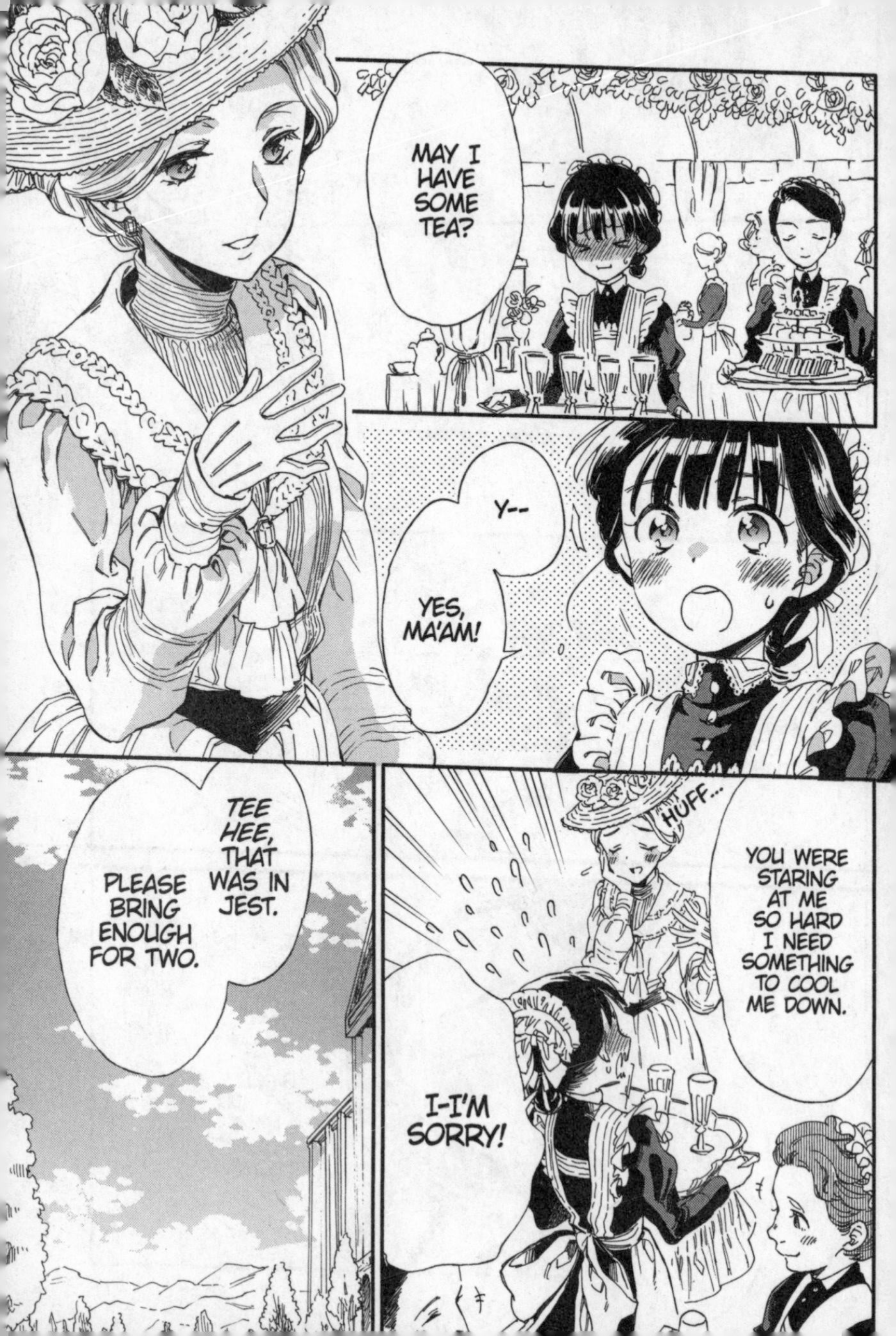
MAY I HAVE SOME TEA?
Y--
YES, MA'AM!
YOU WERE STARING AT ME SO HARD I NEED SOMETHING TO COOL ME DOWN.
HUFF...
I-I'M SORRY!
TEE HEE, THAT WAS IN JEST.
PLEASE BRING ENOUGH FOR TWO.

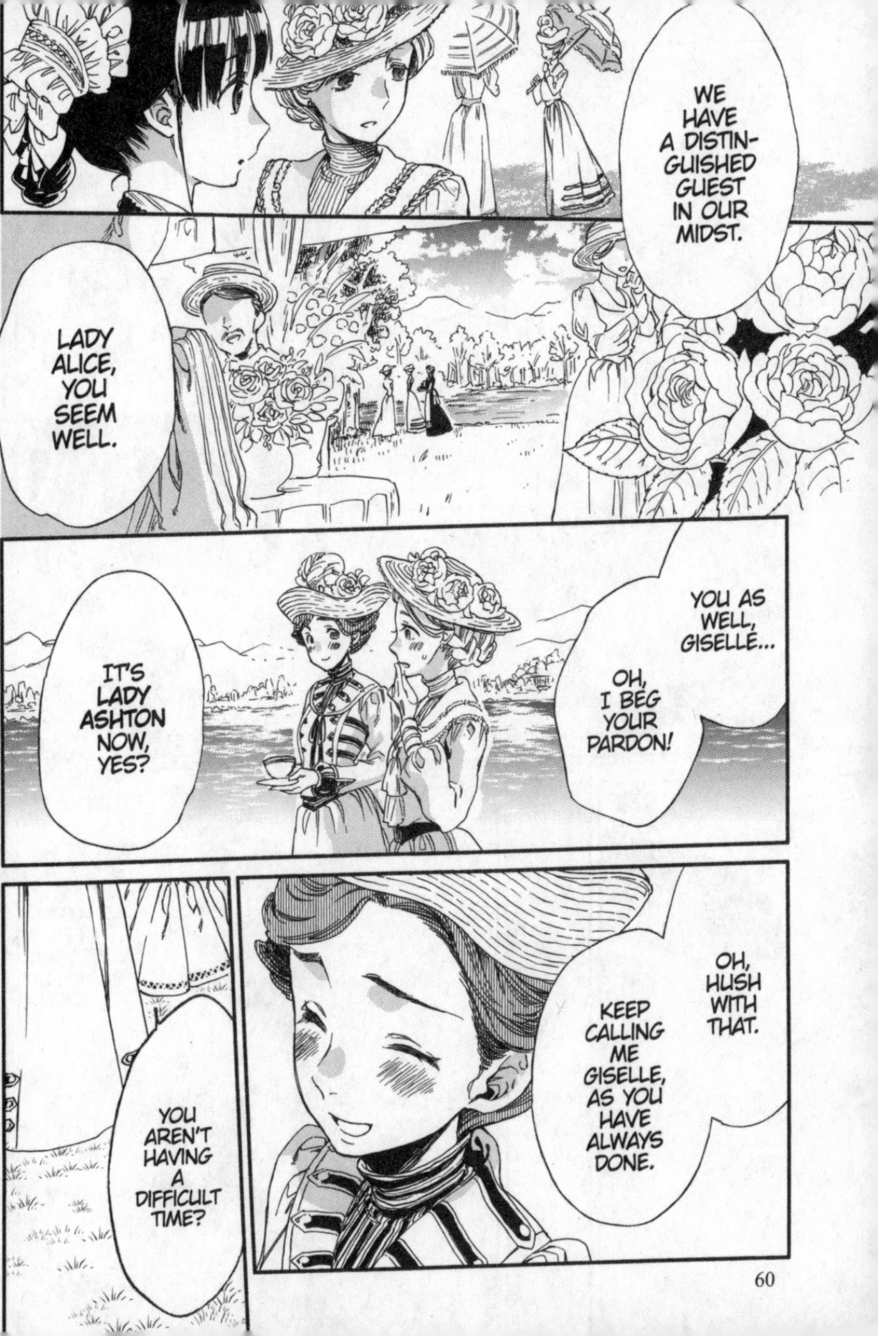
WE HAVE A DISTINGUISHED GUEST IN OUR MIDST.
LADY ALICE, YOU SEEM WELL.
YOU AS WELL, GISELLE...
OH, I BEG YOUR PARDON!
IT'S LADY ASHTON NOW, YES?
OH, HUSH WITH THAT.
KEEP CALLING ME GISELLE, AS YOU HAVE ALWAYS DONE.
YOU AREN'T HAVING A DIFFICULT TIME?

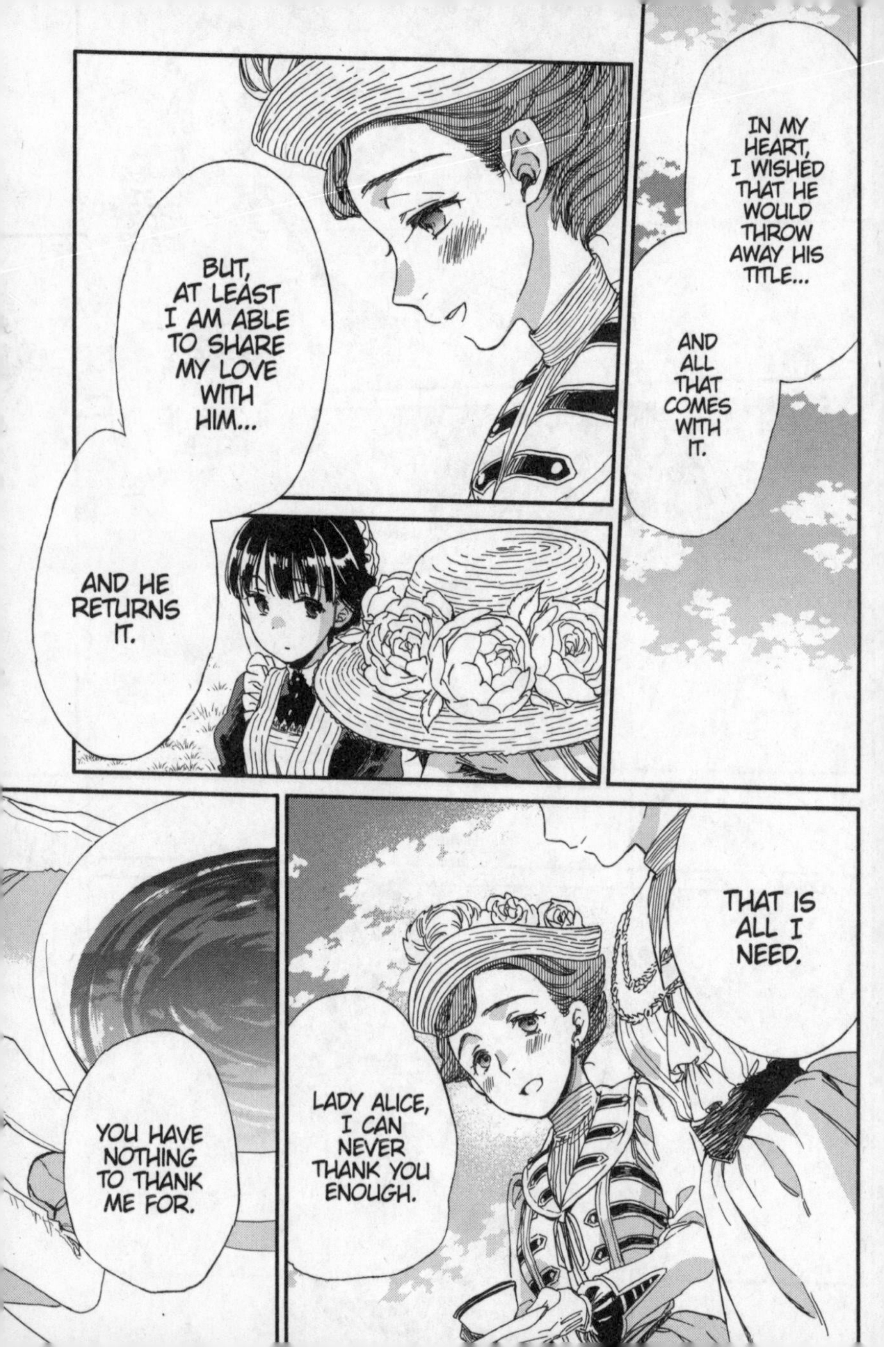
IN MY HEART, I WISHED THAT HE WOULD THROW AWAY HIS TITLE...
AND ALL THAT COMES WITH IT.
BUT, AT LEAST I AM ABLE TO SHARE MY LOVE WITH HIM...
AND HE RETURNS IT.
THAT IS ALL I NEED.
LADY ALICE, I CAN NEVER THANK YOU ENOUGH.
YOU HAVE NOTHING TO THANK ME FOR.

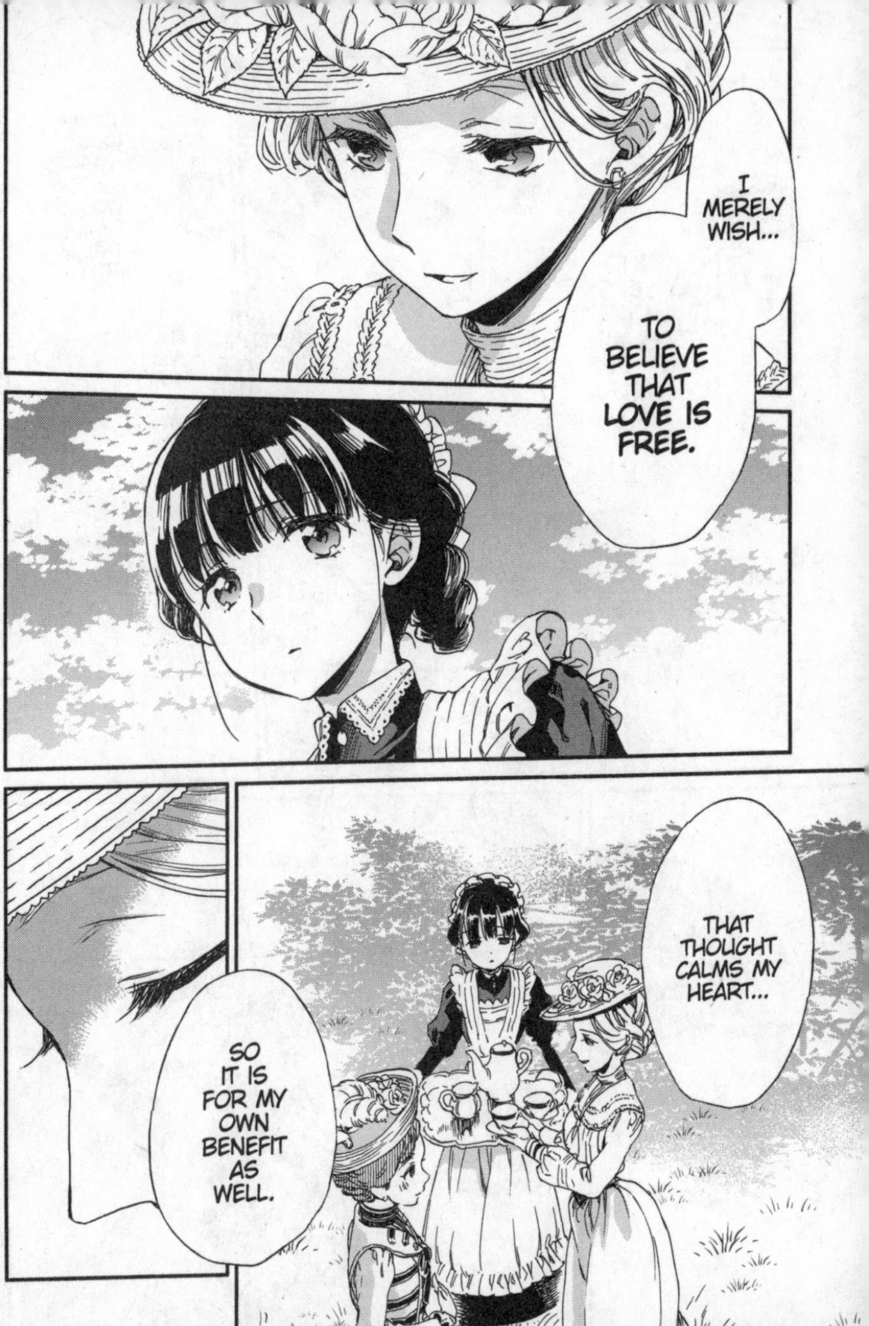
I MERELY WISH...
TO BELIEVE THAT LOVE IS FREE.
THAT THOUGHT CALMS MY HEART...
SO IT IS FOR MY OWN BENEFIT AS WELL.

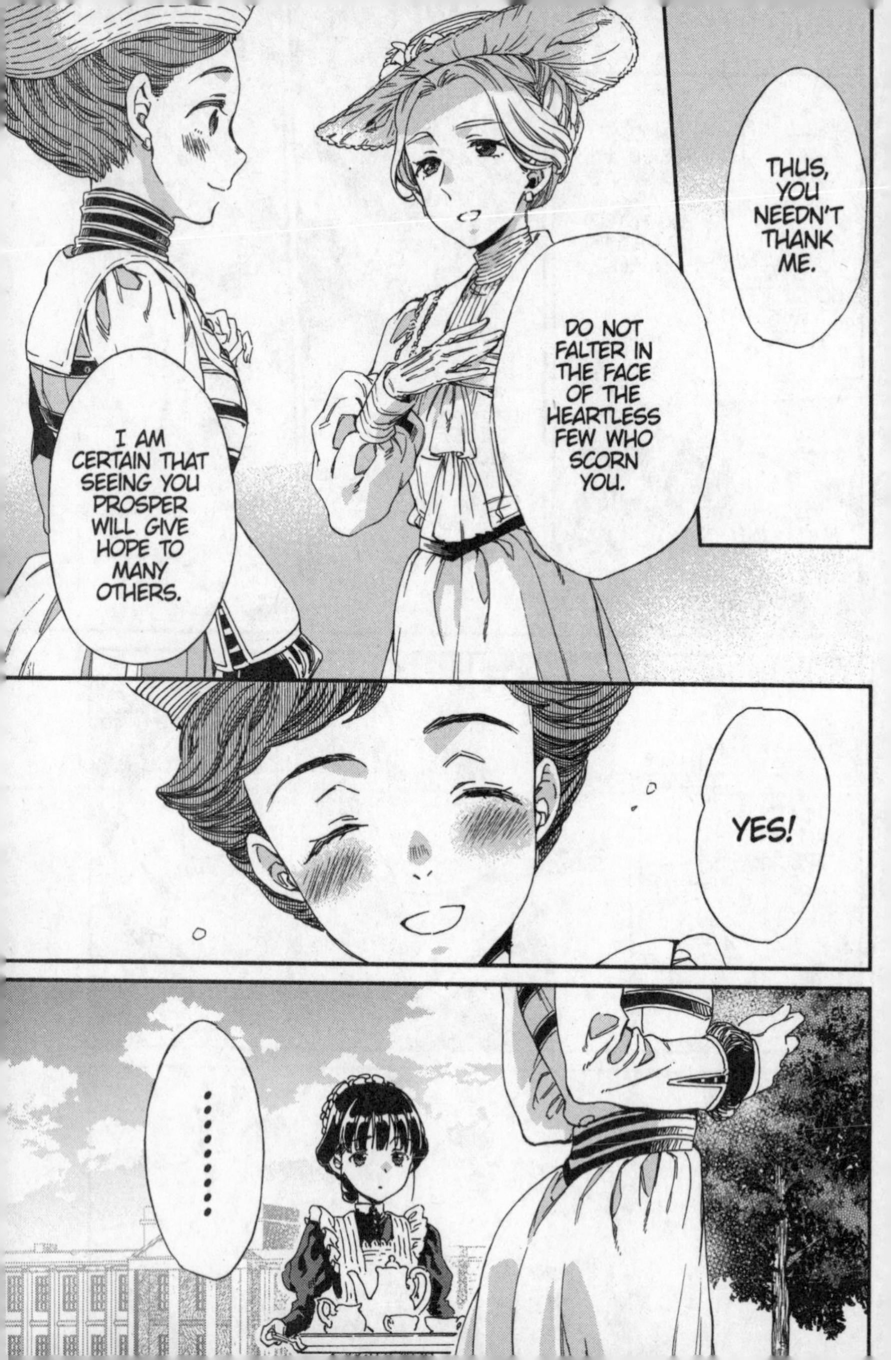
THUS, YOU NEEDN'T THANK ME.
DO NOT FALTER IN THE FACE OF THE HEARTLESS FEW WHO SCORN YOU.
I AM CERTAIN THAT SEEING YOU PROSPER WILL GIVE HOPE TO MANY OTHERS.
YES!
....

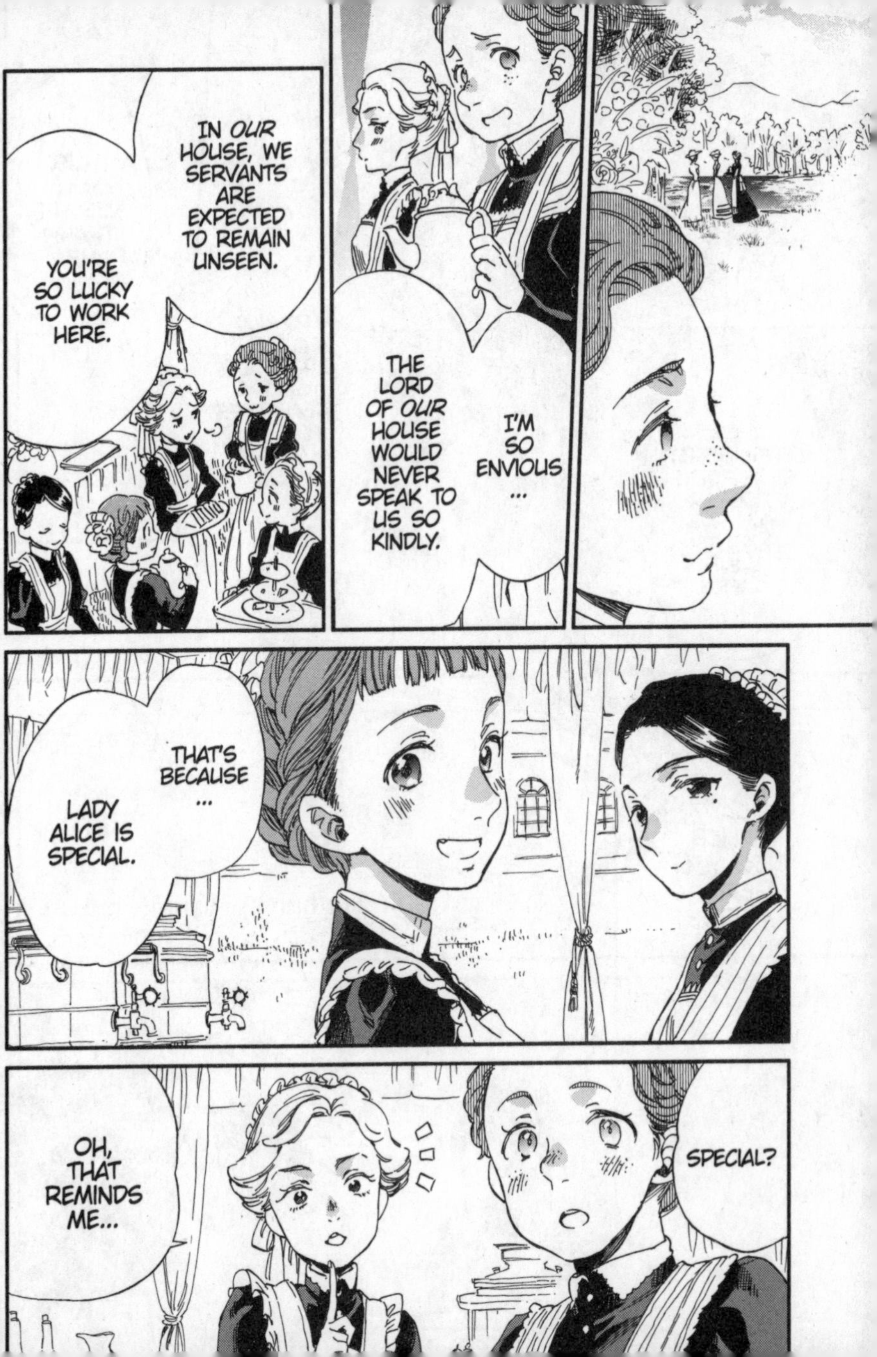
I'M SO ENVIOUS...
THE LORD OF OUR HOUSE WOULD NEVER SPEAK TO US SO KINDLY.
IN OUR HOUSE, WE SERVANTS ARE EXPECTED TO REMAIN UNSEEN.
YOU'RE SO LUCKY TO WORK HERE.
THAT'S BECAUSE...
LADY ALICE IS SPECIAL.
SPECIAL?
OH, THAT REMINDS ME...

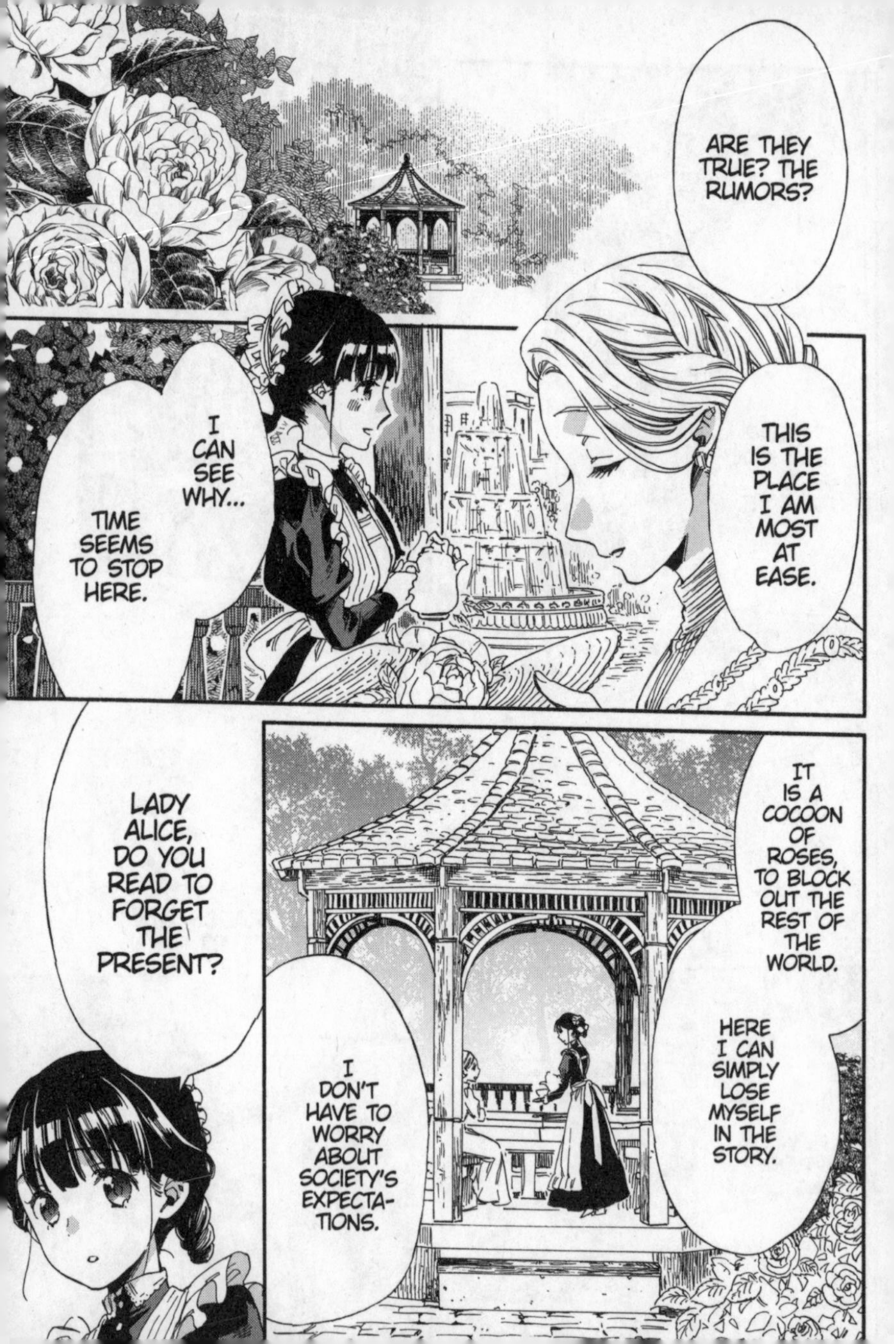
ARE THEY TRUE? THE RUMORS?
THIS IS THE PLACE I AM MOST AT EASE.
I CAN SEE WHY...
TIME SEEMS TO STOP HERE.
IT IS A COCOON OF ROSES, TO BLOCK OUT THE REST OF THE WORLD.
HERE I CAN SIMPLY LOSE MYSELF IN THE STORY.
I DON'T HAVE TO WORRY ABOUT SOCIETY'S EXPECTATIONS.
LADY ALICE, DO YOU READ TO FORGET THE PRESENT?

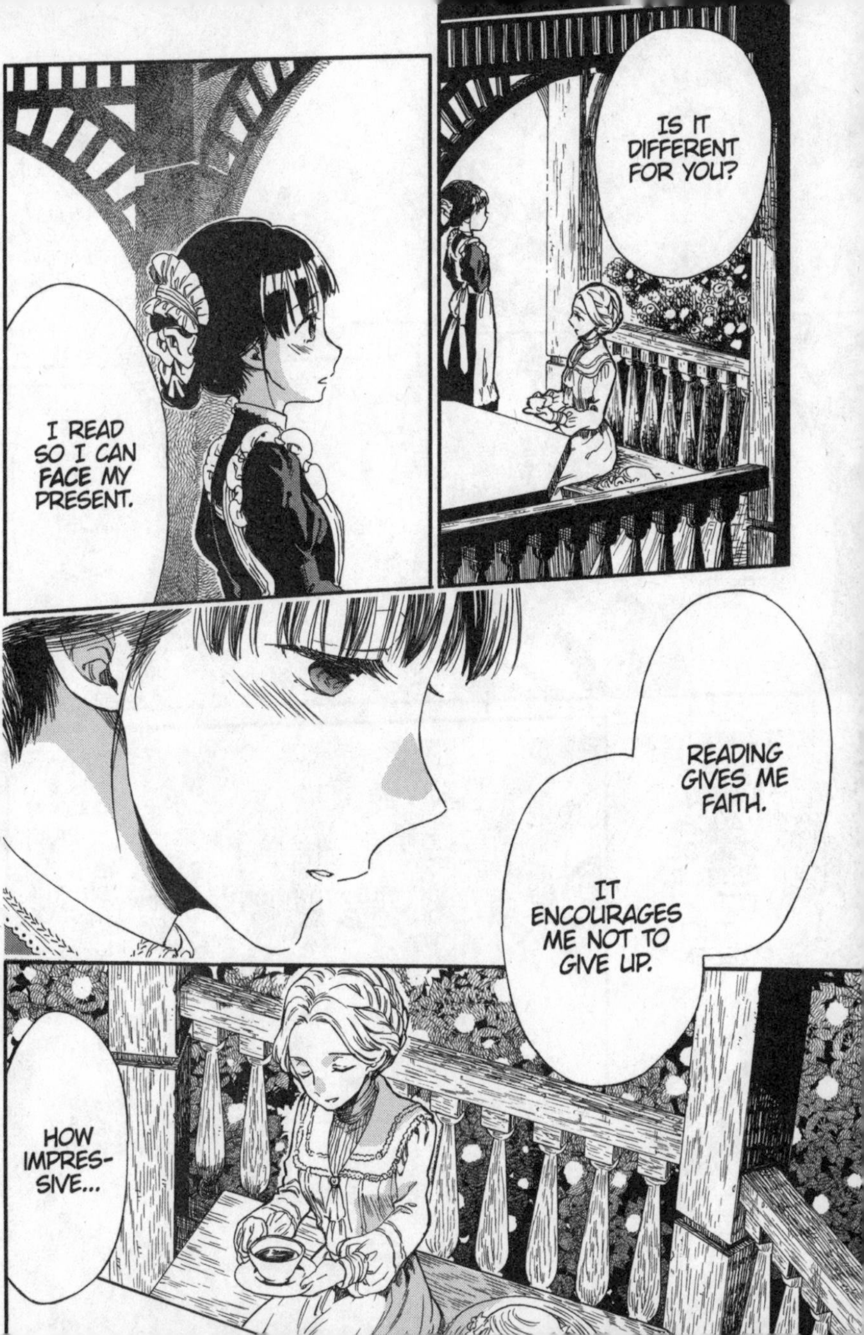
IS IT DIFFERENT FOR YOU?
I READ SO I CAN FACE MY PRESENT.
READING GIVES ME FAITH.
IT ENCOURAGES ME NOT TO GIVE UP.
HOW IMPRES-SIVE...

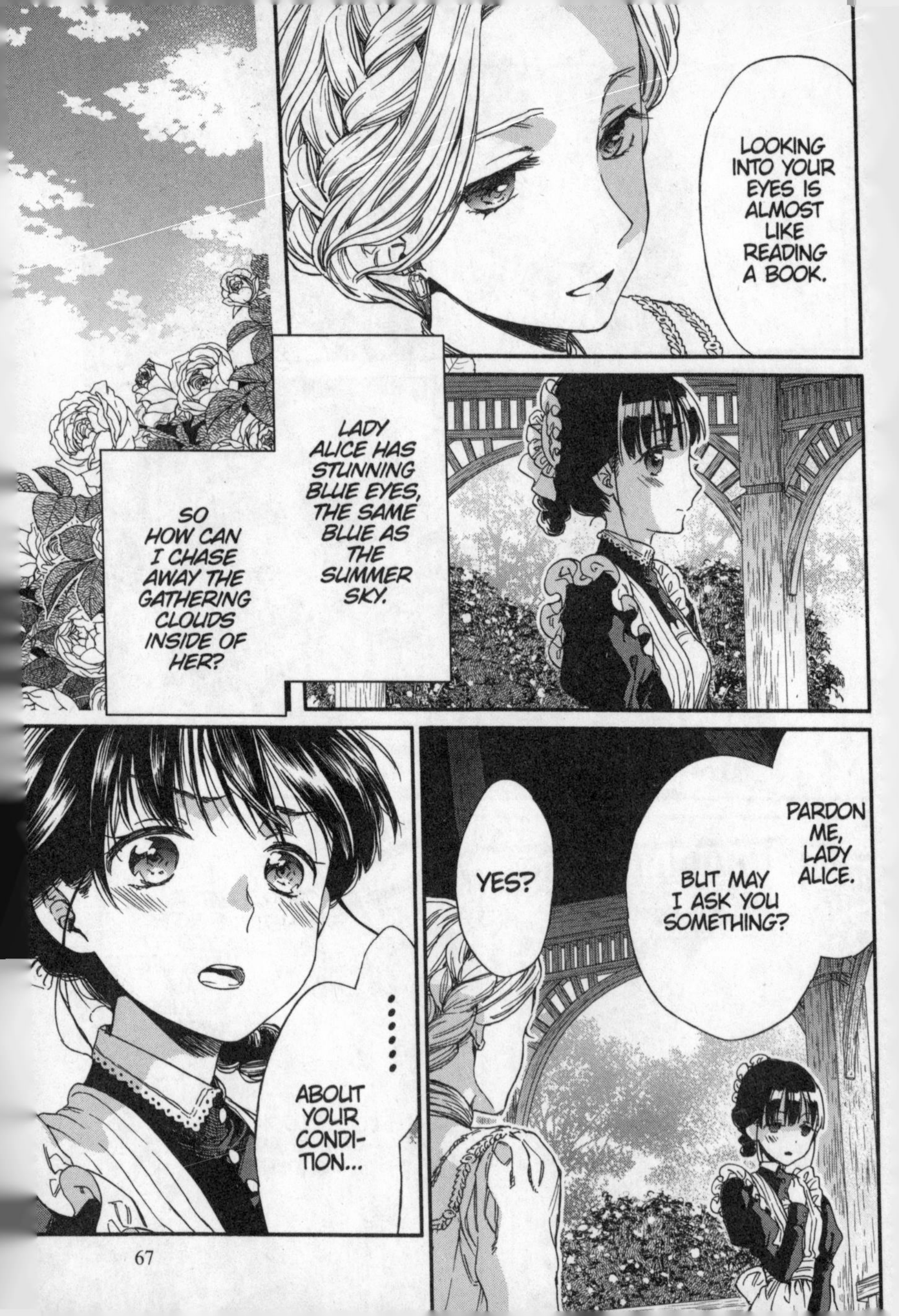
LOOKING INTO YOUR EYES IS ALMOST LIKE READING A BOOK.
LADY ALICE HAS STUNNING BLUE EYES, THE SAME BLUE AS THE SUMMER SKY.
SO HOW CAN I CHASE AWAY THE GATHERING CLOUDS INSIDE OF HER?
PARDON ME, LADY ALICE.
BUT MAY I ASK YOU SOMETHING?
YES?
......
ABOUT YOUR CONDITION...

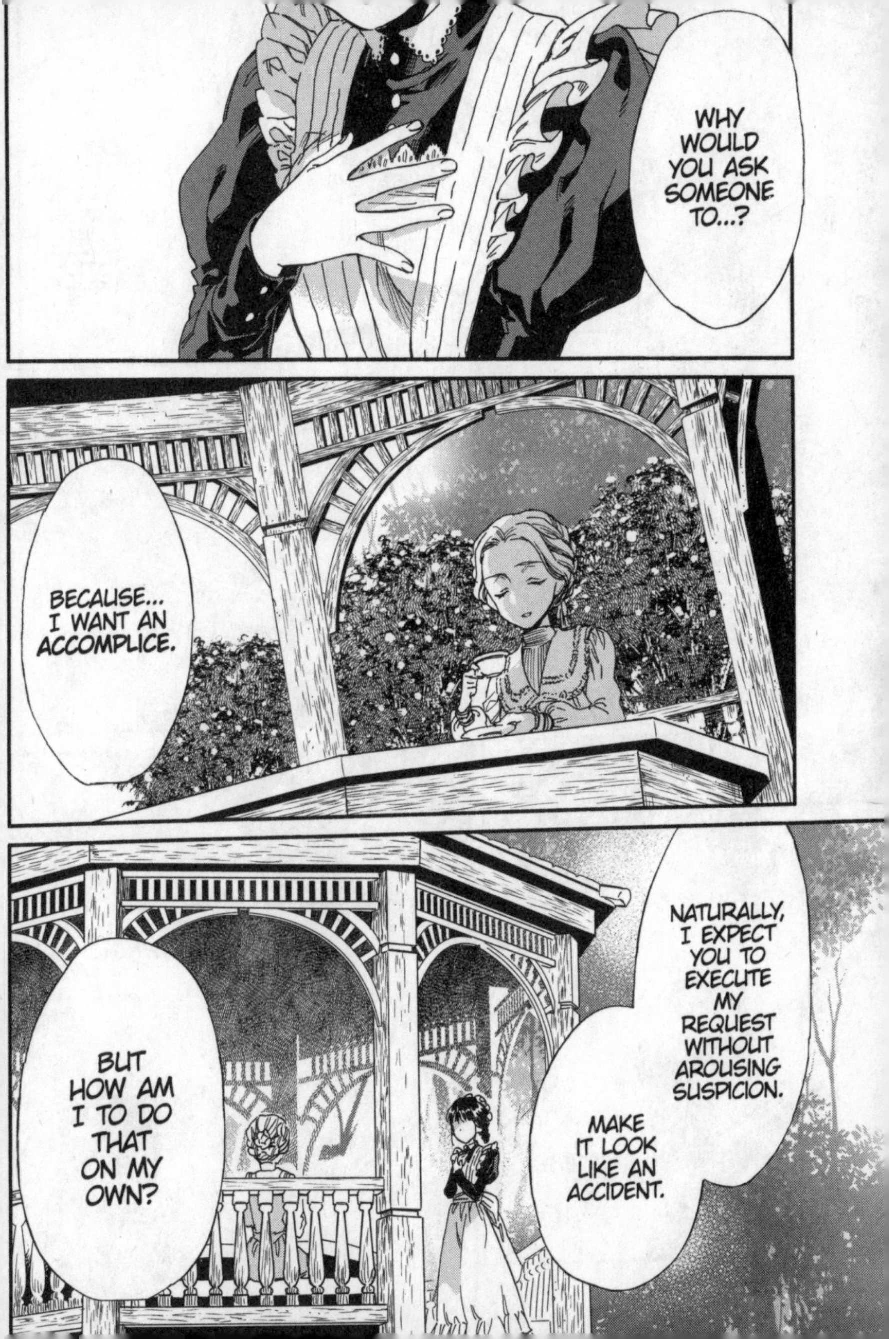
WHY WOULD YOU ASK SOMEONE TO...?
BECAUSE... I WANT AN ACCOMPLICE.
NATURALLY, I EXPECT YOU TO EXECUTE MY REQUEST WITHOUT AROUSING SUSPICION.
MAKE IT LOOK LIKE AN ACCIDENT.
BUT HOW AM I TO DO THAT ON MY OWN?

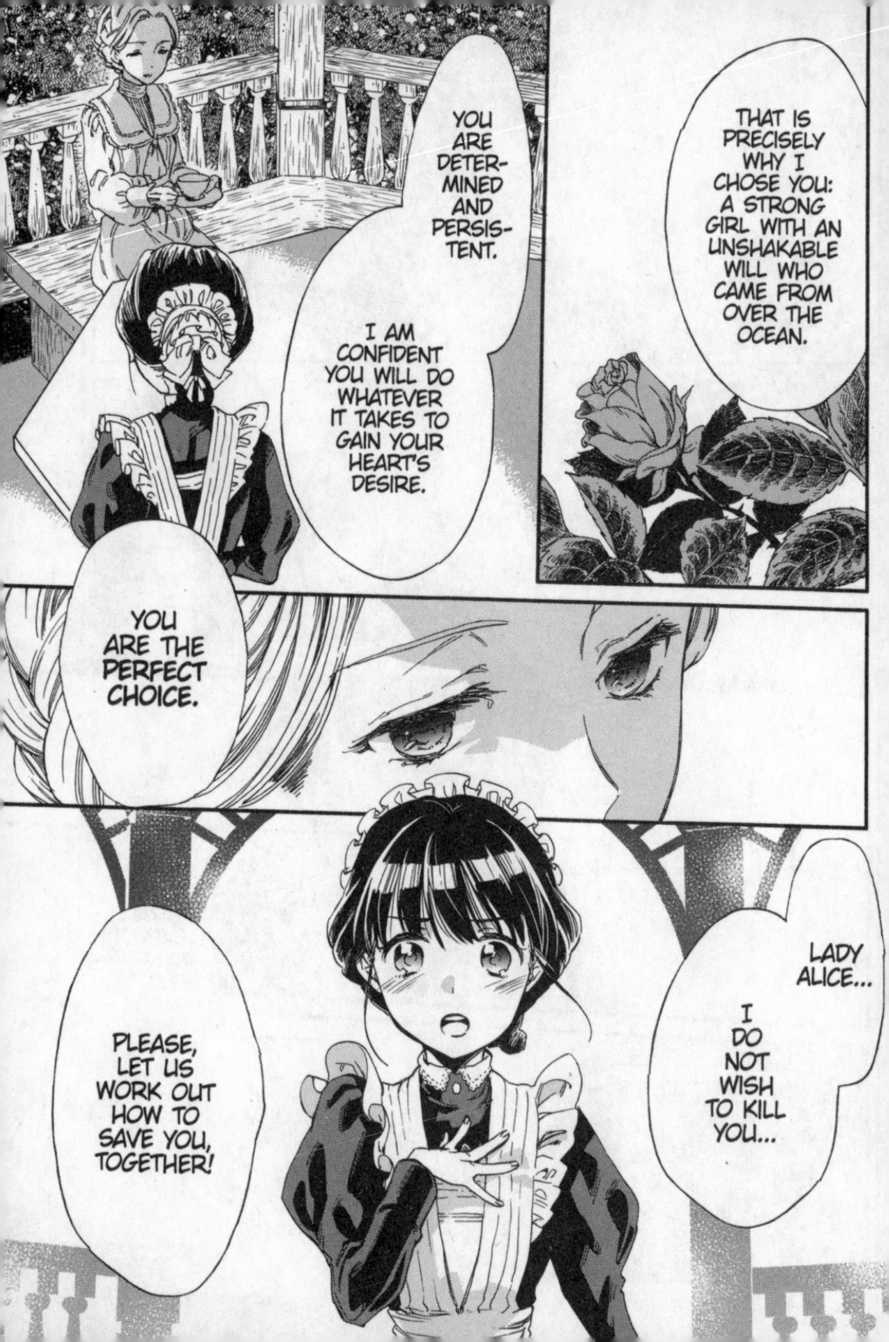
THAT IS PRECISELY WHY I CHOSE YOU: A STRONG GIRL WITH AN UNSHAKABLE WILL WHO CAME FROM OVER THE OCEAN.
YOU ARE DETERMINED AND PERSISTENT.
I AM CONFIDENT YOU WILL DO WHATEVER IT TAKES TO GAIN YOUR HEART'S DESIRE.
YOU ARE THE PERFECT CHOICE.
LADY ALICE...
I DO NOT WISH TO KILL YOU...
PLEASE, LET US WORK OUT HOW TO SAVE YOU, TOGETHER!

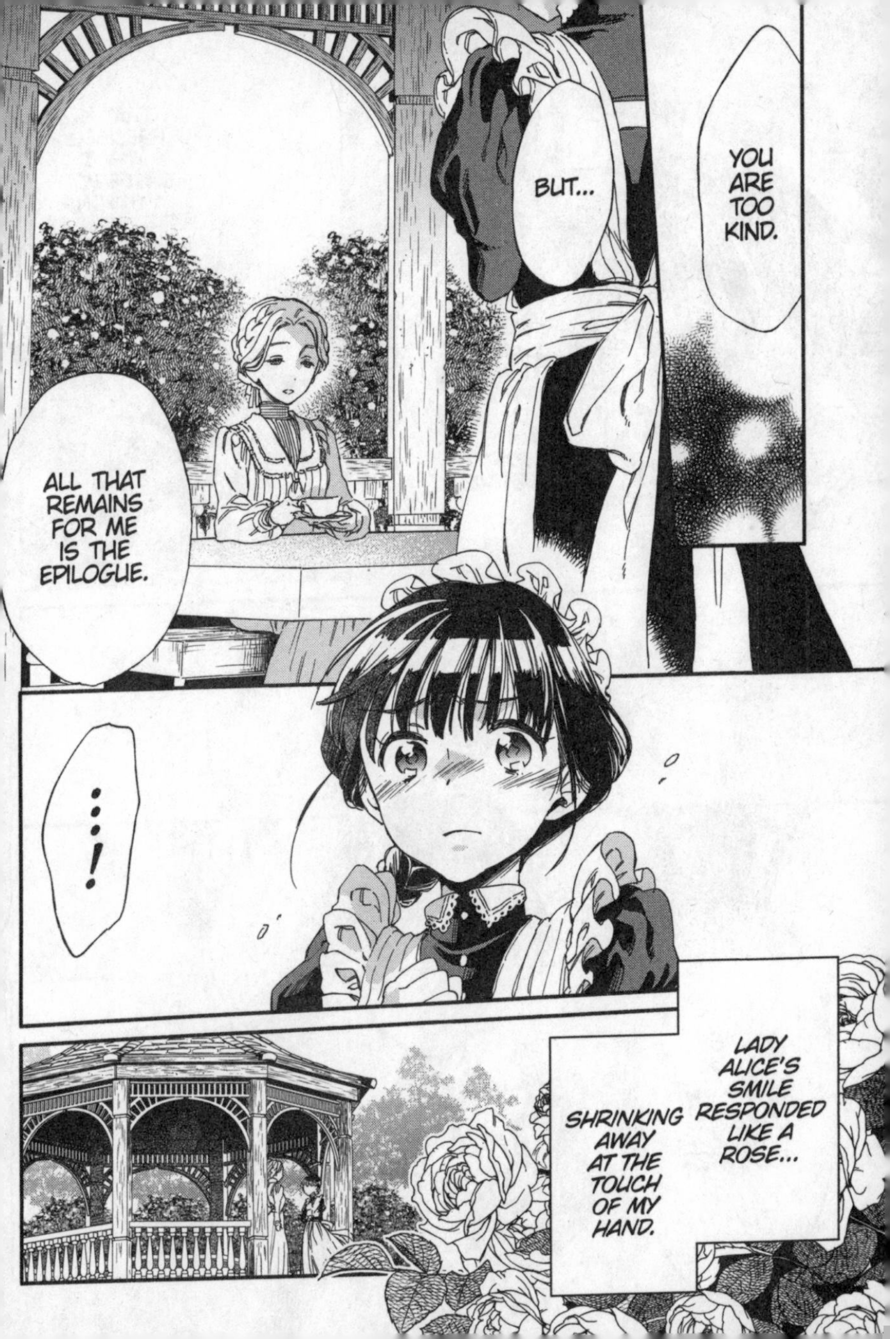
YOU ARE TOO KIND.
BUT...
ALL THAT REMAINS FOR ME IS THE EPILOGUE.
...!
LADY ALICE'S SMILE RESPONDED LIKE A ROSE...
SHRINKING AWAY AT THE TOUCH OF MY HAND.

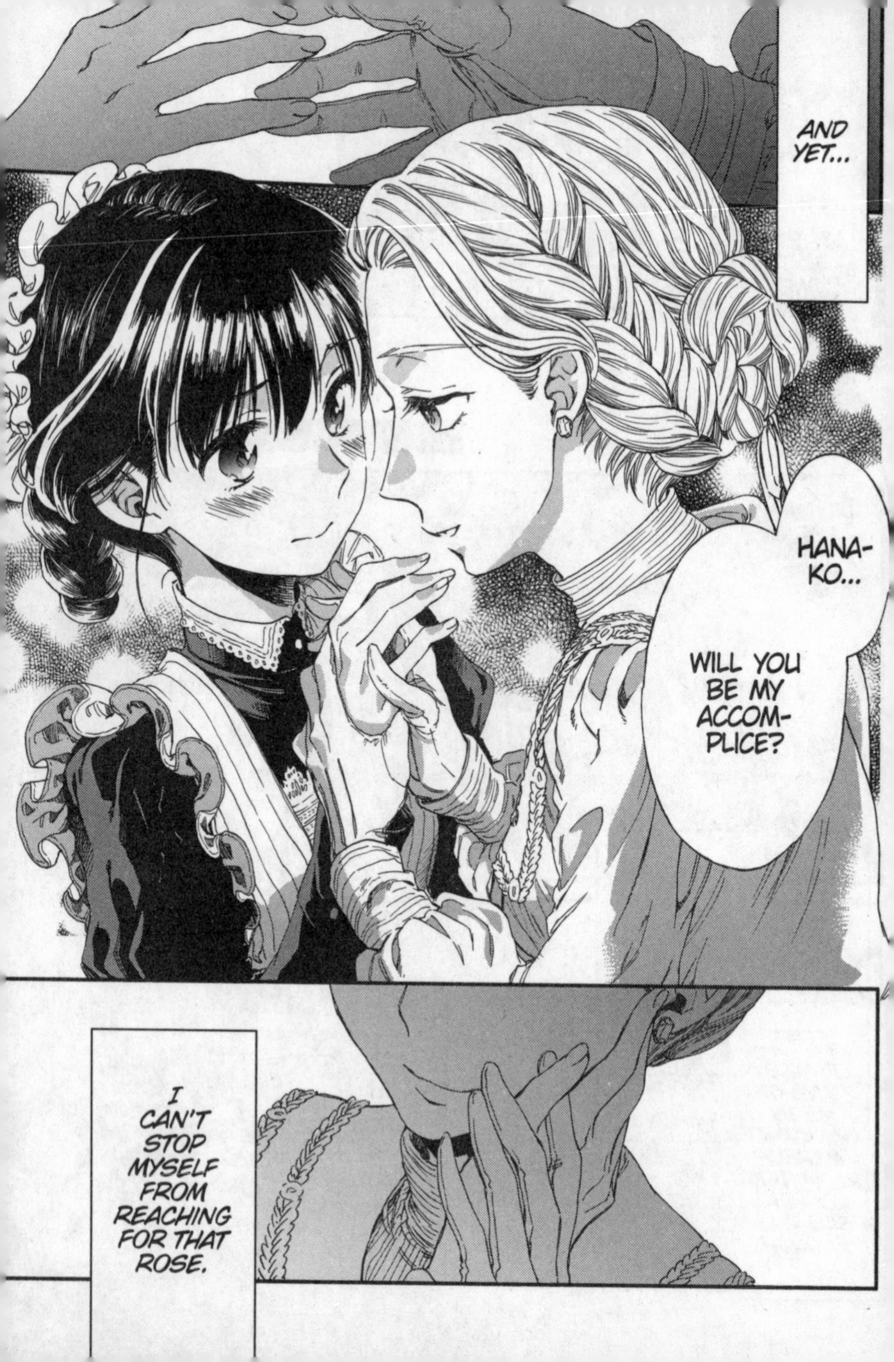
AND YET...
HANA-KO...
WILL YOU BE MY ACCOMPLICE?
I CAN'T STOP MYSELF FROM REACHING FOR THAT ROSE.

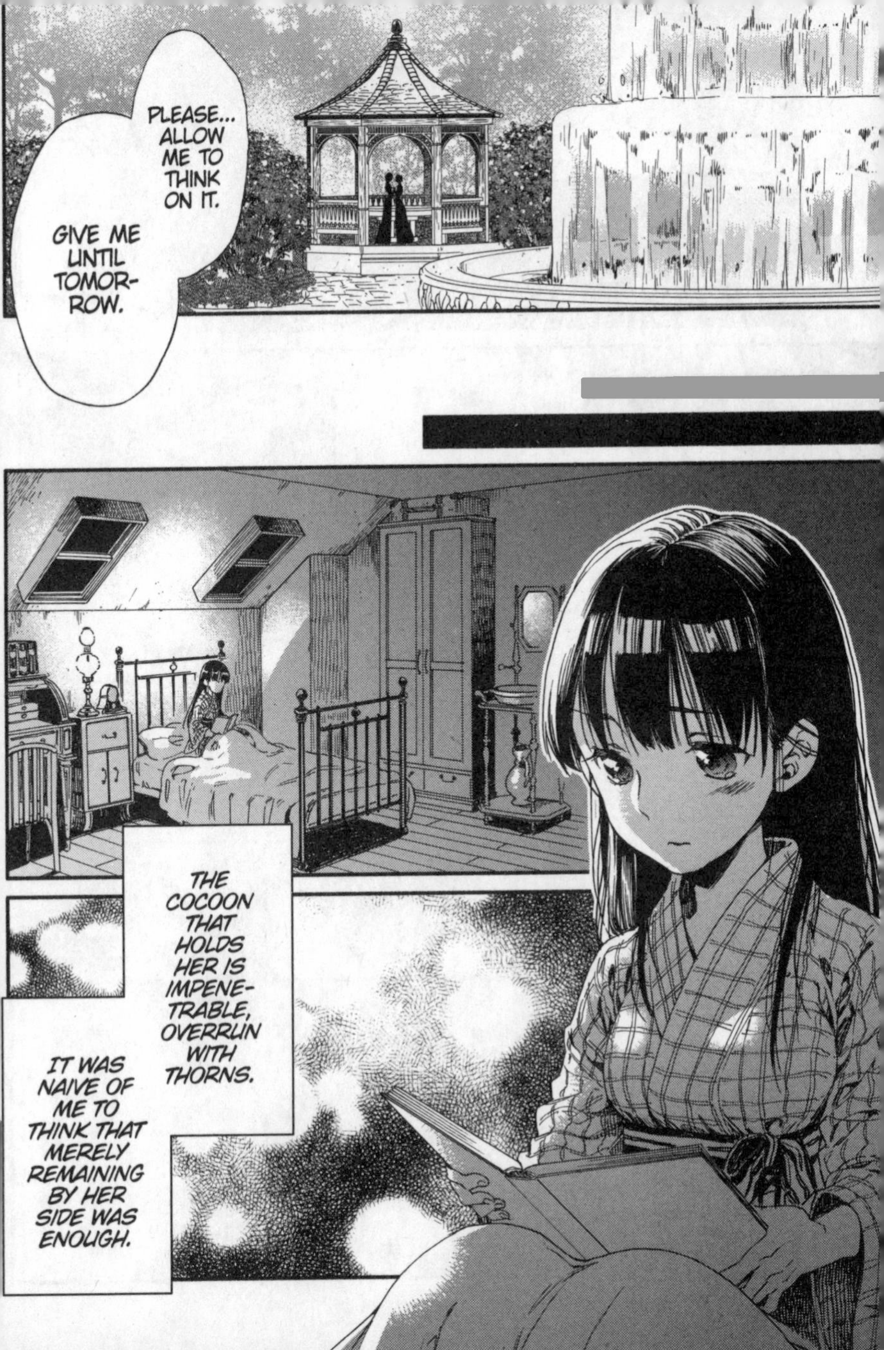
PLEASE... ALLOW ME TO THINK ON IT.
GIVE ME UNTIL TOMOR-ROW.
THE COCOON THAT HOLDS HER IS IMPENE-TRABLE, OVERRUN WITH THORNS.
IT WAS NAIVE OF ME TO THINK THAT MERELY REMAINING BY HER SIDE WAS ENOUGH.

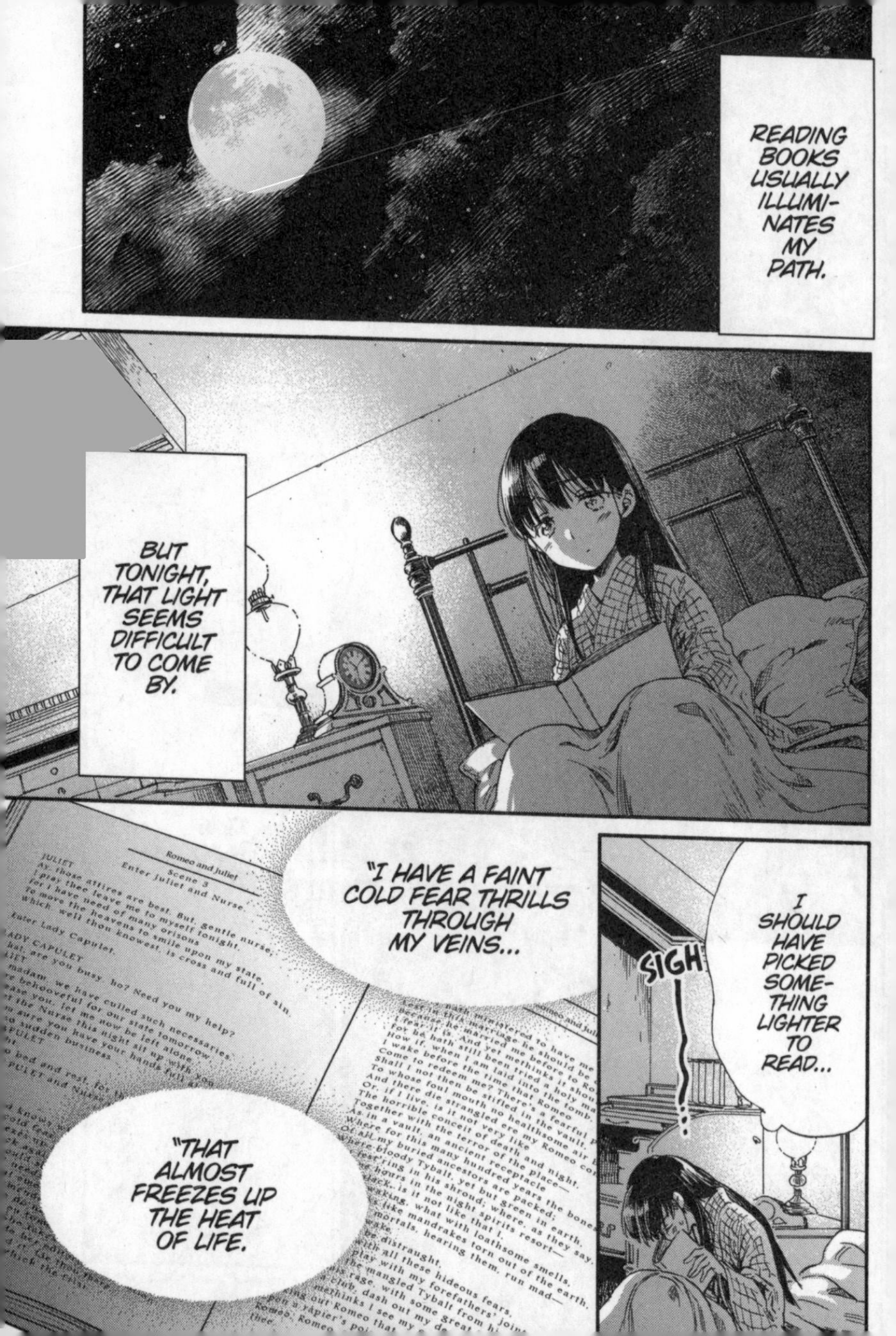
READING BOOKS USUALLY ILLUMINATES MY PATH.
BUT TONIGHT, THAT LIGHT SEEMS DIFFICULT TO COME BY.
I SHOULD HAVE PICKED SOMETHING LIGHTER TO READ...
SIGH
"I HAVE A FAINT COLD FEAR THRILLS THROUGH MY VEINS...
"THAT ALMOST FREEZES UP THE HEAT OF LIFE.

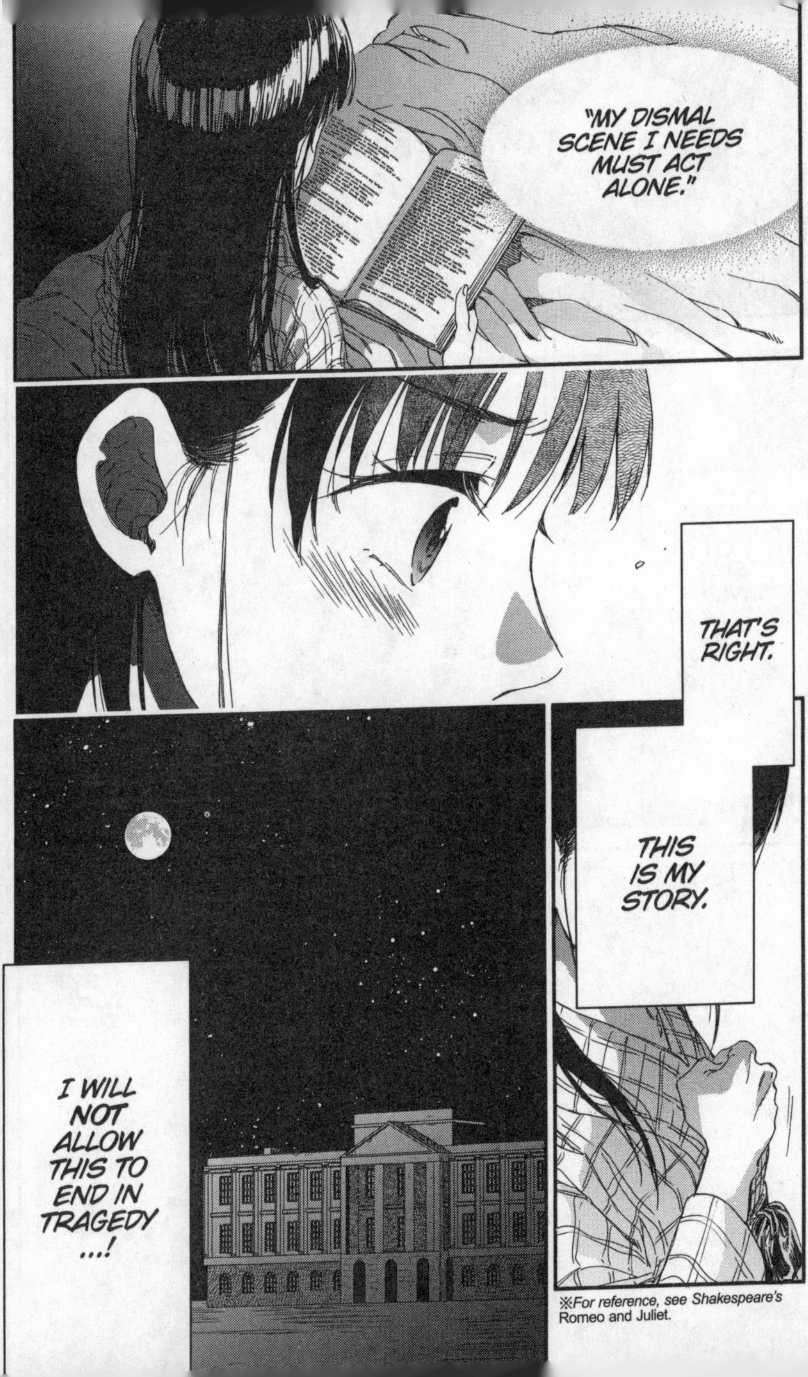
"MY DISMAL SCENE I NEEDS MUST ACT ALONE."
THAT'S RIGHT.
THIS IS MY STORY.
I WILL NOT ALLOW THIS TO END IN TRAGEDY ...!

※For reference, see Shakespeare's Romeo and Juliet.

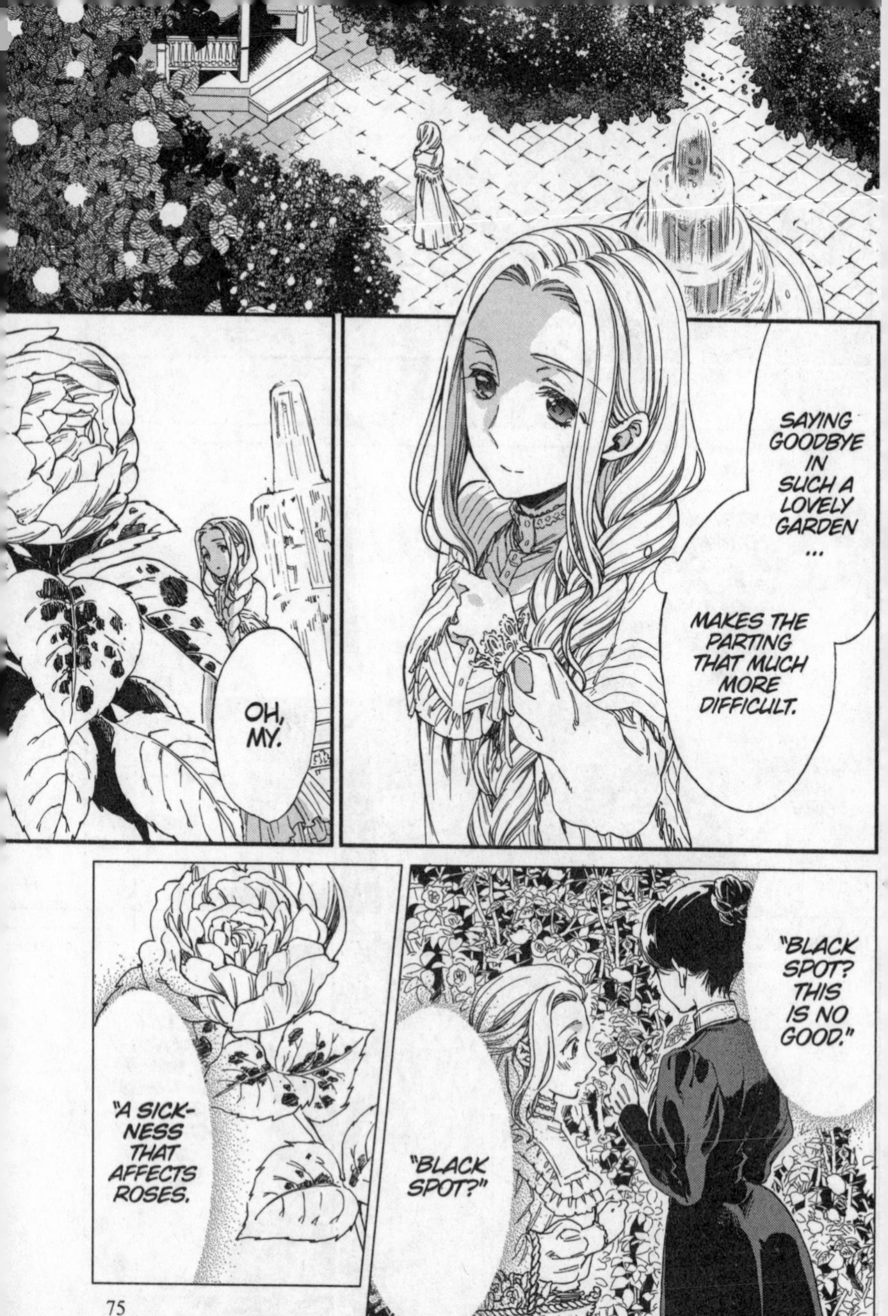
SAYING GOODBYE IN SUCH A LOVELY GARDEN ...
MAKES THE PARTING THAT MUCH MORE DIFFICULT.
OH, MY.
"BLACK SPOT? THIS IS NO GOOD."
"BLACK SPOT?"
"A SICKNESS THAT AFFECTS ROSES.

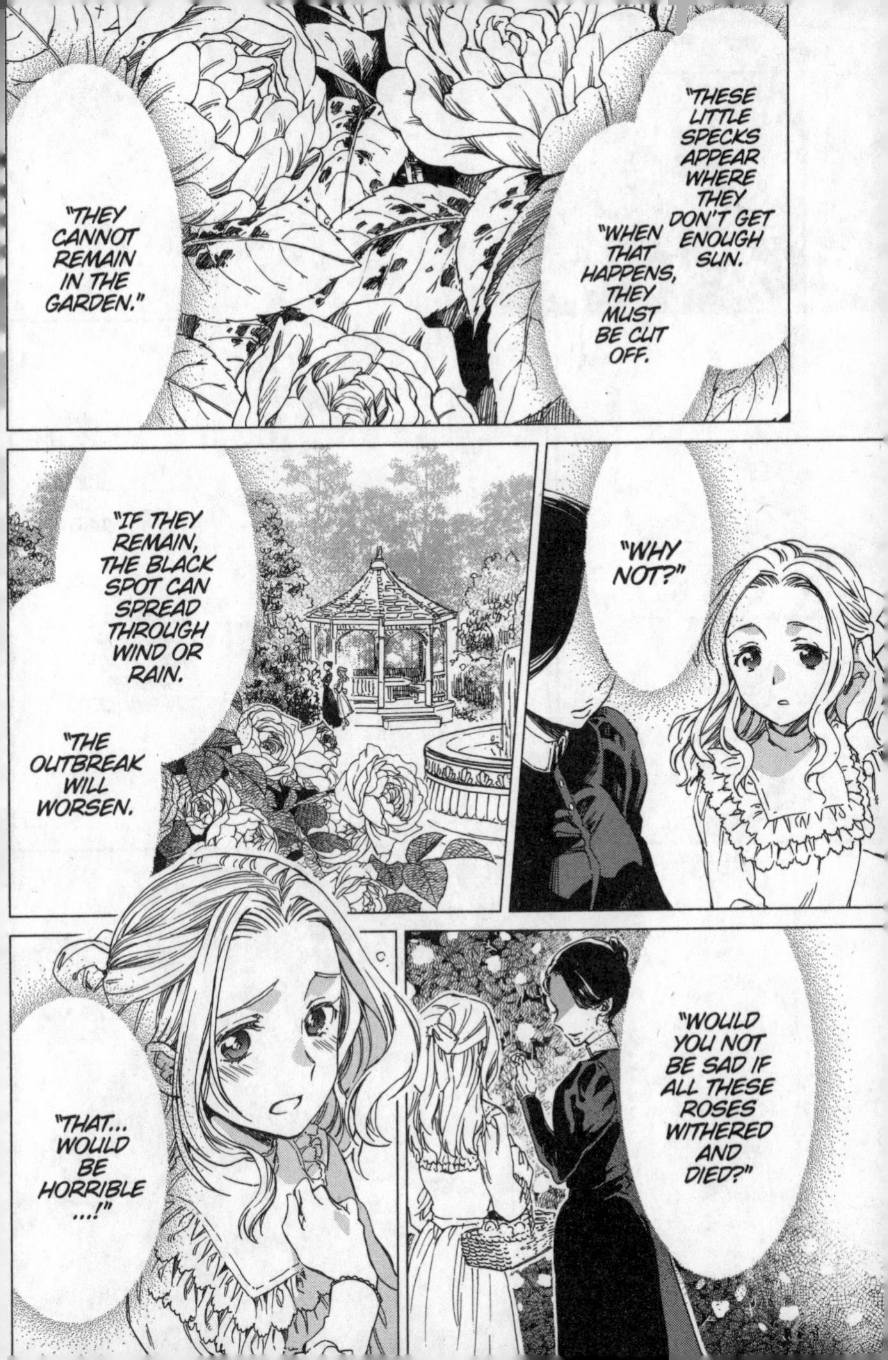
"THESE LITTLE SPECKS APPEAR WHERE THEY DON'T GET ENOUGH SUN.
"WHEN THAT HAPPENS, THEY MUST BE CUT OFF.
"THEY CANNOT REMAIN IN THE GARDEN."
"WHY NOT?"
"IF THEY REMAIN, THE BLACK SPOT CAN SPREAD THROUGH WIND OR RAIN.
"THE OUTBREAK WILL WORSEN.
"WOULD YOU NOT BE SAD IF ALL THESE ROSES WITHERED AND DIED?"
"THAT... WOULD BE HORRIBLE ...!"

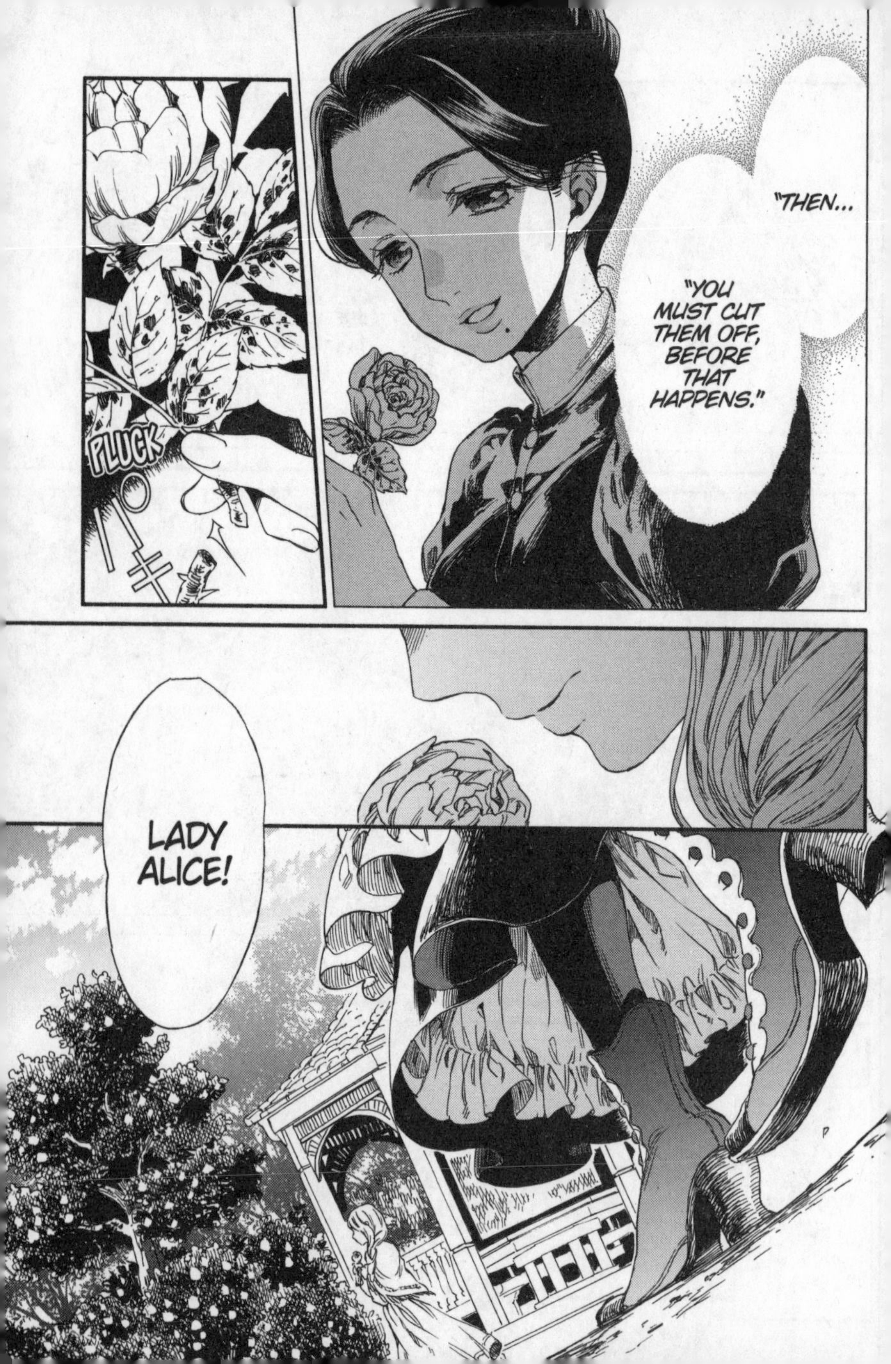
"THEN...
"YOU MUST CUT THEM OFF, BEFORE THAT HAPPENS."
PLUCK
LADY ALICE!

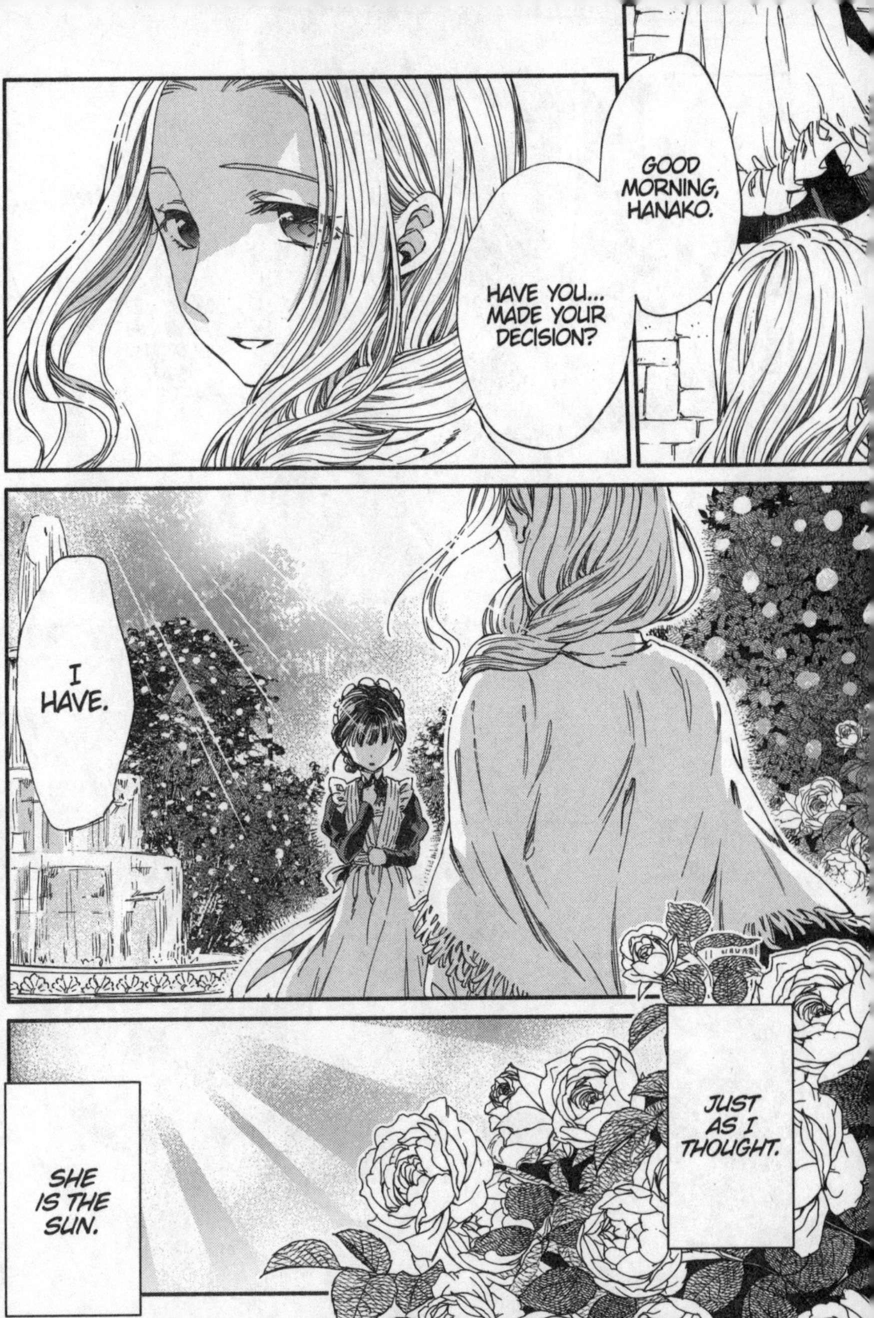
GOOD MORNING, HANAKO.
HAVE YOU... MADE YOUR DECISION?
I HAVE.
JUST AS I THOUGHT.
SHE IS THE SUN.

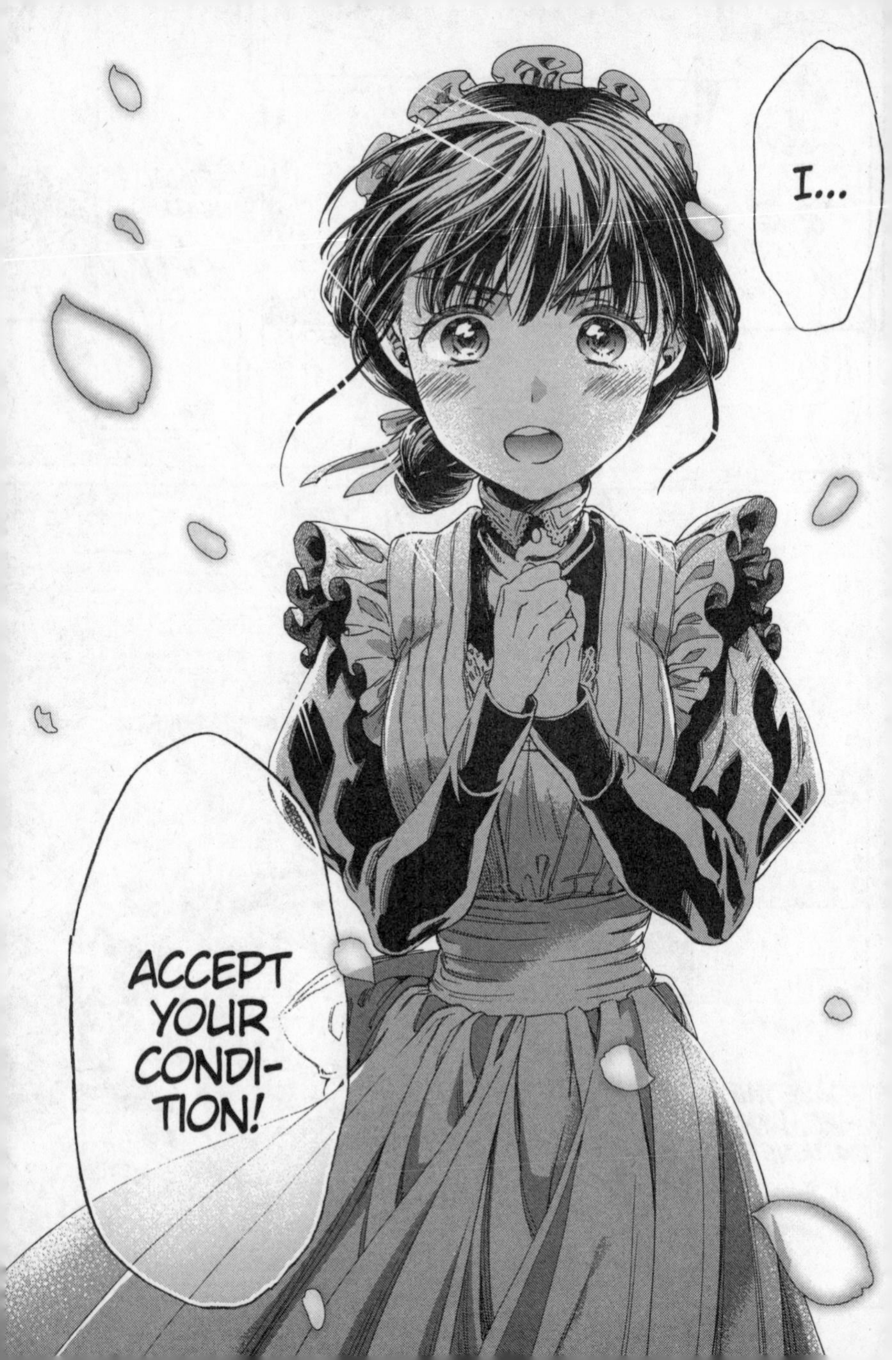
I...
ACCEPT YOUR CONDI-TION!

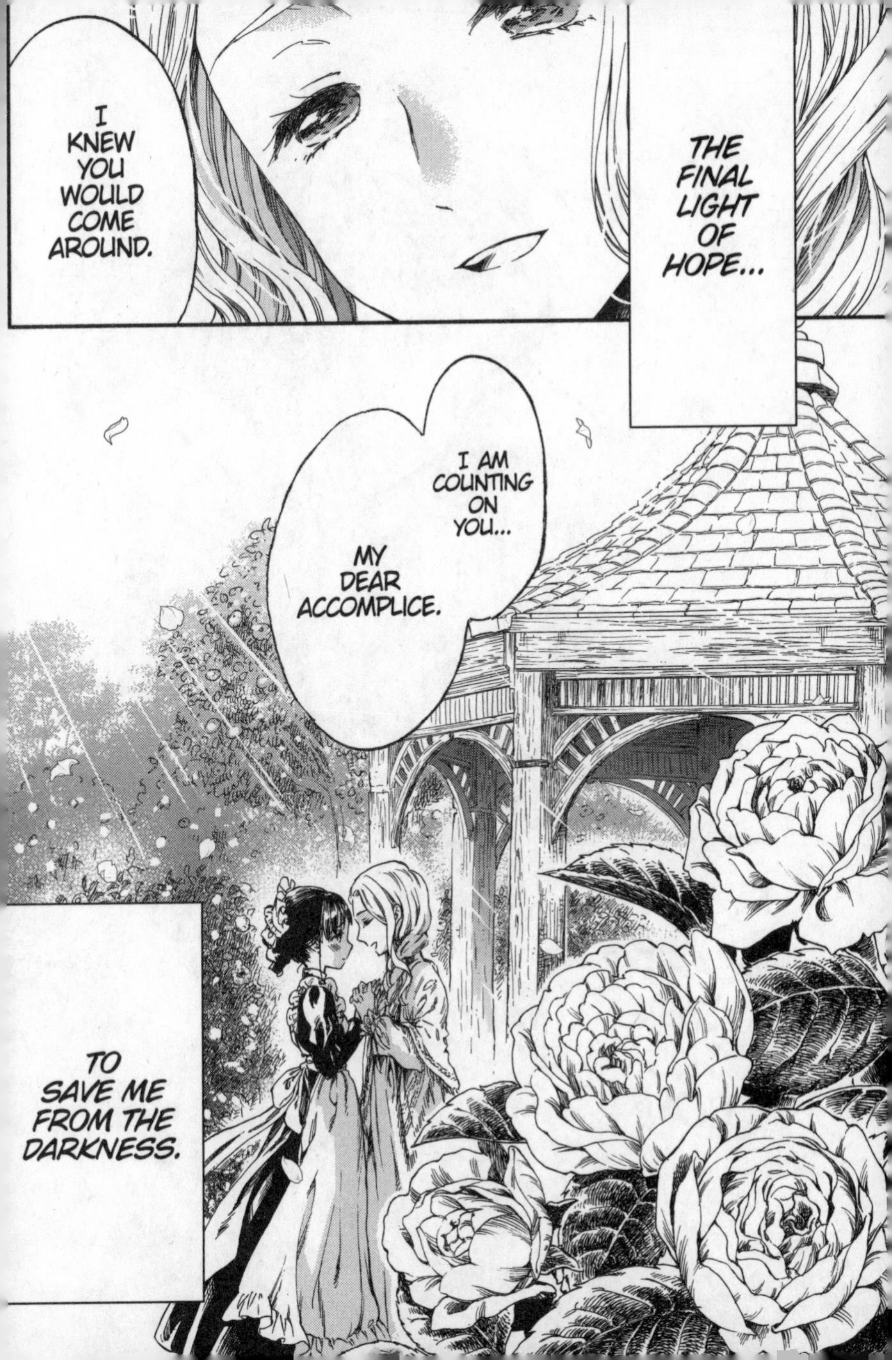
THE FINAL LIGHT OF HOPE...
I KNEW YOU WOULD COME AROUND.
I AM COUNTING ON YOU...
MY DEAR ACCOMPLICE.
TO SAVE ME FROM THE DARKNESS.

{ Chapter 3 }

The Black Spot That Devours Me

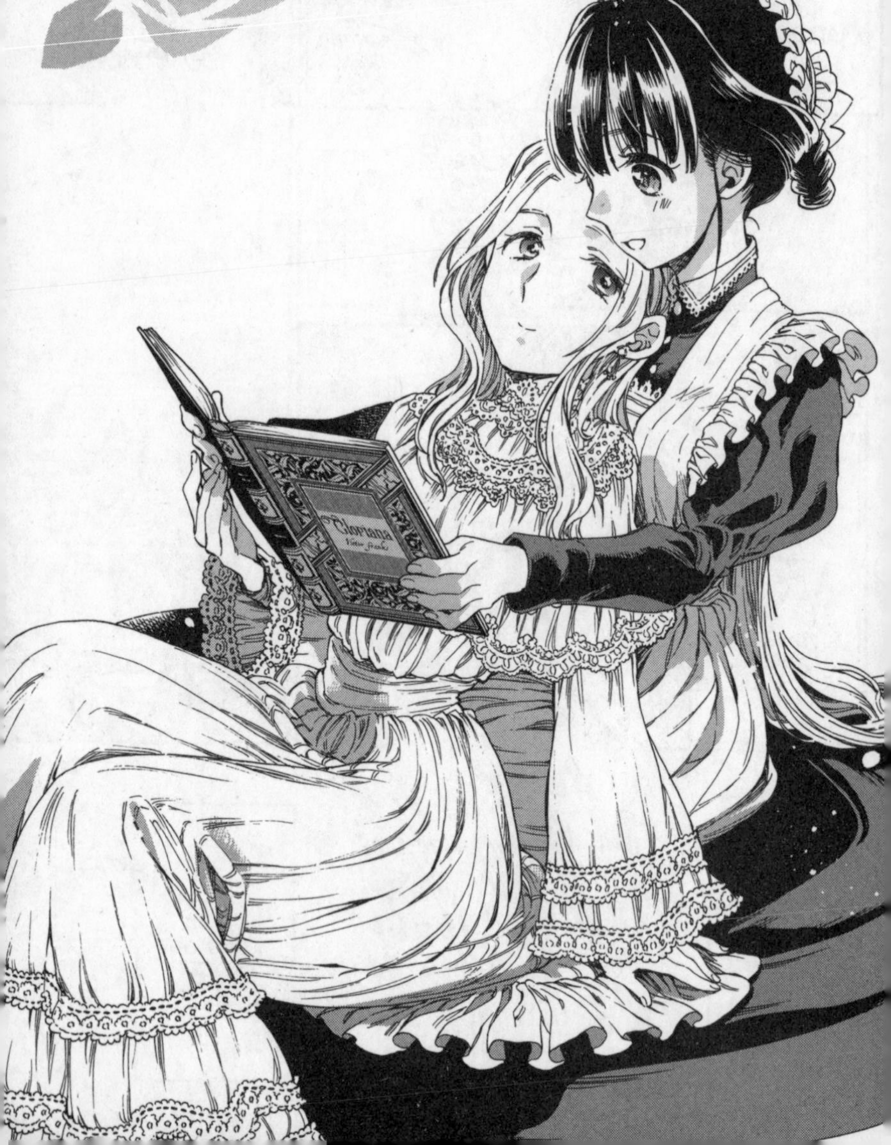
Gloriana

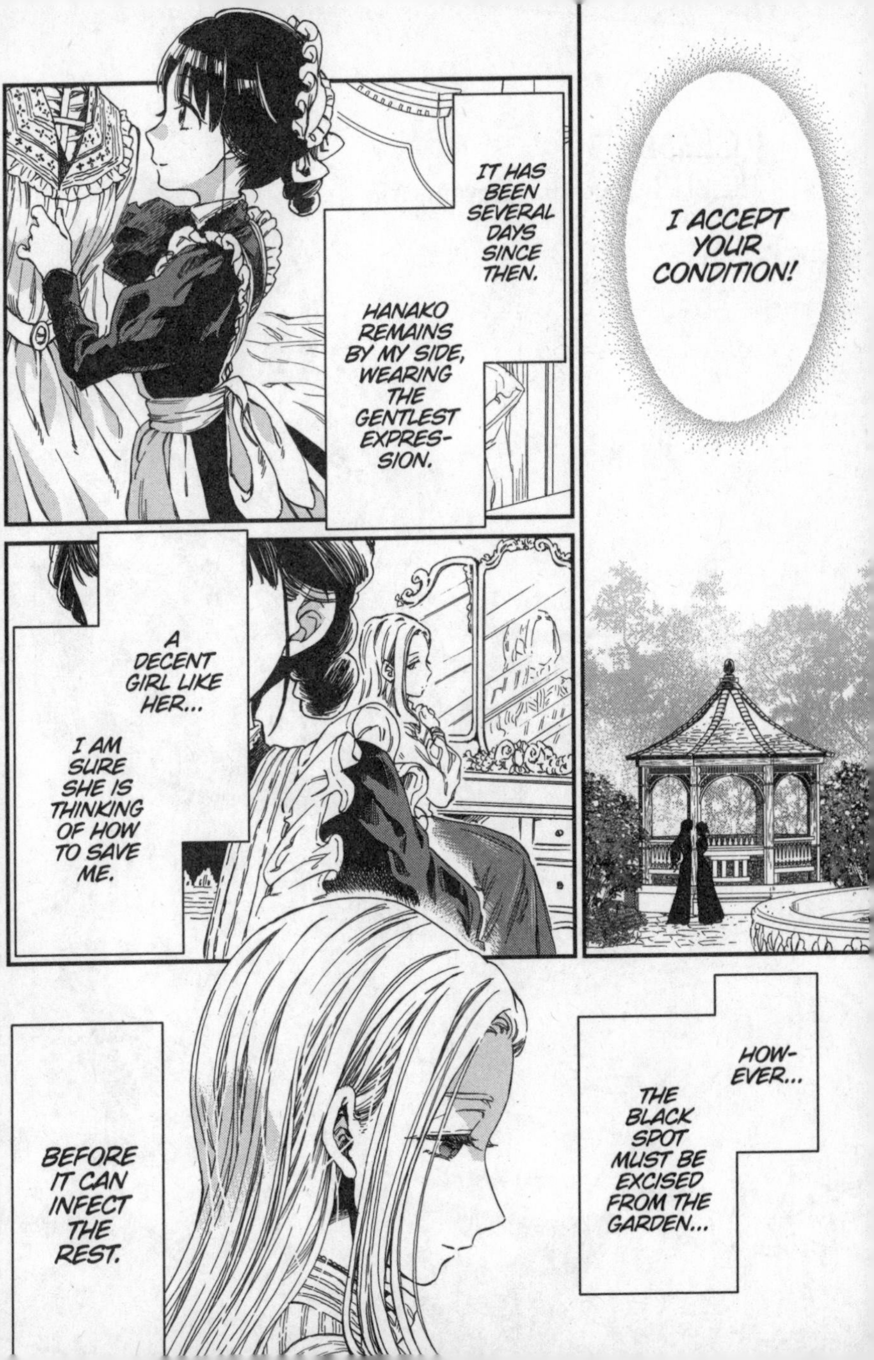

I ACCEPT YOUR CONDITION!
IT HAS BEEN SEVERAL DAYS SINCE THEN.
HANAKO REMAINS BY MY SIDE, WEARING THE GENTLEST EXPRESSION.
A DECENT GIRL LIKE HER...
I AM SURE SHE IS THINKING OF HOW TO SAVE ME.
HOWEVER...
THE BLACK SPOT MUST BE EXCISED FROM THE GARDEN...
BEFORE IT CAN INFECT THE REST.

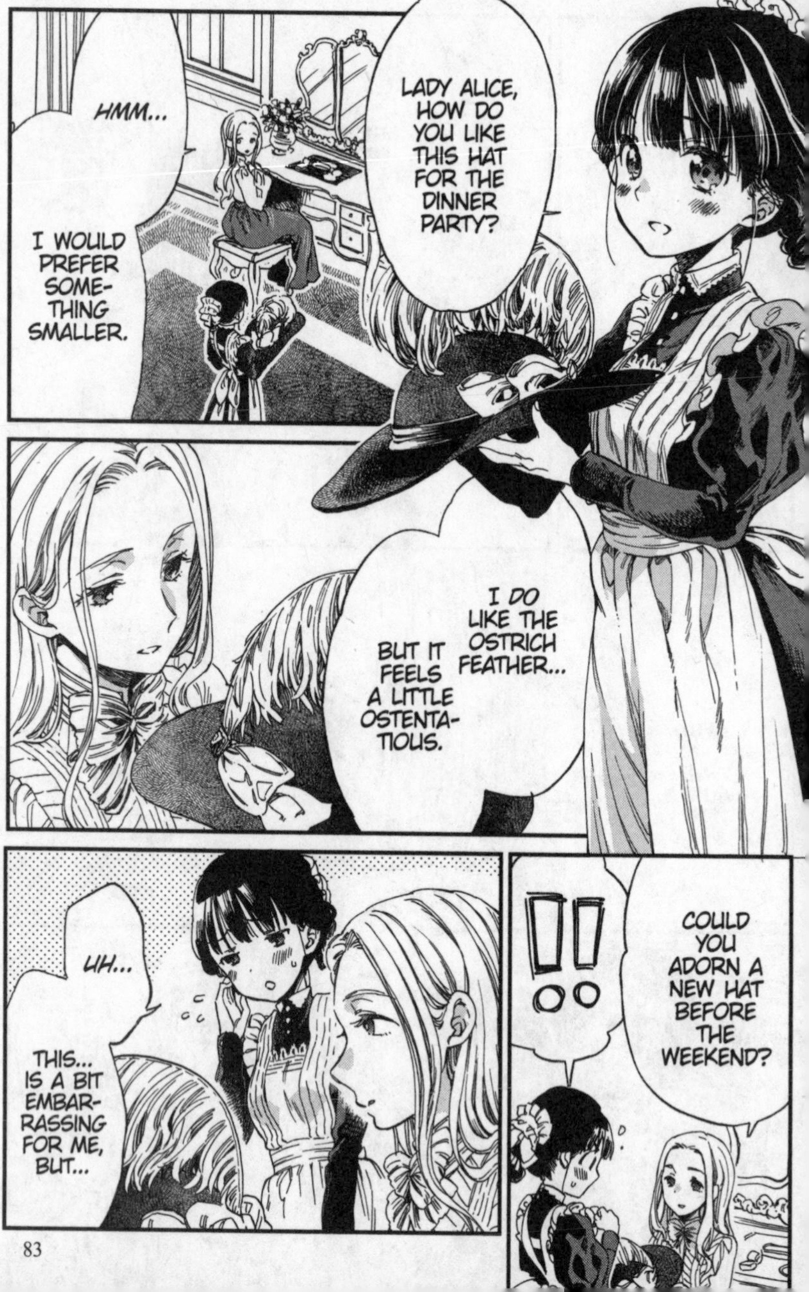
LADY ALICE, HOW DO YOU LIKE THIS HAT FOR THE DINNER PARTY?
HMM...
I WOULD PREFER SOME-THING SMALLER.
I DO LIKE THE OSTRICH FEATHER...
BUT IT FEELS A LITTLE OSTENTA-TIOUS.
COULD YOU ADORN A NEW HAT BEFORE THE WEEKEND?
!!
UH...
THIS... IS A BIT EMBAR-RASSING FOR ME, BUT...

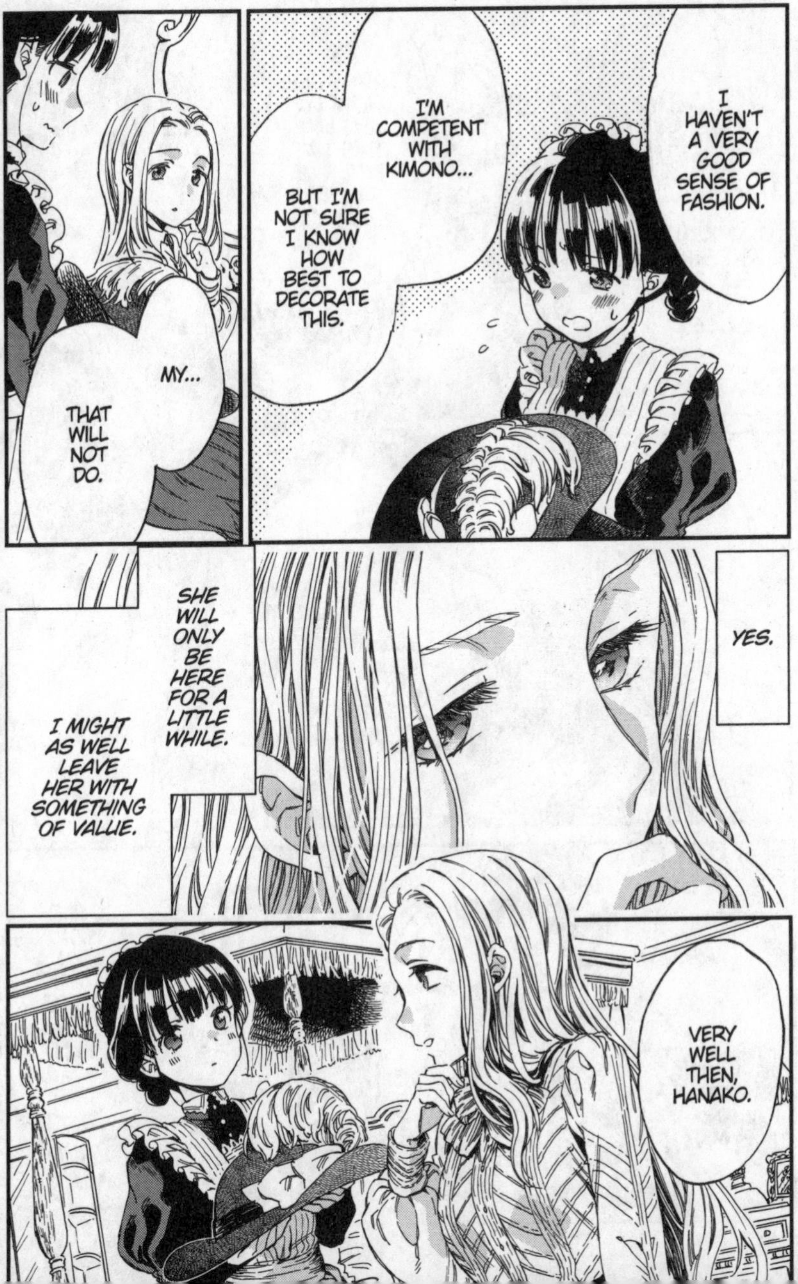
I HAVEN'T A VERY GOOD SENSE OF FASHION.
I'M COMPETENT WITH KIMONO...
BUT I'M NOT SURE I KNOW HOW BEST TO DECORATE THIS.
MY...
THAT WILL NOT DO.
YES.
SHE WILL ONLY BE HERE FOR A LITTLE WHILE.
I MIGHT AS WELL LEAVE HER WITH SOMETHING OF VALUE.
VERY WELL THEN, HANAKO.

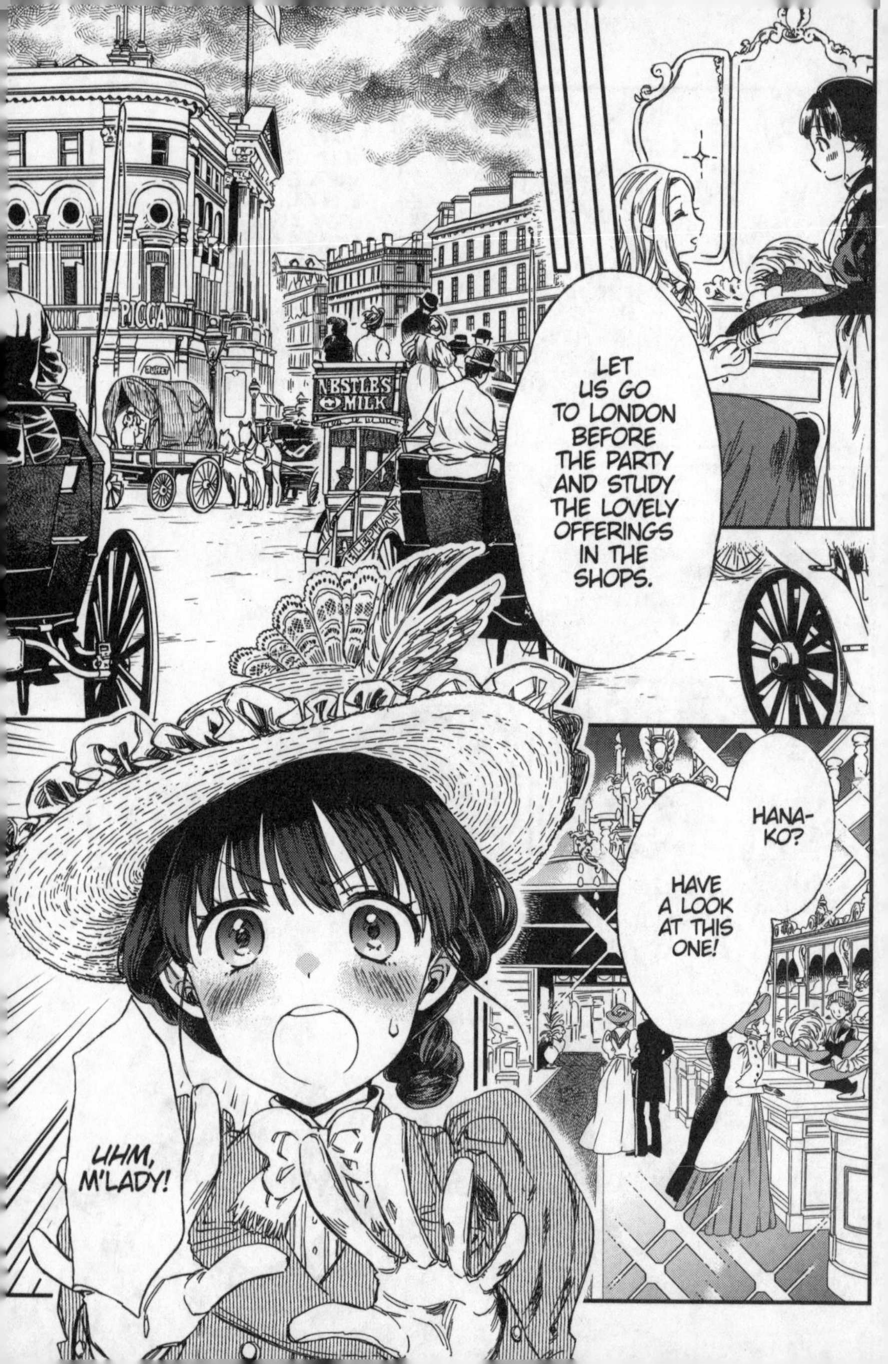
LET US GO TO LONDON BEFORE THE PARTY AND STUDY THE LOVELY OFFERINGS IN THE SHOPS.
NESTLE'S MILK
PICCA
HANA-KO?
HAVE A LOOK AT THIS ONE!
UHM, M'LADY!

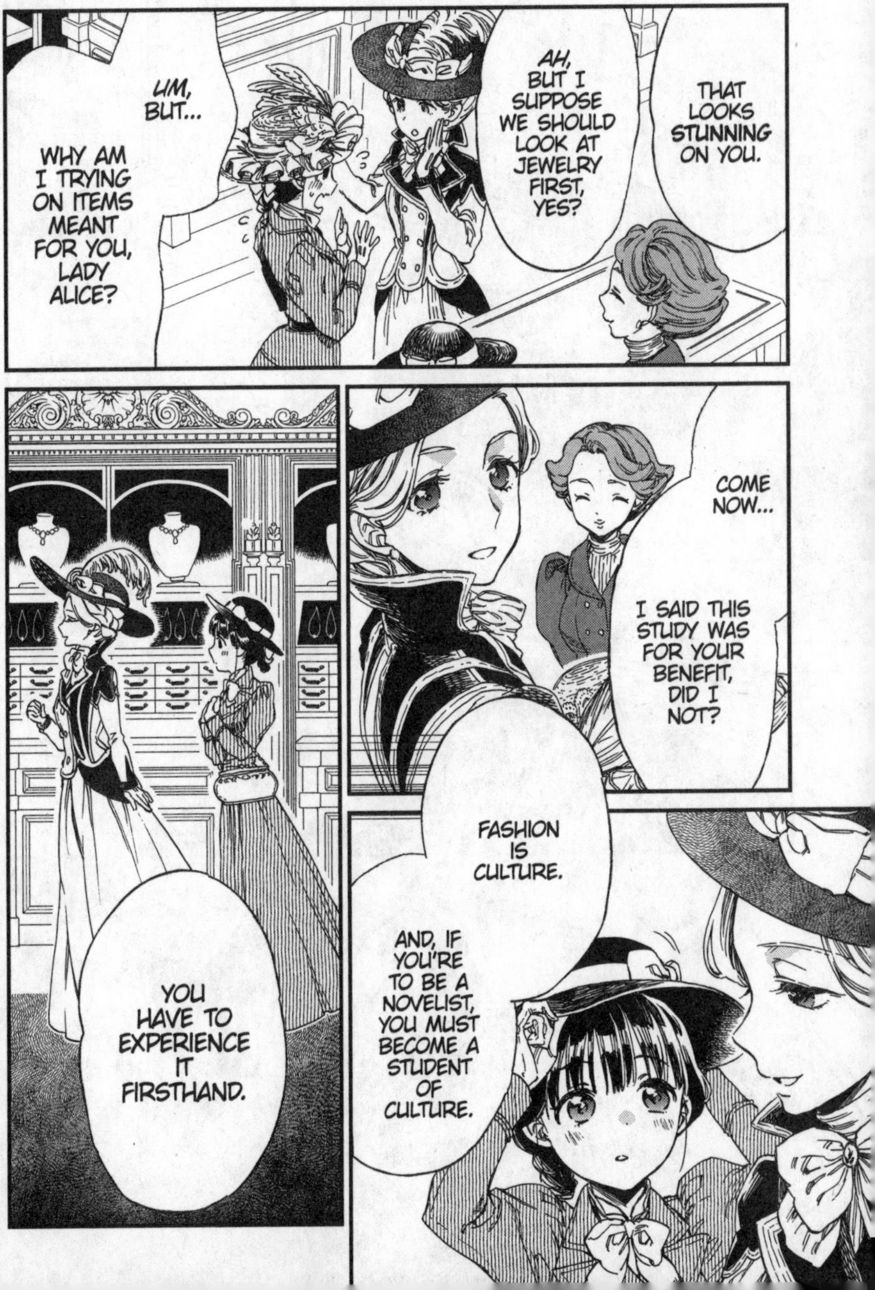
THAT LOOKS STUNNING ON YOU.
AH, BUT I SUPPOSE WE SHOULD LOOK AT JEWELRY FIRST, YES?
UM, BUT...
WHY AM I TRYING ON ITEMS MEANT FOR YOU, LADY ALICE?
COME NOW...
I SAID THIS STUDY WAS FOR YOUR BENEFIT, DID I NOT?
FASHION IS CULTURE.
AND, IF YOU'RE TO BE A NOVELIST, YOU MUST BECOME A STUDENT OF CULTURE.
YOU HAVE TO EXPERIENCE IT FIRSTHAND.

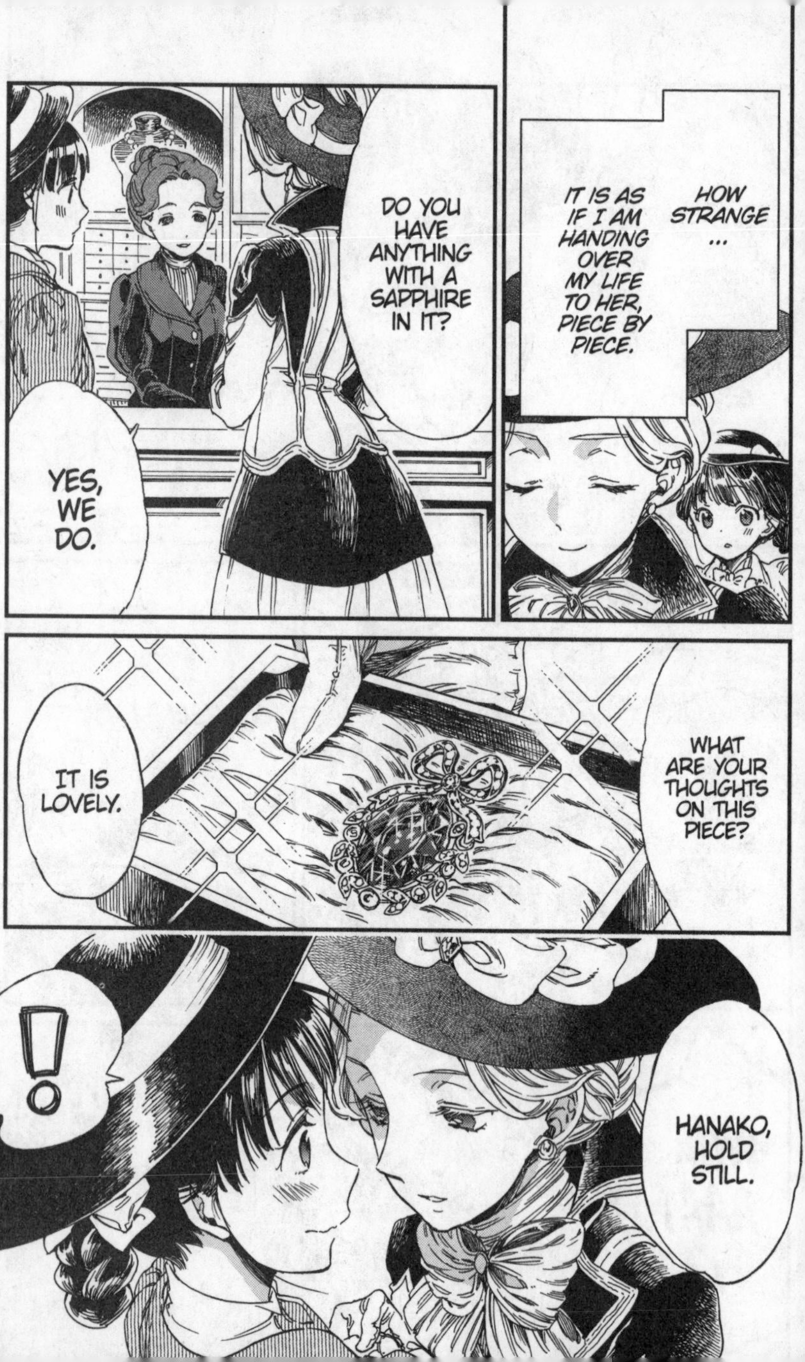
HOW STRANGE ...
IT IS AS IF I AM HANDING OVER MY LIFE TO HER, PIECE BY PIECE.
DO YOU HAVE ANYTHING WITH A SAPPHIRE IN IT?
YES, WE DO.
WHAT ARE YOUR THOUGHTS ON THIS PIECE?
IT IS LOVELY.
HANAKO, HOLD STILL.
!

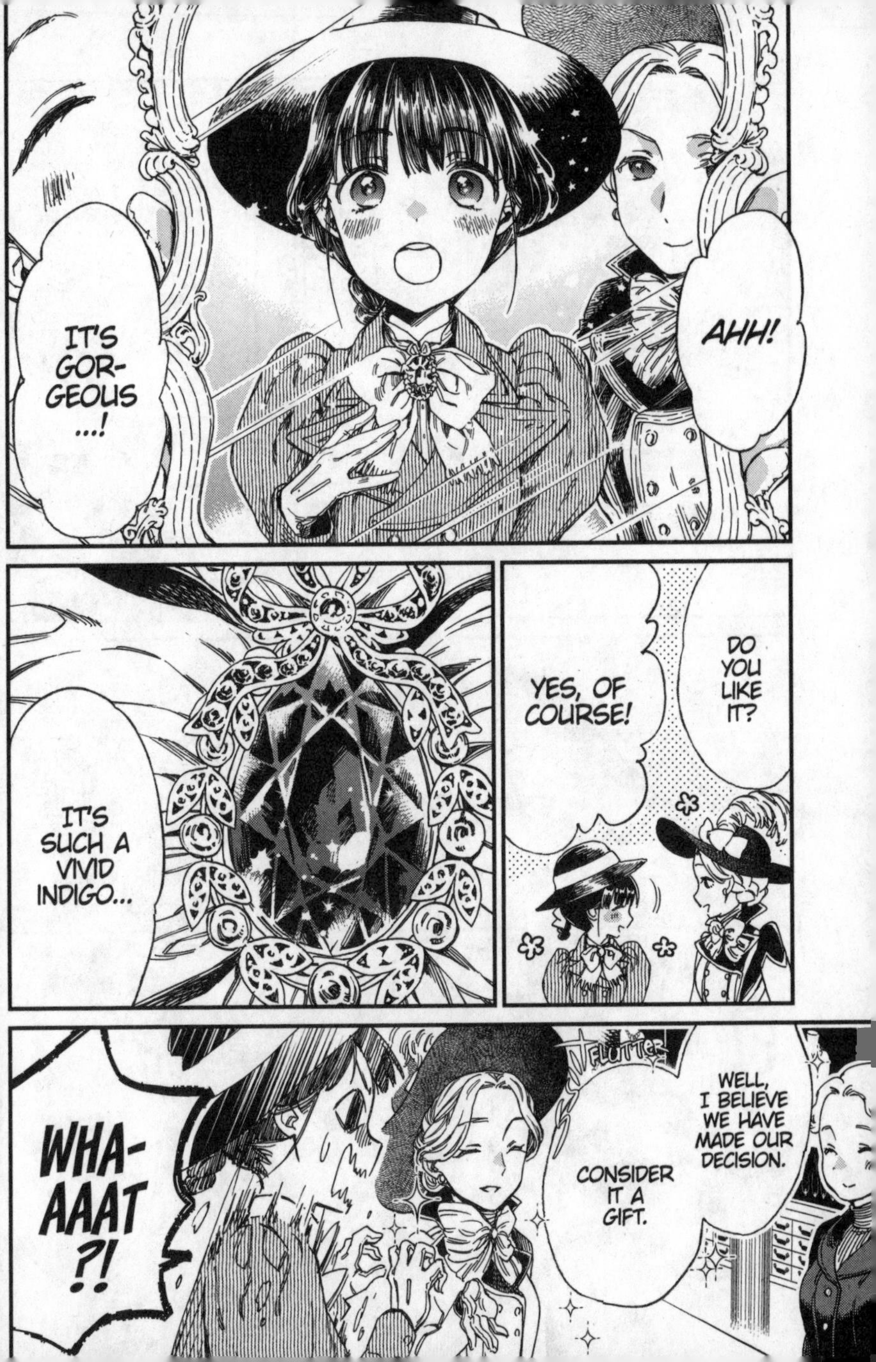
AHH!
IT'S GOR-GEOUS ...!
DO YOU LIKE IT?
YES, OF COURSE!
IT'S SUCH A VIVID INDIGO...
WELL, I BELIEVE WE HAVE MADE OUR DECISION.
FLUTTER
CONSIDER IT A GIFT.
WHA-AAAT?!

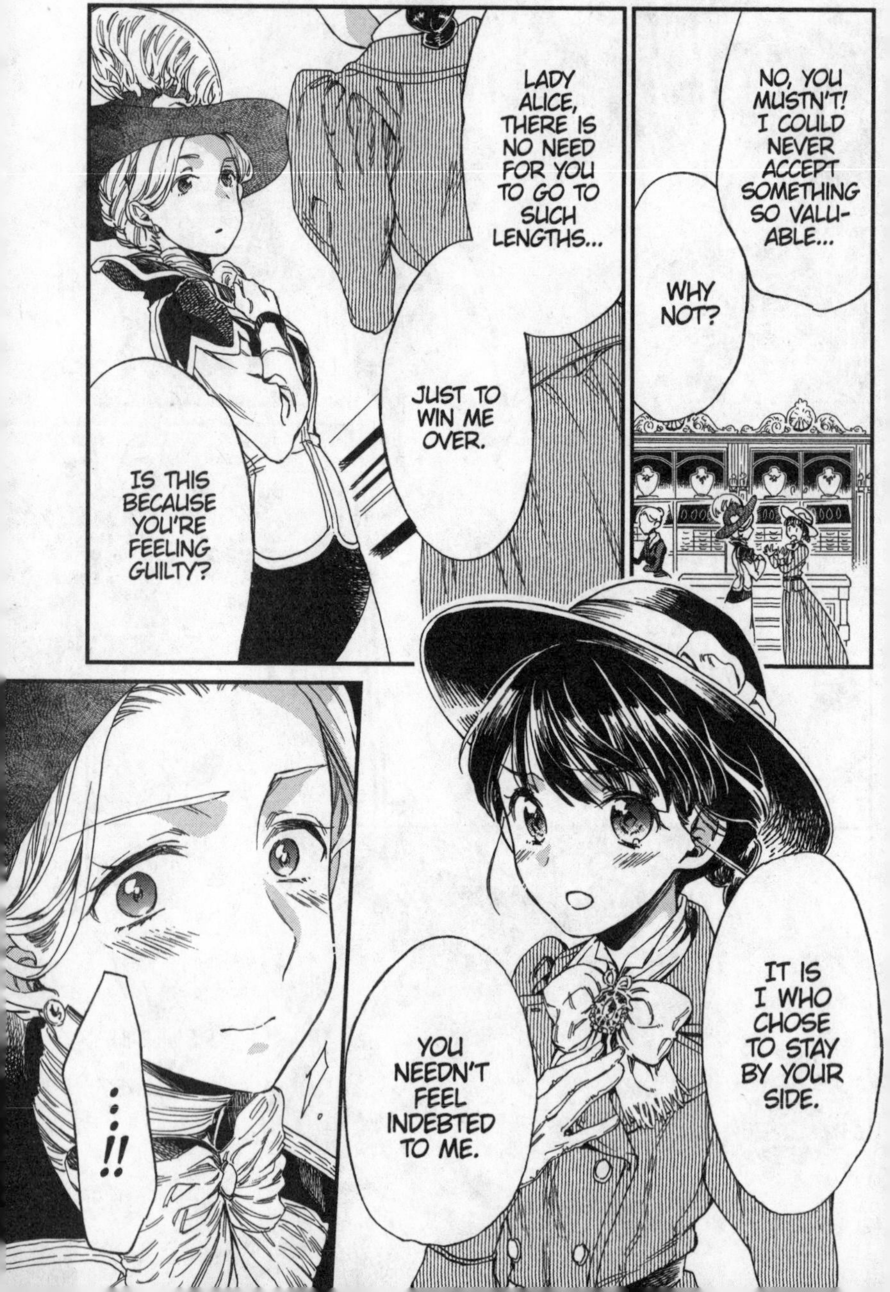
NO, YOU MUSTN'T! I COULD NEVER ACCEPT SOMETHING SO VALU-ABLE...
WHY NOT?
LADY ALICE, THERE IS NO NEED FOR YOU TO GO TO SUCH LENGTHS...
JUST TO WIN ME OVER.
IS THIS BECAUSE YOU'RE FEELING GUILTY?
IT IS I WHO CHOSE TO STAY BY YOUR SIDE.
YOU NEEDN'T FEEL INDEBTED TO ME.
...!!

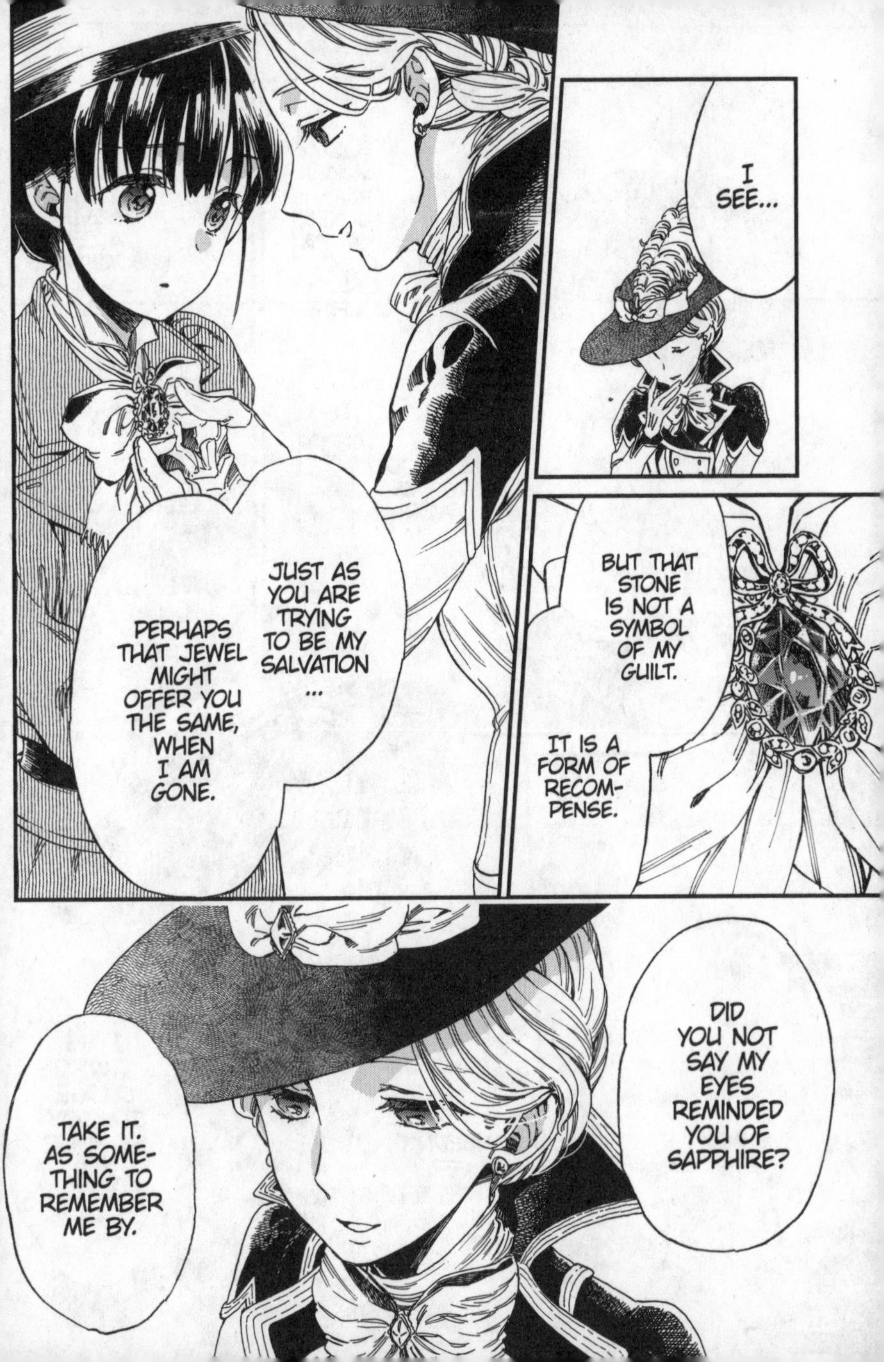
I SEE...
BUT THAT STONE IS NOT A SYMBOL OF MY GUILT.
IT IS A FORM OF RECOM-PENSE.
JUST AS YOU ARE TRYING TO BE MY SALVATION ...
PERHAPS THAT JEWEL MIGHT OFFER YOU THE SAME, WHEN I AM GONE.
DID YOU NOT SAY MY EYES REMINDED YOU OF SAPPHIRE?
TAKE IT. AS SOME-THING TO REMEMBER ME BY.

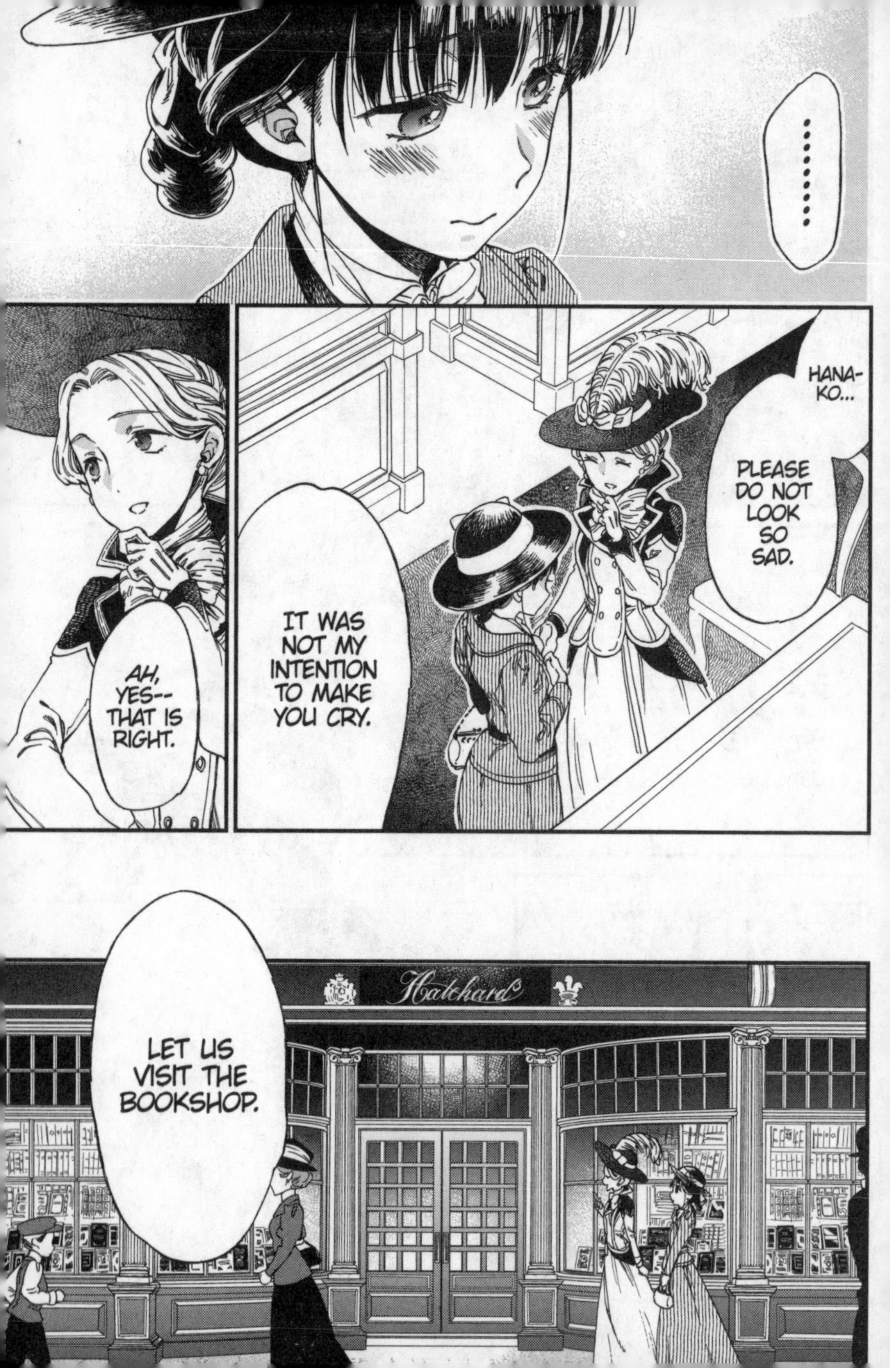
....
HANA-KO...
PLEASE DO NOT LOOK SO SAD.
IT WAS NOT MY INTENTION TO MAKE YOU CRY.
AH, YES--THAT IS RIGHT.
Hatchards
LET US VISIT THE BOOKSHOP.

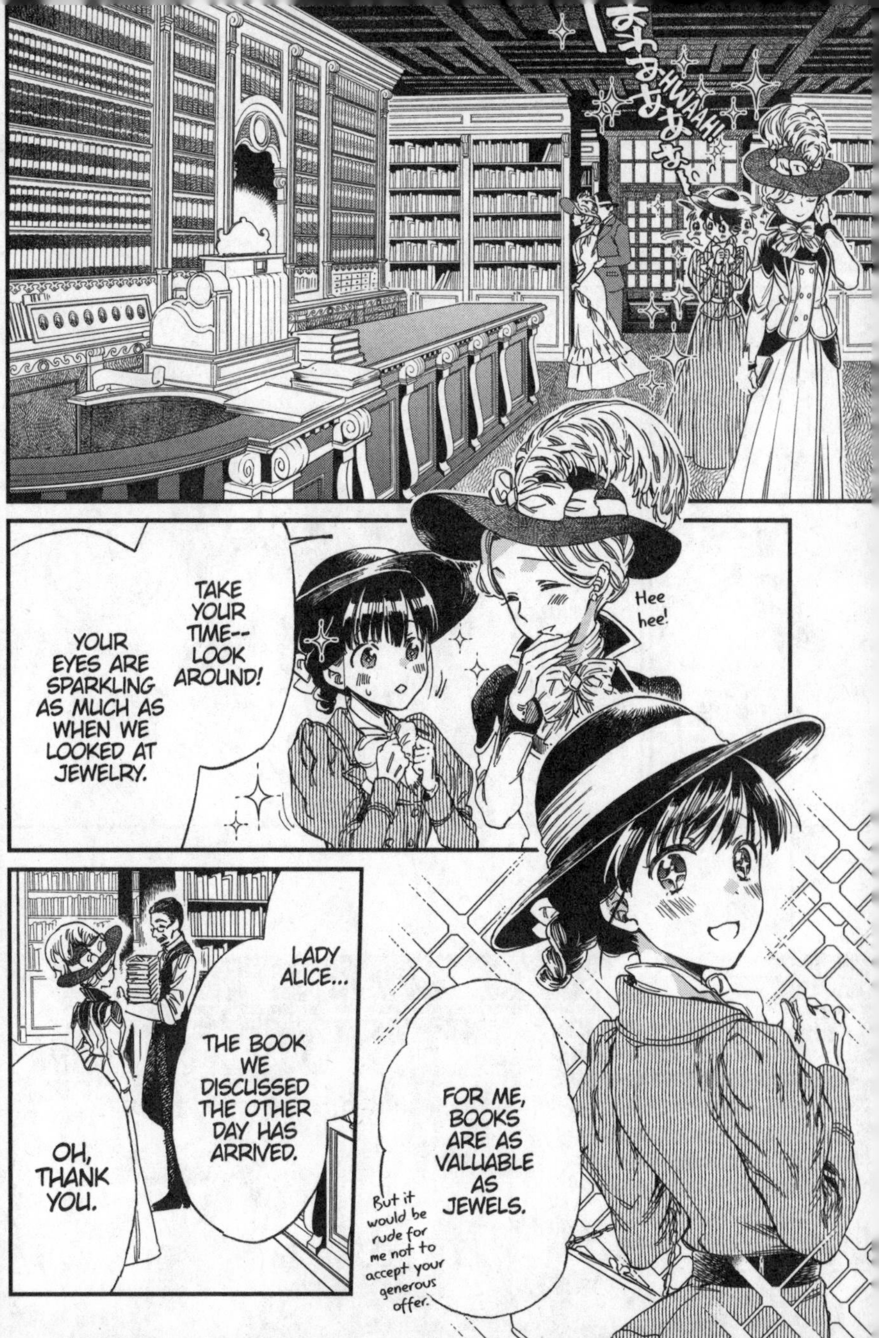
HWAAAH!
Hee hee!
TAKE YOUR TIME-- LOOK AROUND!
YOUR EYES ARE SPARKLING AS MUCH AS WHEN WE LOOKED AT JEWELRY.
FOR ME, BOOKS ARE AS VALUABLE AS JEWELS.
But it would be rude for me not to accept your generous offer.
LADY ALICE...
THE BOOK WE DISCUSSED THE OTHER DAY HAS ARRIVED.
OH, THANK YOU.

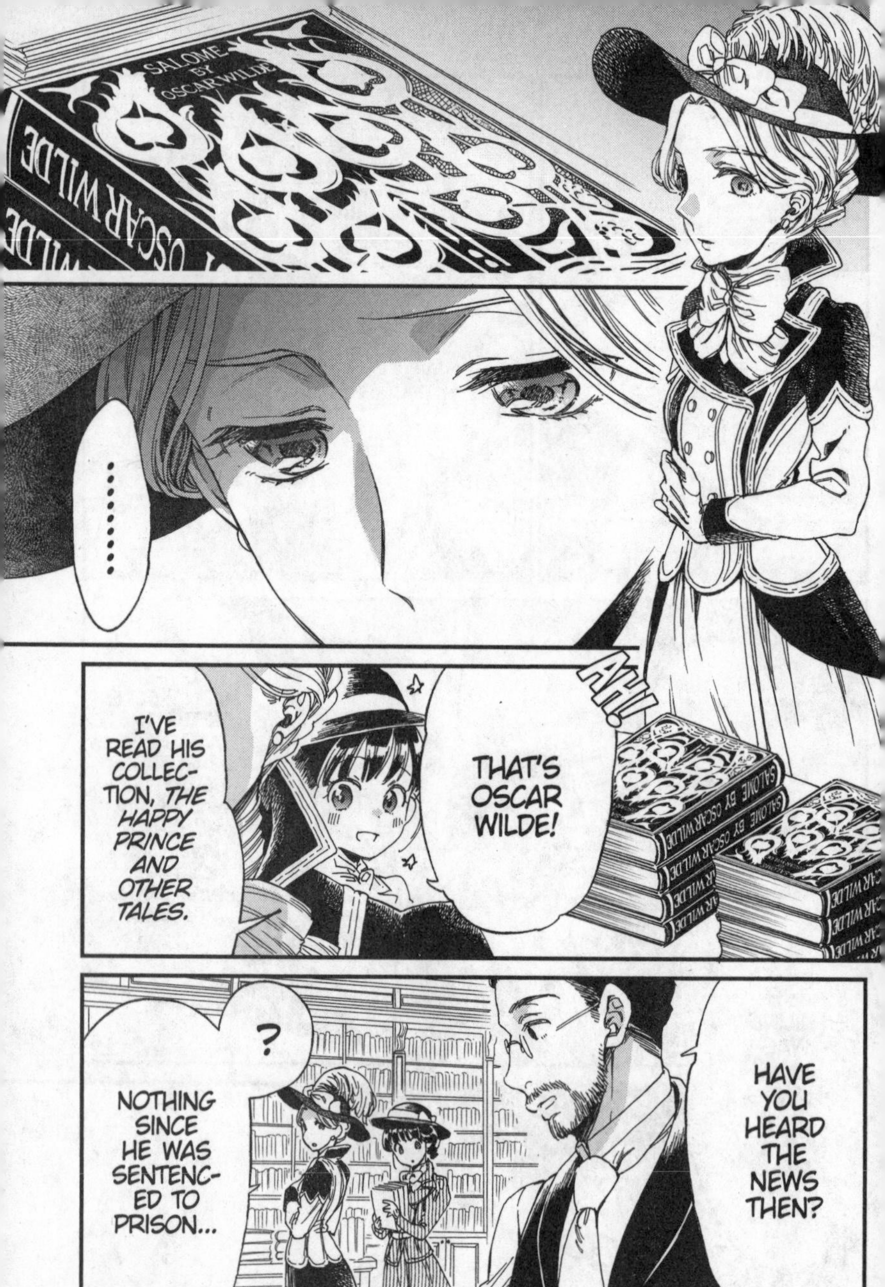
SALOME BY OSCAR WILDE
....
AH!
THAT'S OSCAR WILDE!
I'VE READ HIS COLLECTION, *THE HAPPY PRINCE AND OTHER TALES.*
SALOME BY OSCAR WILDE
HAVE YOU HEARD THE NEWS THEN?
?
NOTHING SINCE HE WAS SENTENCED TO PRISON...

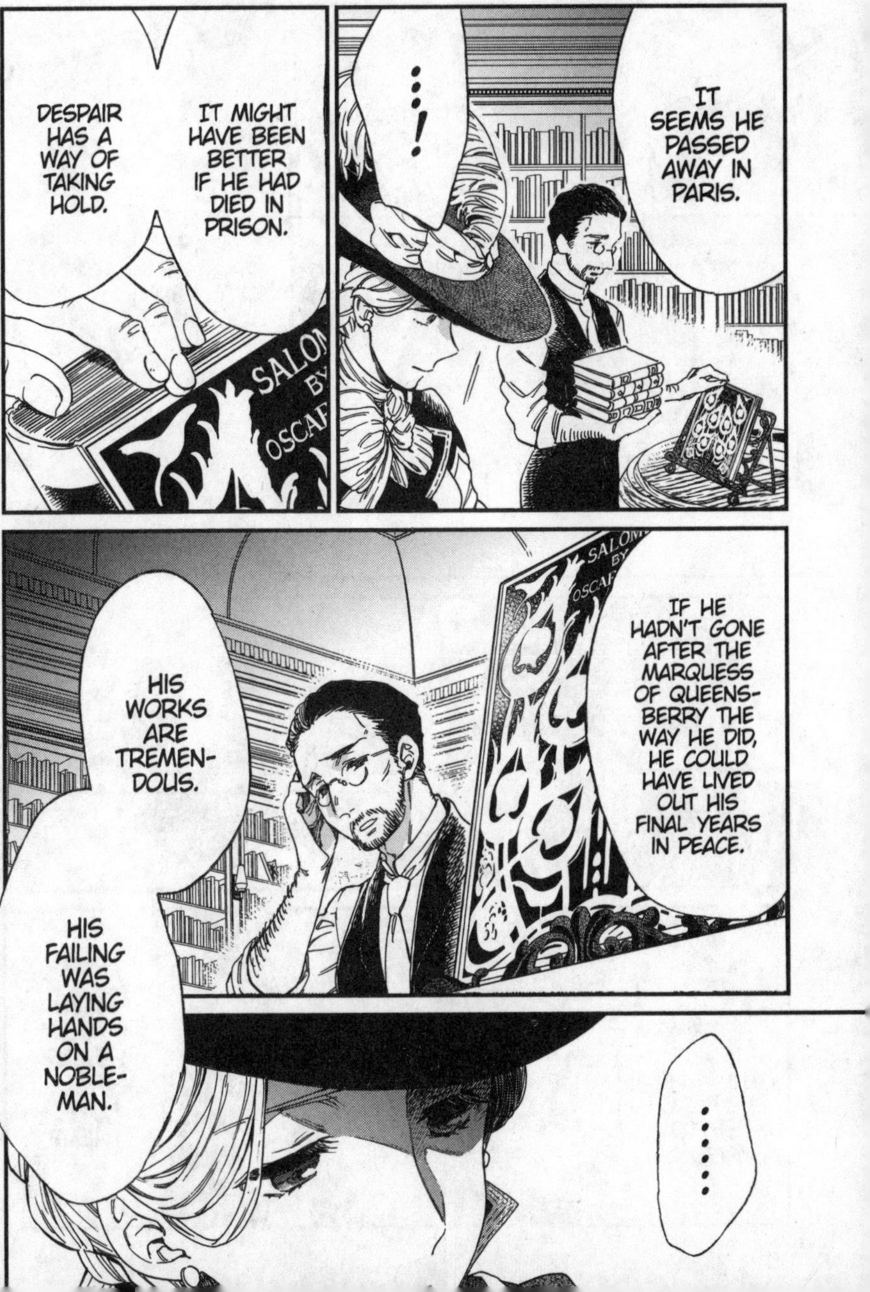
IT SEEMS HE PASSED AWAY IN PARIS.
...!
IT MIGHT HAVE BEEN BETTER IF HE HAD DIED IN PRISON.
DESPAIR HAS A WAY OF TAKING HOLD.
IF HE HADN'T GONE AFTER THE MARQUESS OF QUEENS-BERRY THE WAY HE DID, HE COULD HAVE LIVED OUT HIS FINAL YEARS IN PEACE.
HIS WORKS ARE TREMEN-DOUS.
HIS FAILING WAS LAYING HANDS ON A NOBLE-MAN.
......

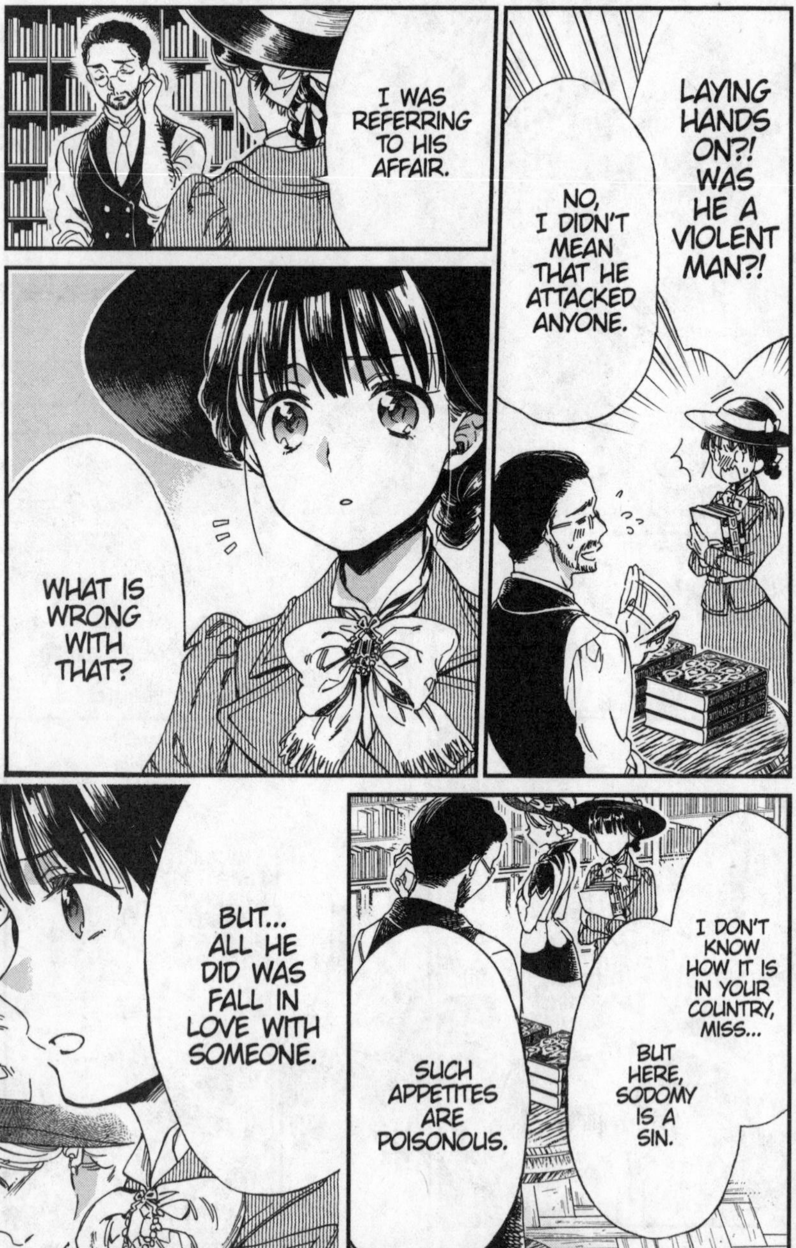
LAYING HANDS ON?! WAS HE A VIOLENT MAN?!
NO, I DIDN'T MEAN THAT HE ATTACKED ANYONE.
I WAS REFERRING TO HIS AFFAIR.
WHAT IS WRONG WITH THAT?
I DON'T KNOW HOW IT IS IN YOUR COUNTRY, MISS...
BUT HERE, SODOMY IS A SIN.
SUCH APPETITES ARE POISONOUS.
BUT... ALL HE DID WAS FALL IN LOVE WITH SOMEONE.

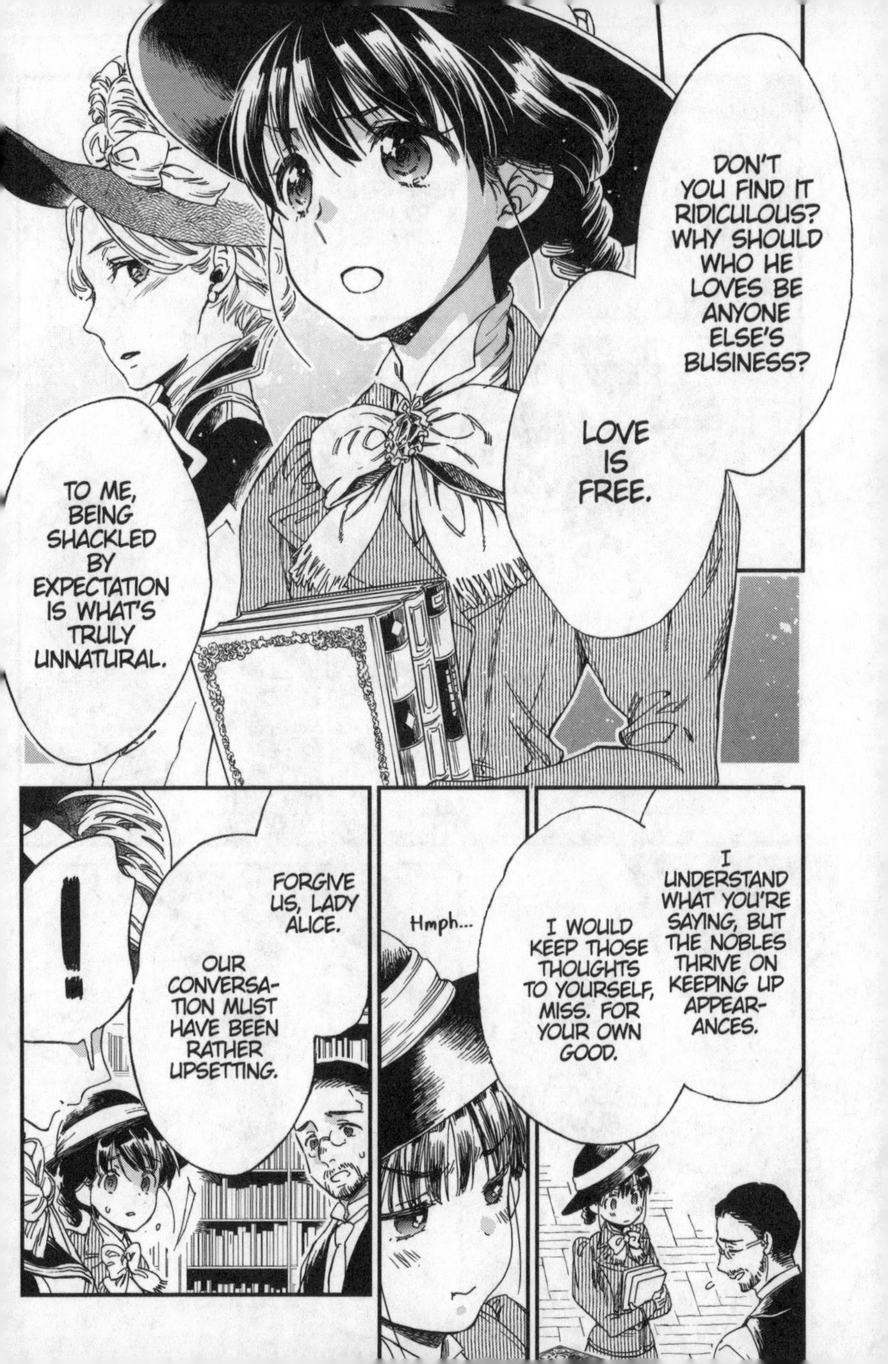
DON'T YOU FIND IT RIDICULOUS? WHY SHOULD WHO HE LOVES BE ANYONE ELSE'S BUSINESS?
LOVE IS FREE.
TO ME, BEING SHACKLED BY EXPECTATION IS WHAT'S TRULY UNNATURAL.
I UNDERSTAND WHAT YOU'RE SAYING, BUT THE NOBLES THRIVE ON KEEPING UP APPEARANCES.
I WOULD KEEP THOSE THOUGHTS TO YOURSELF, MISS. FOR YOUR OWN GOOD.
Hmph...
FORGIVE US, LADY ALICE.
OUR CONVERSATION MUST HAVE BEEN RATHER UPSETTING.
!

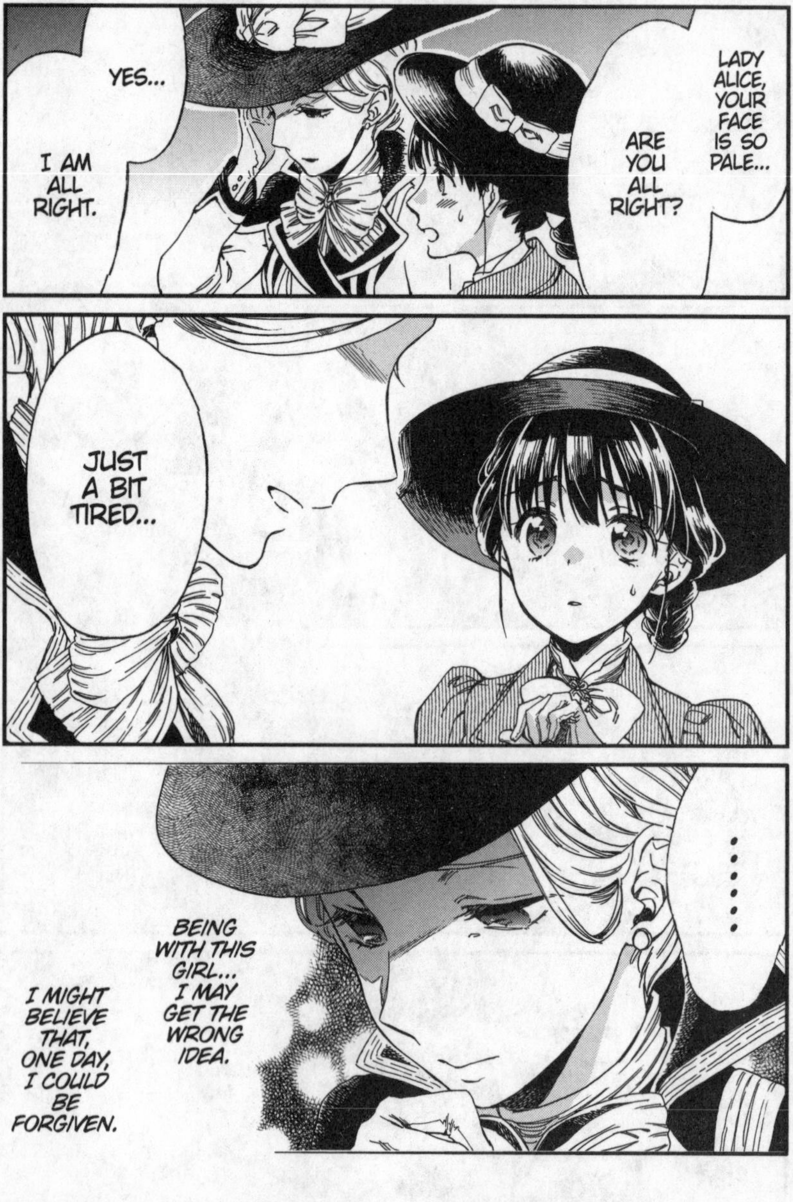
LADY ALICE, YOUR FACE IS SO PALE...
ARE YOU ALL RIGHT?
YES...
I AM ALL RIGHT.
JUST A BIT TIRED...
......
BEING WITH THIS GIRL... I MAY GET THE WRONG IDEA.
I MIGHT BELIEVE THAT, ONE DAY, I COULD BE FORGIVEN.

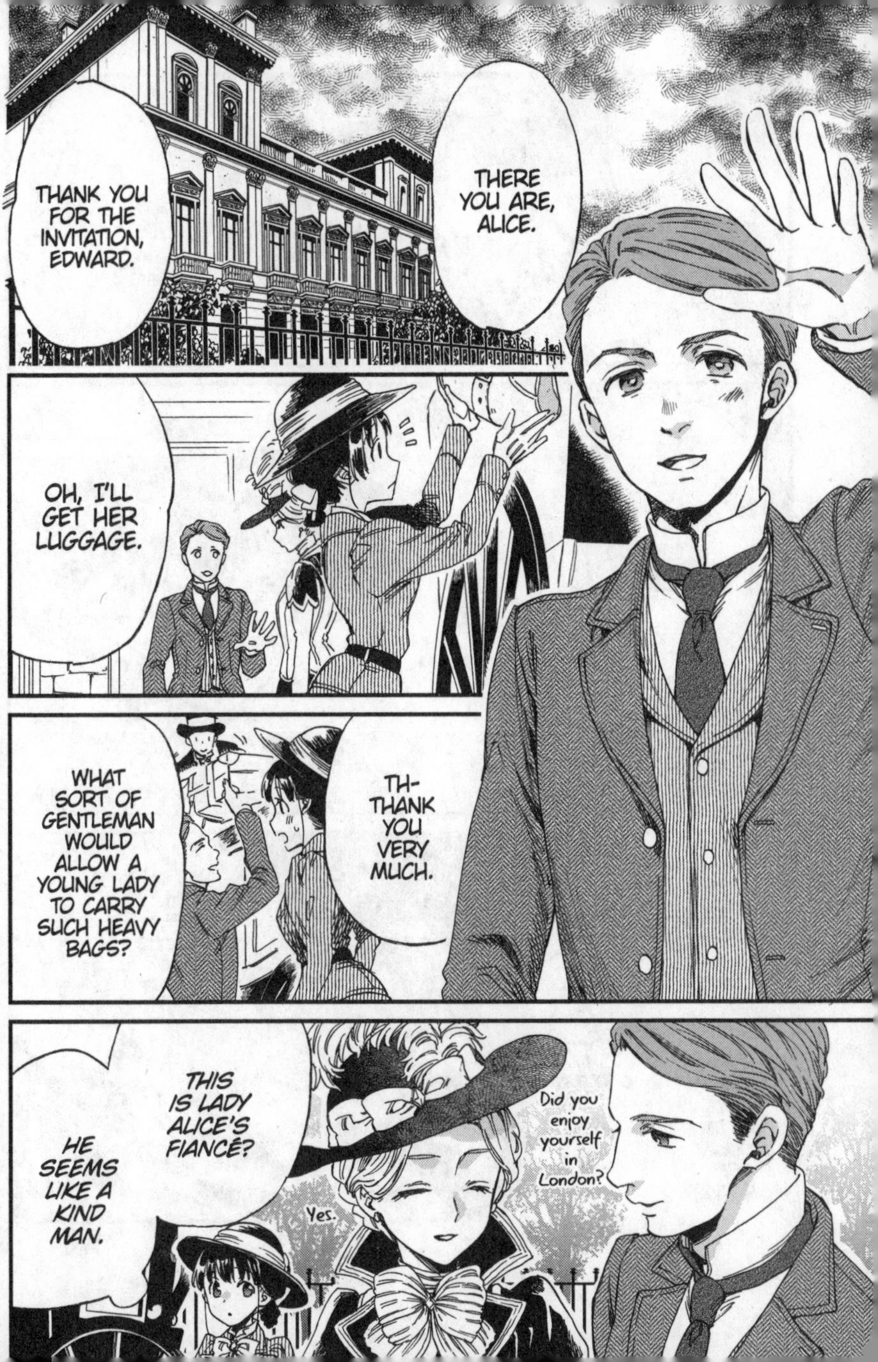

THERE YOU ARE, ALICE.
THANK YOU FOR THE INVITATION, EDWARD.
OH, I'LL GET HER LUGGAGE.
TH- THANK YOU VERY MUCH.
WHAT SORT OF GENTLEMAN WOULD ALLOW A YOUNG LADY TO CARRY SUCH HEAVY BAGS?
Did you enjoy yourself in London?
Yes.
THIS IS LADY ALICE'S FIANCÉ?
HE SEEMS LIKE A KIND MAN.

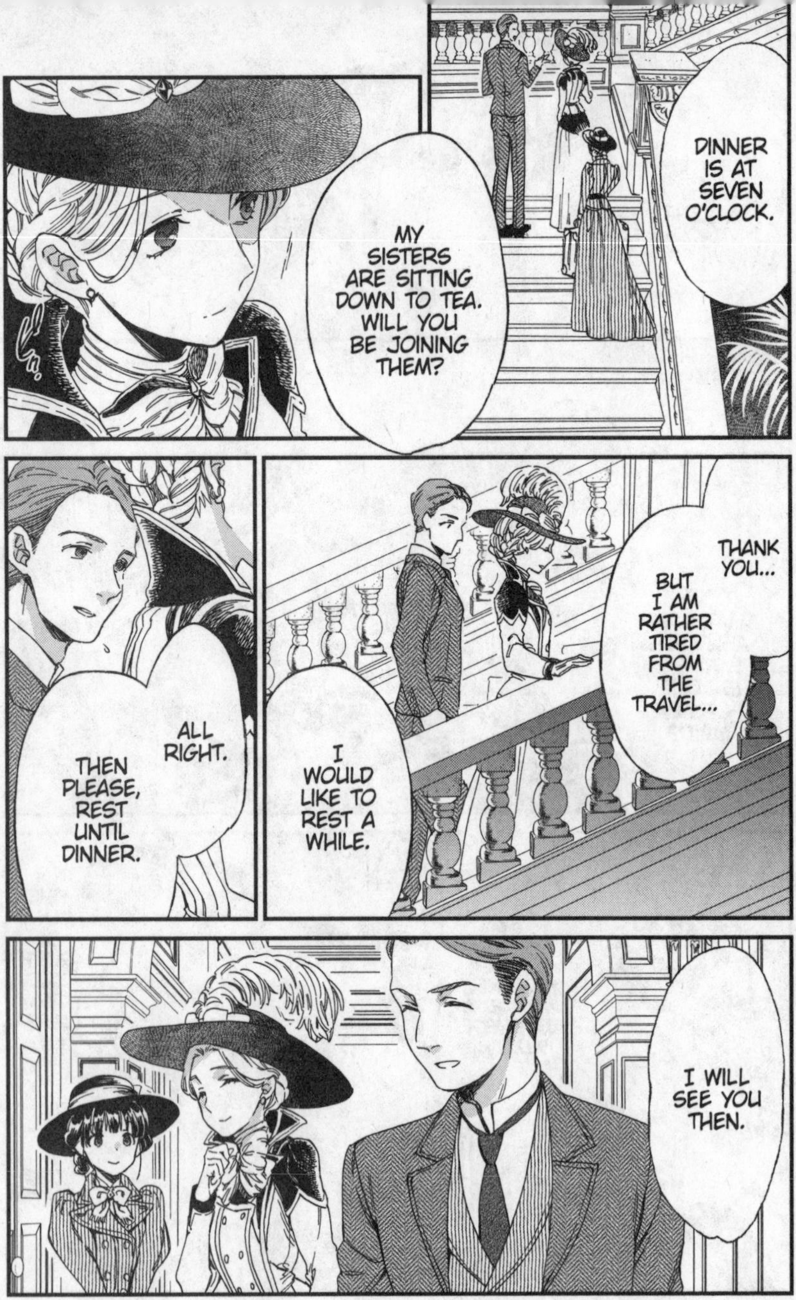
DINNER IS AT SEVEN O'CLOCK.
MY SISTERS ARE SITTING DOWN TO TEA. WILL YOU BE JOINING THEM?
THANK YOU...
BUT I AM RATHER TIRED FROM THE TRAVEL...
I WOULD LIKE TO REST A WHILE.
ALL RIGHT.
THEN PLEASE, REST UNTIL DINNER.
I WILL SEE YOU THEN.

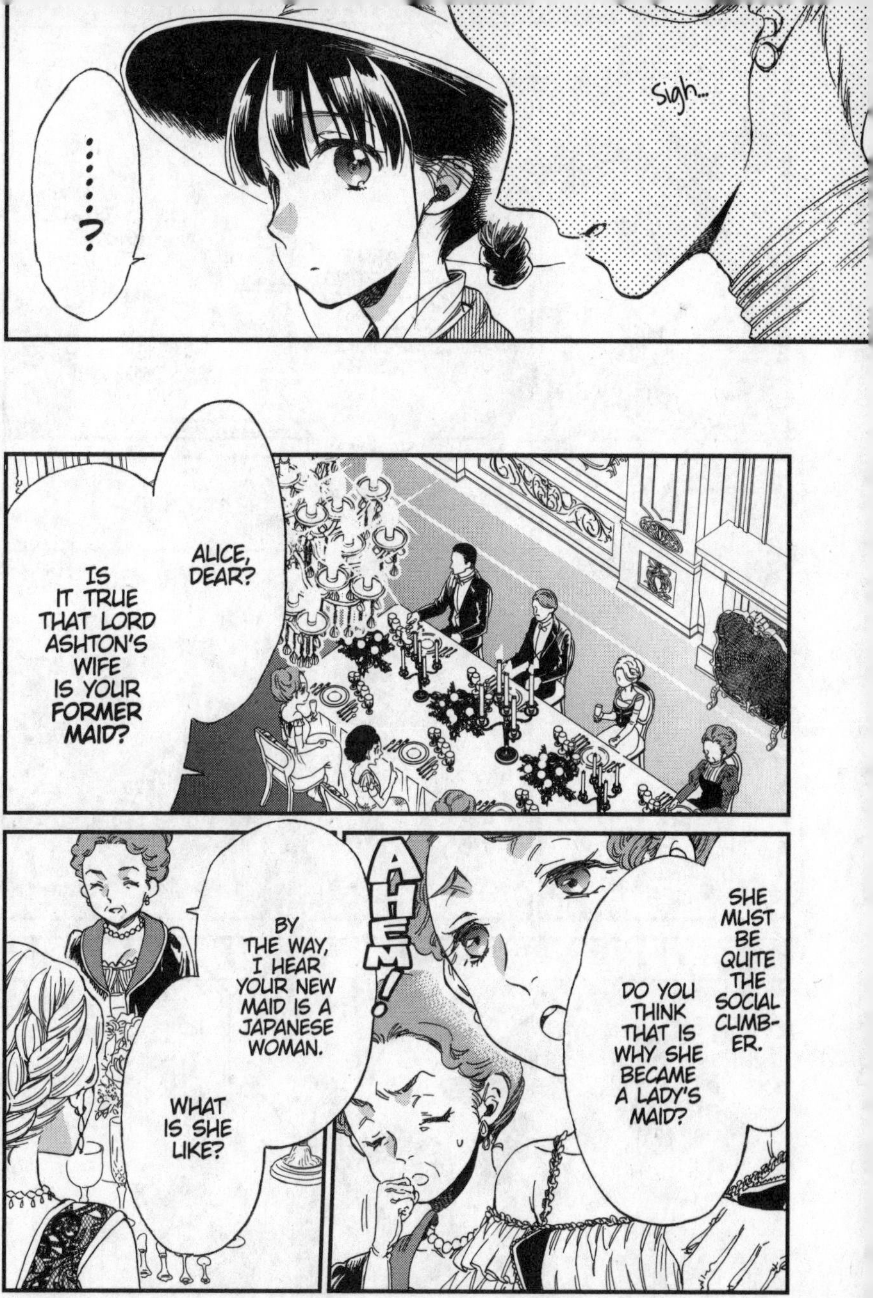
Sigh...
......?
ALICE, DEAR?
IS IT TRUE THAT LORD ASHTON'S WIFE IS YOUR FORMER MAID?
SHE MUST BE QUITE THE SOCIAL CLIMBER.
DO YOU THINK THAT IS WHY SHE BECAME A LADY'S MAID?
AHEM!
BY THE WAY, I HEAR YOUR NEW MAID IS A JAPANESE WOMAN.
WHAT IS SHE LIKE?

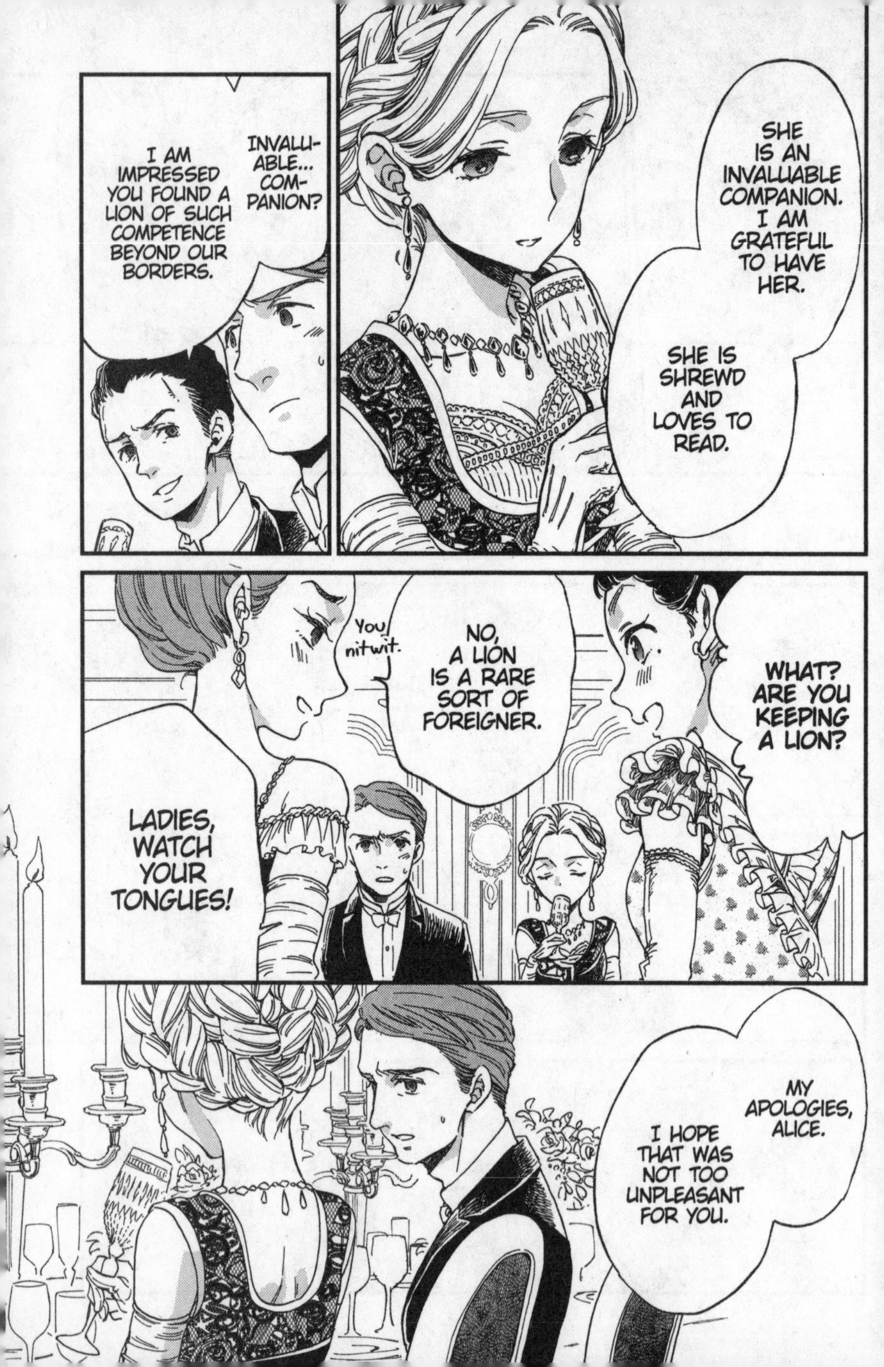
SHE IS AN INVALUABLE COMPANION. I AM GRATEFUL TO HAVE HER.
SHE IS SHREWD AND LOVES TO READ.
INVALU-ABLE... COM-PANION?
I AM IMPRESSED YOU FOUND A LION OF SUCH COMPETENCE BEYOND OUR BORDERS.
WHAT? ARE YOU KEEPING A LION?
NO, A LION IS A RARE SORT OF FOREIGNER.
You nitwit.
LADIES, WATCH YOUR TONGUES!
MY APOLOGIES, ALICE.
I HOPE THAT WAS NOT TOO UNPLEASANT FOR YOU.

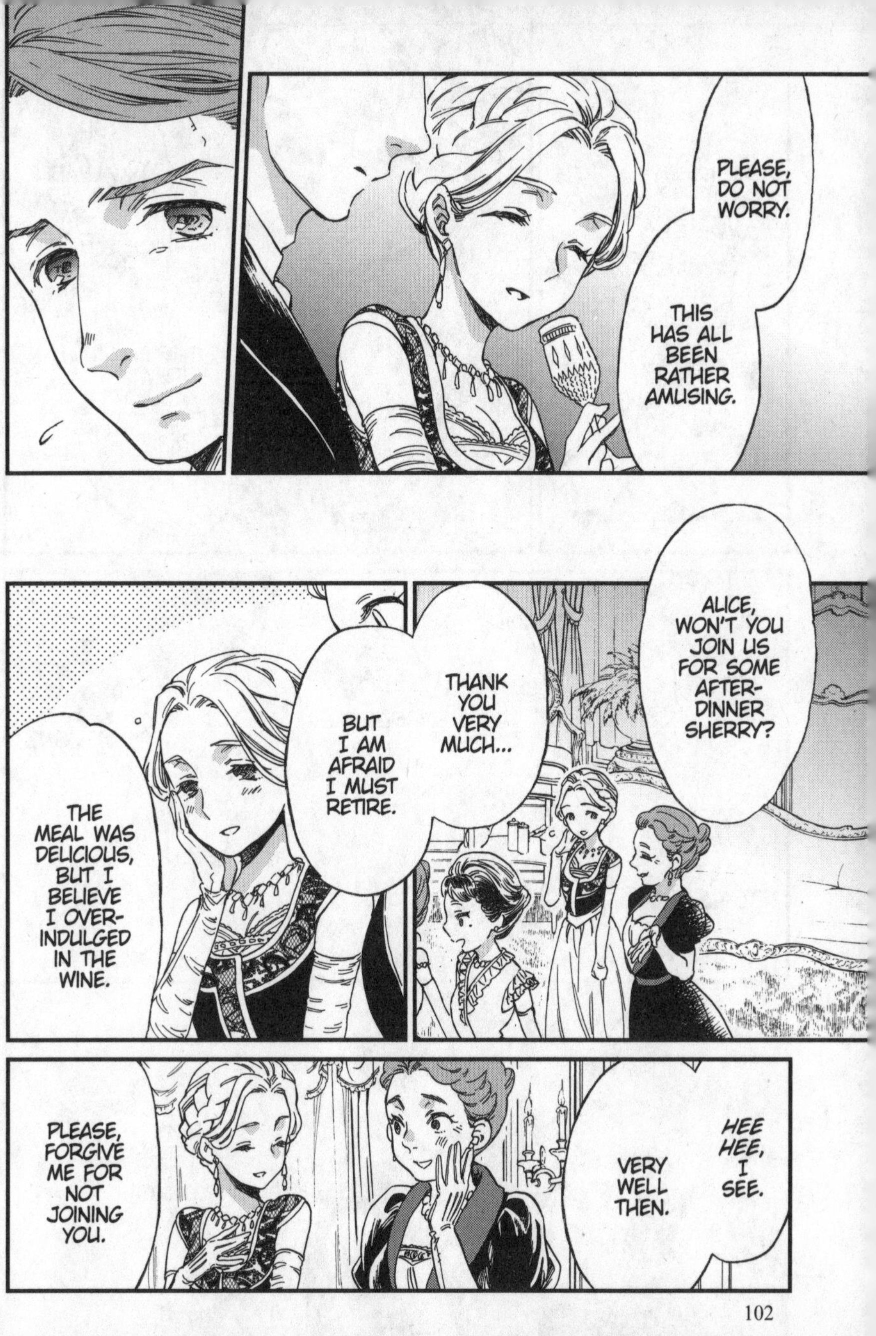
PLEASE, DO NOT WORRY.
THIS HAS ALL BEEN RATHER AMUSING.
ALICE, WON'T YOU JOIN US FOR SOME AFTER-DINNER SHERRY?
THANK YOU VERY MUCH...
BUT I AM AFRAID I MUST RETIRE.
THE MEAL WAS DELICIOUS, BUT I BELIEVE I OVER-INDULGED IN THE WINE.
HEE HEE, I SEE.
VERY WELL THEN.
PLEASE, FORGIVE ME FOR NOT JOINING YOU.

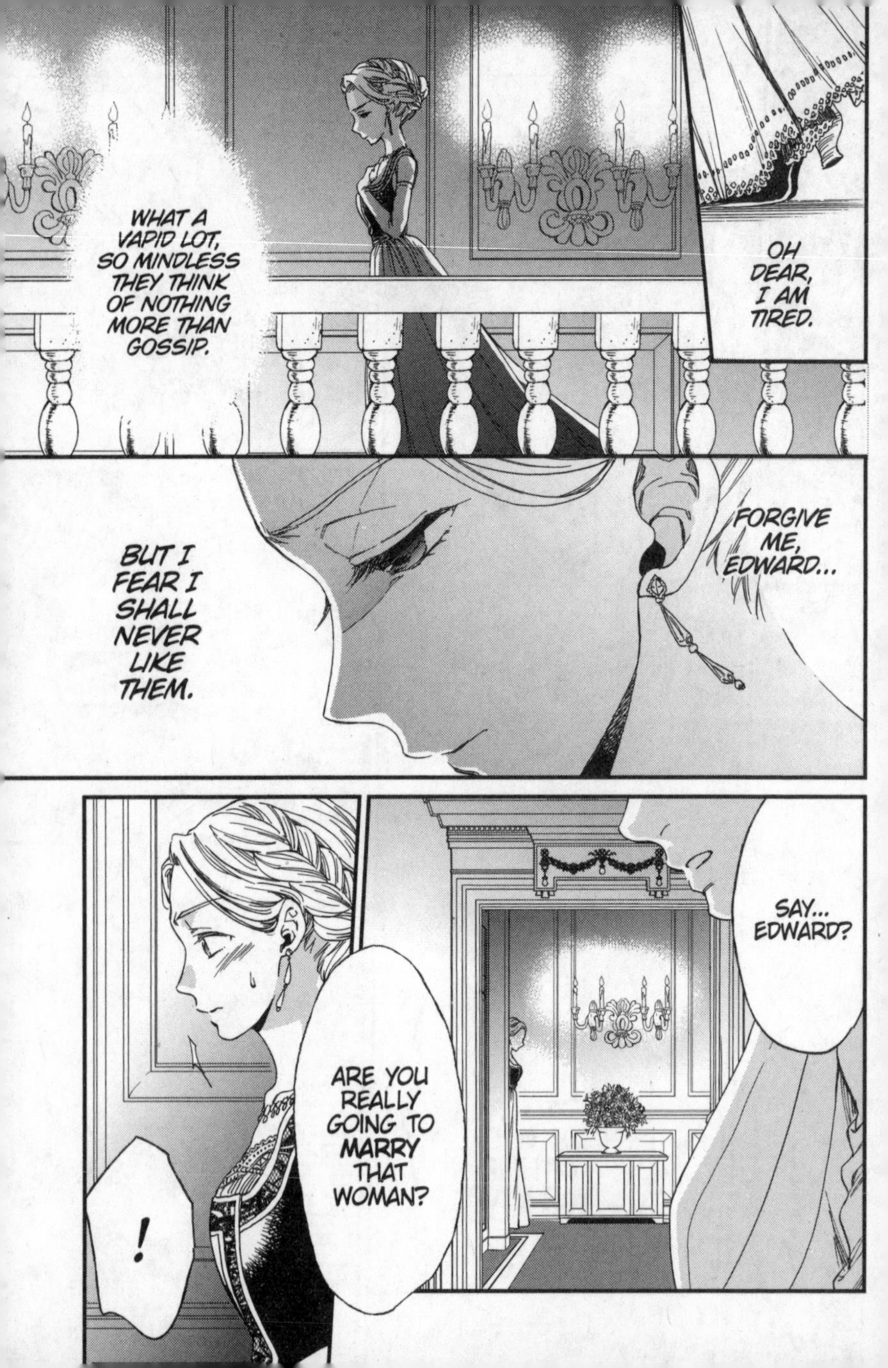
OH DEAR, I AM TIRED.
WHAT A VAPID LOT, SO MINDLESS THEY THINK OF NOTHING MORE THAN GOSSIP.
FORGIVE ME, EDWARD...
BUT I FEAR I SHALL NEVER LIKE THEM.
SAY... EDWARD?
ARE YOU REALLY GOING TO MARRY THAT WOMAN?
!

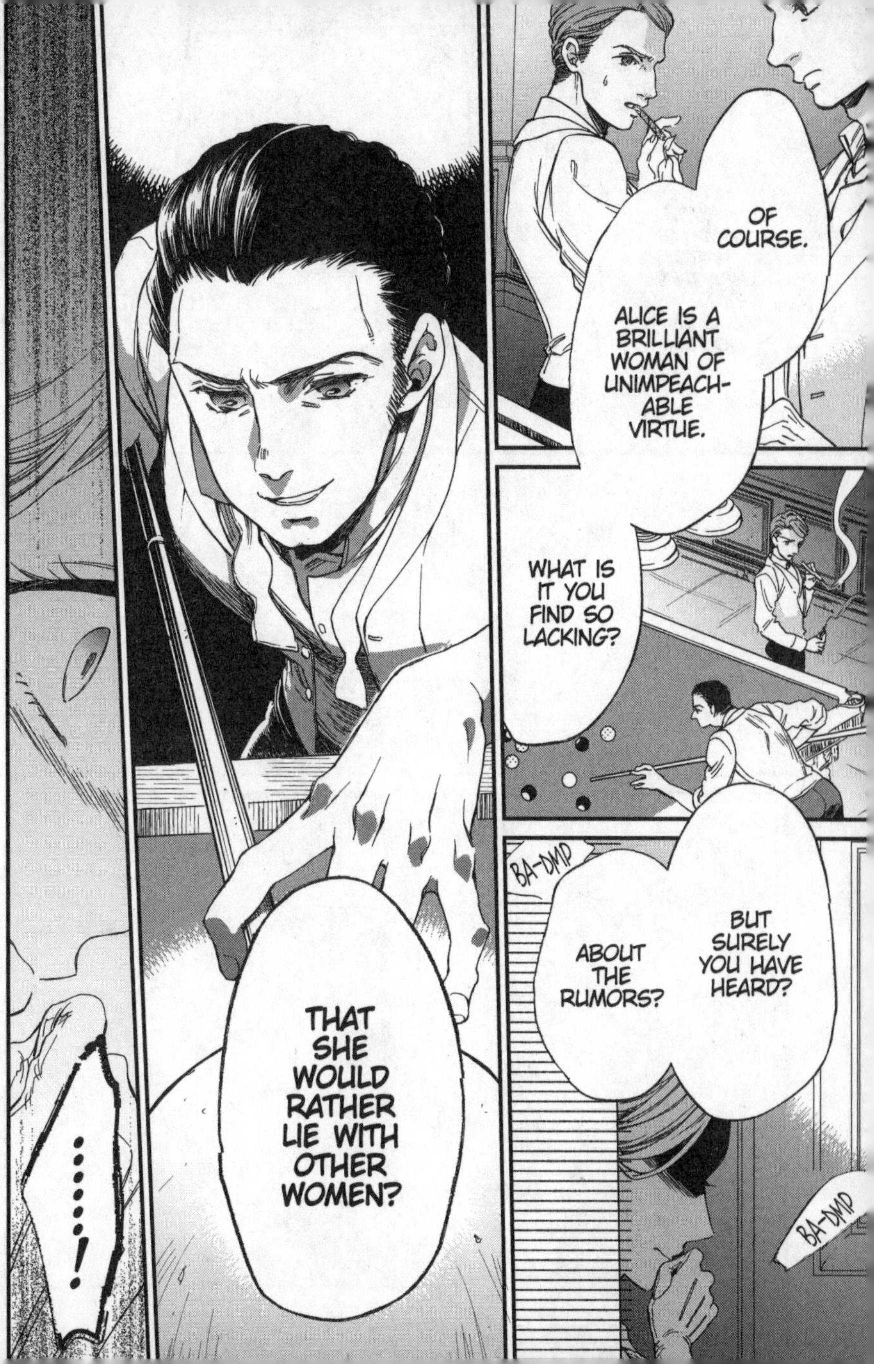
OF COURSE.
ALICE IS A BRILLIANT WOMAN OF UNIMPEACHABLE VIRTUE.
WHAT IS IT YOU FIND SO LACKING?
BA-DMP
BUT SURELY YOU HAVE HEARD?
ABOUT THE RUMORS?
BA-DMP
THAT SHE WOULD RATHER LIE WITH OTHER WOMEN?
......!

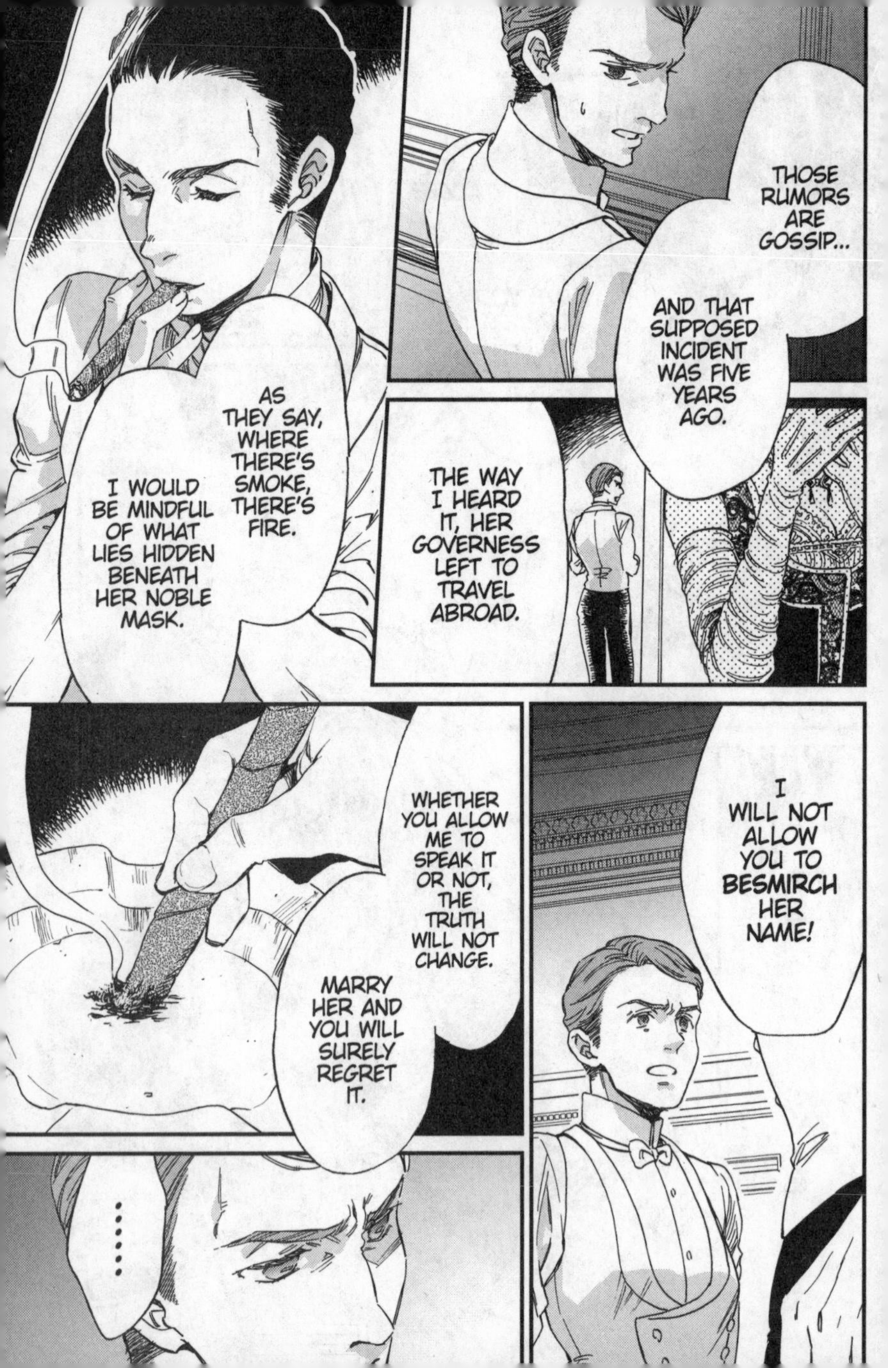

THOSE RUMORS ARE GOSSIP...
AND THAT SUPPOSED INCIDENT WAS FIVE YEARS AGO.
THE WAY I HEARD IT, HER GOVERNESS LEFT TO TRAVEL ABROAD.
AS THEY SAY, WHERE THERE'S SMOKE, THERE'S FIRE.
I WOULD BE MINDFUL OF WHAT LIES HIDDEN BENEATH HER NOBLE MASK.
I WILL NOT ALLOW YOU TO BESMIRCH HER NAME!
WHETHER YOU ALLOW ME TO SPEAK IT OR NOT, THE TRUTH WILL NOT CHANGE.
MARRY HER AND YOU WILL SURELY REGRET IT.
......

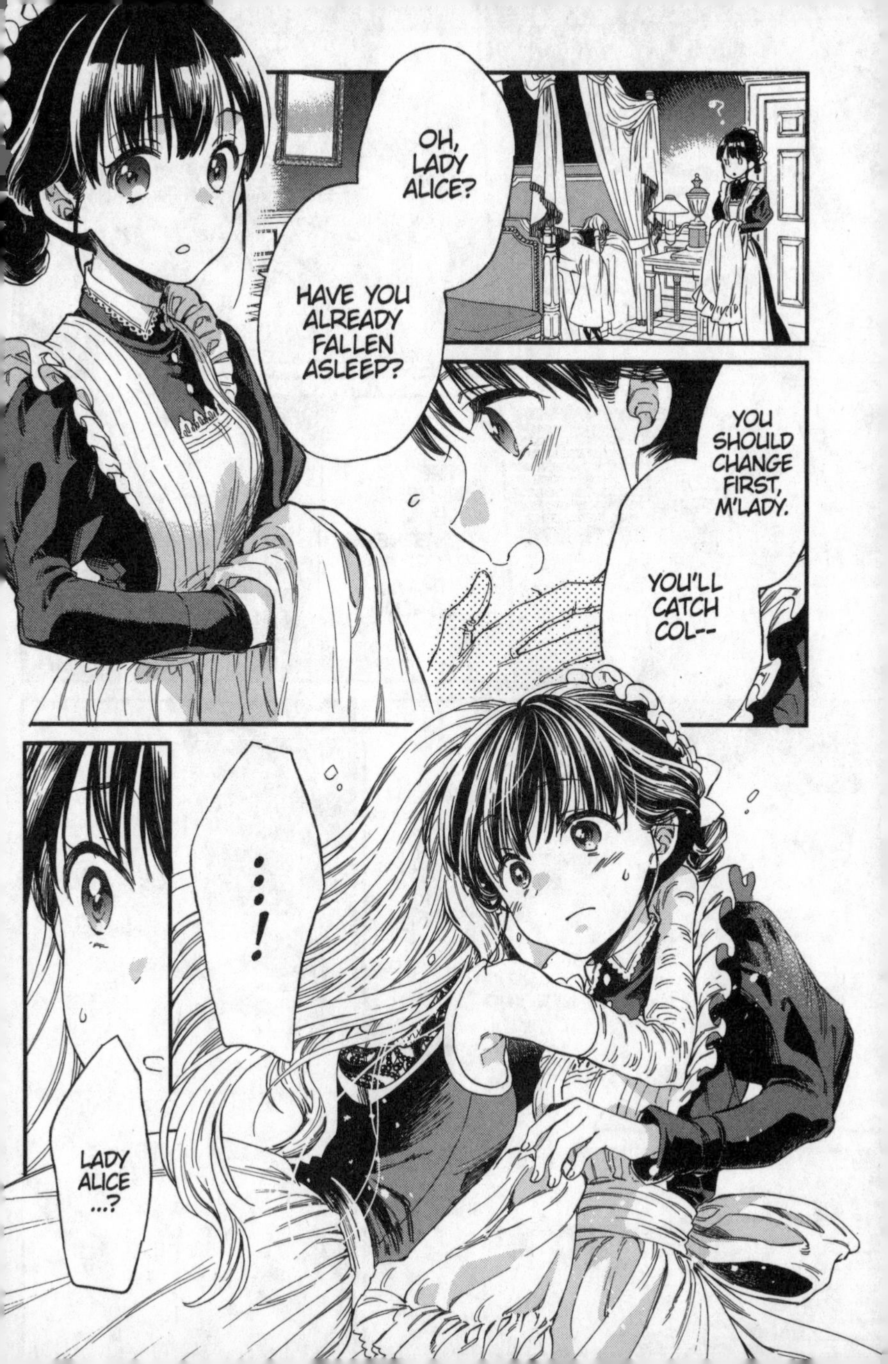
?
OH, LADY ALICE?
HAVE YOU ALREADY FALLEN ASLEEP?
YOU SHOULD CHANGE FIRST, M'LADY.
YOU'LL CATCH COL--
...!
LADY ALICE ...?

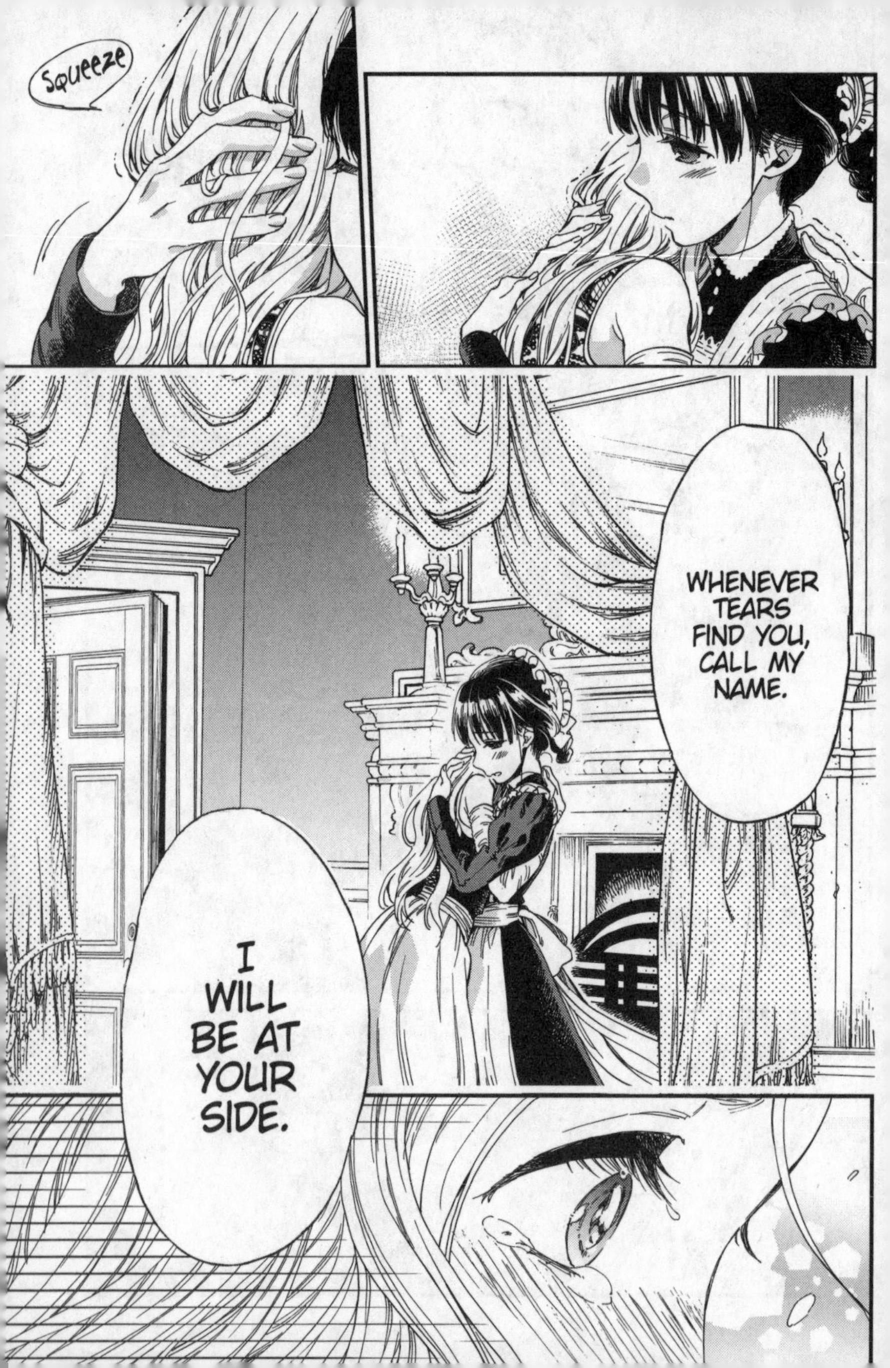
Squeeze
WHENEVER TEARS FIND YOU, CALL MY NAME.
I WILL BE AT YOUR SIDE.

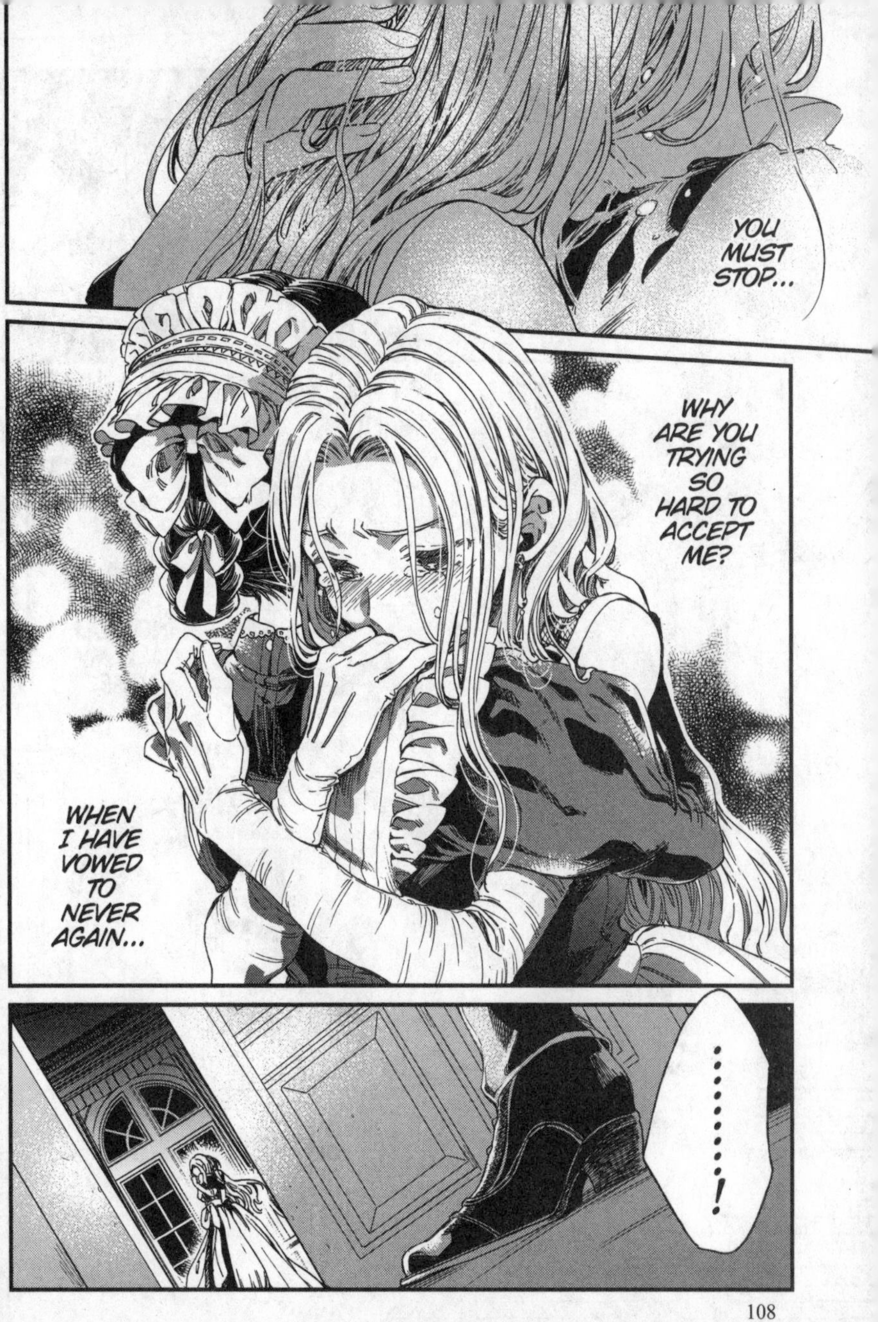
YOU MUST STOP...
WHY ARE YOU TRYING SO HARD TO ACCEPT ME?
WHEN I HAVE VOWED TO NEVER AGAIN...
.........!

{ Chapter 4 }
Nameless Beast, Nameless Bud

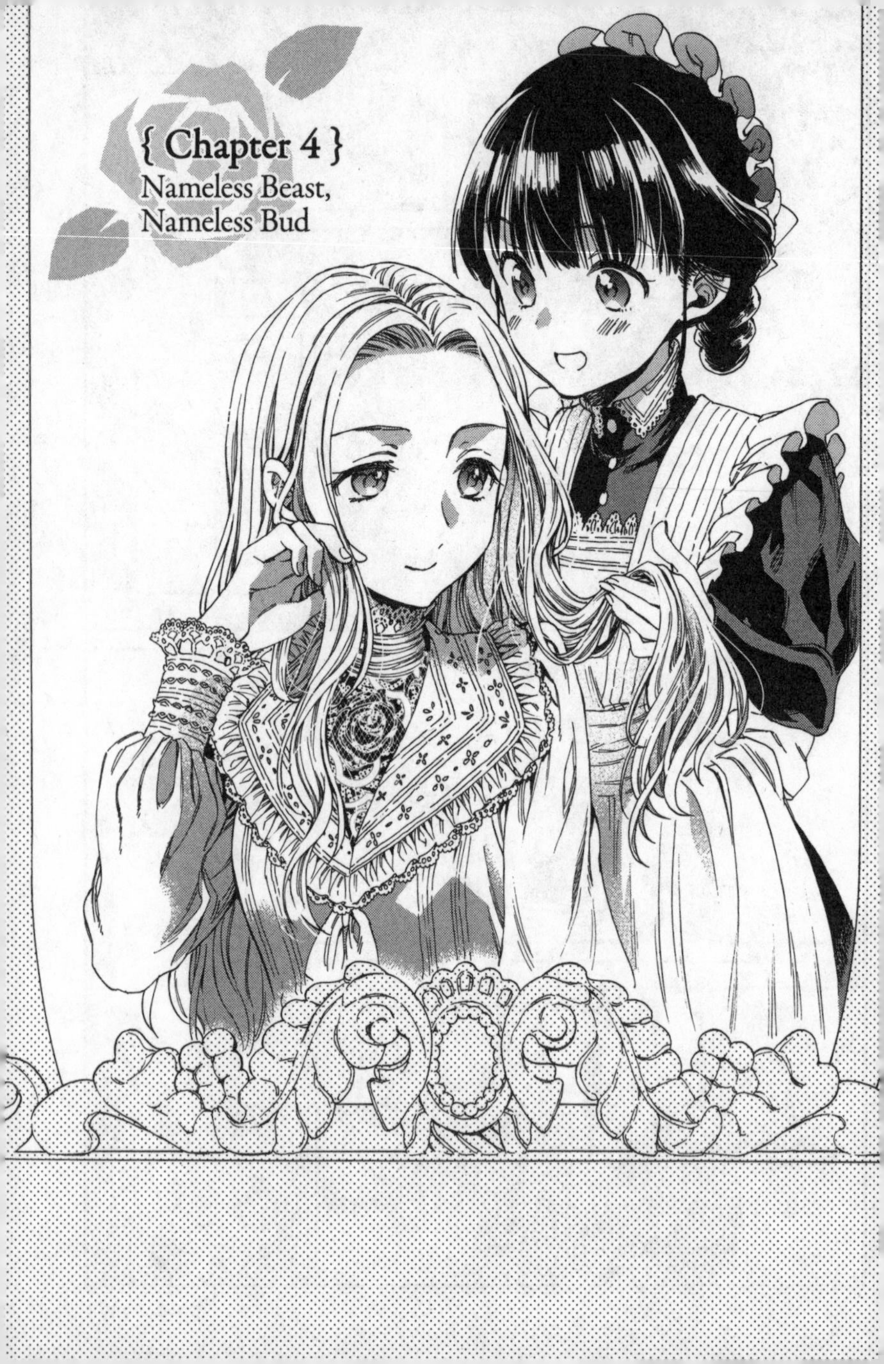

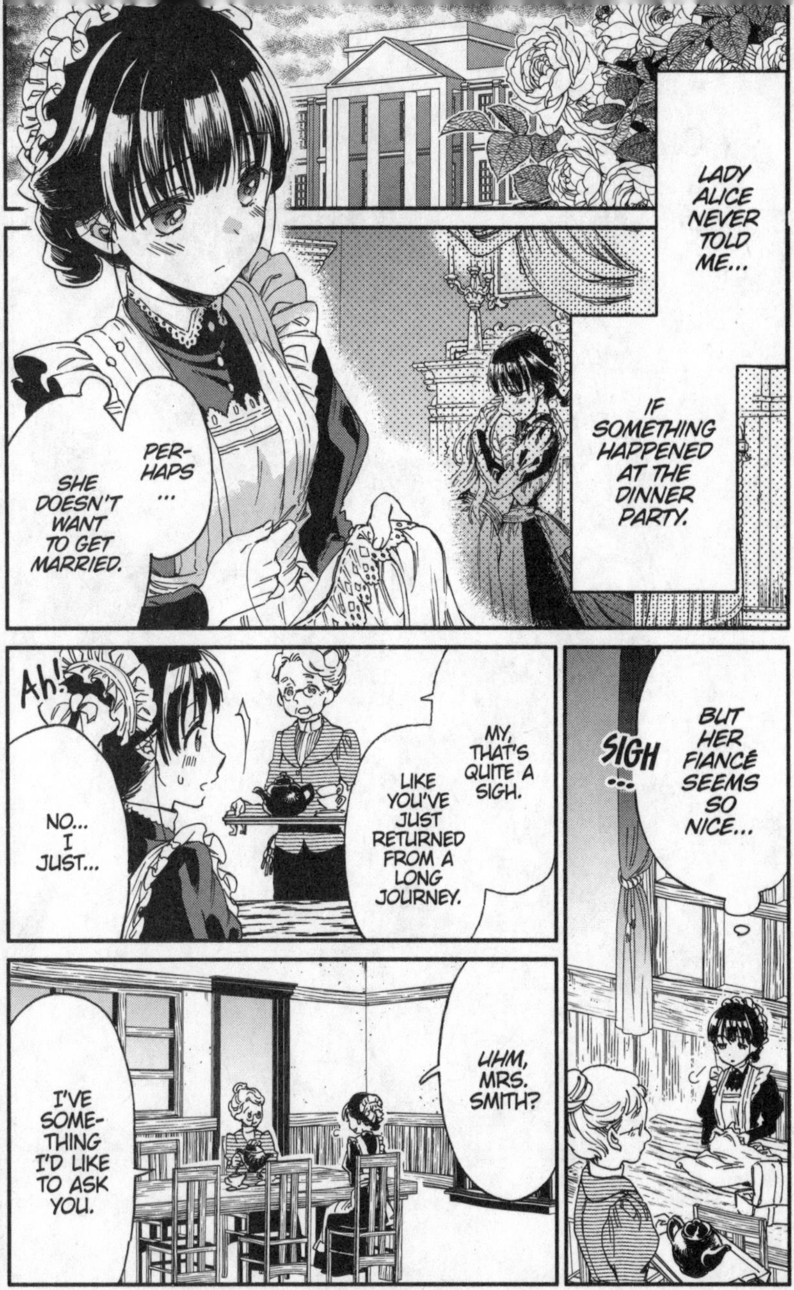
LADY ALICE NEVER TOLD ME...
IF SOMETHING HAPPENED AT THE DINNER PARTY.
PER-HAPS... SHE DOESN'T WANT TO GET MARRIED.
SIGH...
BUT HER FIANCE SEEMS SO NICE...
MY, THAT'S QUITE A SIGH.
LIKE YOU'VE JUST RETURNED FROM A LONG JOURNEY.
Ah!
NO... I JUST...
UHM, MRS. SMITH?
I'VE SOME-THING I'D LIKE TO ASK YOU.

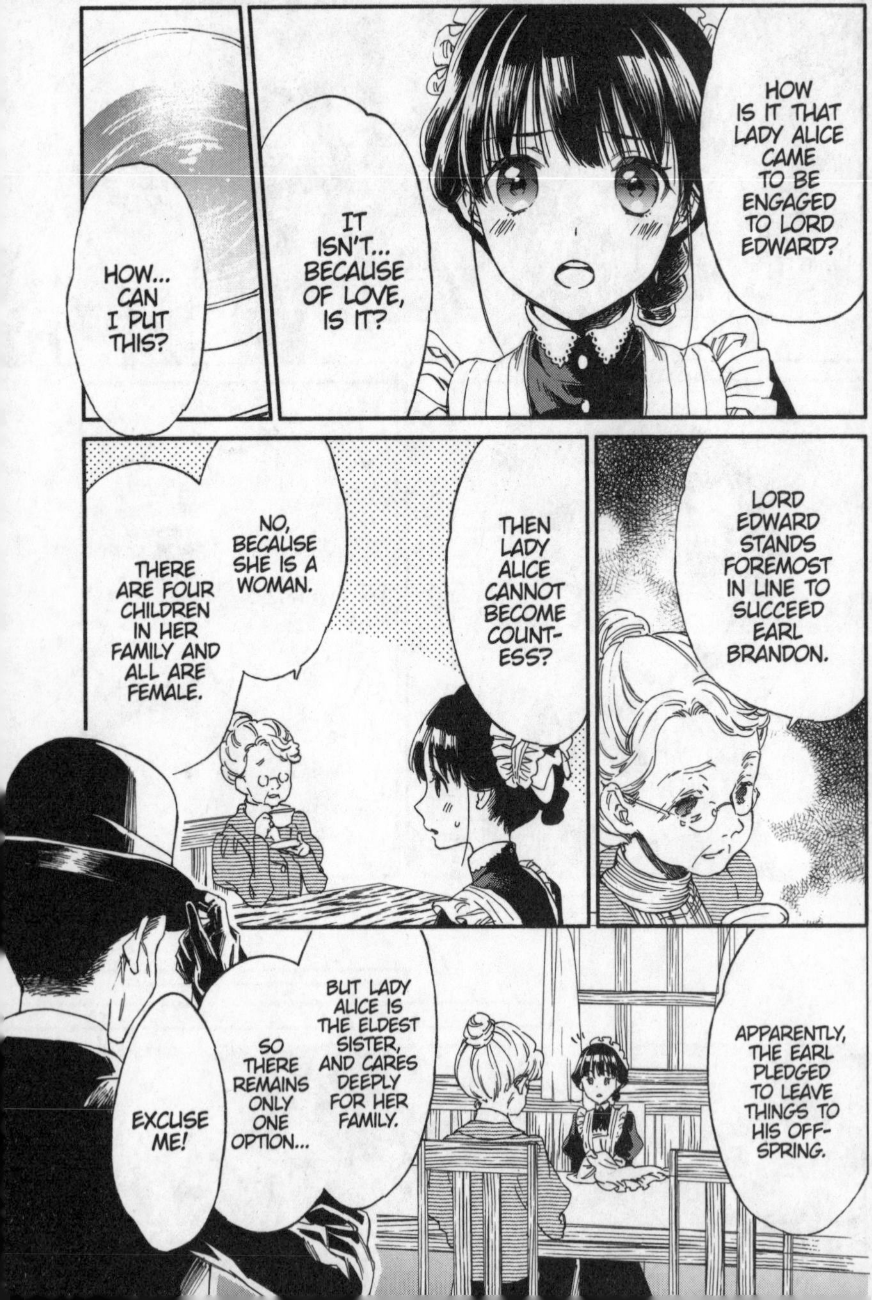
HOW IS IT THAT LADY ALICE CAME TO BE ENGAGED TO LORD EDWARD?
IT ISN'T... BECAUSE OF LOVE, IS IT?
HOW... CAN I PUT THIS?
LORD EDWARD STANDS FOREMOST IN LINE TO SUCCEED EARL BRANDON.
THEN LADY ALICE CANNOT BECOME COUNT-ESS?
NO, BECAUSE SHE IS A WOMAN.
THERE ARE FOUR CHILDREN IN HER FAMILY AND ALL ARE FEMALE.
APPARENTLY, THE EARL PLEDGED TO LEAVE THINGS TO HIS OFF-SPRING.
BUT LADY ALICE IS THE ELDEST SISTER, AND CARES DEEPLY FOR HER FAMILY.
SO THERE REMAINS ONLY ONE OPTION...
EXCUSE ME!

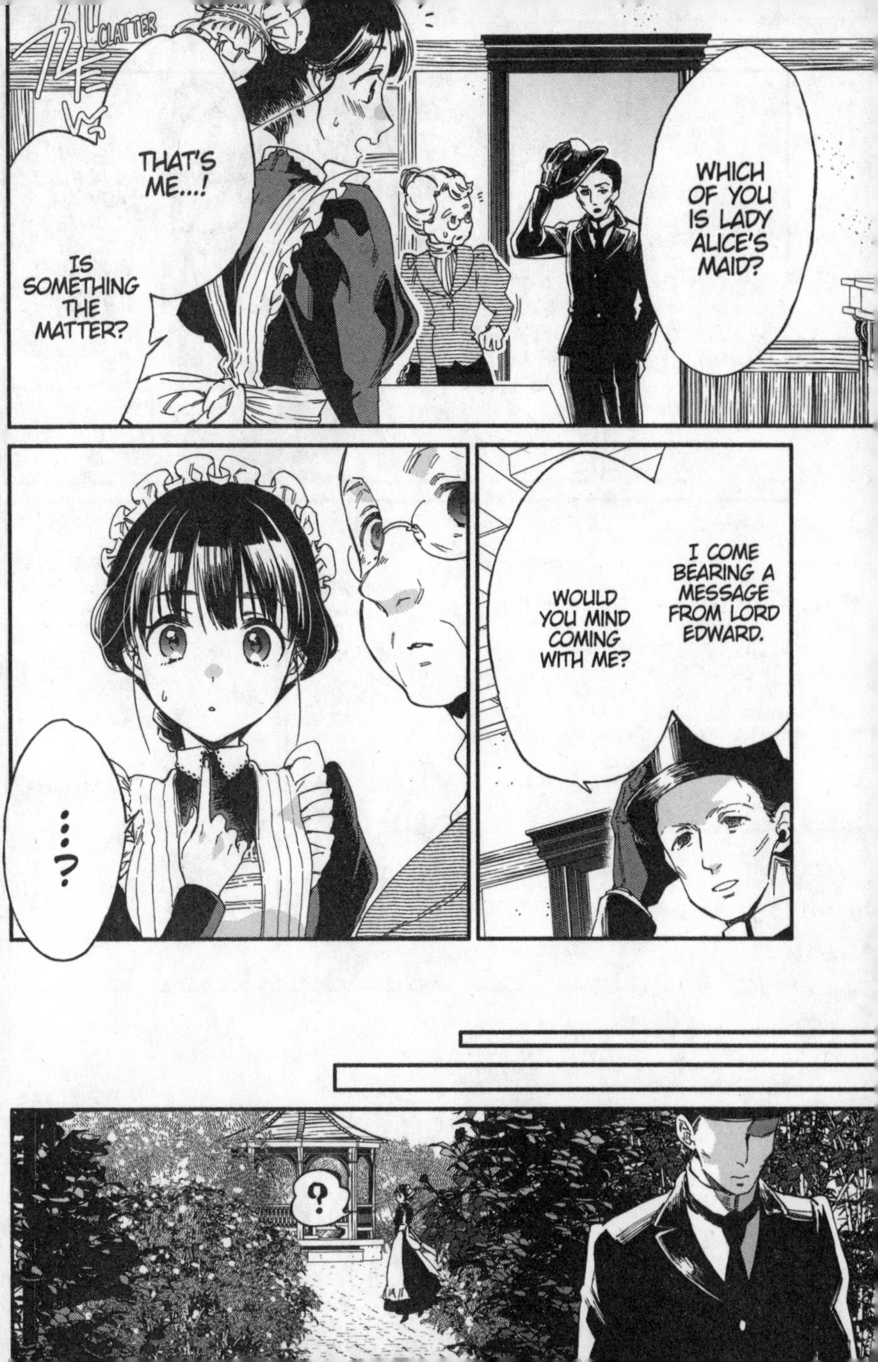
WHICH OF YOU IS LADY ALICE'S MAID?
CLATTER
THAT'S ME...!
IS SOMETHING THE MATTER?
I COME BEARING A MESSAGE FROM LORD EDWARD.
WOULD YOU MIND COMING WITH ME?
...?
?

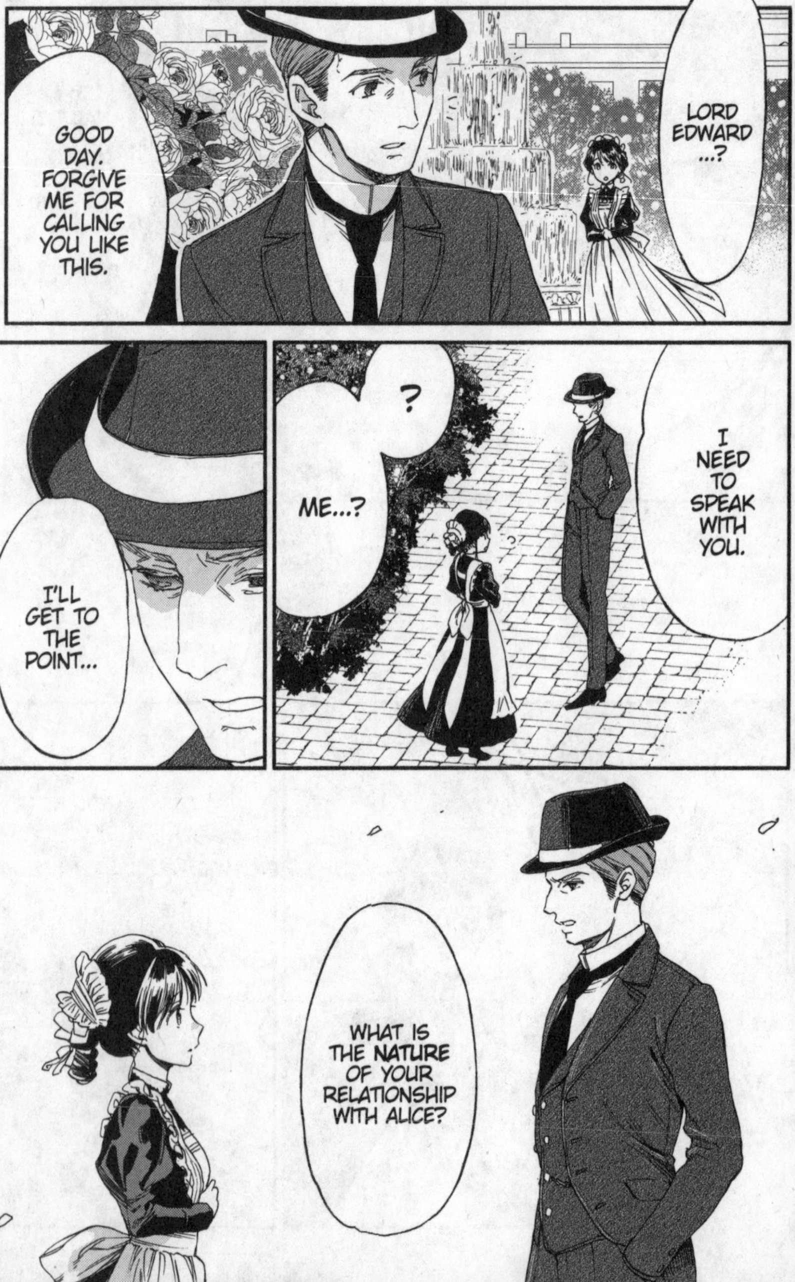
LORD EDWARD ...?
GOOD DAY. FORGIVE ME FOR CALLING YOU LIKE THIS.
I NEED TO SPEAK WITH YOU.
?
ME...?
I'LL GET TO THE POINT...
WHAT IS THE NATURE OF YOUR RELATIONSHIP WITH ALICE?

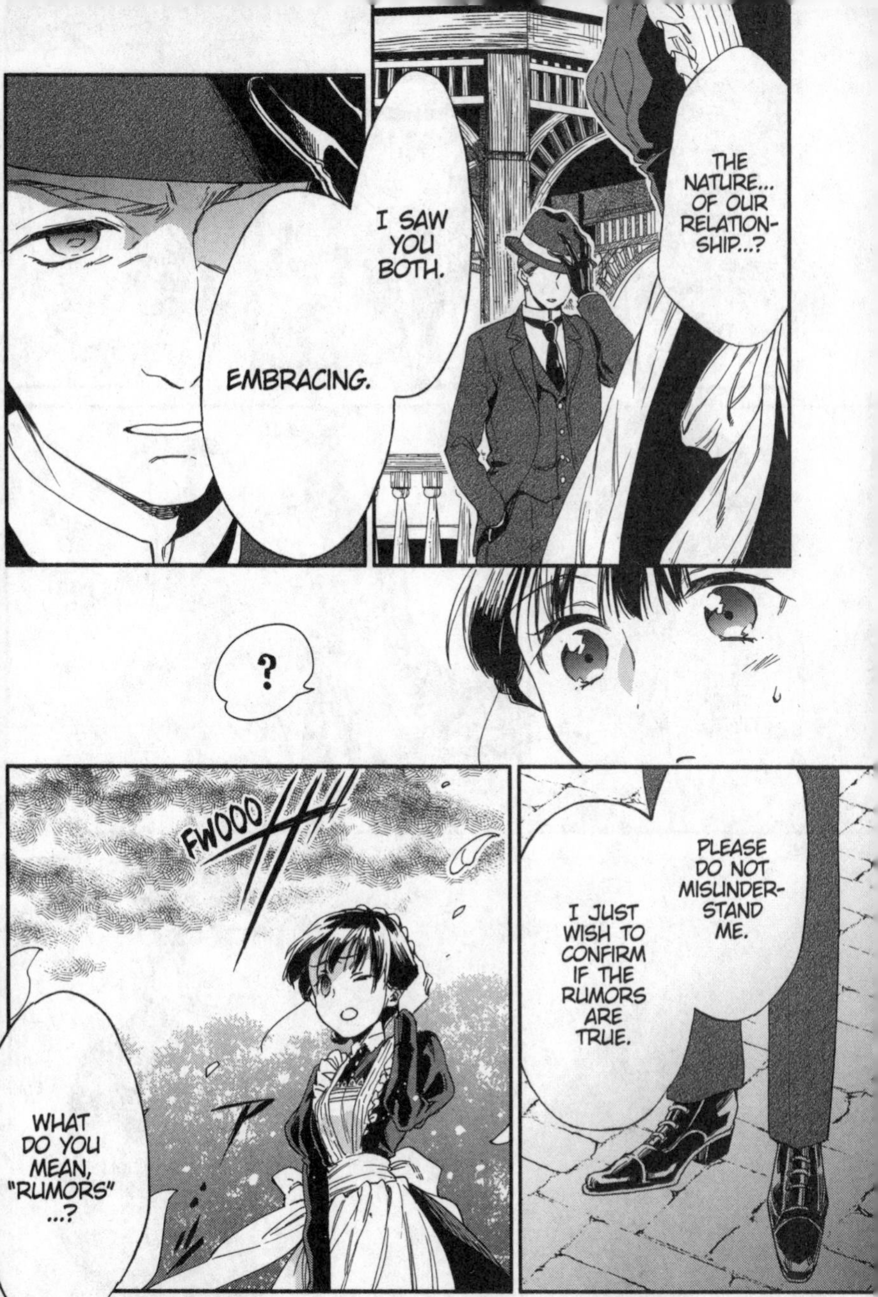
THE NATURE... OF OUR RELATION-SHIP...?
I SAW YOU BOTH.
EMBRACING.
?
PLEASE DO NOT MISUNDER-STAND ME.
I JUST WISH TO CONFIRM IF THE RUMORS ARE TRUE.
FWOOOH
WHAT DO YOU MEAN, "RUMORS" ...?

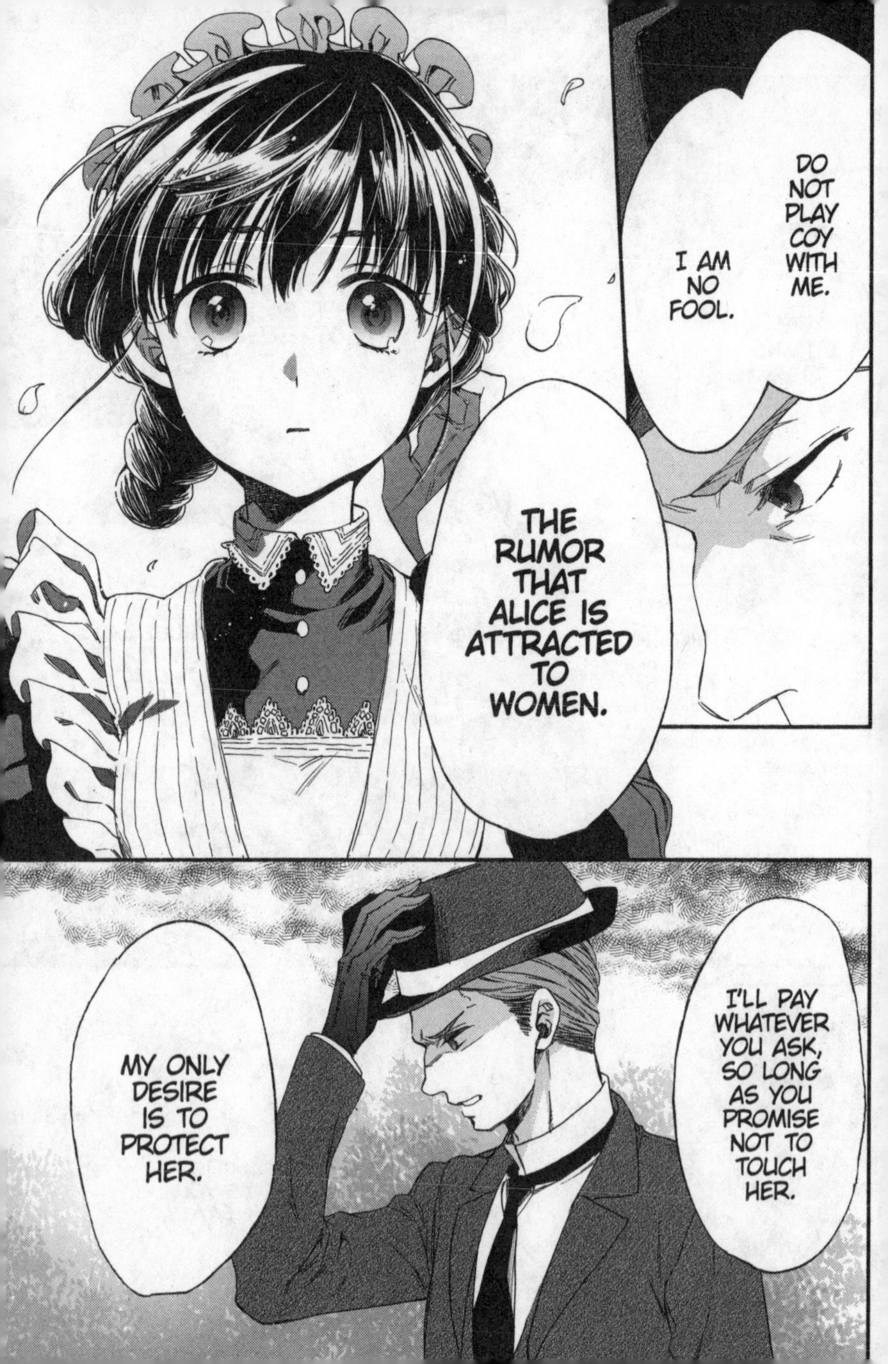
DO NOT PLAY COY WITH ME.
I AM NO FOOL.
THE RUMOR THAT ALICE IS ATTRACTED TO WOMEN.
I'LL PAY WHATEVER YOU ASK, SO LONG AS YOU PROMISE NOT TO TOUCH HER.
MY ONLY DESIRE IS TO PROTECT HER.

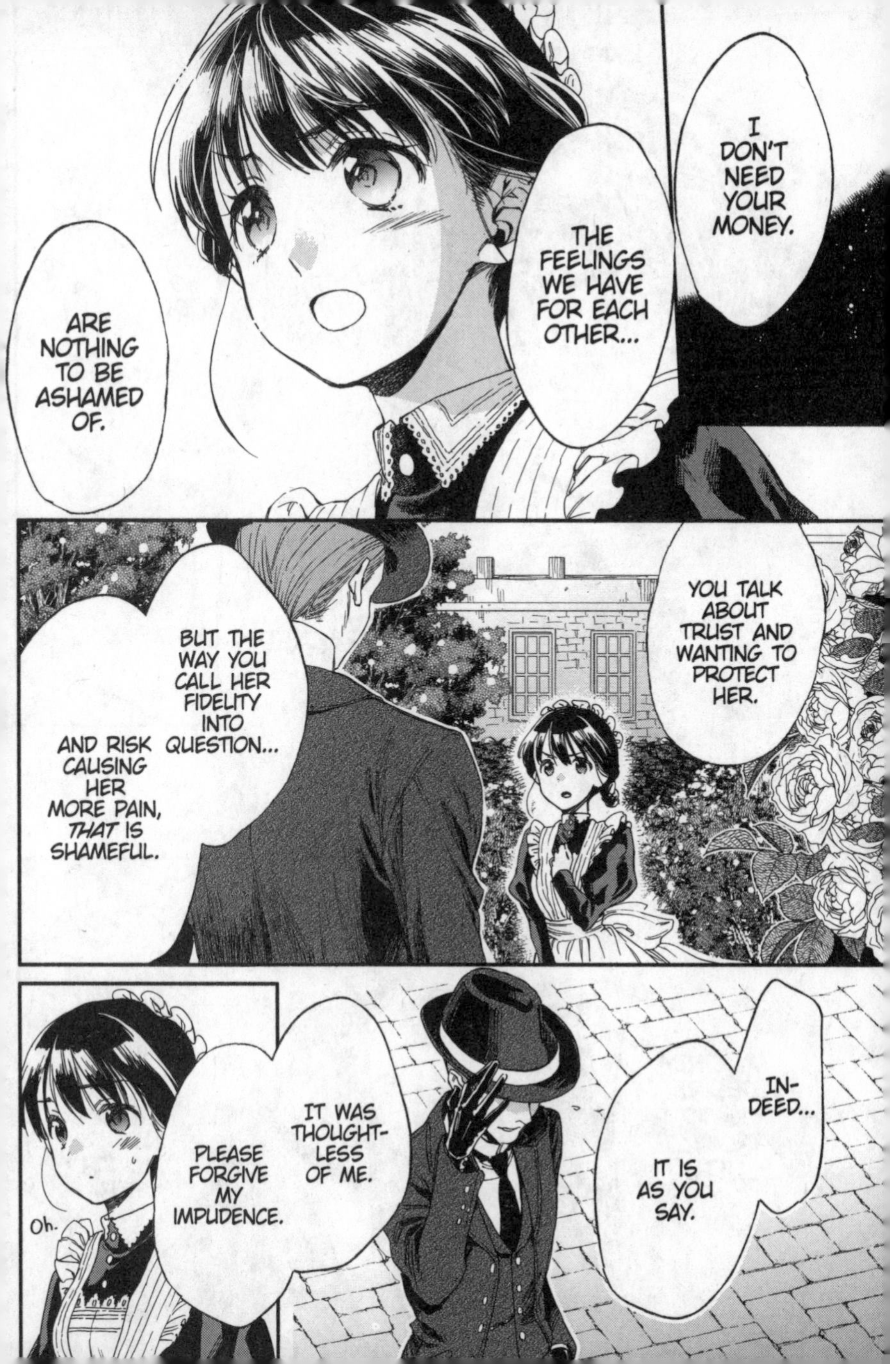
I DON'T NEED YOUR MONEY.
THE FEELINGS WE HAVE FOR EACH OTHER...
ARE NOTHING TO BE ASHAMED OF.
YOU TALK ABOUT TRUST AND WANTING TO PROTECT HER.
BUT THE WAY YOU CALL HER FIDELITY INTO QUESTION...
AND RISK CAUSING HER MORE PAIN, *THAT* IS SHAMEFUL.
IN-DEED...
IT IS AS YOU SAY.
IT WAS THOUGHT-LESS OF ME.
PLEASE FORGIVE MY IMPUDENCE.
Oh.

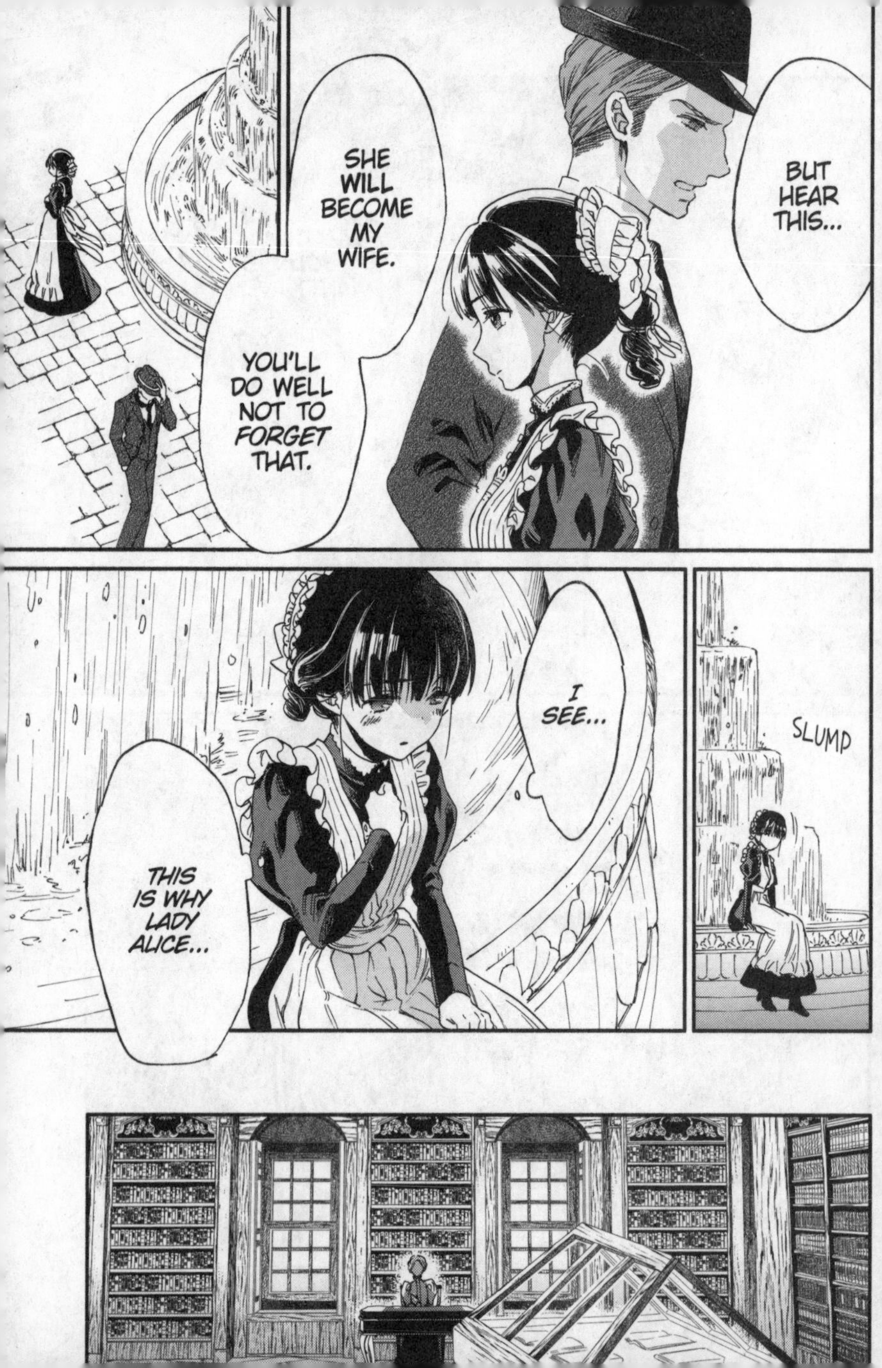
BUT HEAR THIS...
SHE WILL BECOME MY WIFE.
YOU'LL DO WELL NOT TO FORGET THAT.
SLUMP
I SEE...
THIS IS WHY LADY ALICE...

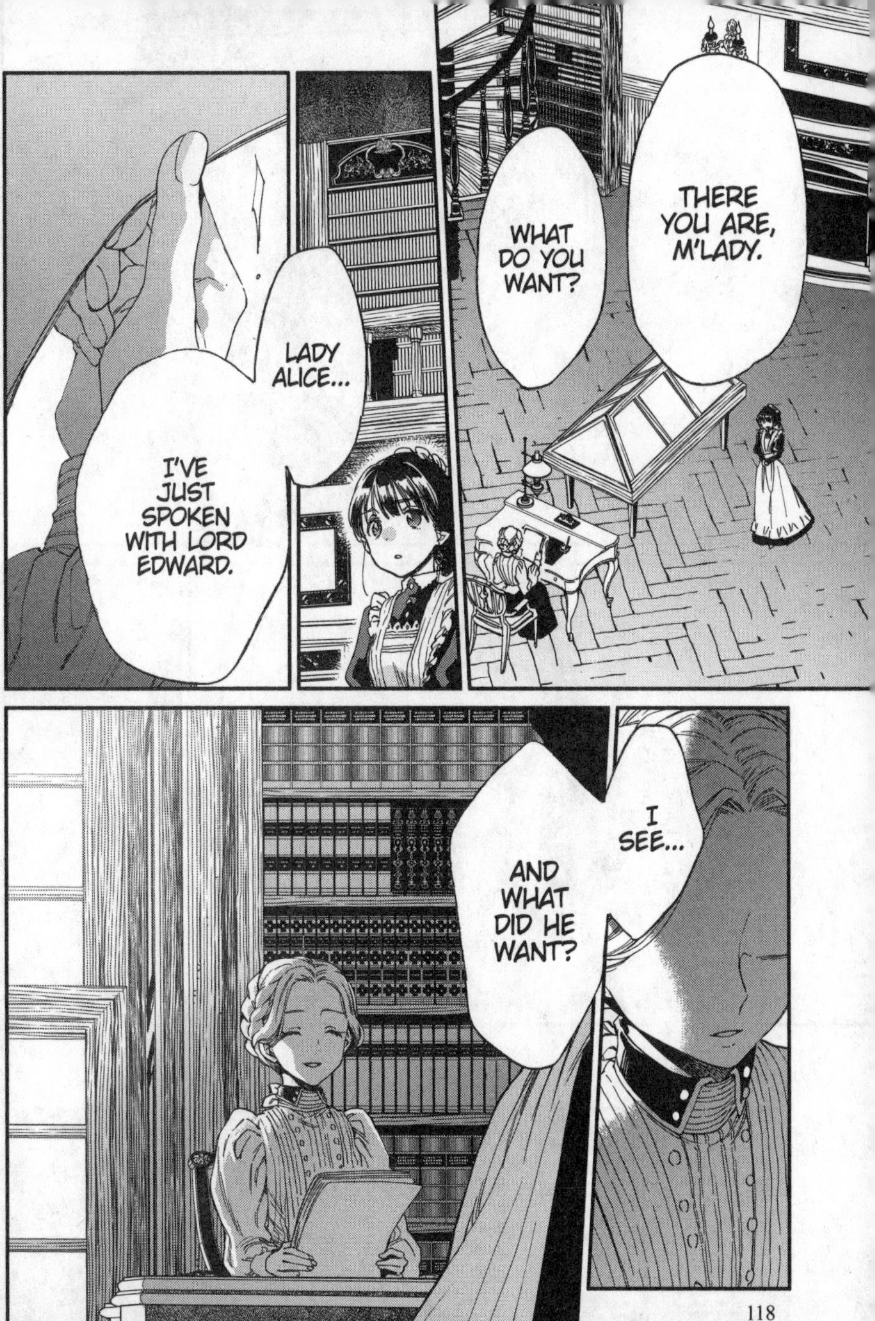
THERE YOU ARE, M'LADY.
WHAT DO YOU WANT?
LADY ALICE...
I'VE JUST SPOKEN WITH LORD EDWARD.
I SEE...
AND WHAT DID HE WANT?

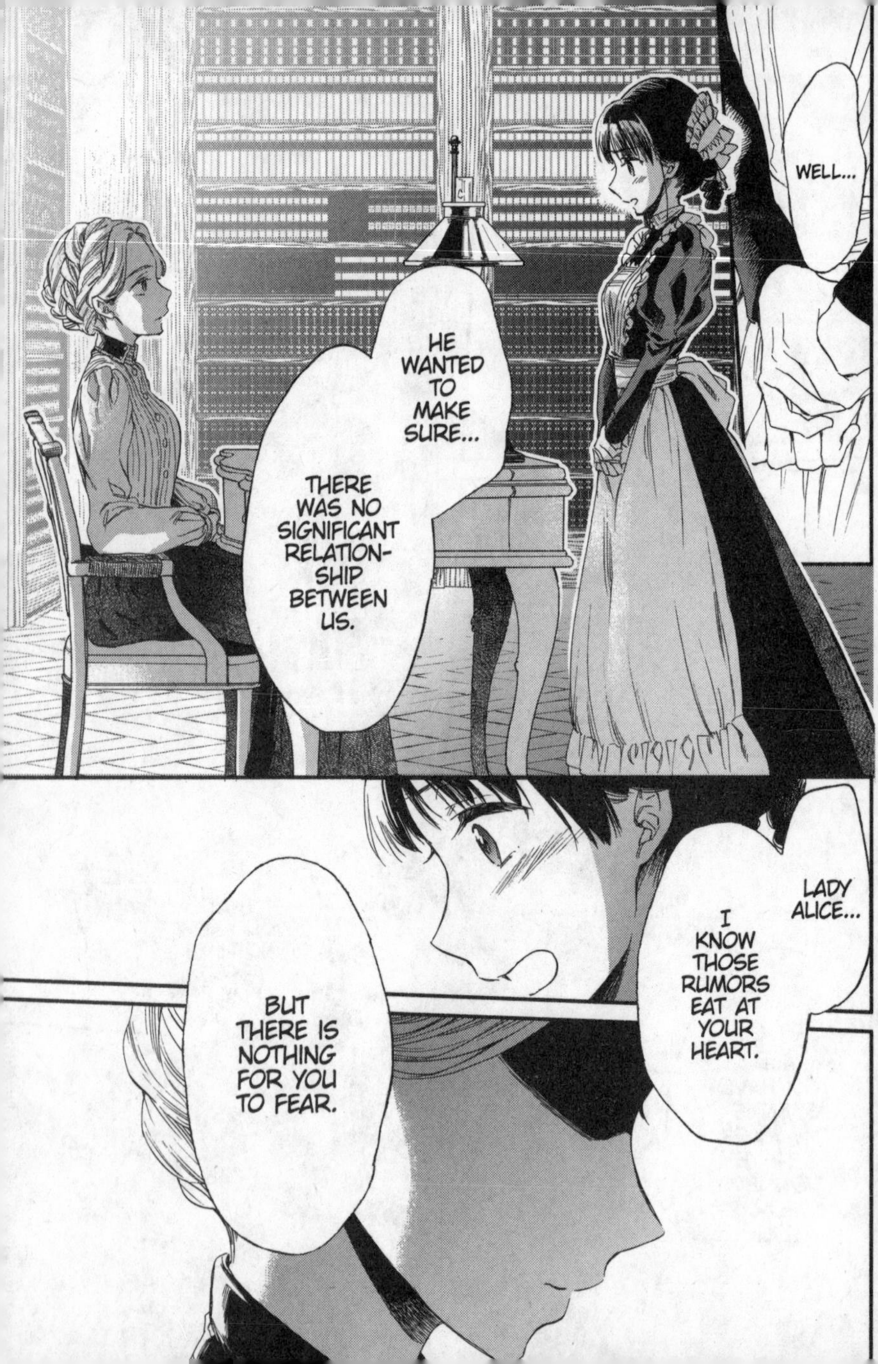
WELL...
HE WANTED TO MAKE SURE...
THERE WAS NO SIGNIFICANT RELATIONSHIP BETWEEN US.
LADY ALICE...
I KNOW THOSE RUMORS EAT AT YOUR HEART.
BUT THERE IS NOTHING FOR YOU TO FEAR.

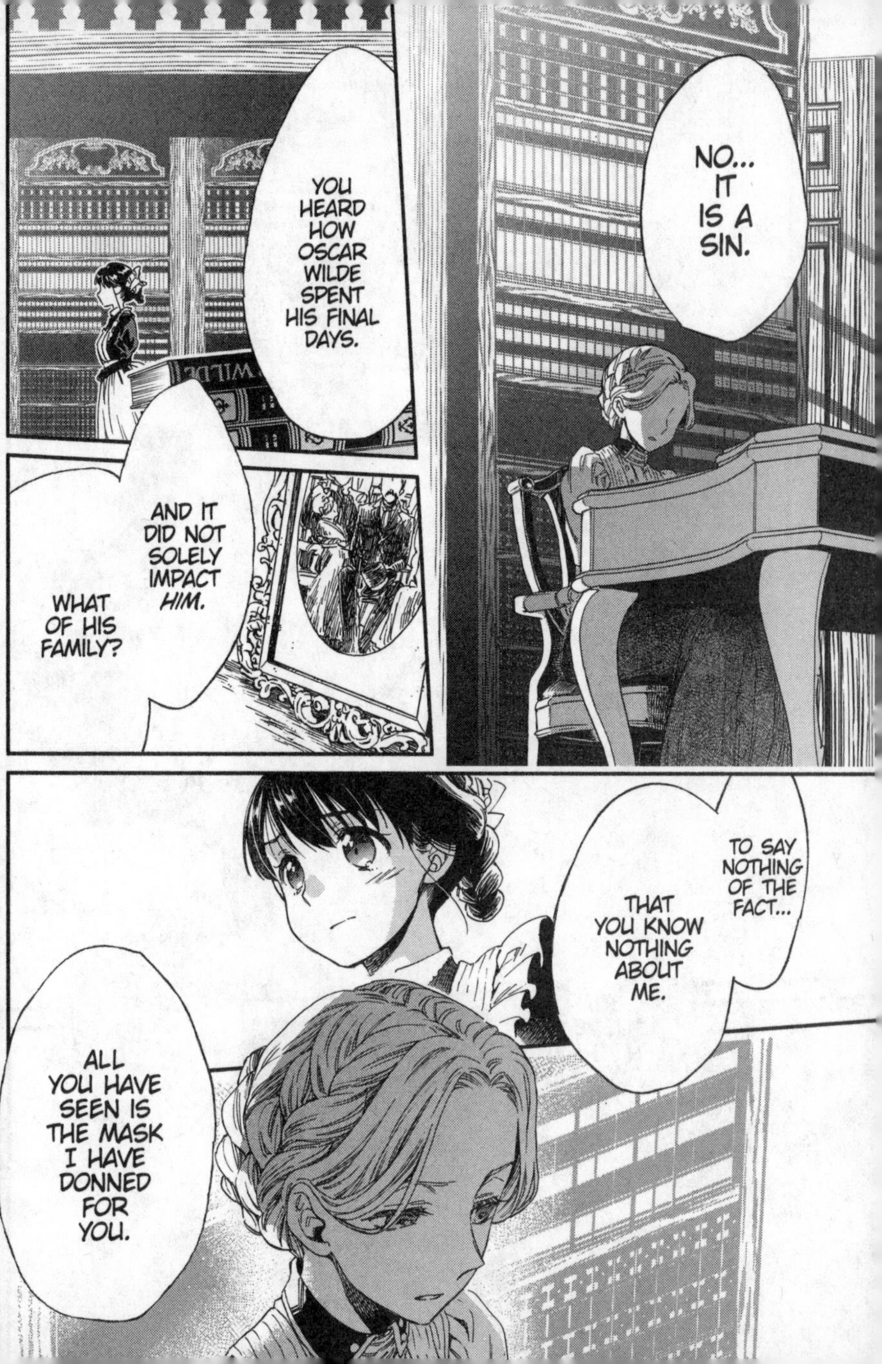
NO... IT IS A SIN.
YOU HEARD HOW OSCAR WILDE SPENT HIS FINAL DAYS.
AND IT DID NOT SOLELY IMPACT *HIM*.
WHAT OF HIS FAMILY?
TO SAY NOTHING OF THE FACT...
THAT YOU KNOW NOTHING ABOUT ME.
ALL YOU HAVE SEEN IS THE MASK I HAVE DONNED FOR YOU.

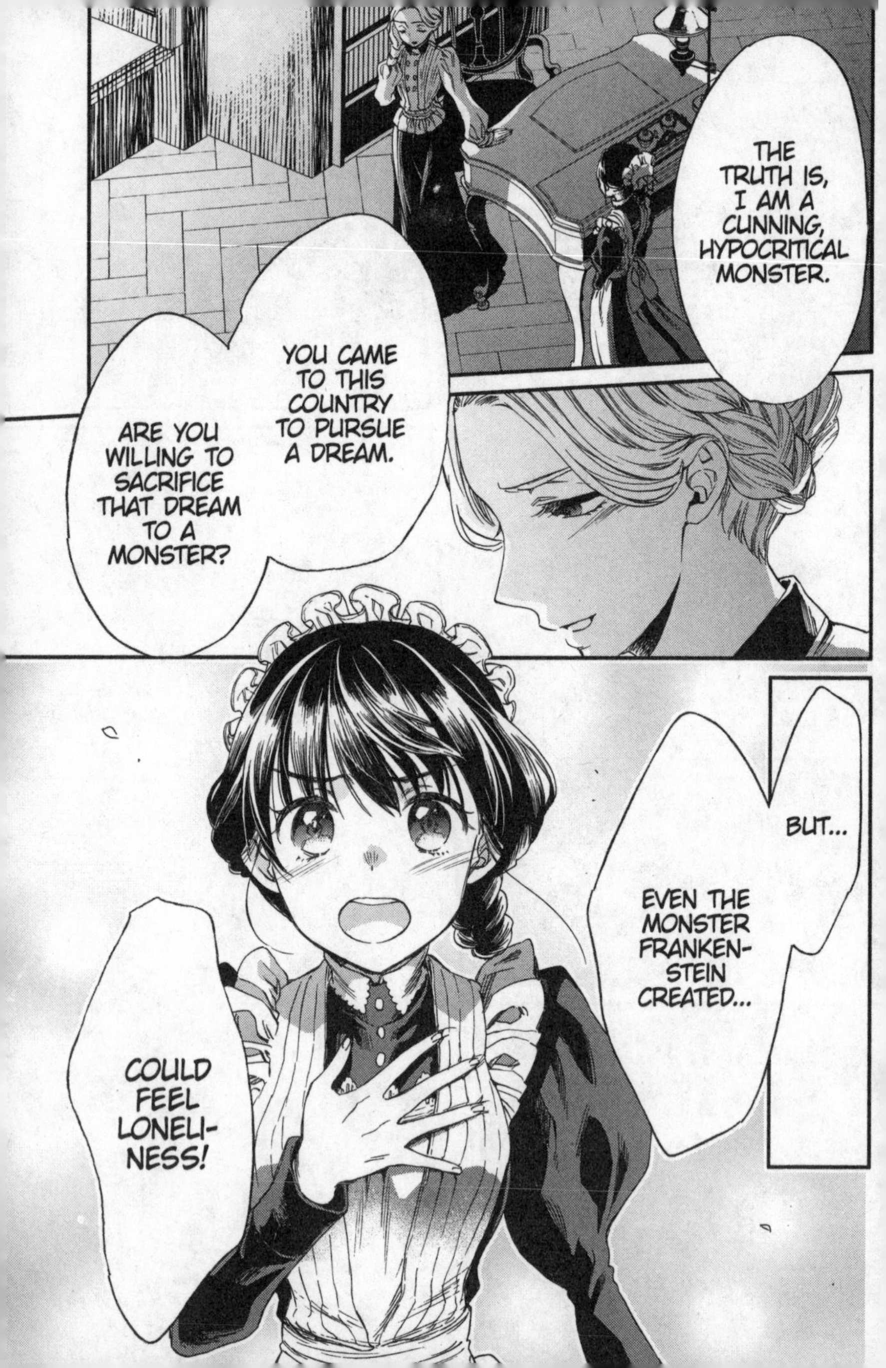
THE TRUTH IS, I AM A CUNNING, HYPOCRITICAL MONSTER.
YOU CAME TO THIS COUNTRY TO PURSUE A DREAM.
ARE YOU WILLING TO SACRIFICE THAT DREAM TO A MONSTER?
BUT...
EVEN THE MONSTER FRANKEN-STEIN CREATED...
COULD FEEL LONELI-NESS!

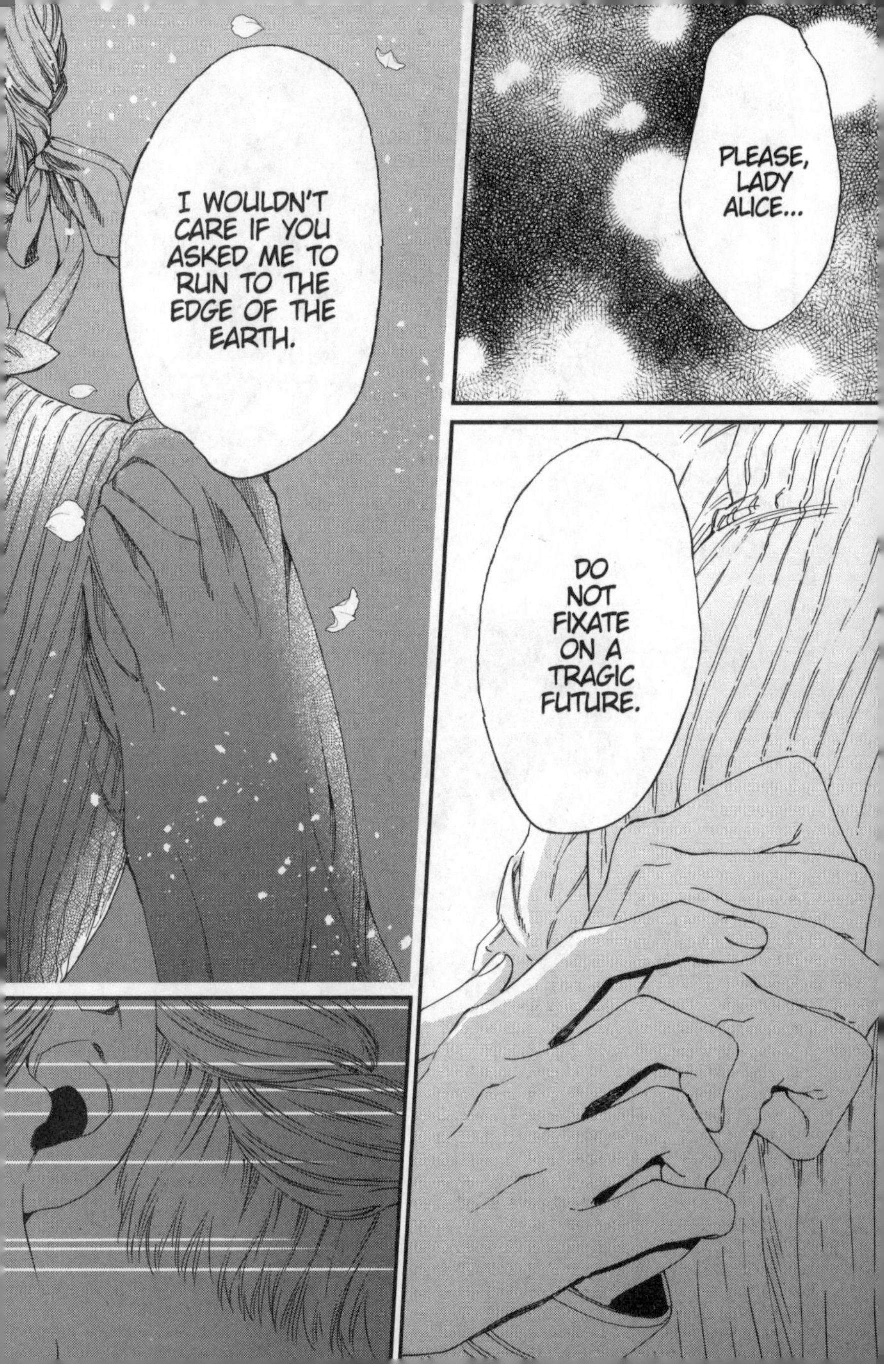
PLEASE, LADY ALICE...
I WOULDN'T CARE IF YOU ASKED ME TO RUN TO THE EDGE OF THE EARTH.
DO NOT FIXATE ON A TRAGIC FUTURE.

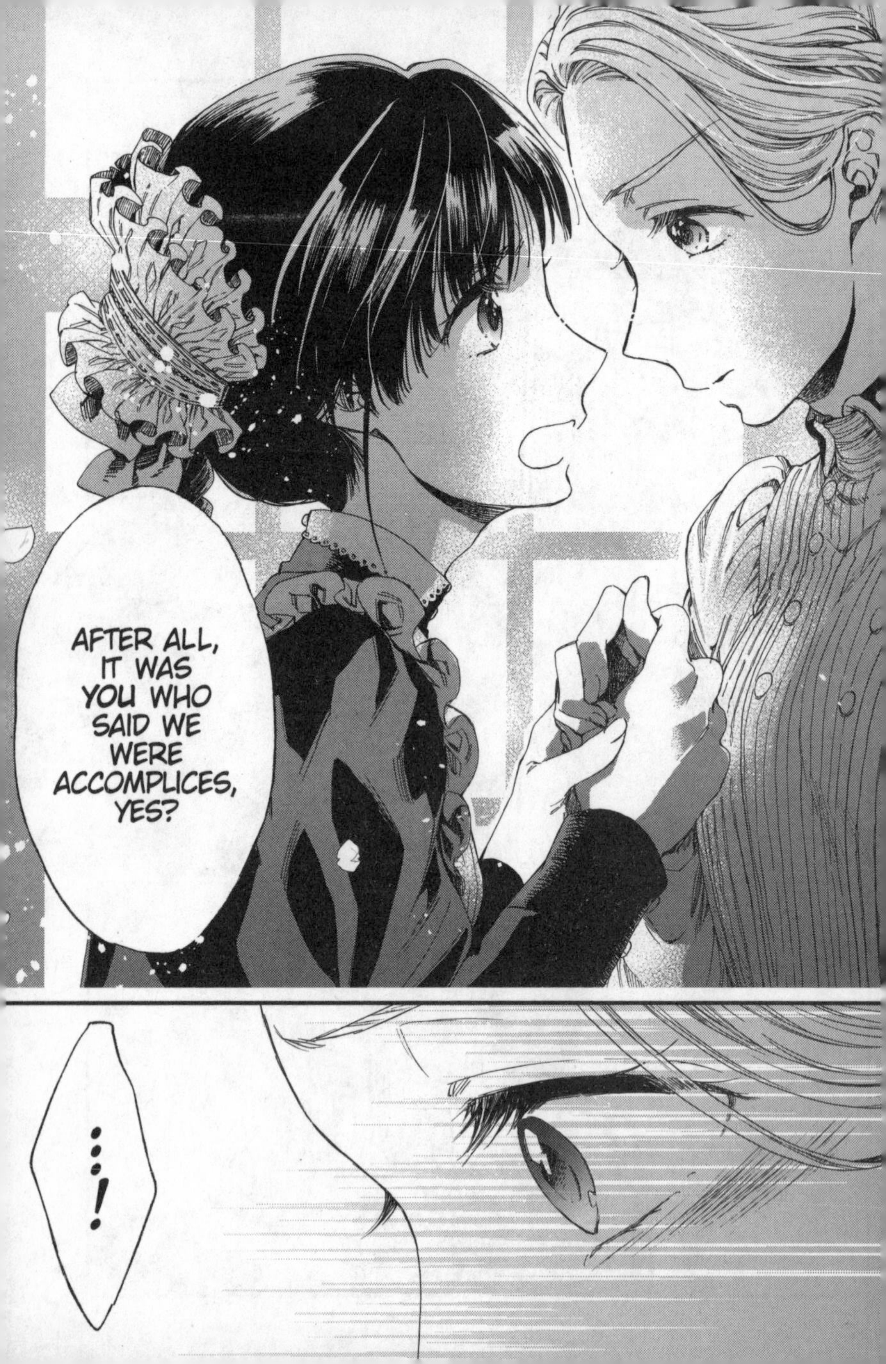
AFTER ALL, IT WAS YOU WHO SAID WE WERE ACCOMPLICES, YES?
...!

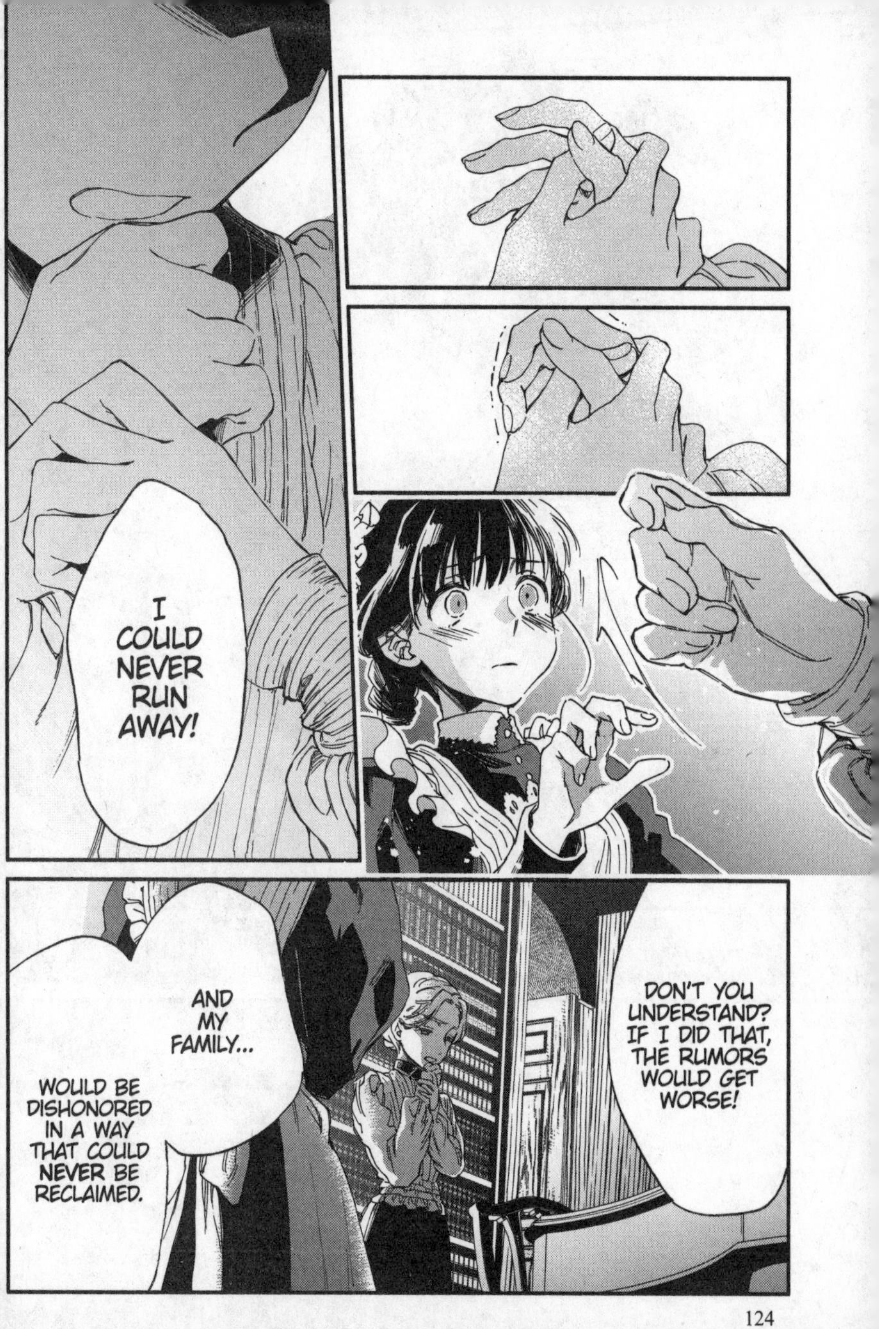
I COULD NEVER RUN AWAY!
DON'T YOU UNDERSTAND? IF I DID THAT, THE RUMORS WOULD GET WORSE!
AND MY FAMILY...
WOULD BE DISHONORED IN A WAY THAT COULD NEVER BE RECLAIMED.

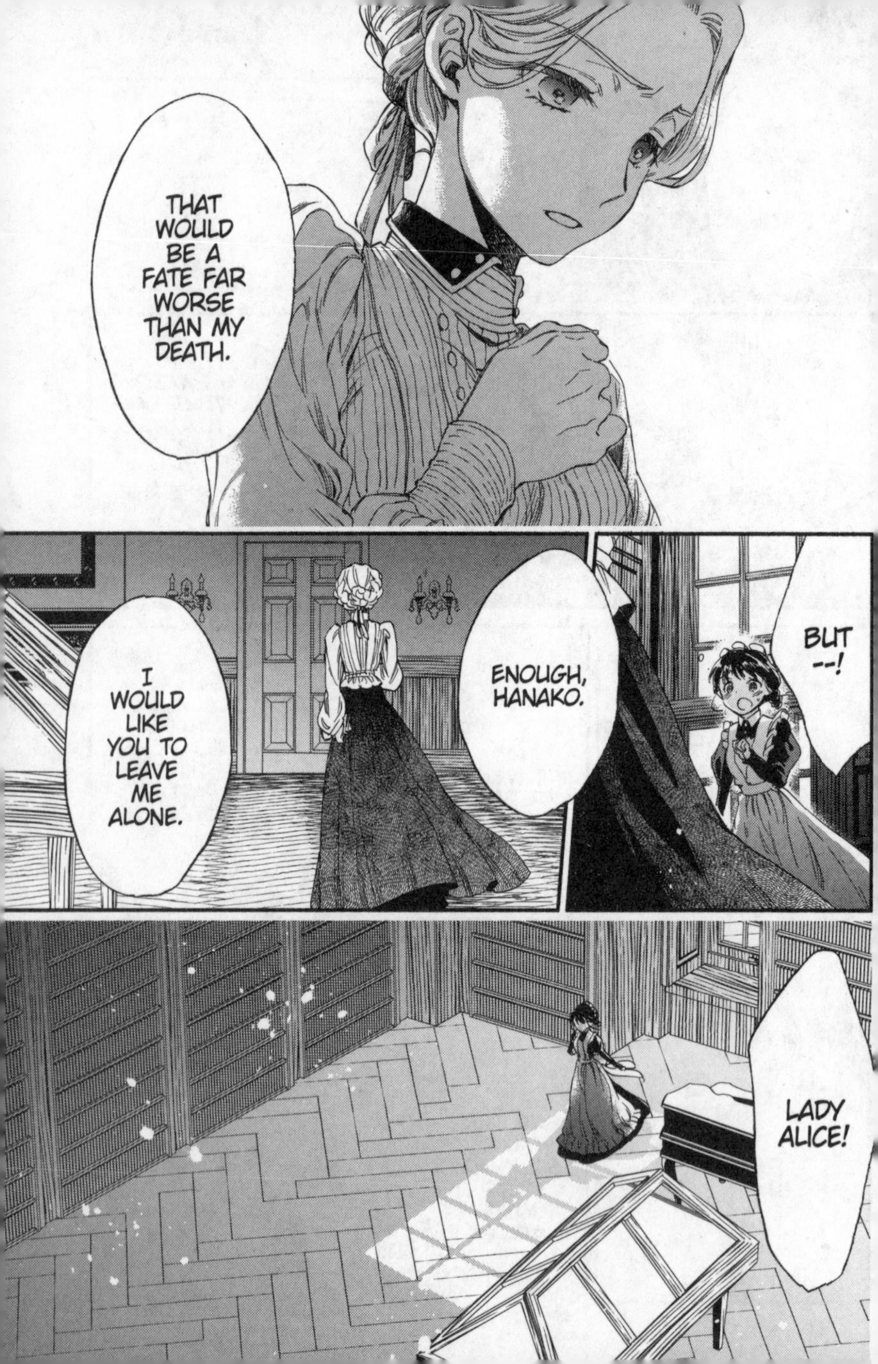
THAT WOULD BE A FATE FAR WORSE THAN MY DEATH.
BUT --!
ENOUGH, HANAKO.
I WOULD LIKE YOU TO LEAVE ME ALONE.
LADY ALICE!

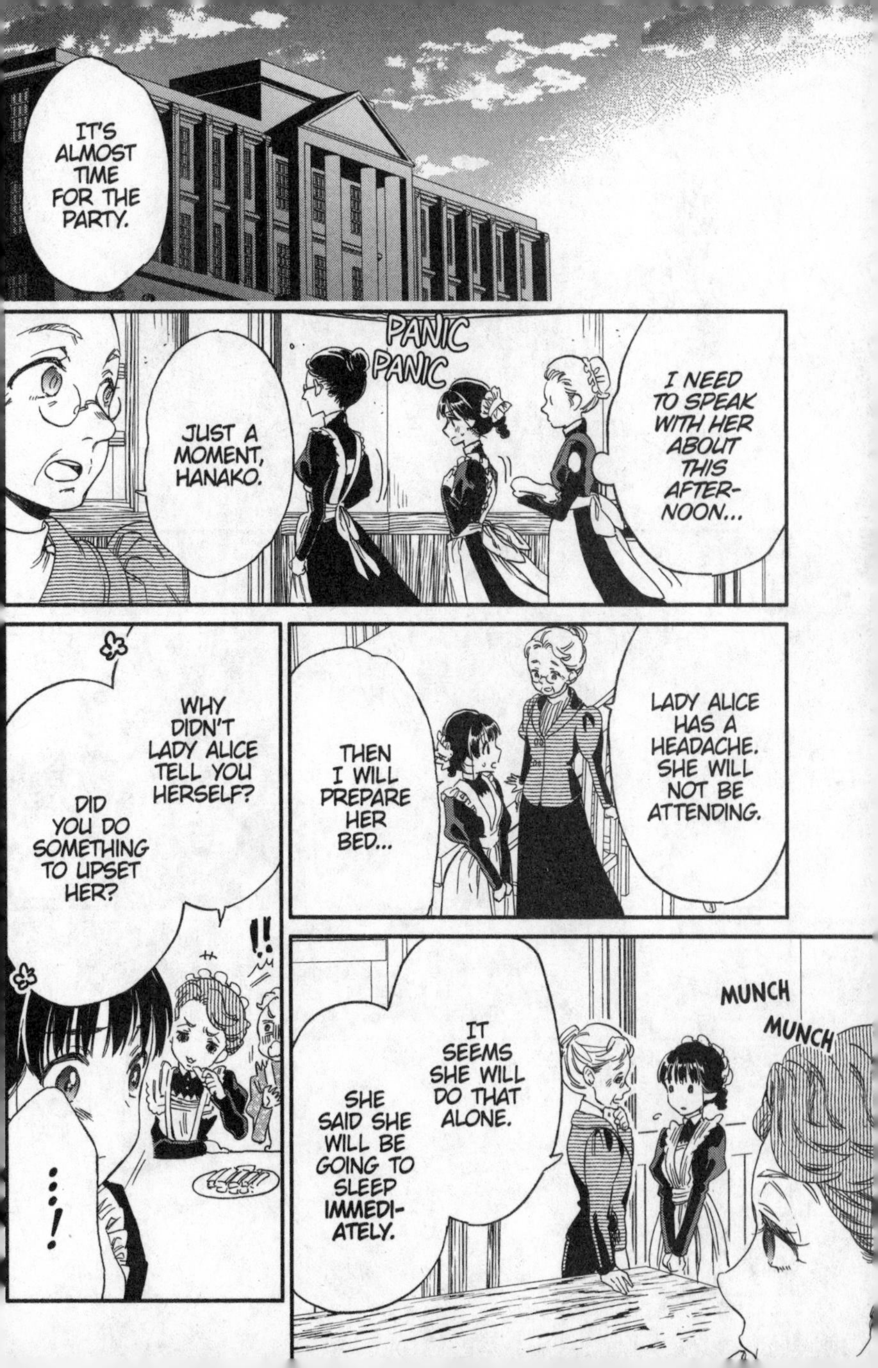
IT'S ALMOST TIME FOR THE PARTY.
I NEED TO SPEAK WITH HER ABOUT THIS AFTERNOON...
PANIC PANIC
JUST A MOMENT, HANAKO.
LADY ALICE HAS A HEADACHE. SHE WILL NOT BE ATTENDING.
THEN I WILL PREPARE HER BED...
MUNCH MUNCH
IT SEEMS SHE WILL DO THAT ALONE.
SHE SAID SHE WILL BE GOING TO SLEEP IMMEDIATELY.
WHY DIDN'T LADY ALICE TELL YOU HERSELF?
DID YOU DO SOMETHING TO UPSET HER?
!!
...!

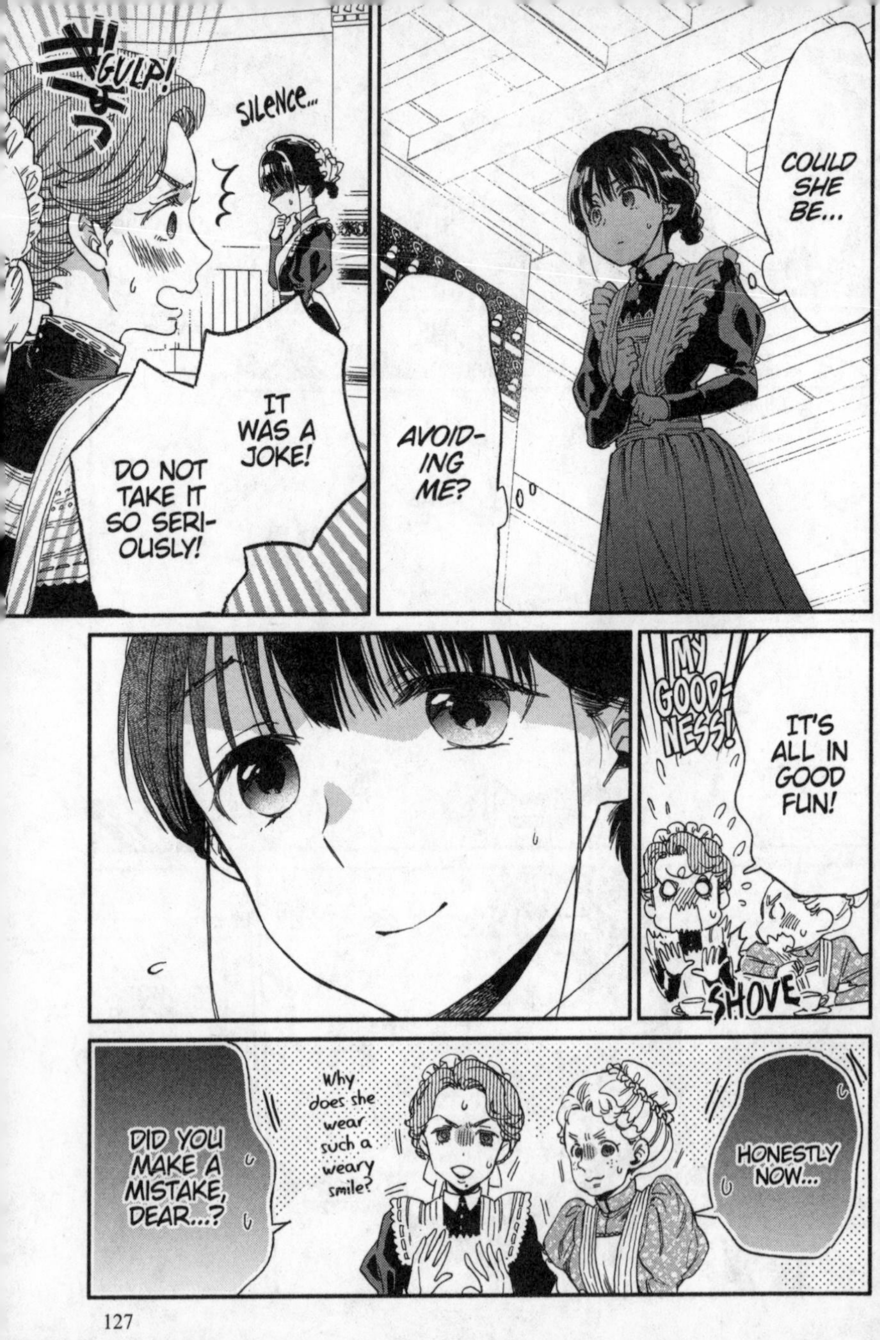
COULD SHE BE...
AVOIDING ME?
GULP!
SILENCE...
IT WAS A JOKE!
DO NOT TAKE IT SO SERIOUSLY!
MY GOODNESS!
IT'S ALL IN GOOD FUN!
SHOVE
HONESTLY NOW...
Why does she wear such a weary smile?
DID YOU MAKE A MISTAKE, DEAR...?

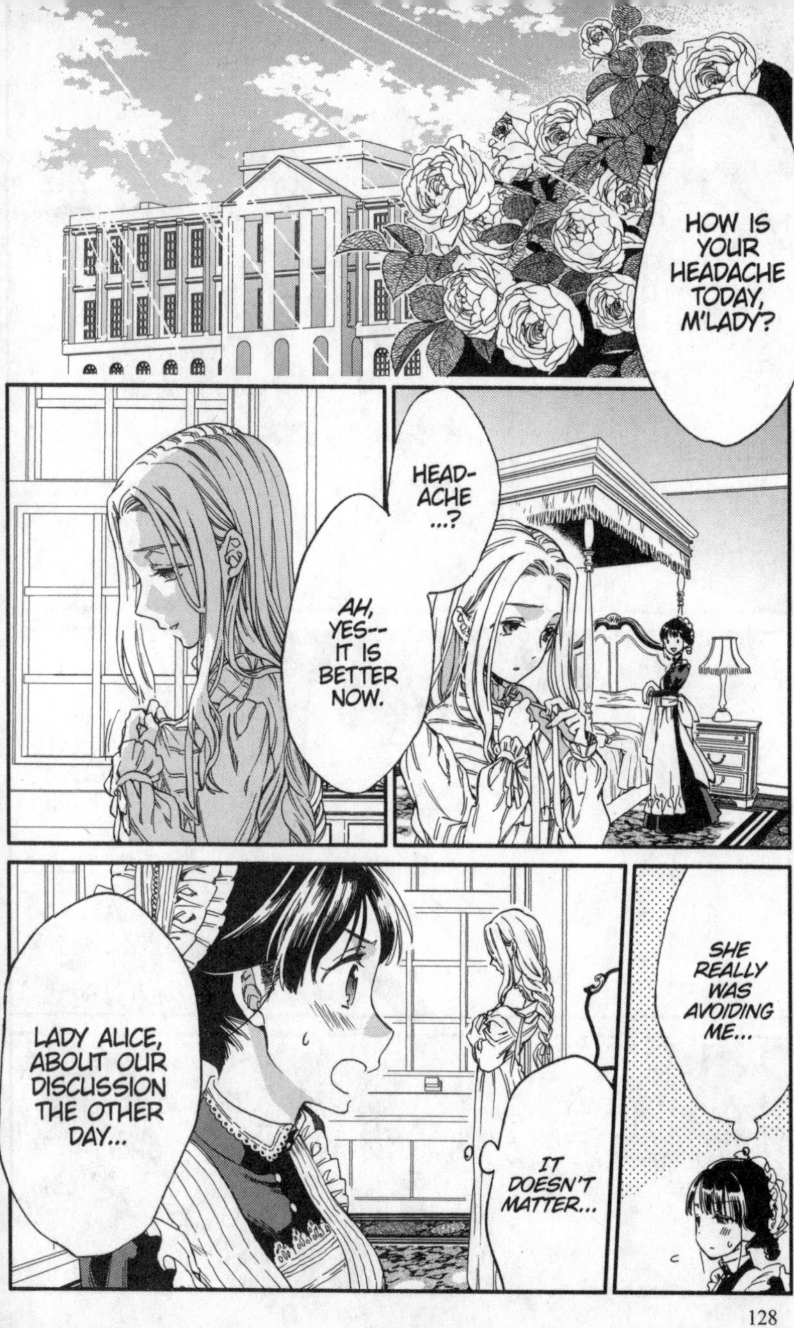
HOW IS YOUR HEADACHE TODAY, M'LADY?
HEAD-ACHE ...?
AH, YES-- IT IS BETTER NOW.
SHE REALLY WAS AVOIDING ME...
LADY ALICE, ABOUT OUR DISCUSSION THE OTHER DAY...
IT DOESN'T MATTER...

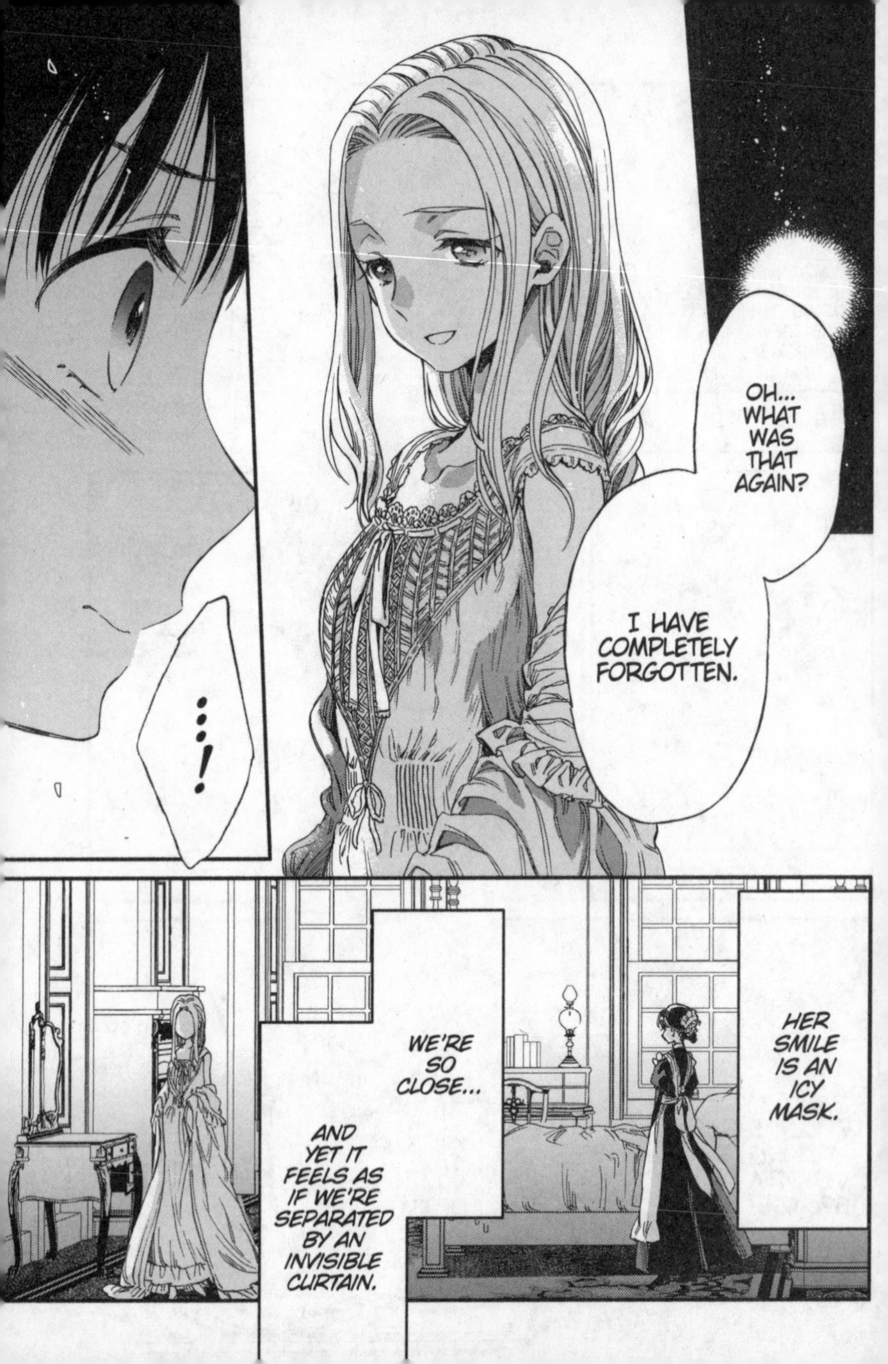
OH... WHAT WAS THAT AGAIN?
I HAVE COMPLETELY FORGOTTEN.
...!
HER SMILE IS AN ICY MASK.
WE'RE SO CLOSE...
AND YET IT FEELS AS IF WE'RE SEPARATED BY AN INVISIBLE CURTAIN.

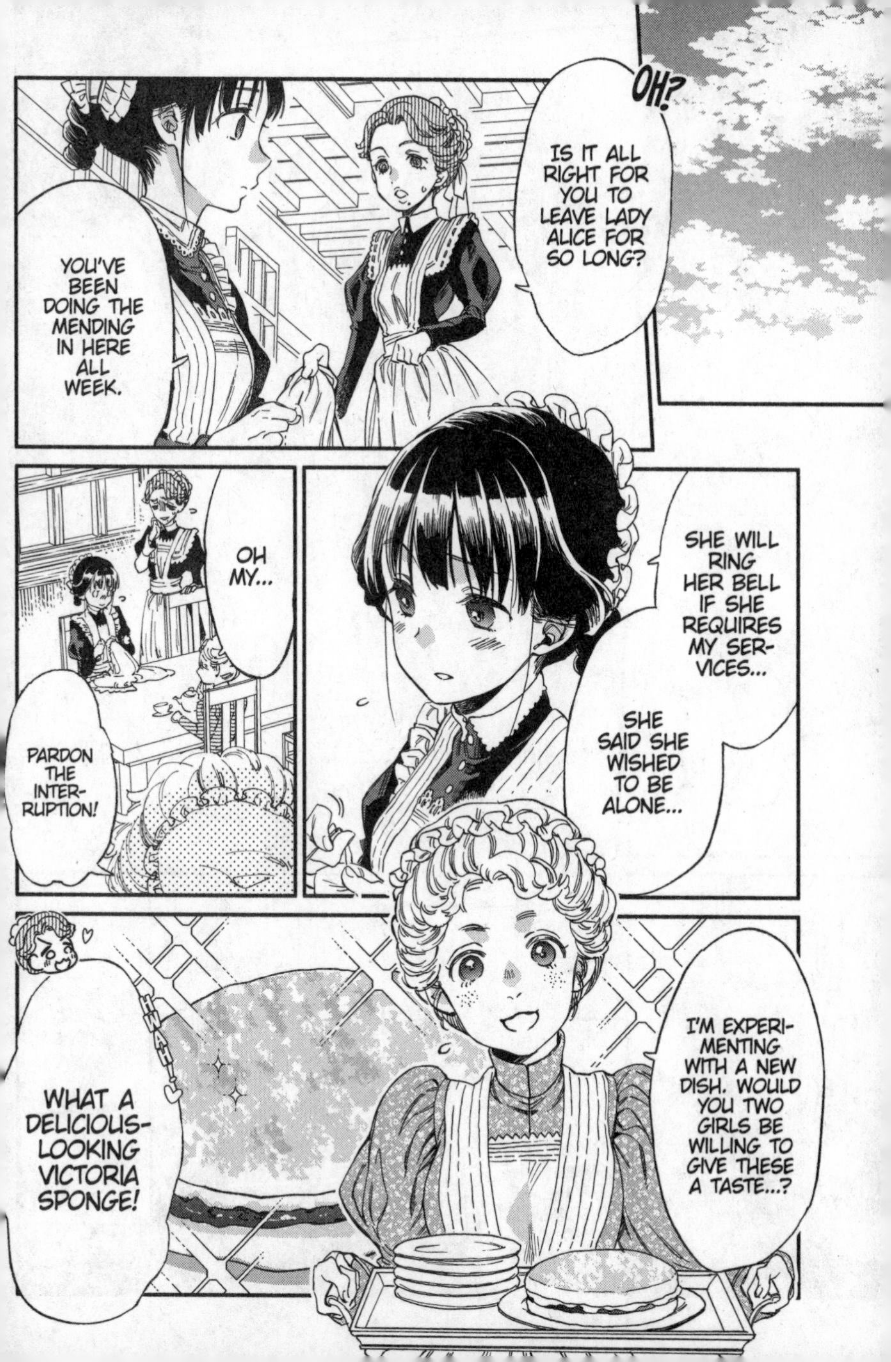
OH?
IS IT ALL RIGHT FOR YOU TO LEAVE LADY ALICE FOR SO LONG?
YOU'VE BEEN DOING THE MENDING IN HERE ALL WEEK.
SHE WILL RING HER BELL IF SHE REQUIRES MY SER-VICES...
SHE SAID SHE WISHED TO BE ALONE...
OH MY...
PARDON THE INTER-RUPTION!
I'M EXPERI-MENTING WITH A NEW DISH. WOULD YOU TWO GIRLS BE WILLING TO GIVE THESE A TASTE...?
HWAH!
WHAT A DELICIOUS-LOOKING VICTORIA SPONGE!

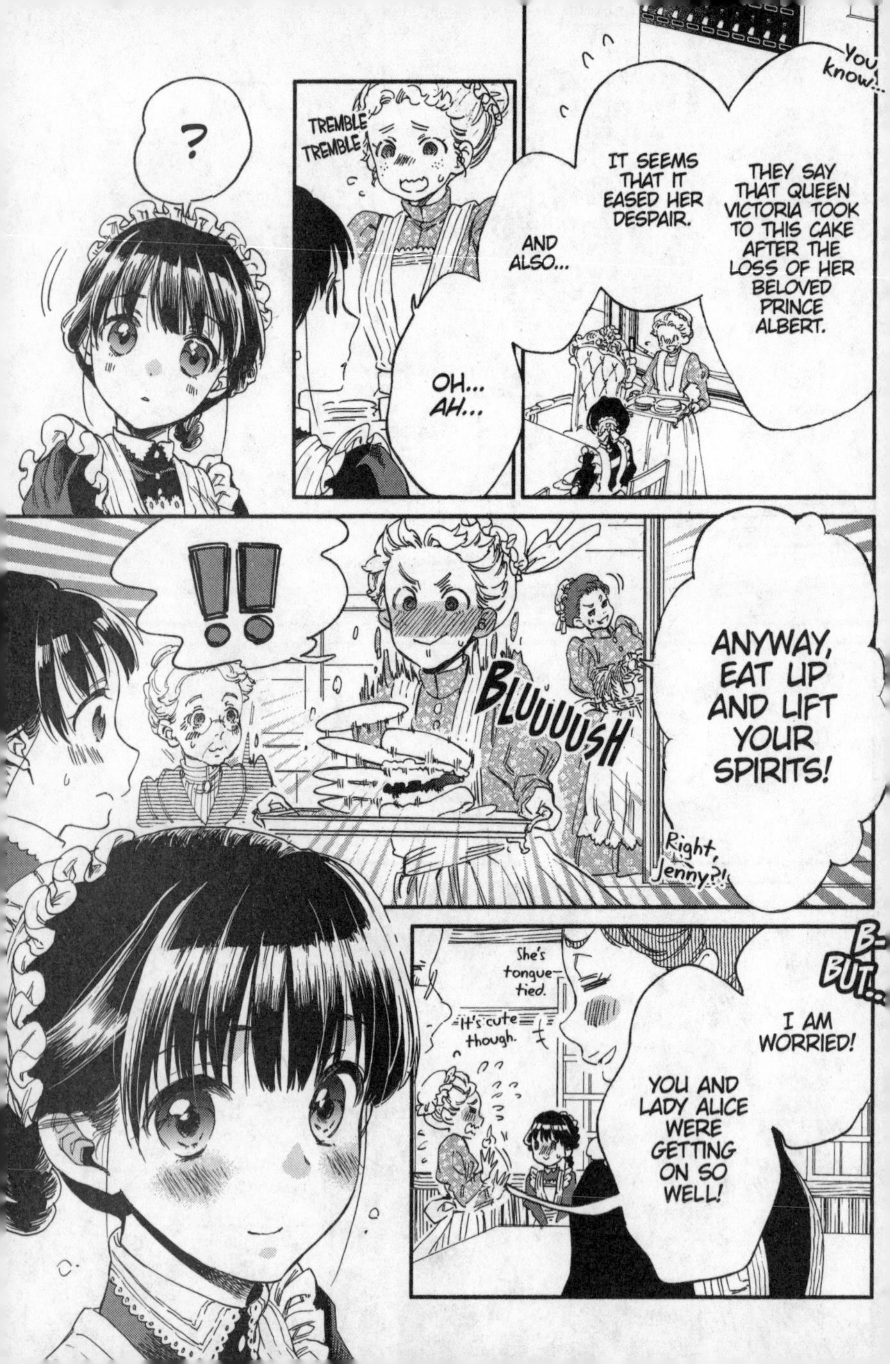
You know!..
THEY SAY THAT QUEEN VICTORIA TOOK TO THIS CAKE AFTER THE LOSS OF HER BELOVED PRINCE ALBERT.
IT SEEMS THAT IT EASED HER DESPAIR.
AND ALSO...
TREMBLE TREMBLE
OH... AH...
?
ANYWAY, EAT UP AND LIFT YOUR SPIRITS!
Right, Jenny?!
BLUUUUSH
!!
B-BUT..
I AM WORRIED!
YOU AND LADY ALICE WERE GETTING ON SO WELL!
She's tongue-tied.
It's cute though.

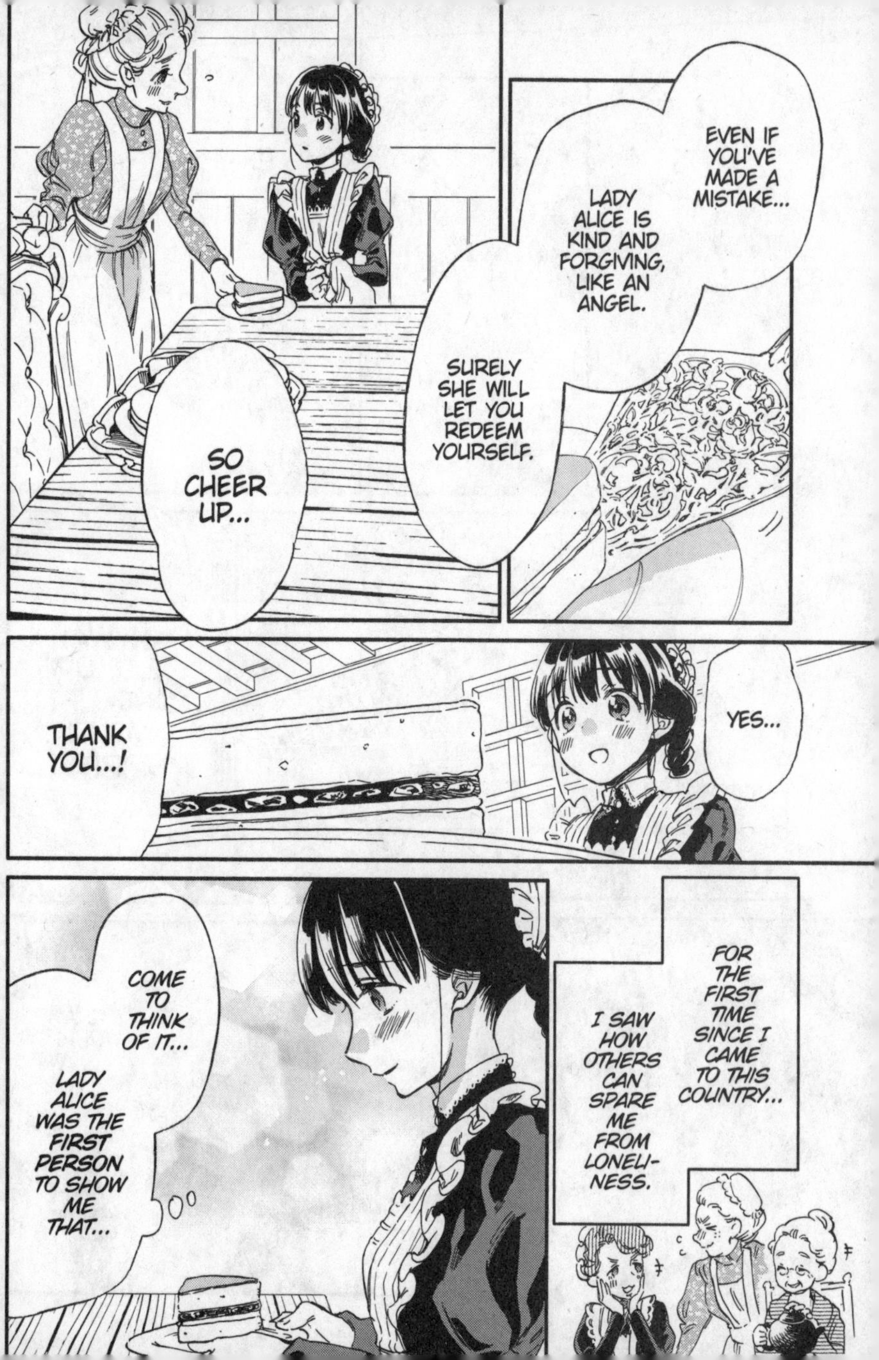
EVEN IF YOU'VE MADE A MISTAKE...
LADY ALICE IS KIND AND FORGIVING, LIKE AN ANGEL.
SURELY SHE WILL LET YOU REDEEM YOURSELF.
SO CHEER UP...
YES...
THANK YOU...!
FOR THE FIRST TIME SINCE I CAME TO THIS COUNTRY...
I SAW HOW OTHERS CAN SPARE ME FROM LONELI-NESS.
COME TO THINK OF IT...
LADY ALICE WAS THE FIRST PERSON TO SHOW ME THAT...

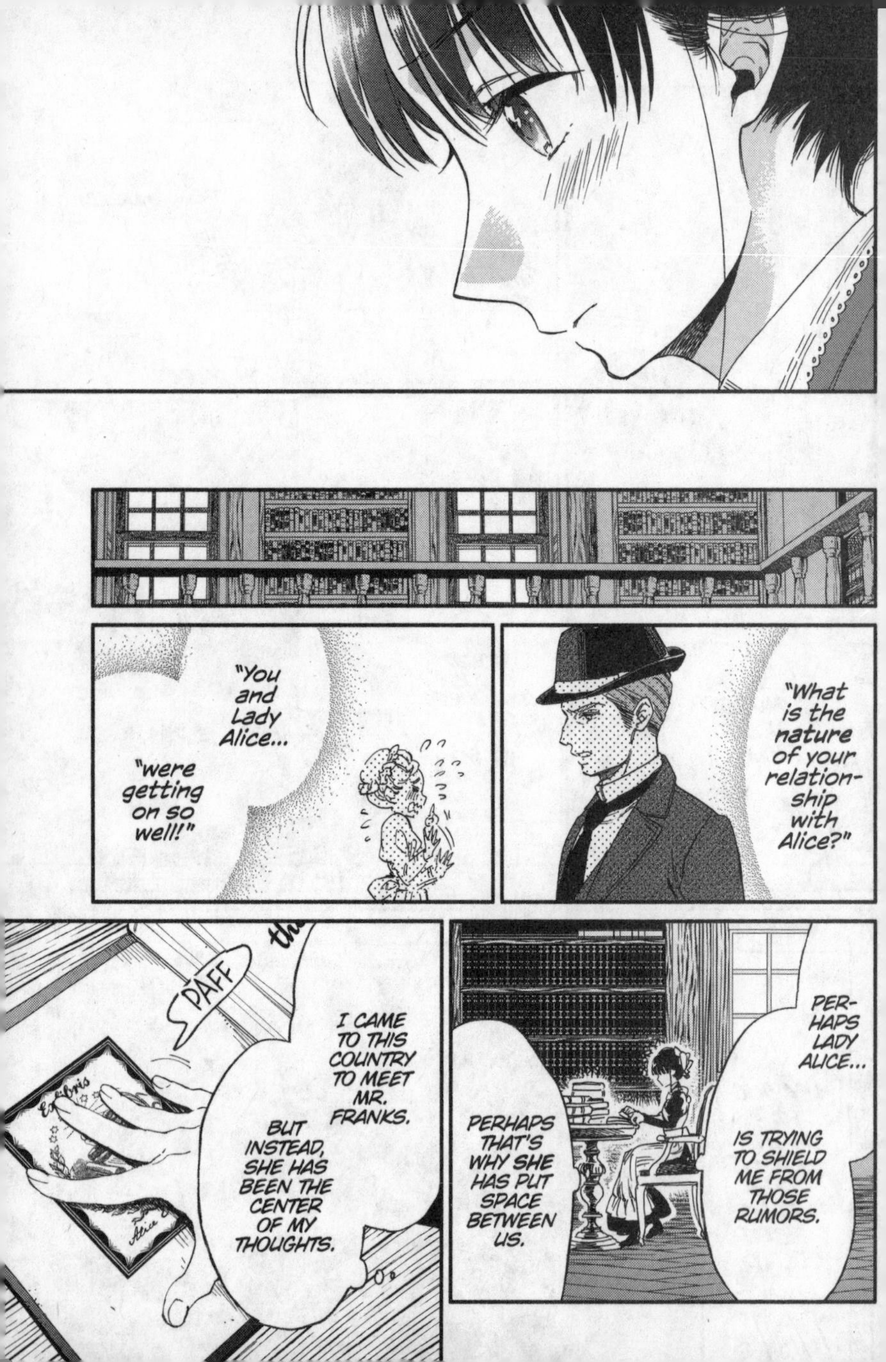
"What is the nature of your relationship with Alice?"
"You and Lady Alice...
"were getting on so well!"
PERHAPS LADY ALICE...
IS TRYING TO SHIELD ME FROM THOSE RUMORS.
PERHAPS THAT'S WHY SHE HAS PUT SPACE BETWEEN US.
PAFF
I CAME TO THIS COUNTRY TO MEET MR. FRANKS.
BUT INSTEAD, SHE HAS BEEN THE CENTER OF MY THOUGHTS.

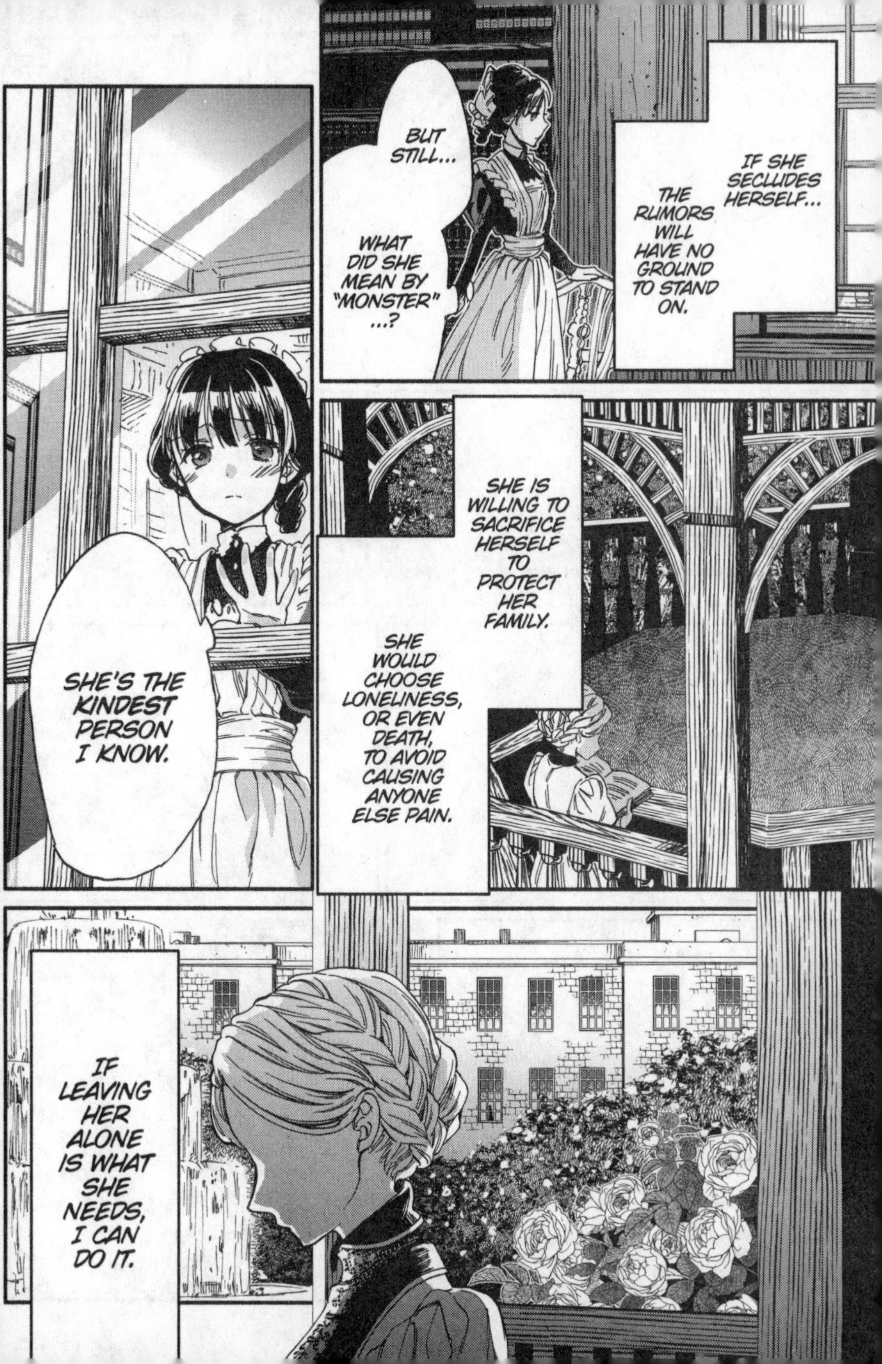
IF SHE SECLUDES HERSELF...
THE RUMORS WILL HAVE NO GROUND TO STAND ON.
BUT STILL...
WHAT DID SHE MEAN BY "MONSTER"...?
SHE IS WILLING TO SACRIFICE HERSELF TO PROTECT HER FAMILY.
SHE WOULD CHOOSE LONELINESS, OR EVEN DEATH, TO AVOID CAUSING ANYONE ELSE PAIN.
SHE'S THE KINDEST PERSON I KNOW.
IF LEAVING HER ALONE IS WHAT SHE NEEDS, I CAN DO IT.

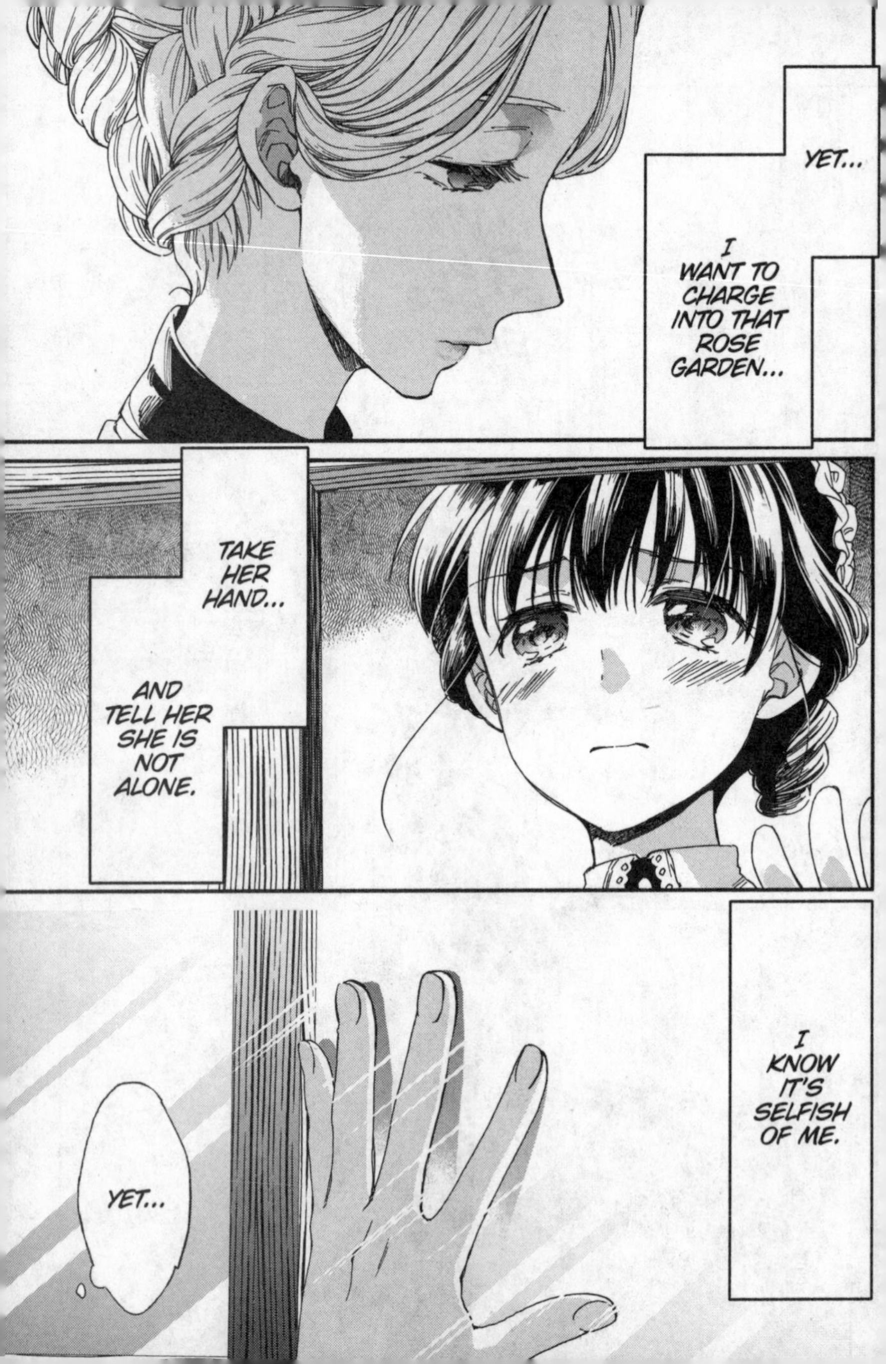
YET...
I WANT TO CHARGE INTO THAT ROSE GARDEN...
TAKE HER HAND...
AND TELL HER SHE IS NOT ALONE.
I KNOW IT'S SELFISH OF ME.
YET...

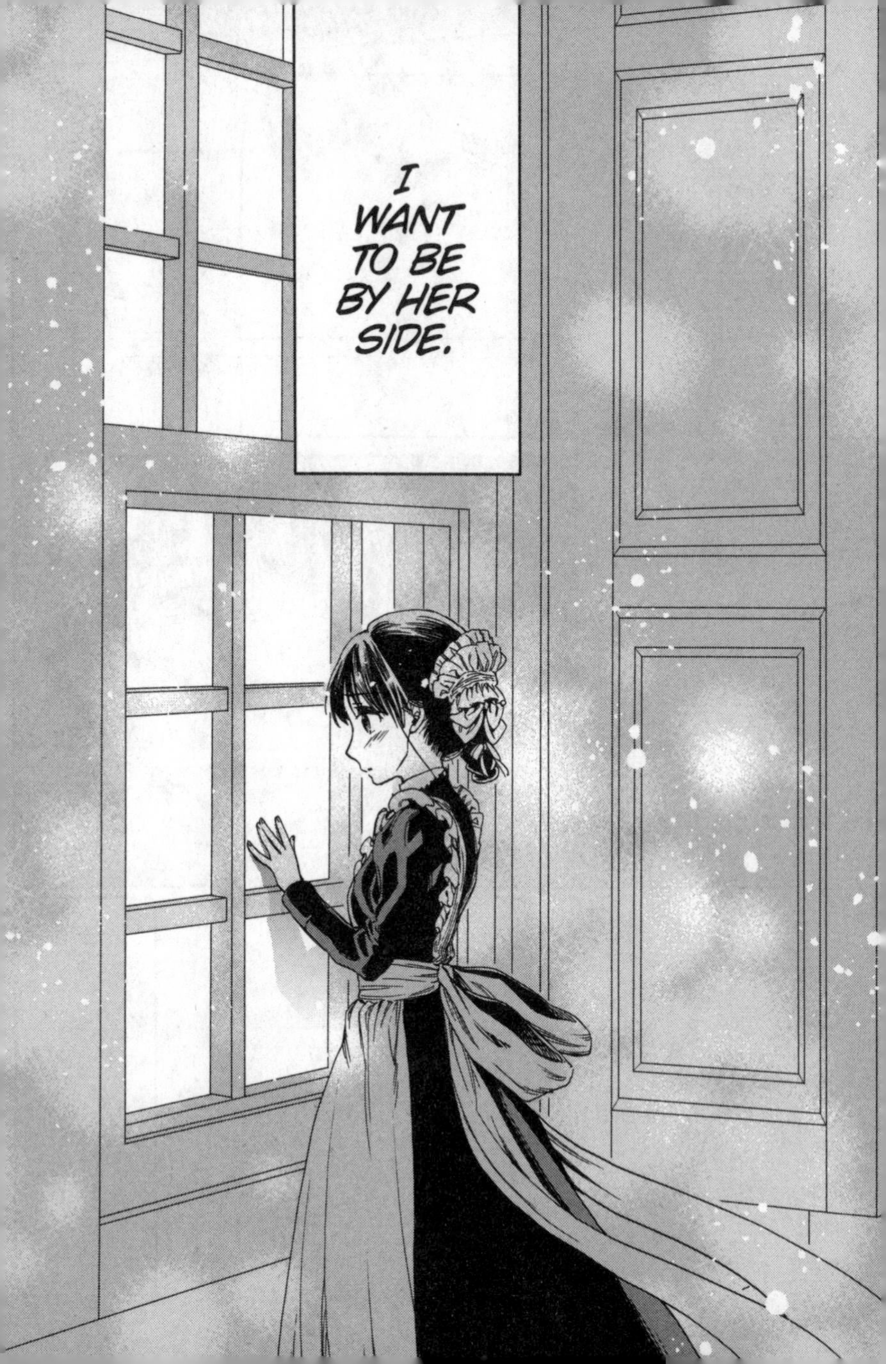
I WANT TO BE BY HER SIDE.

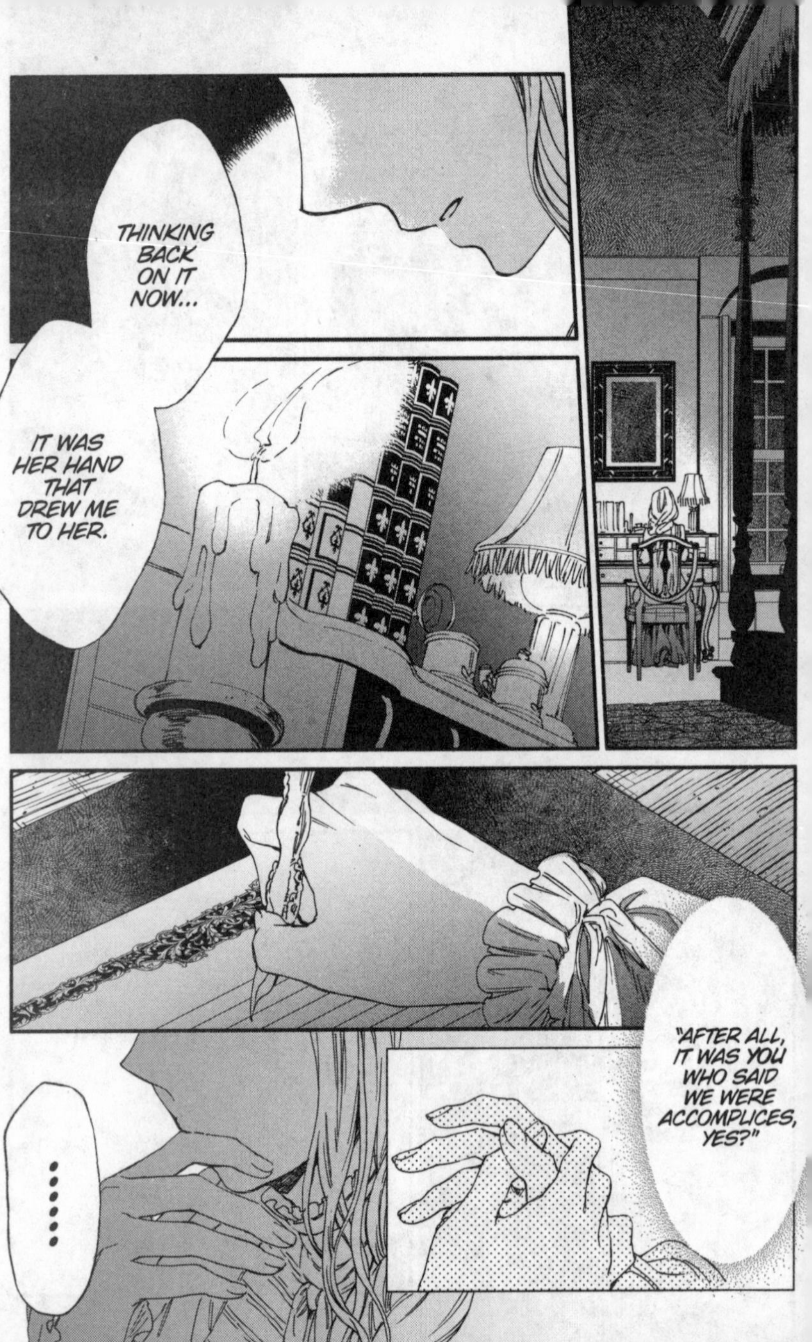
THINKING BACK ON IT NOW...
IT WAS HER HAND THAT DREW ME TO HER.
"AFTER ALL, IT WAS YOU WHO SAID WE WERE ACCOMPLICES, YES?"
......

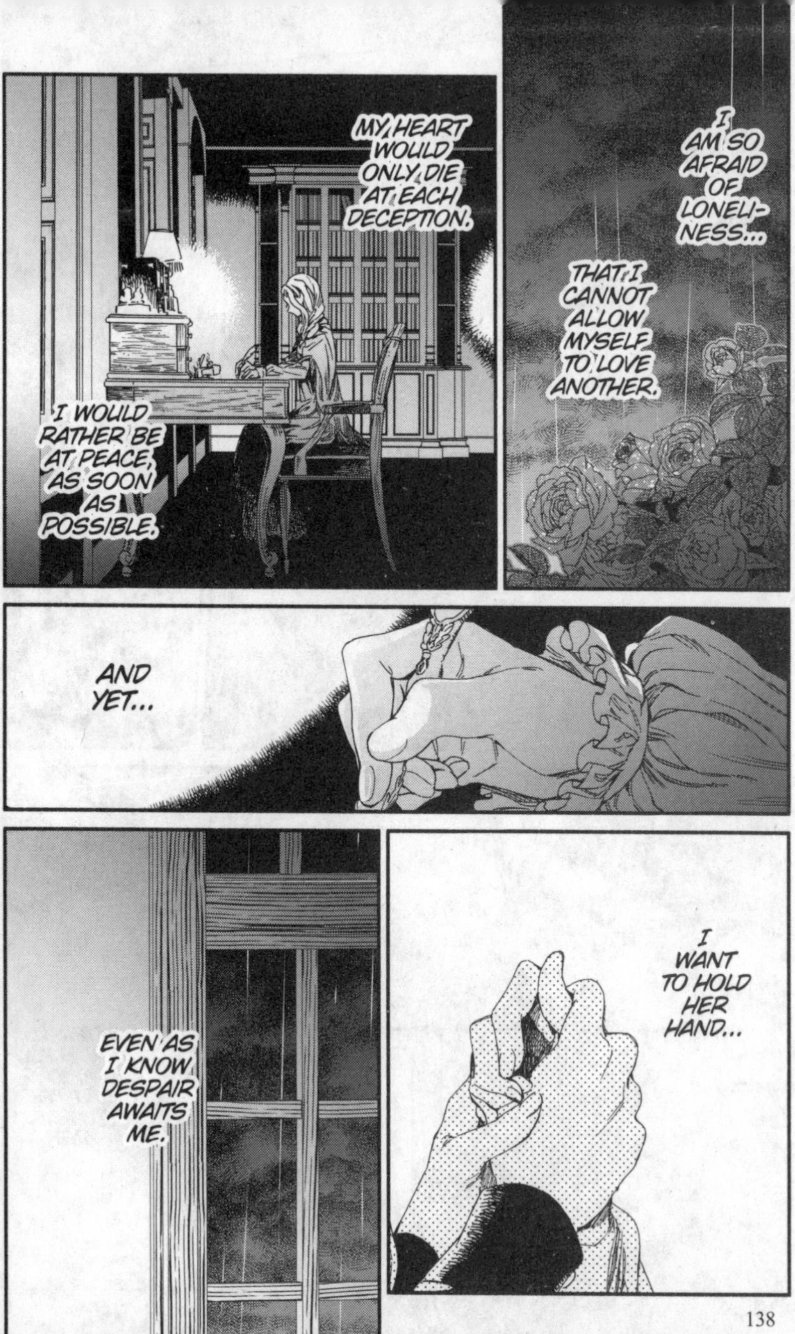
I AM SO AFRAID OF LONELI-NESS...
THAT I CANNOT ALLOW MYSELF TO LOVE ANOTHER.
MY HEART WOULD ONLY DIE AT EACH DECEPTION.
I WOULD RATHER BE AT PEACE, AS SOON AS POSSIBLE.
AND YET...
I WANT TO HOLD HER HAND...
EVEN AS I KNOW DESPAIR AWAITS ME.

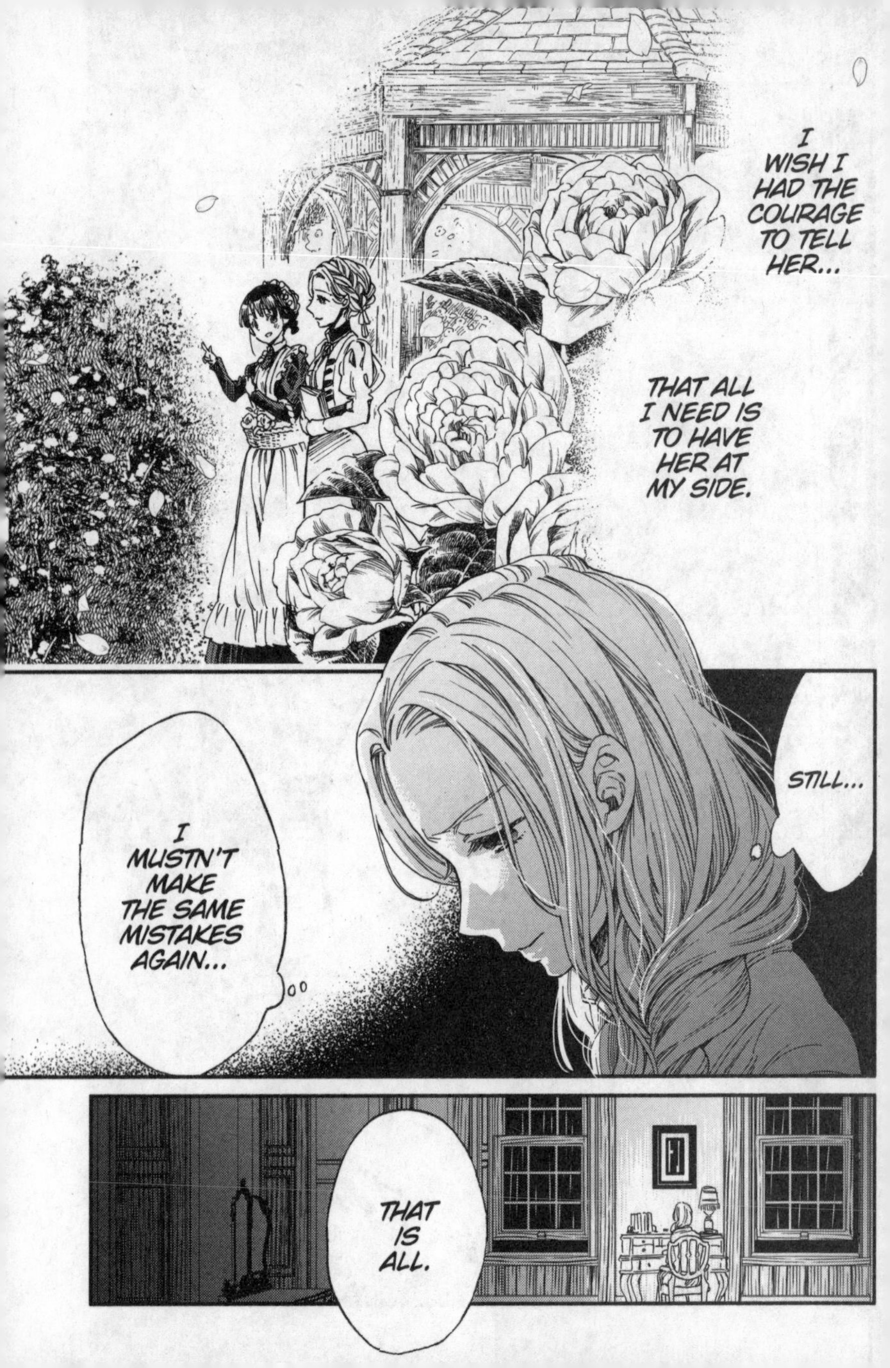
I WISH I HAD THE COURAGE TO TELL HER...
THAT ALL I NEED IS TO HAVE HER AT MY SIDE.
STILL...
I MUSTN'T MAKE THE SAME MISTAKES AGAIN...
THAT IS ALL.

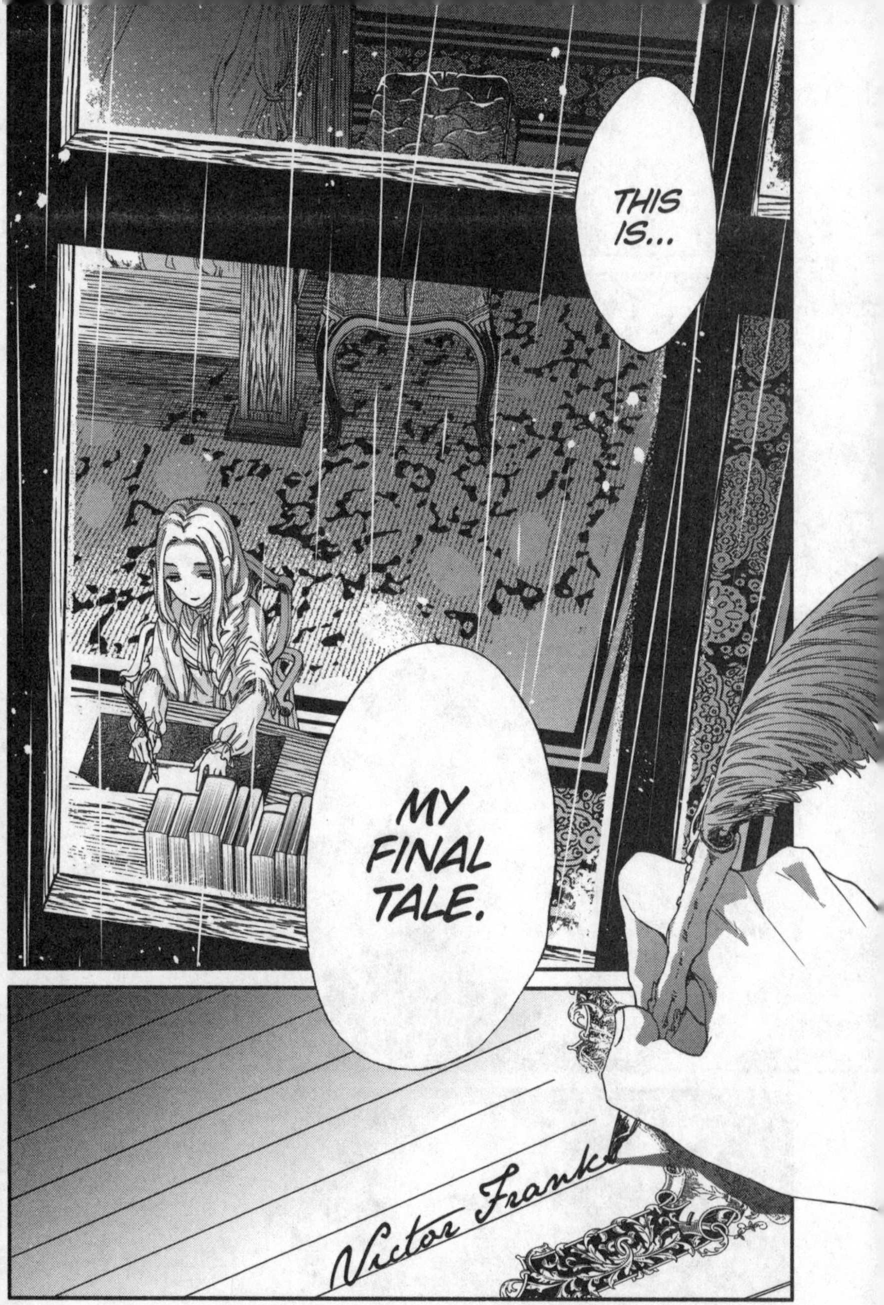
THIS IS...
MY FINAL TALE.
Victor Frank

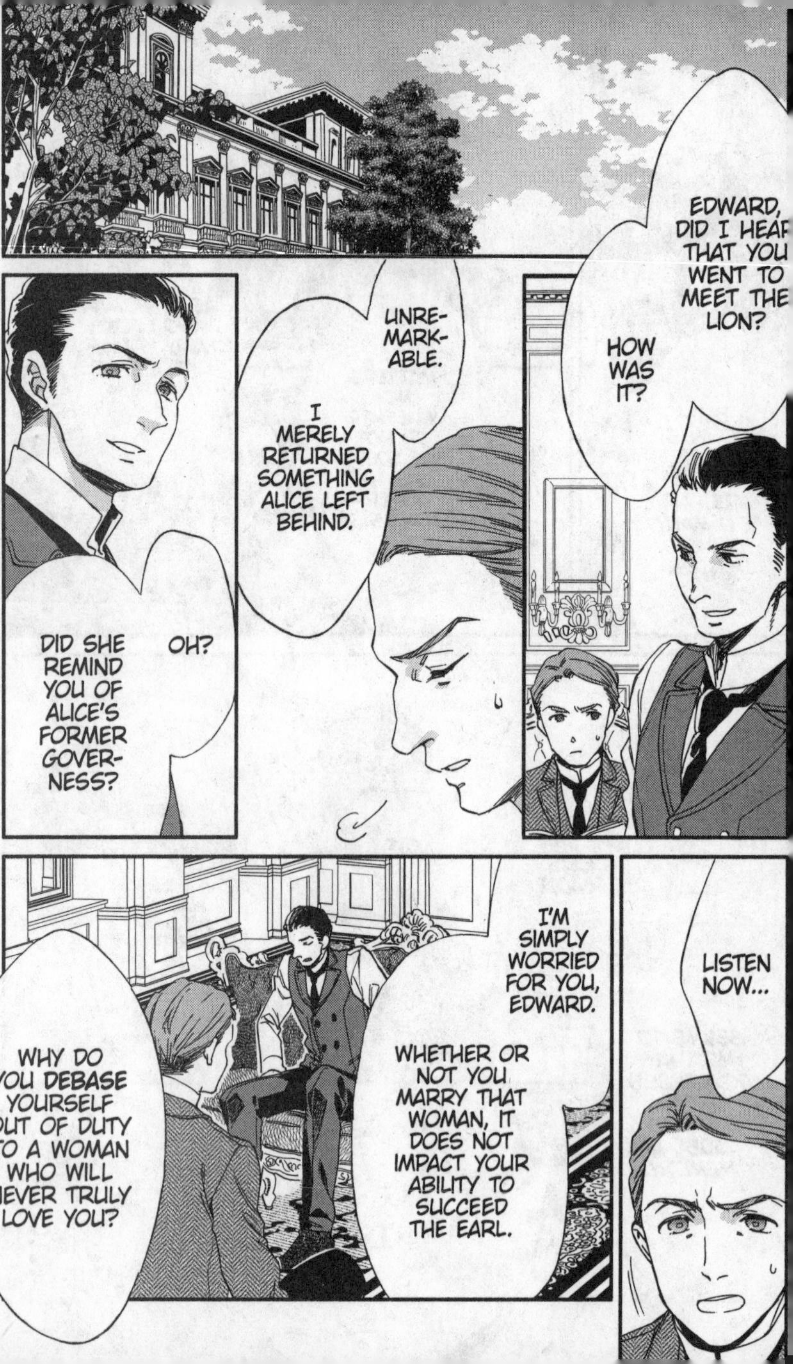
EDWARD, DID I HEAR THAT YOU WENT TO MEET THE LION?
HOW WAS IT?
UNRE-MARK-ABLE.
I MERELY RETURNED SOMETHING ALICE LEFT BEHIND.
OH?
DID SHE REMIND YOU OF ALICE'S FORMER GOVER-NESS?
LISTEN NOW...
I'M SIMPLY WORRIED FOR YOU, EDWARD.
WHETHER OR NOT YOU MARRY THAT WOMAN, IT DOES NOT IMPACT YOUR ABILITY TO SUCCEED THE EARL.
WHY DO YOU DEBASE YOURSELF OUT OF DUTY TO A WOMAN WHO WILL NEVER TRULY LOVE YOU?

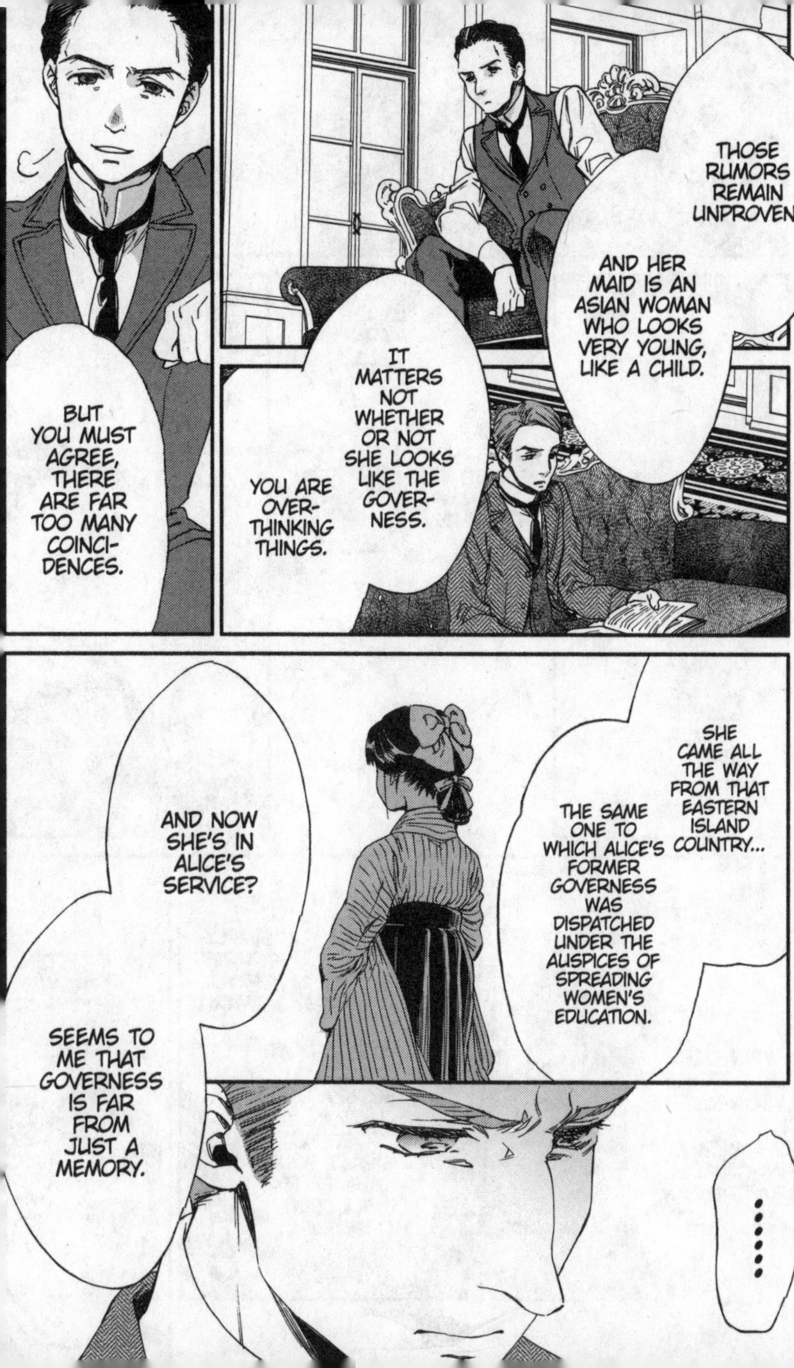
THOSE RUMORS REMAIN UNPROVEN.
AND HER MAID IS AN ASIAN WOMAN WHO LOOKS VERY YOUNG, LIKE A CHILD.
IT MATTERS NOT WHETHER OR NOT SHE LOOKS LIKE THE GOVER-NESS.
YOU ARE OVER-THINKING THINGS.
BUT YOU MUST AGREE, THERE ARE FAR TOO MANY COINCI-DENCES.
SHE CAME ALL THE WAY FROM THAT EASTERN ISLAND COUNTRY...
THE SAME ONE TO WHICH ALICE'S FORMER GOVERNESS WAS DISPATCHED UNDER THE AUSPICES OF SPREADING WOMEN'S EDUCATION.
AND NOW SHE'S IN ALICE'S SERVICE?
......
SEEMS TO ME THAT GOVERNESS IS FAR FROM JUST A MEMORY.

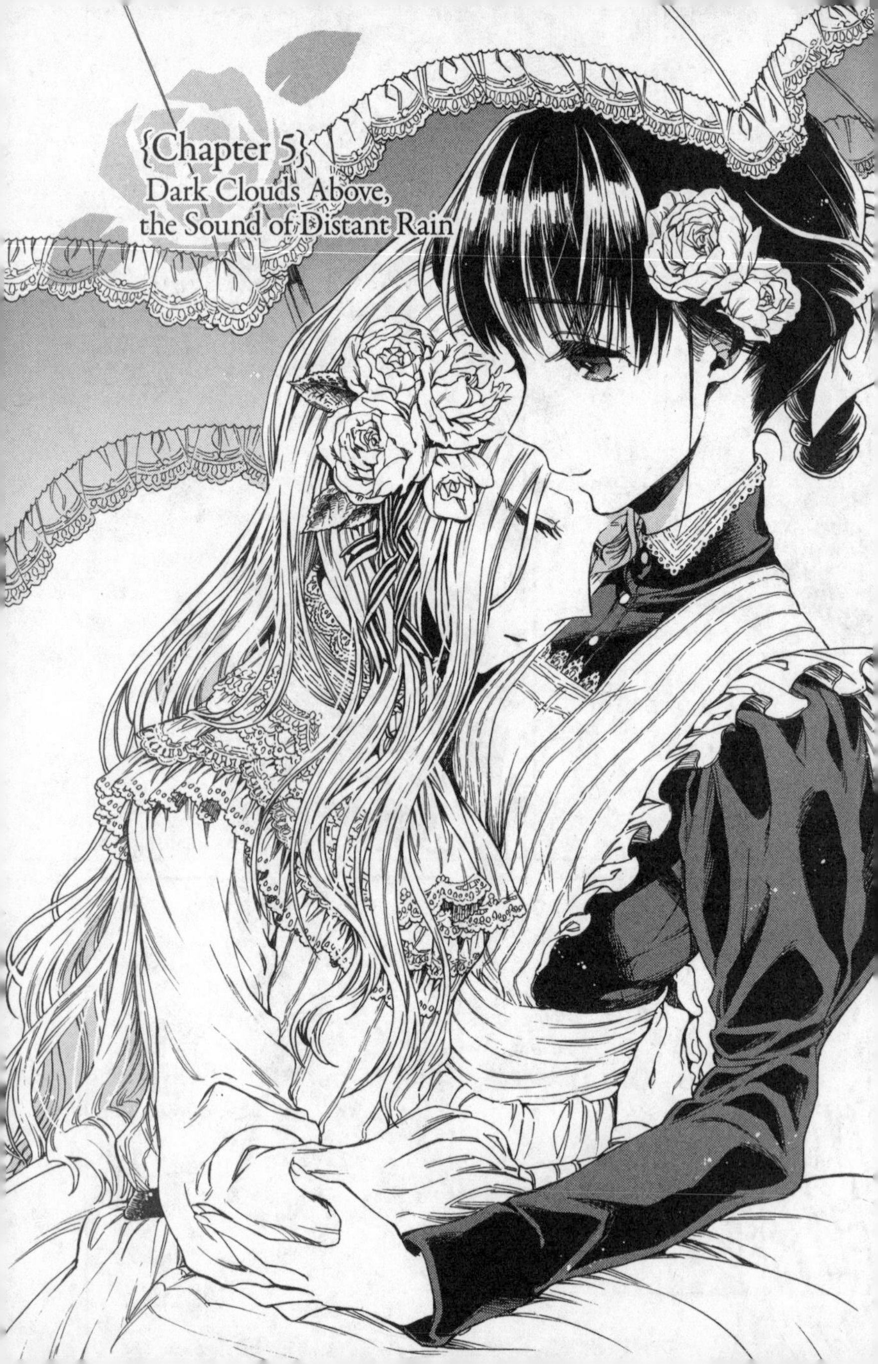
{Chapter 5}
Dark Clouds Above,
the Sound of Distant Rain

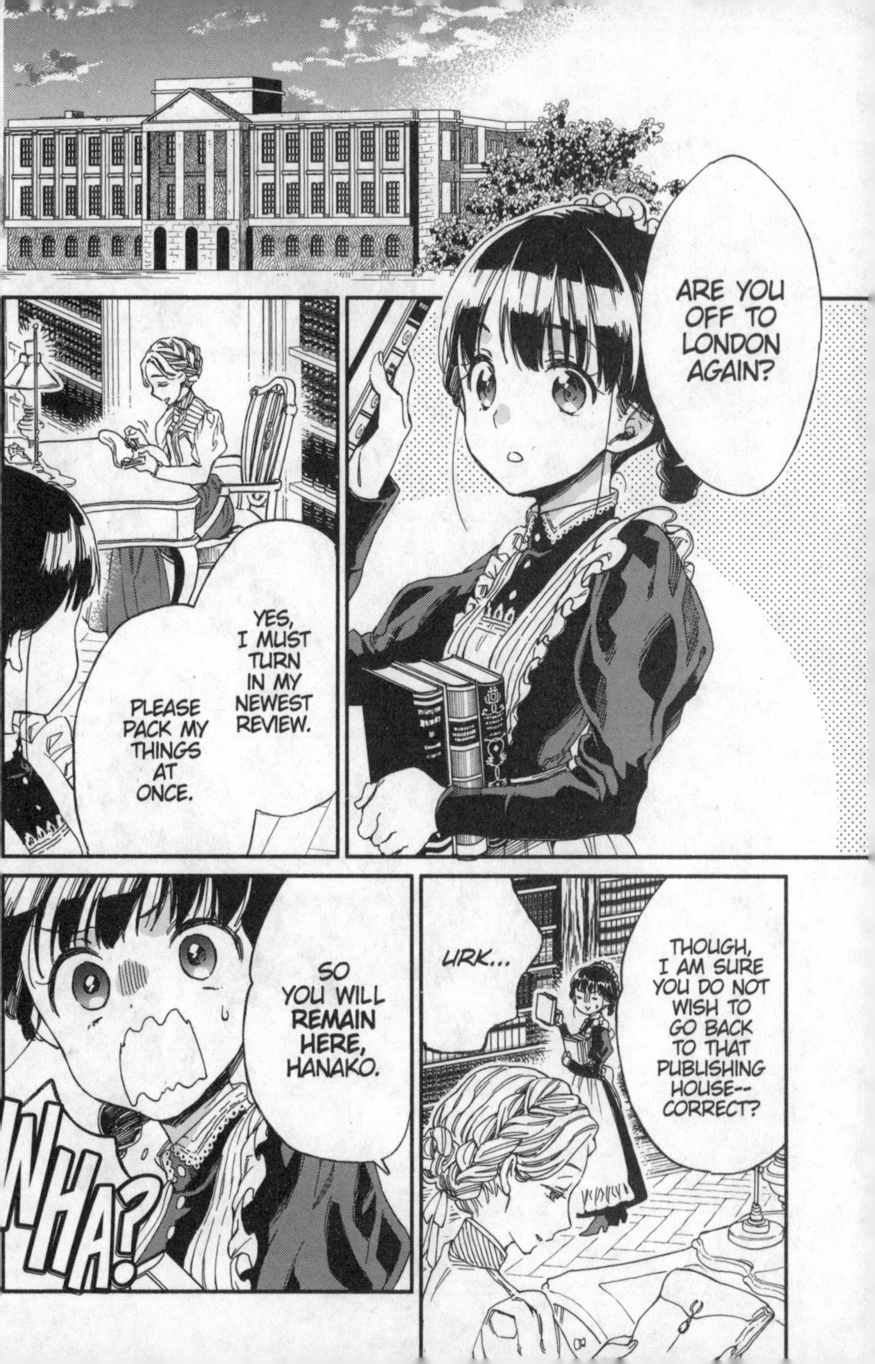
ARE YOU OFF TO LONDON AGAIN?
YES, I MUST TURN IN MY NEWEST REVIEW.
PLEASE PACK MY THINGS AT ONCE.
THOUGH, I AM SURE YOU DO NOT WISH TO GO BACK TO THAT PUBLISHING HOUSE--CORRECT?
URK...
SO YOU WILL REMAIN HERE, HANAKO.
NHA?!

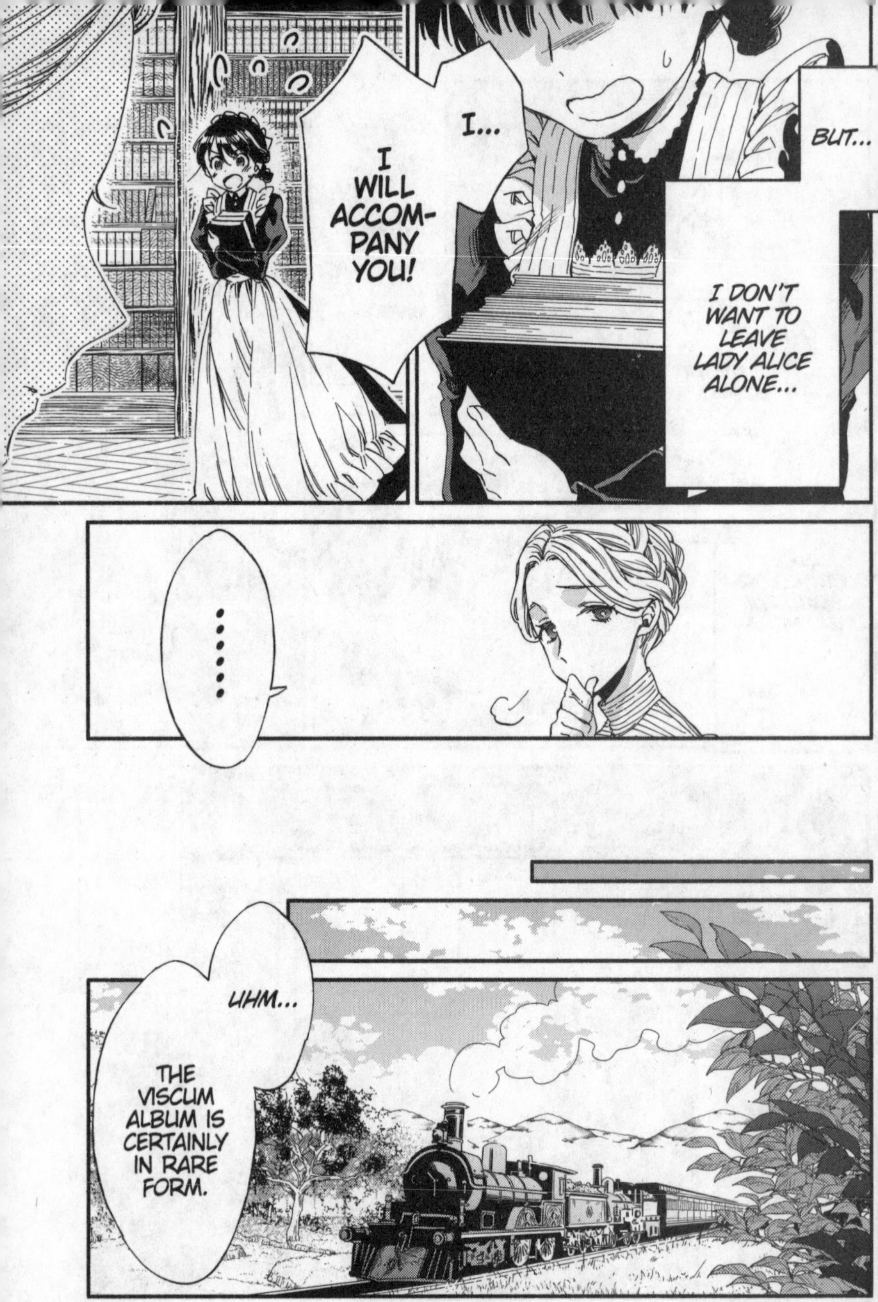
BUT...
I DON'T WANT TO LEAVE LADY ALICE ALONE...
I...
I WILL ACCOMPANY YOU!
......
UHM...
THE VISCUM ALBUM IS CERTAINLY IN RARE FORM.

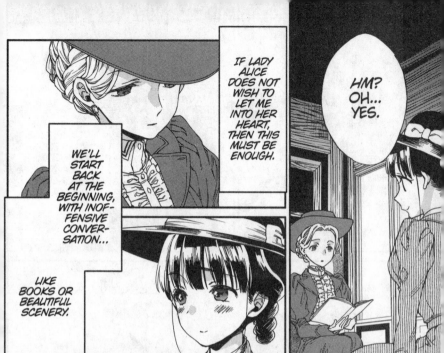

IF LADY ALICE DOES NOT WISH TO LET ME INTO HER HEART, THEN THIS MUST BE ENOUGH.

HM? OH... YES.

WE'LL START BACK AT THE BEGINNING, WITH INOFFENSIVE CONVERSATION...

LIKE BOOKS OR BEAUTIFUL SCENERY.

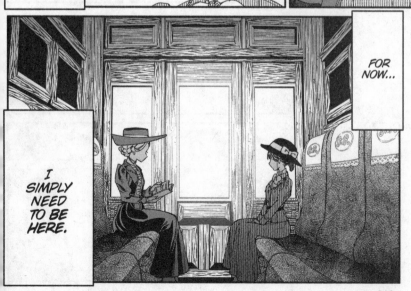

FOR NOW...

I SIMPLY NEED TO BE HERE.

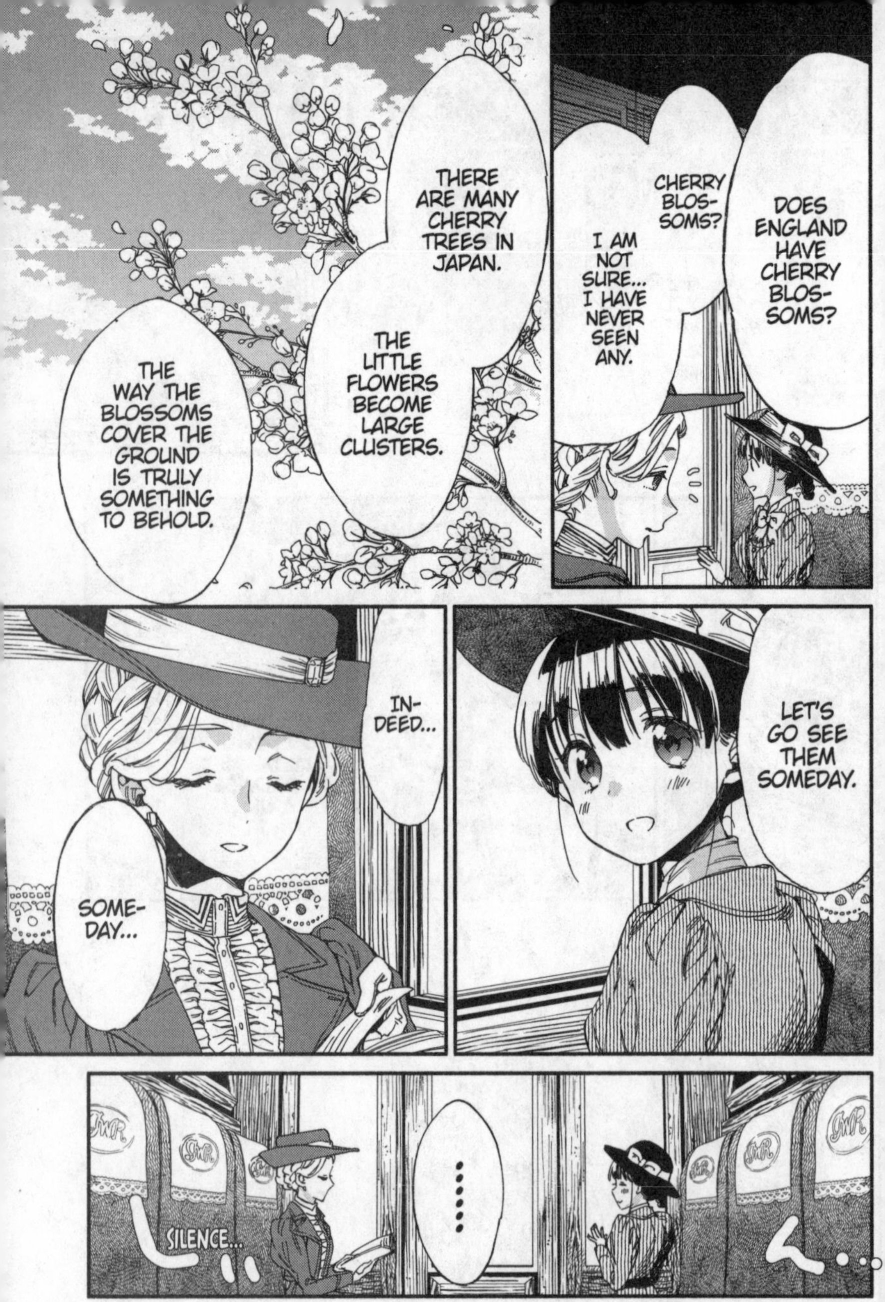
DOES ENGLAND HAVE CHERRY BLOSSOMS?
CHERRY BLOSSOMS?
I AM NOT SURE... I HAVE NEVER SEEN ANY.
THERE ARE MANY CHERRY TREES IN JAPAN.
THE LITTLE FLOWERS BECOME LARGE CLUSTERS.
THE WAY THE BLOSSOMS COVER THE GROUND IS TRULY SOMETHING TO BEHOLD.
LET'S GO SEE THEM SOMEDAY.
INDEED...
SOMEDAY...
......
SILENCE...

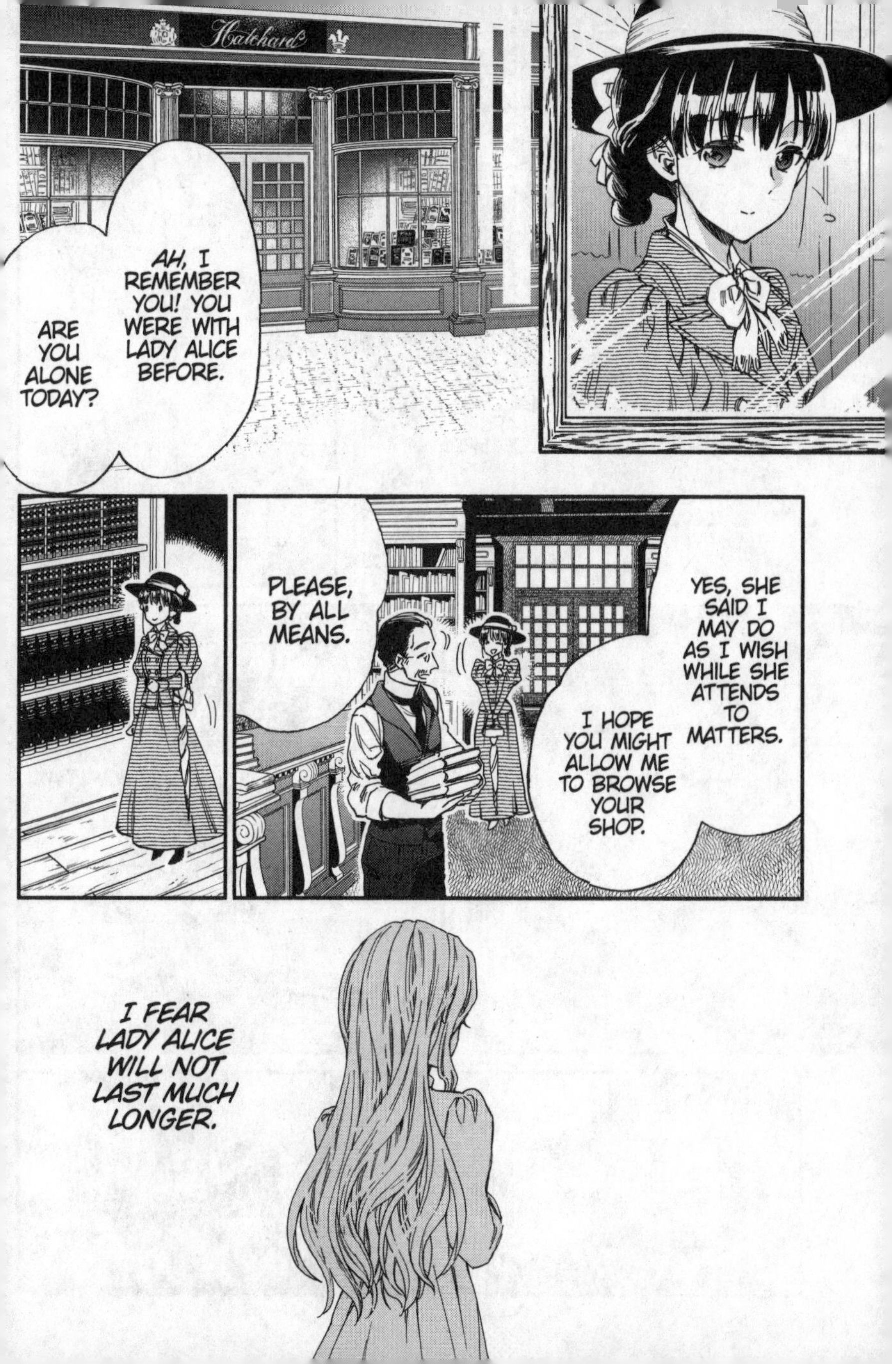
Hatchard
AH, I REMEMBER YOU! YOU WERE WITH LADY ALICE BEFORE.
ARE YOU ALONE TODAY?
YES, SHE SAID I MAY DO AS I WISH WHILE SHE ATTENDS TO MATTERS.
I HOPE YOU MIGHT ALLOW ME TO BROWSE YOUR SHOP.
PLEASE, BY ALL MEANS.
I FEAR LADY ALICE WILL NOT LAST MUCH LONGER.

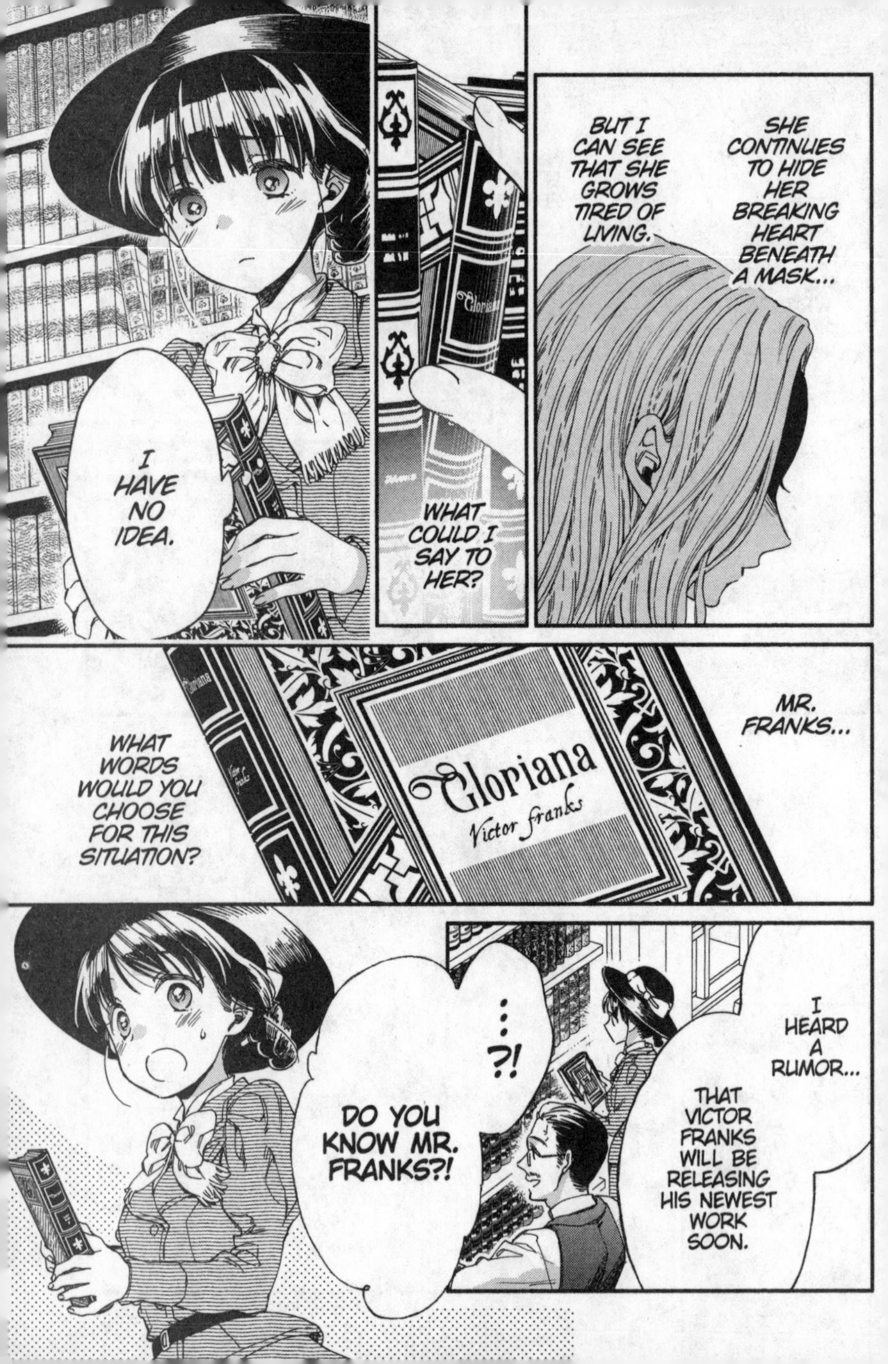

SHE CONTINUES TO HIDE HER BREAKING HEART BENEATH A MASK...
BUT I CAN SEE THAT SHE GROWS TIRED OF LIVING.
WHAT COULD I SAY TO HER?
I HAVE NO IDEA.
MR. FRANKS...
Gloriana
Victor franks
WHAT WORDS WOULD YOU CHOOSE FOR THIS SITUATION?
I HEARD A RUMOR...
THAT VICTOR FRANKS WILL BE RELEASING HIS NEWEST WORK SOON.
...?!
DO YOU KNOW MR. FRANKS?!

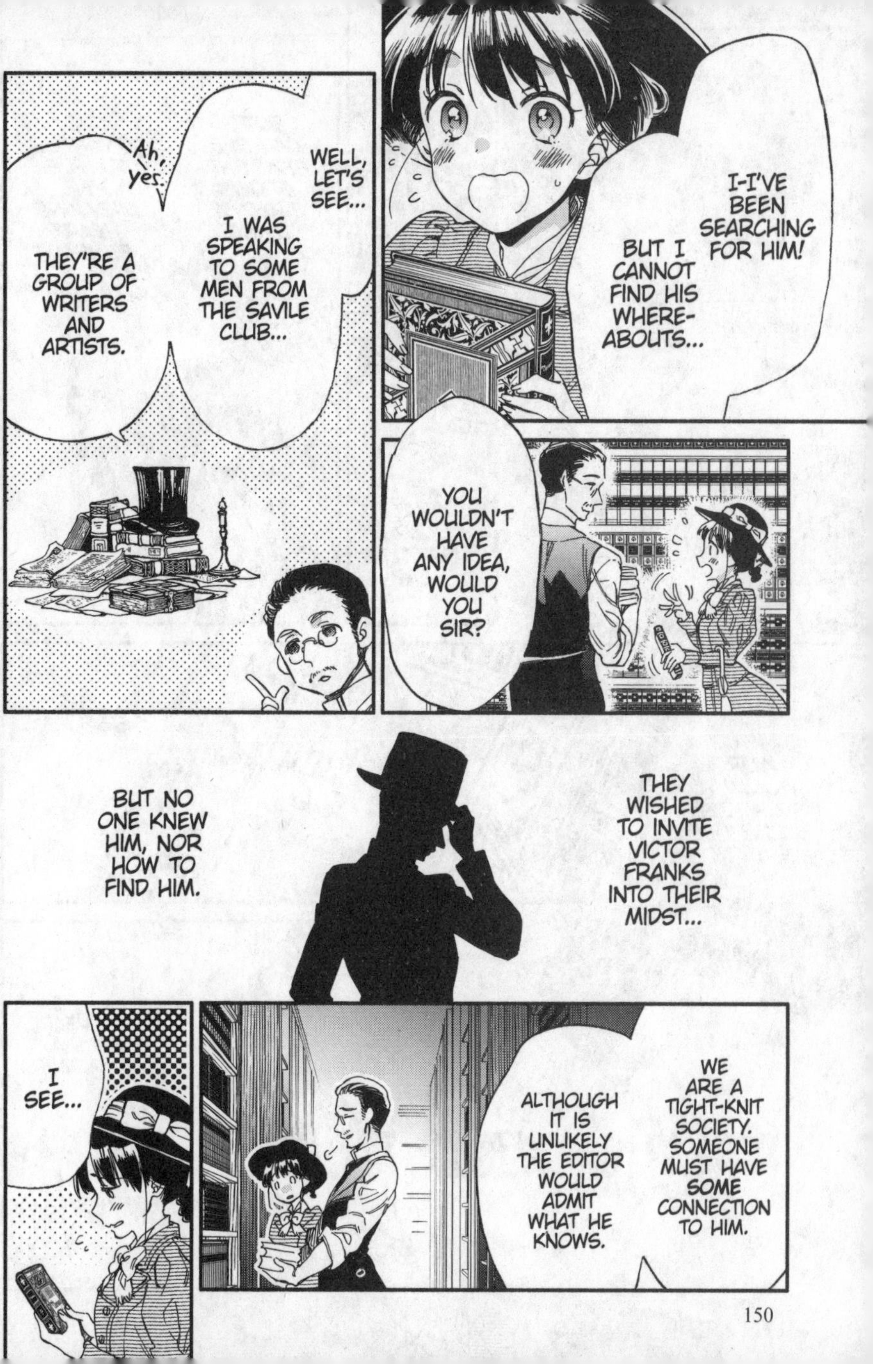
I-I'VE BEEN SEARCHING FOR HIM!
BUT I CANNOT FIND HIS WHERE-ABOUTS...
YOU WOULDN'T HAVE ANY IDEA, WOULD YOU SIR?
WELL, LET'S SEE...
Ah, yes.
I WAS SPEAKING TO SOME MEN FROM THE SAVILE CLUB...
THEY'RE A GROUP OF WRITERS AND ARTISTS.
THEY WISHED TO INVITE VICTOR FRANKS INTO THEIR MIDST...
BUT NO ONE KNEW HIM, NOR HOW TO FIND HIM.
WE ARE A TIGHT-KNIT SOCIETY. SOMEONE MUST HAVE SOME CONNECTION TO HIM.
ALTHOUGH IT IS UNLIKELY THE EDITOR WOULD ADMIT WHAT HE KNOWS.
I SEE...

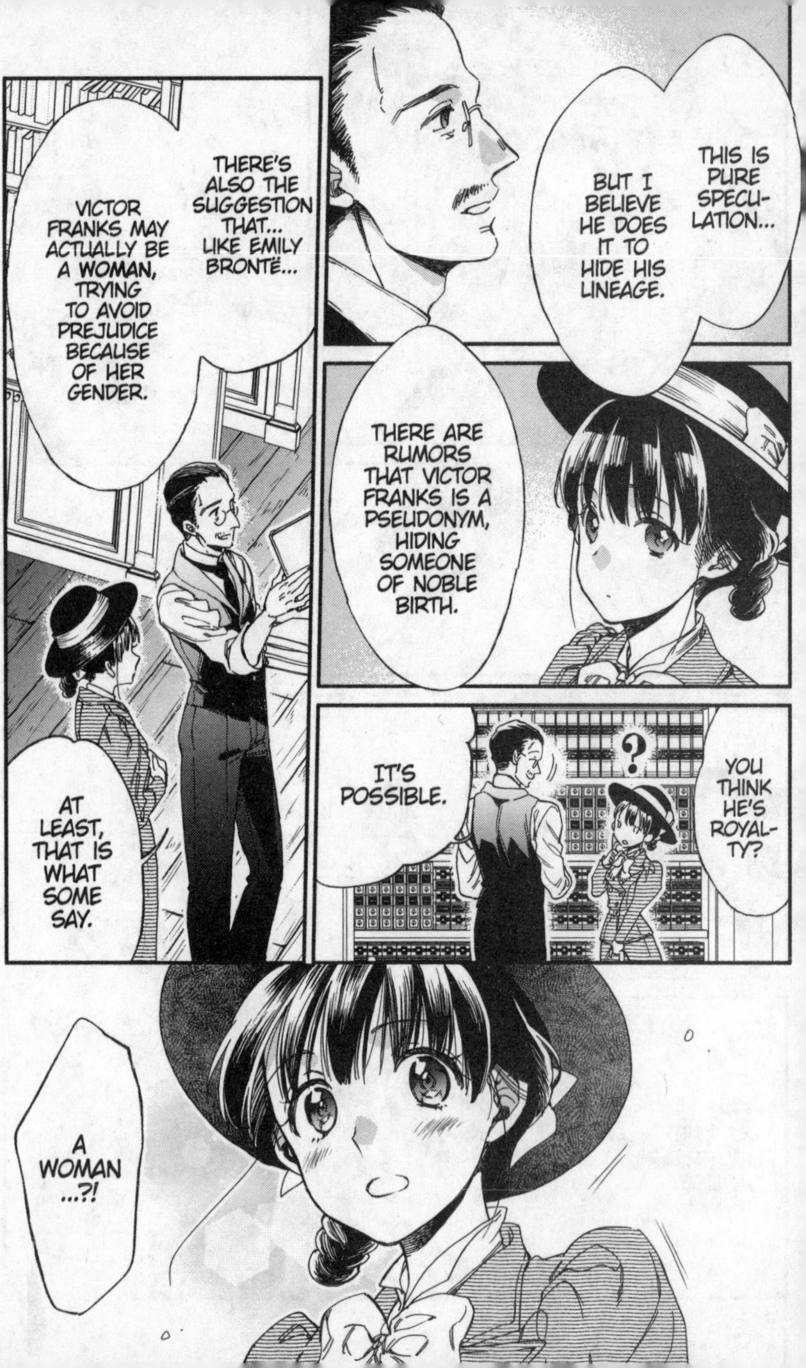

THIS IS PURE SPECULATION...
BUT I BELIEVE HE DOES IT TO HIDE HIS LINEAGE.
THERE ARE RUMORS THAT VICTOR FRANKS IS A PSEUDONYM, HIDING SOMEONE OF NOBLE BIRTH.
YOU THINK HE'S ROYALTY?
IT'S POSSIBLE.
THERE'S ALSO THE SUGGESTION THAT... LIKE EMILY BRONTË...
VICTOR FRANKS MAY ACTUALLY BE A WOMAN, TRYING TO AVOID PREJUDICE BECAUSE OF HER GENDER.
AT LEAST, THAT IS WHAT SOME SAY.
A WOMAN ...?!

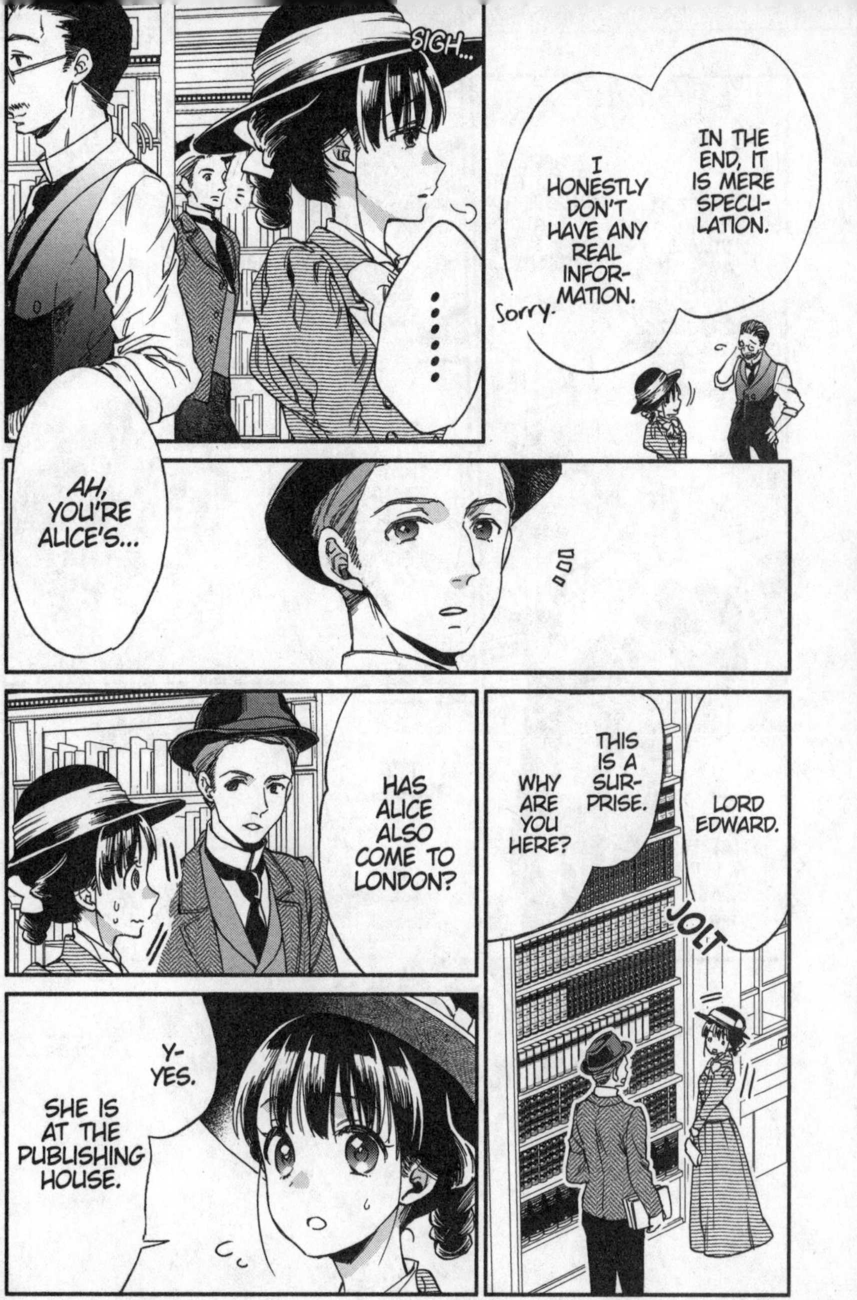
IN THE END, IT IS MERE SPECULATION.
I HONESTLY DON'T HAVE ANY REAL INFORMATION.
Sorry.
SIGH...
......
AH, YOU'RE ALICE'S...
LORD EDWARD.
JOLT
THIS IS A SURPRISE.
WHY ARE YOU HERE?
HAS ALICE ALSO COME TO LONDON?
Y-YES.
SHE IS AT THE PUBLISHING HOUSE.

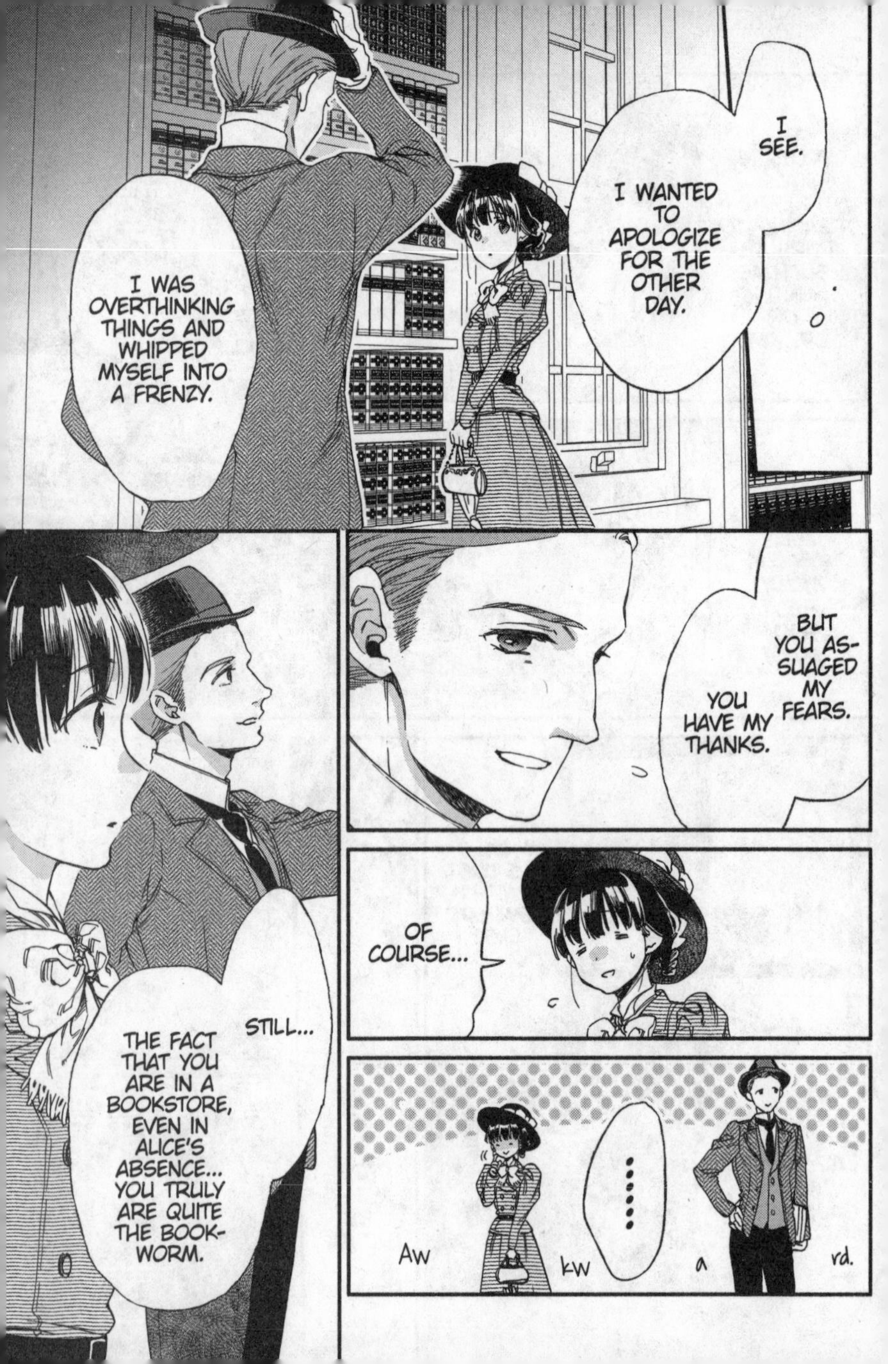
I SEE.
I WANTED TO APOLOGIZE FOR THE OTHER DAY.
I WAS OVERTHINKING THINGS AND WHIPPED MYSELF INTO A FRENZY.
BUT YOU AS-SUAGED MY FEARS.
YOU HAVE MY THANKS.
OF COURSE...
......
Aw kw a rd.
STILL...
THE FACT THAT YOU ARE IN A BOOKSTORE, EVEN IN ALICE'S ABSENCE... YOU TRULY ARE QUITE THE BOOK-WORM.

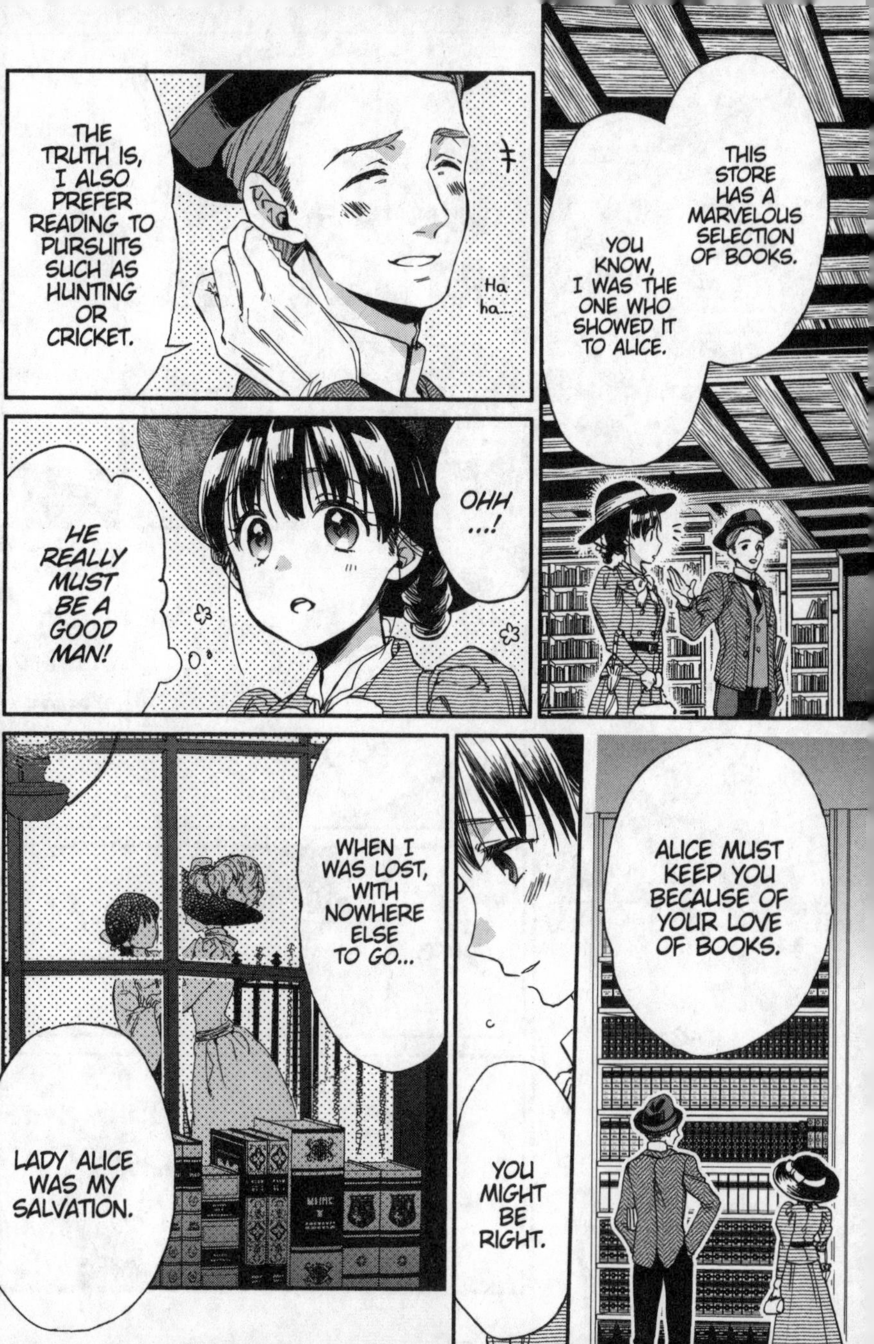

THIS STORE HAS A MARVELOUS SELECTION OF BOOKS.
YOU KNOW, I WAS THE ONE WHO SHOWED IT TO ALICE.
THE TRUTH IS, I ALSO PREFER READING TO PURSUITS SUCH AS HUNTING OR CRICKET.
Ha ha...
OHH ...!
HE REALLY MUST BE A GOOD MAN!
ALICE MUST KEEP YOU BECAUSE OF YOUR LOVE OF BOOKS.
YOU MIGHT BE RIGHT.
WHEN I WAS LOST, WITH NOWHERE ELSE TO GO...
LADY ALICE WAS MY SALVATION.

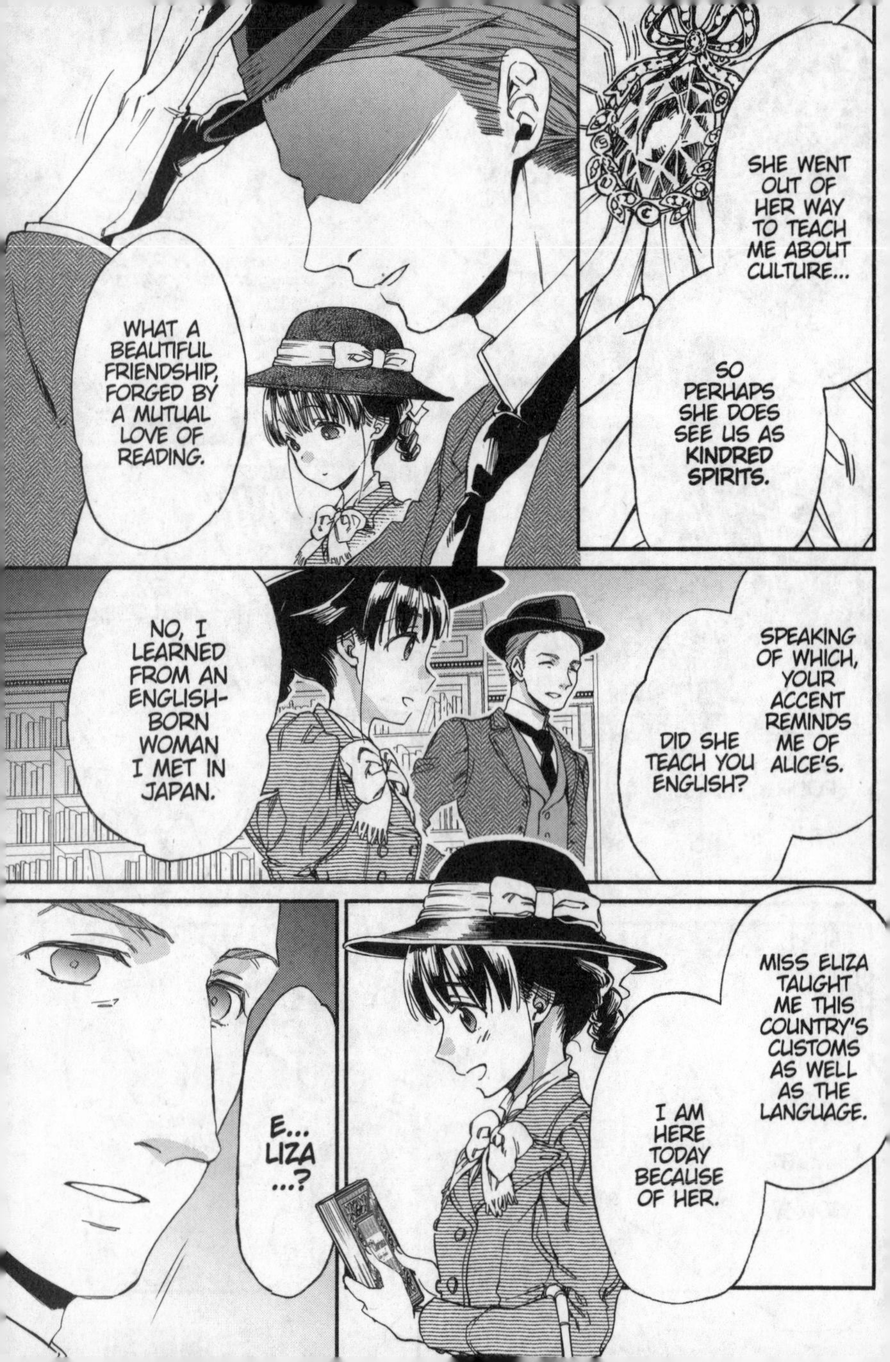
SHE WENT OUT OF HER WAY TO TEACH ME ABOUT CULTURE...
SO PERHAPS SHE DOES SEE US AS KINDRED SPIRITS.
WHAT A BEAUTIFUL FRIENDSHIP, FORGED BY A MUTUAL LOVE OF READING.
SPEAKING OF WHICH, YOUR ACCENT REMINDS ME OF ALICE'S.
DID SHE TEACH YOU ENGLISH?
NO, I LEARNED FROM AN ENGLISH-BORN WOMAN I MET IN JAPAN.
MISS ELIZA TAUGHT ME THIS COUNTRY'S CUSTOMS AS WELL AS THE LANGUAGE.
I AM HERE TODAY BECAUSE OF HER.
E... LIZA ...?

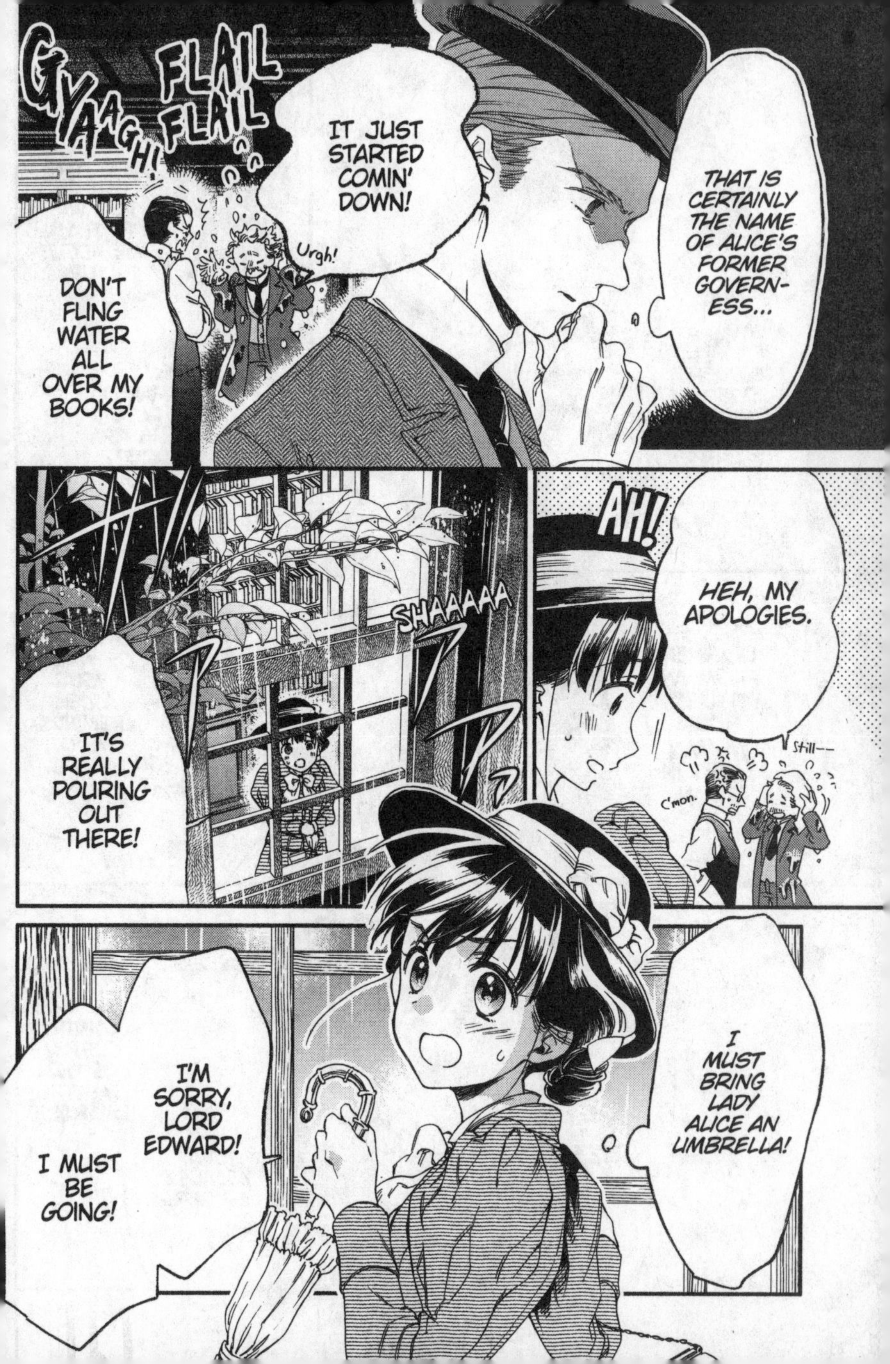
THAT IS CERTAINLY THE NAME OF ALICE'S FORMER GOVERNESS...
IT JUST STARTED COMIN' DOWN!
FLAIL FLAIL
GYAAGH!
Urgh!
DON'T FLING WATER ALL OVER MY BOOKS!
AH!
HEH, MY APOLOGIES.
Still—
C'mon.
SHAAAAA
IT'S REALLY POURING OUT THERE!
I MUST BRING LADY ALICE AN UMBRELLA!
I'M SORRY, LORD EDWARD!
I MUST BE GOING!

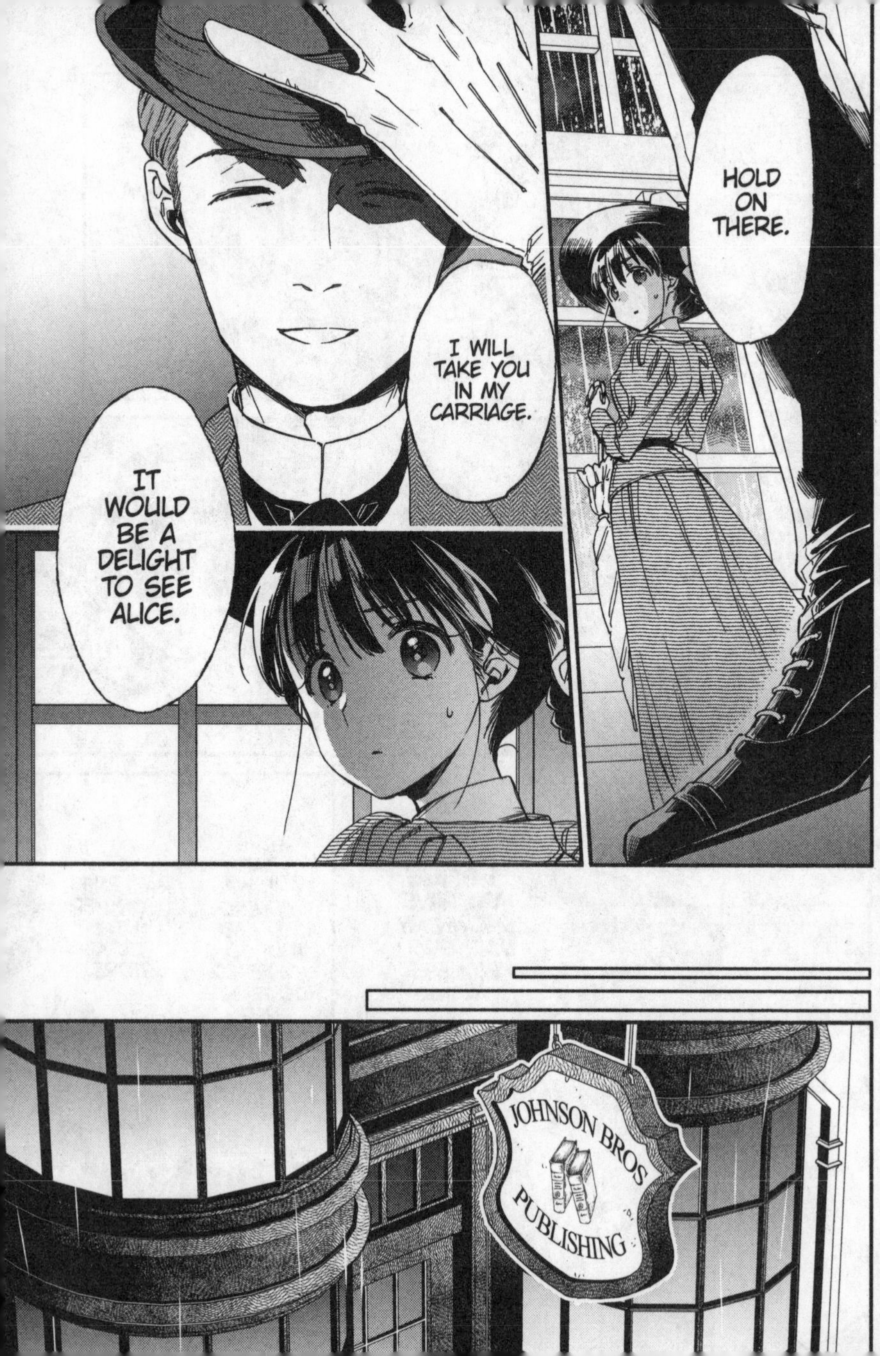
HOLD ON THERE.
I WILL TAKE YOU IN MY CARRIAGE.
IT WOULD BE A DELIGHT TO SEE ALICE.
JOHNSON BROS PUBLISHING

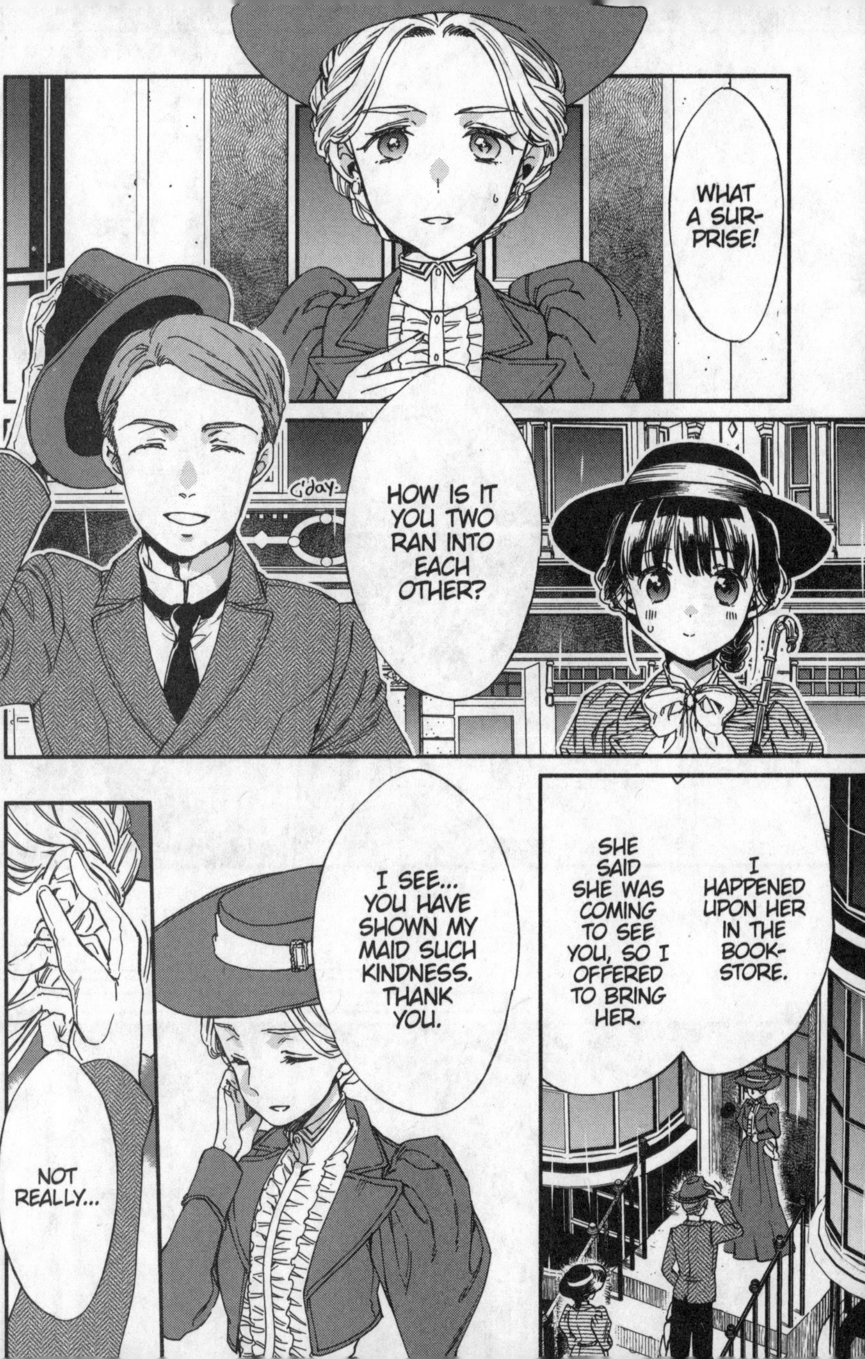
WHAT A SUR-PRISE!
HOW IS IT YOU TWO RAN INTO EACH OTHER?
G'day.
I HAPPENED UPON HER IN THE BOOK-STORE.
SHE SAID SHE WAS COMING TO SEE YOU, SO I OFFERED TO BRING HER.
I SEE... YOU HAVE SHOWN MY MAID SUCH KINDNESS. THANK YOU.
NOT REALLY...

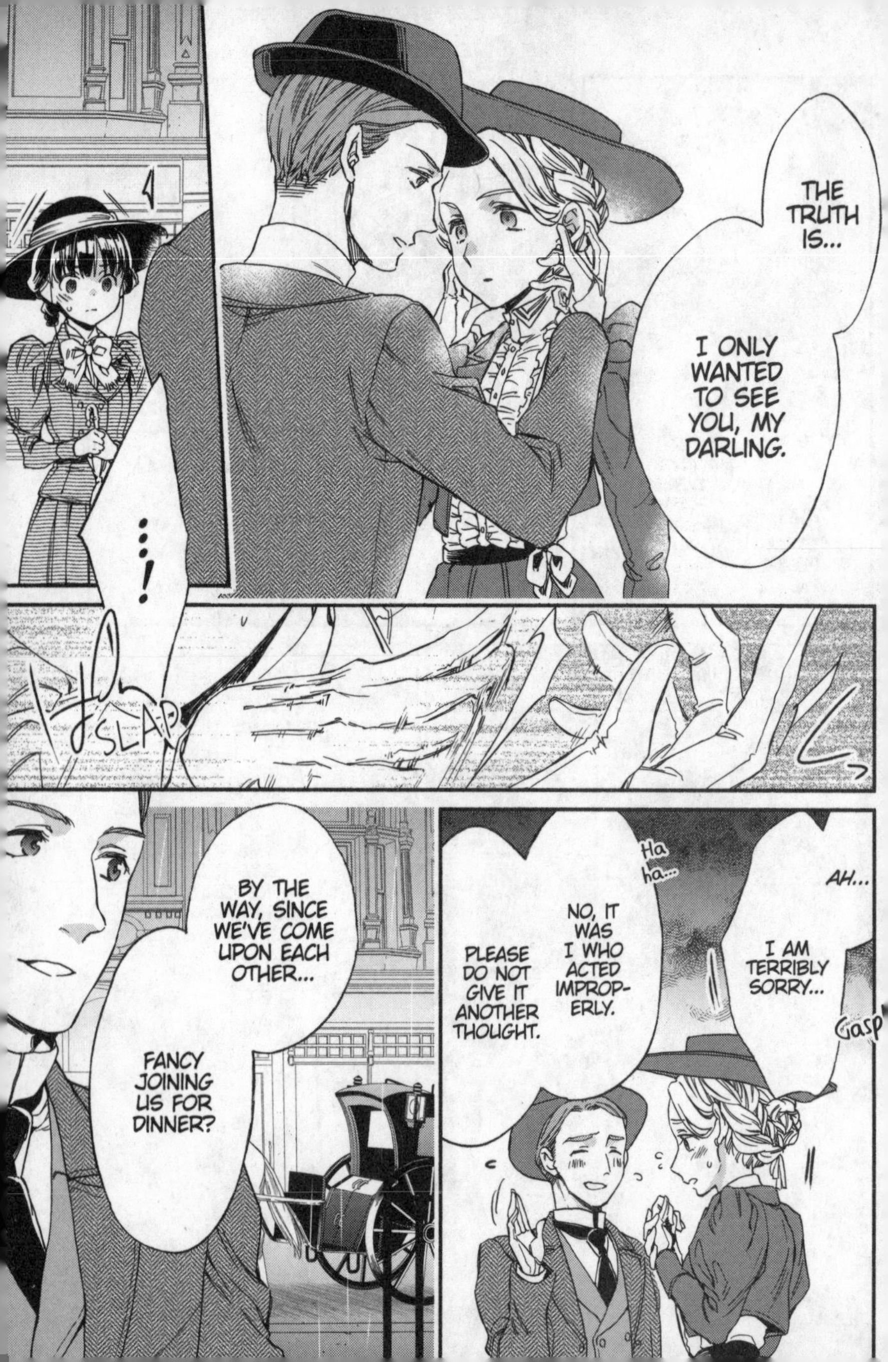
THE TRUTH IS...
I ONLY WANTED TO SEE YOU, MY DARLING.
...!
SLAP
AH...
I AM TERRIBLY SORRY...
Gasp
Ha ha...
NO, IT WAS I WHO ACTED IMPROP-ERLY.
PLEASE DO NOT GIVE IT ANOTHER THOUGHT.
BY THE WAY, SINCE WE'VE COME UPON EACH OTHER...
FANCY JOINING US FOR DINNER?

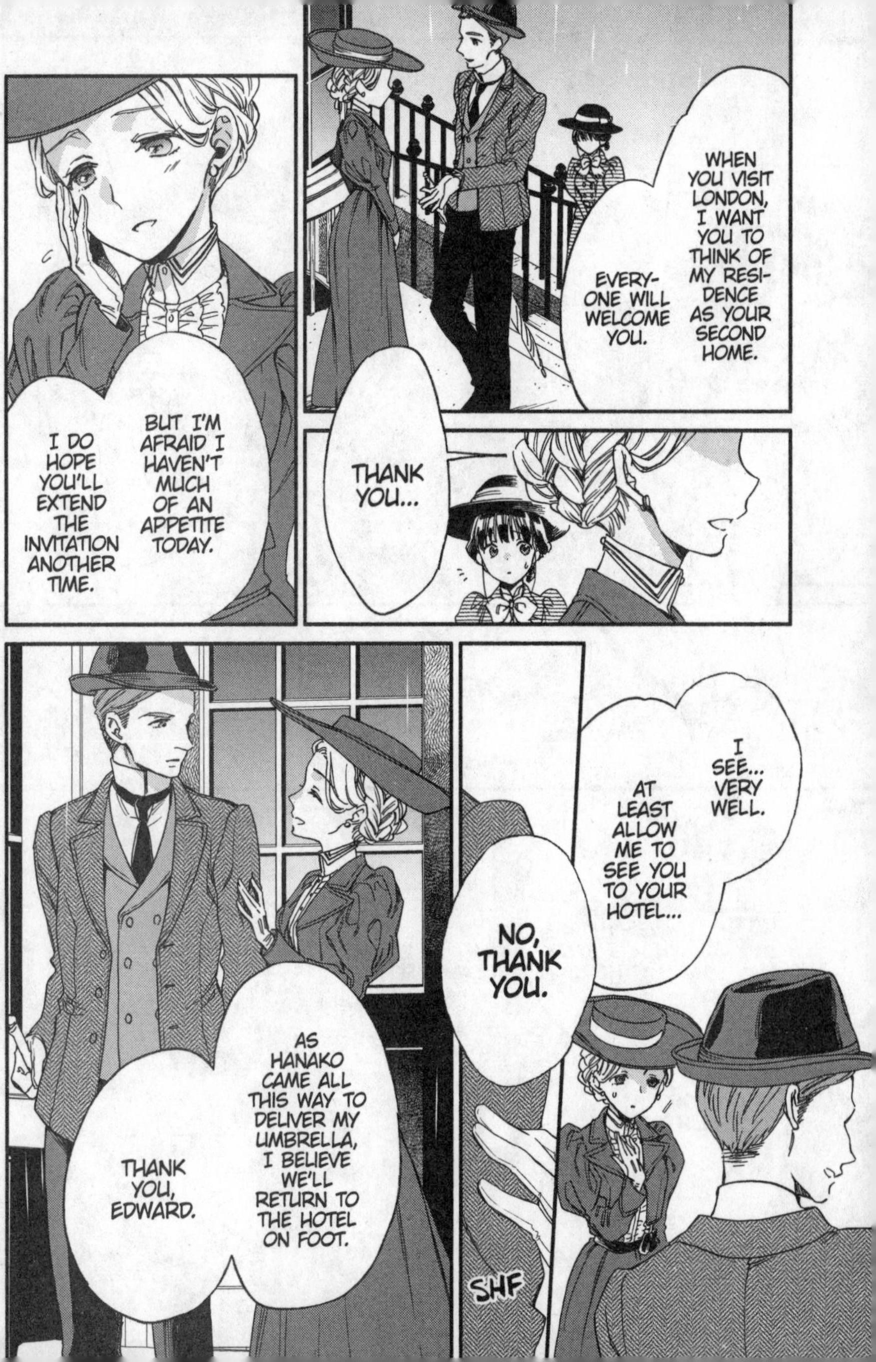
WHEN YOU VISIT LONDON, I WANT YOU TO THINK OF MY RESIDENCE AS YOUR SECOND HOME.
EVERYONE WILL WELCOME YOU.
THANK YOU...
BUT I'M AFRAID I HAVEN'T MUCH OF AN APPETITE TODAY.
I DO HOPE YOU'LL EXTEND THE INVITATION ANOTHER TIME.
I SEE... VERY WELL.
AT LEAST ALLOW ME TO SEE YOU TO YOUR HOTEL...
NO, THANK YOU.
SHF
AS HANAKO CAME ALL THIS WAY TO DELIVER MY UMBRELLA, I BELIEVE WE'LL RETURN TO THE HOTEL ON FOOT.
THANK YOU, EDWARD.

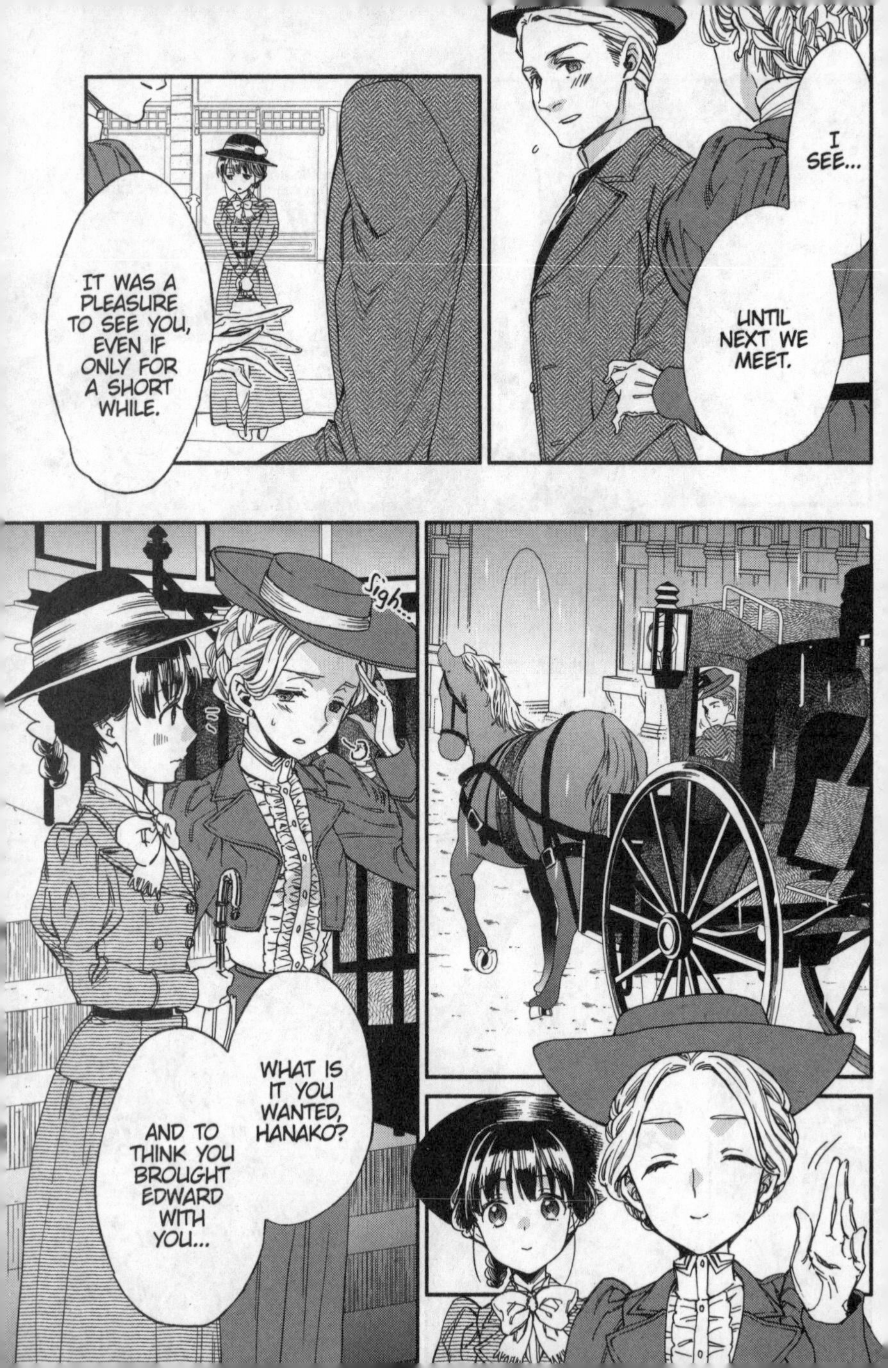
I SEE...
UNTIL NEXT WE MEET.
IT WAS A PLEASURE TO SEE YOU, EVEN IF ONLY FOR A SHORT WHILE.
Sigh...
WHAT IS IT YOU WANTED, HANAKO?
AND TO THINK YOU BROUGHT EDWARD WITH YOU...

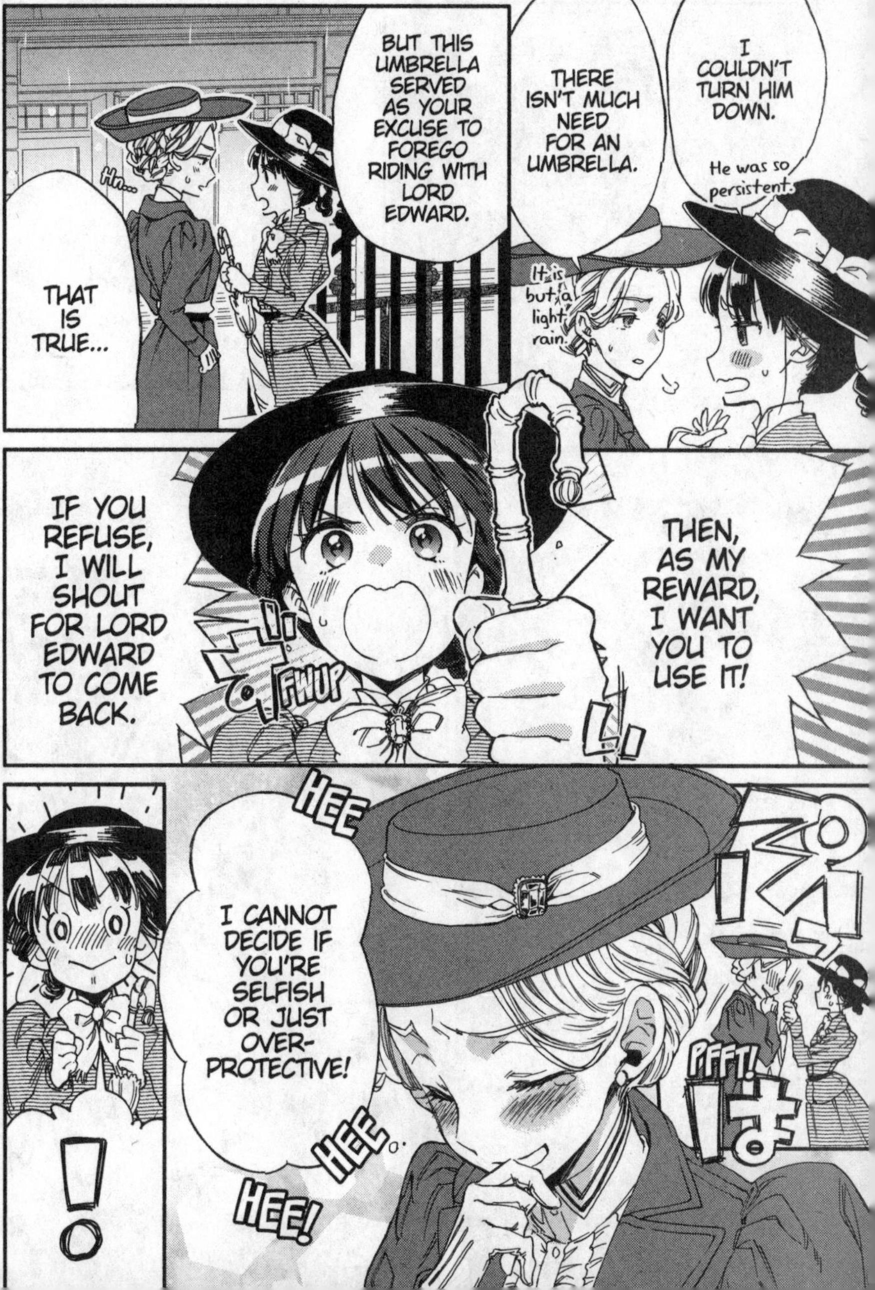
I COULDN'T TURN HIM DOWN.
He was so persistent.
THERE ISN'T MUCH NEED FOR AN UMBRELLA.
It is but a light rain.
BUT THIS UMBRELLA SERVED AS YOUR EXCUSE TO FOREGO RIDING WITH LORD EDWARD.
Hn...
THAT IS TRUE...
THEN, AS MY REWARD, I WANT YOU TO USE IT!
FWUP
IF YOU REFUSE, I WILL SHOUT FOR LORD EDWARD TO COME BACK.
PFFT!
HEE
I CANNOT DECIDE IF YOU'RE SELFISH OR JUST OVER-PROTECTIVE!
HEE
HEE!
!

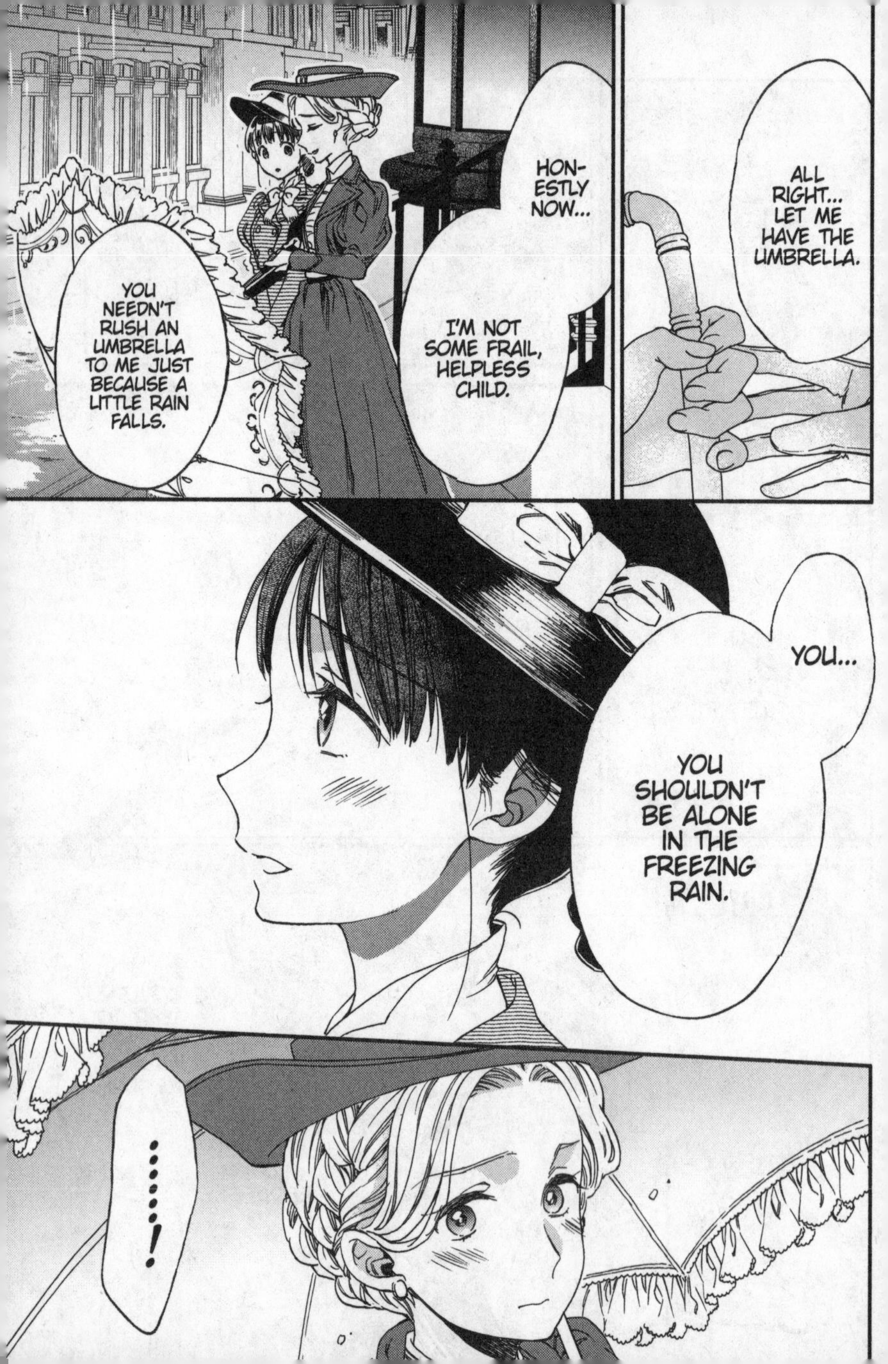
ALL RIGHT... LET ME HAVE THE UMBRELLA.
HON-ESTLY NOW...
I'M NOT SOME FRAIL, HELPLESS CHILD.
YOU NEEDN'T RUSH AN UMBRELLA TO ME JUST BECAUSE A LITTLE RAIN FALLS.
YOU...
YOU SHOULDN'T BE ALONE IN THE FREEZING RAIN.
......!

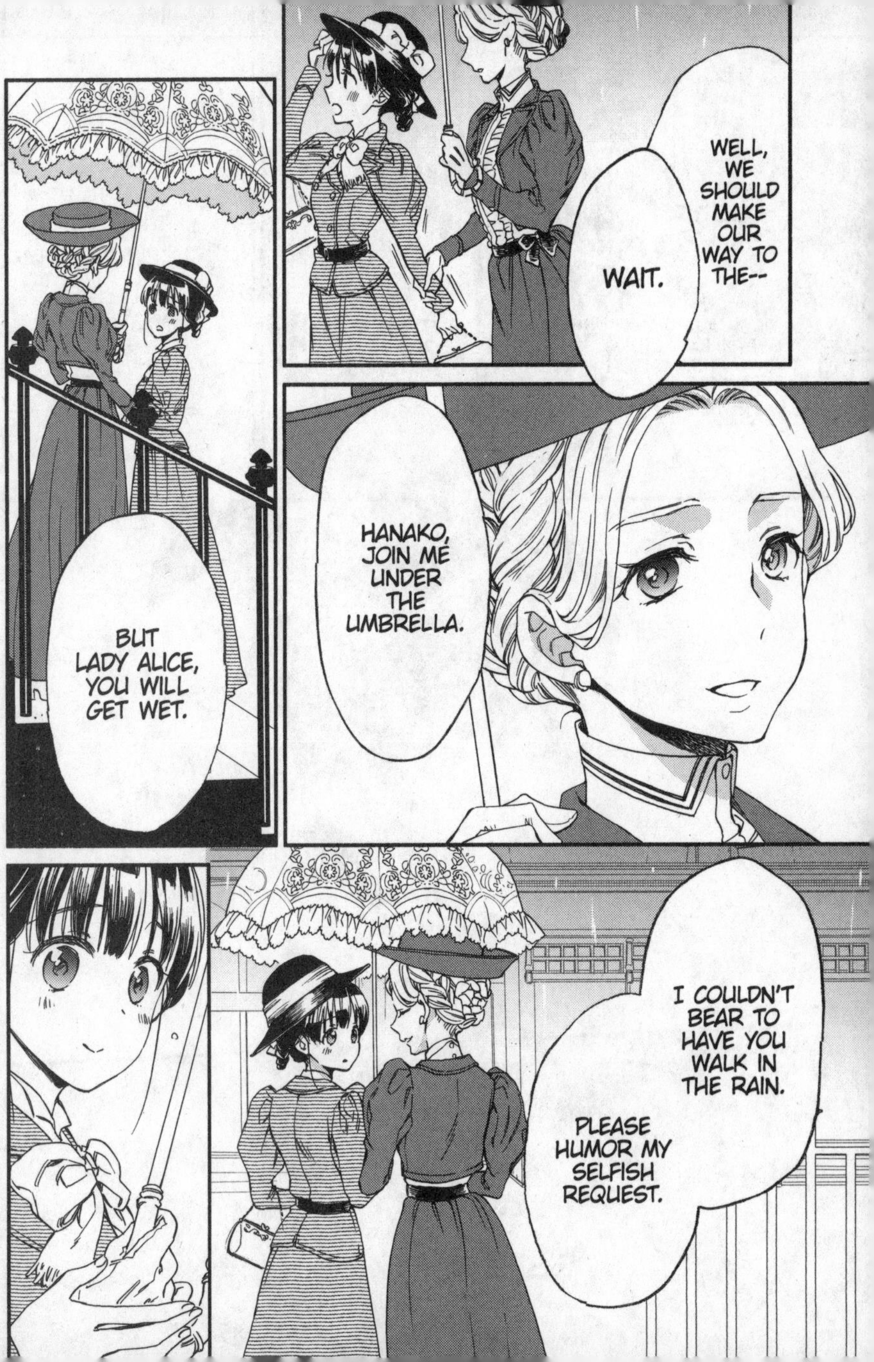
WELL, WE SHOULD MAKE OUR WAY TO THE--
WAIT.
HANAKO, JOIN ME UNDER THE UMBRELLA.
BUT LADY ALICE, YOU WILL GET WET.
I COULDN'T BEAR TO HAVE YOU WALK IN THE RAIN.
PLEASE HUMOR MY SELFISH REQUEST.

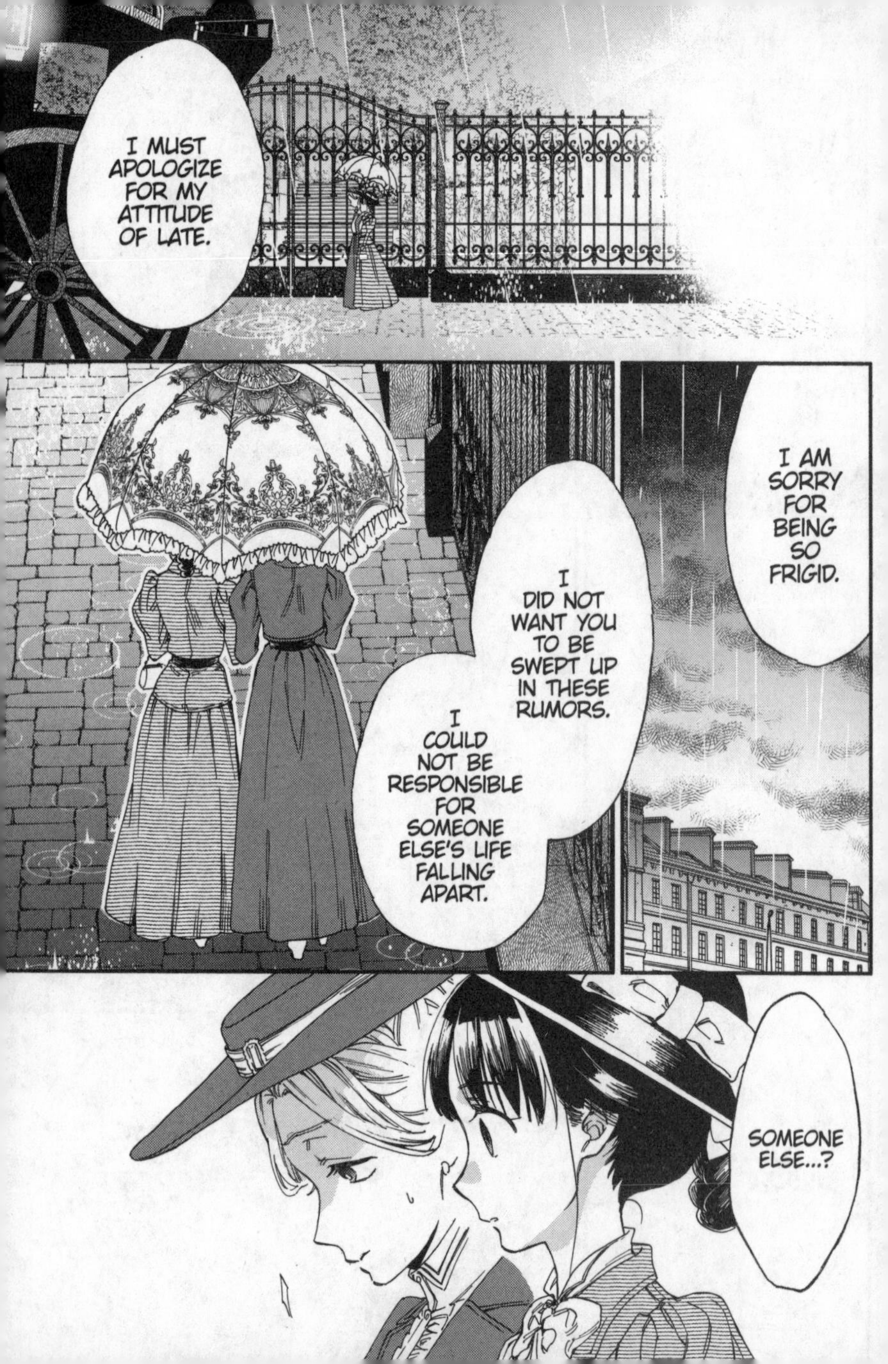
I MUST APOLOGIZE FOR MY ATTITUDE OF LATE.
I AM SORRY FOR BEING SO FRIGID.
I DID NOT WANT YOU TO BE SWEPT UP IN THESE RUMORS.
I COULD NOT BE RESPONSIBLE FOR SOMEONE ELSE'S LIFE FALLING APART.
SOMEONE ELSE...?

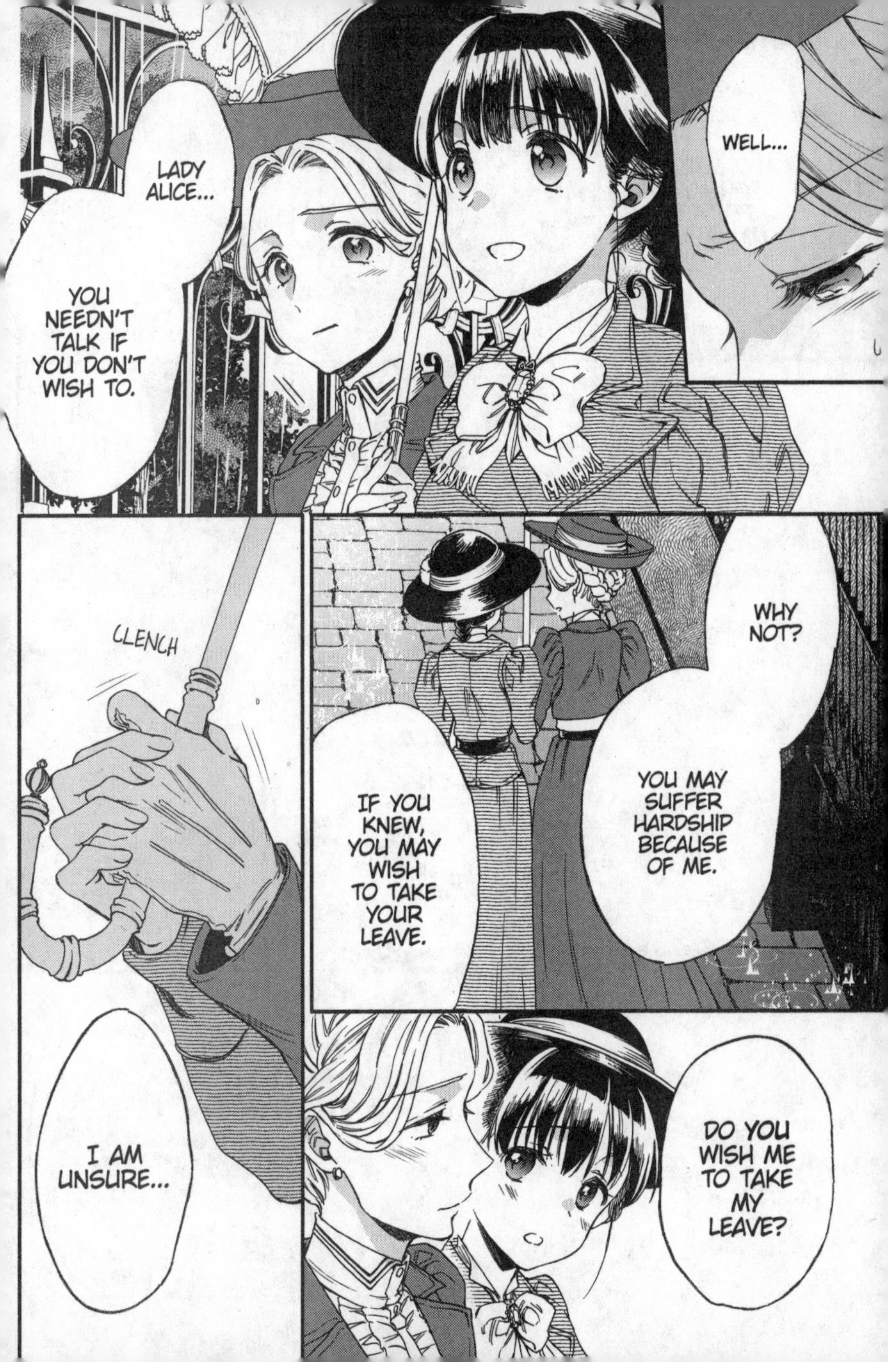
WELL...
LADY ALICE...
YOU NEEDN'T TALK IF YOU DON'T WISH TO.
WHY NOT?
YOU MAY SUFFER HARDSHIP BECAUSE OF ME.
IF YOU KNEW, YOU MAY WISH TO TAKE YOUR LEAVE.
DO YOU WISH ME TO TAKE MY LEAVE?
CLENCH
I AM UNSURE...

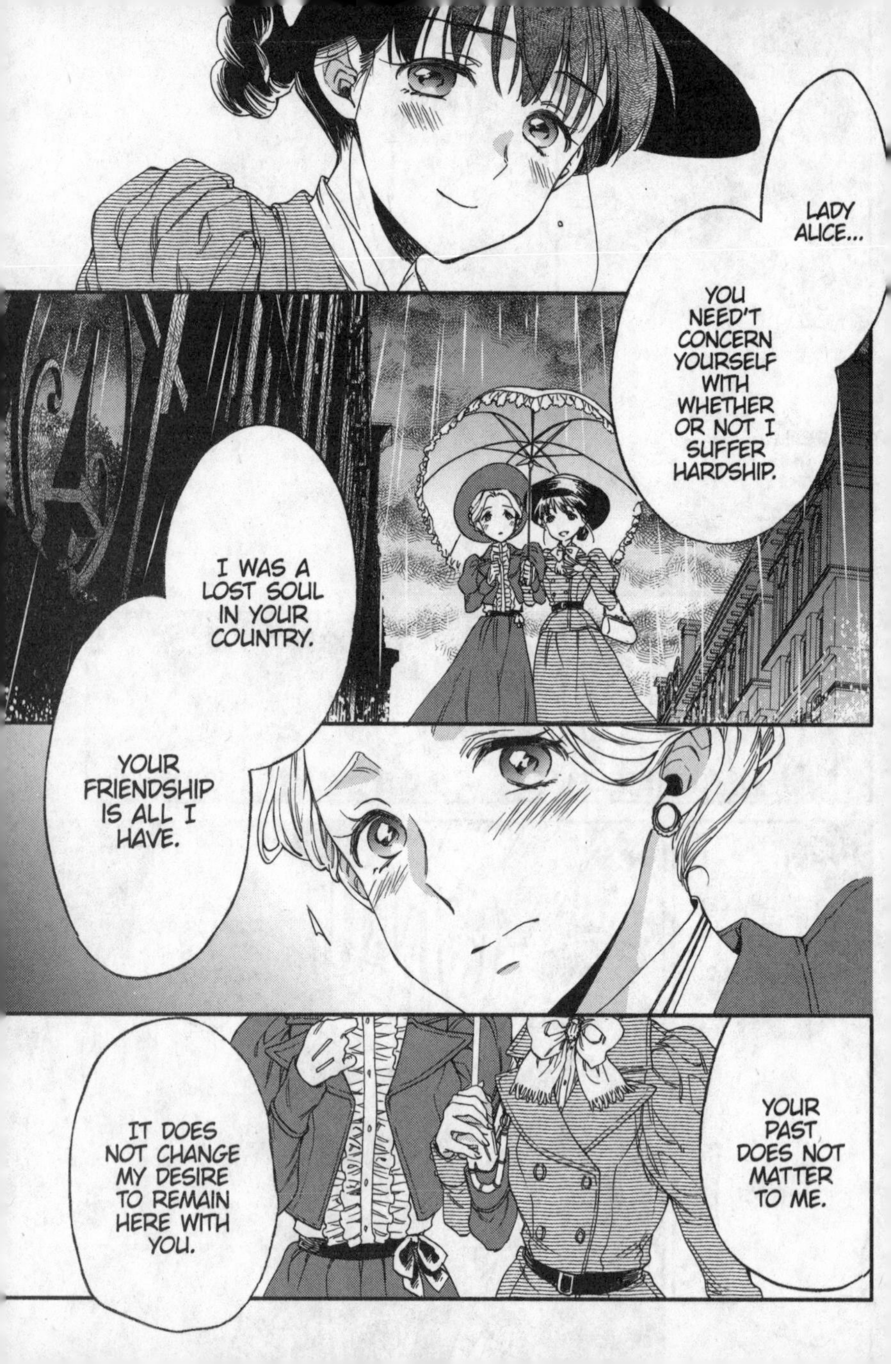
LADY ALICE...
YOU NEED'T CONCERN YOURSELF WITH WHETHER OR NOT I SUFFER HARDSHIP.
I WAS A LOST SOUL IN YOUR COUNTRY.
YOUR FRIENDSHIP IS ALL I HAVE.
YOUR PAST DOES NOT MATTER TO ME.
IT DOES NOT CHANGE MY DESIRE TO REMAIN HERE WITH YOU.

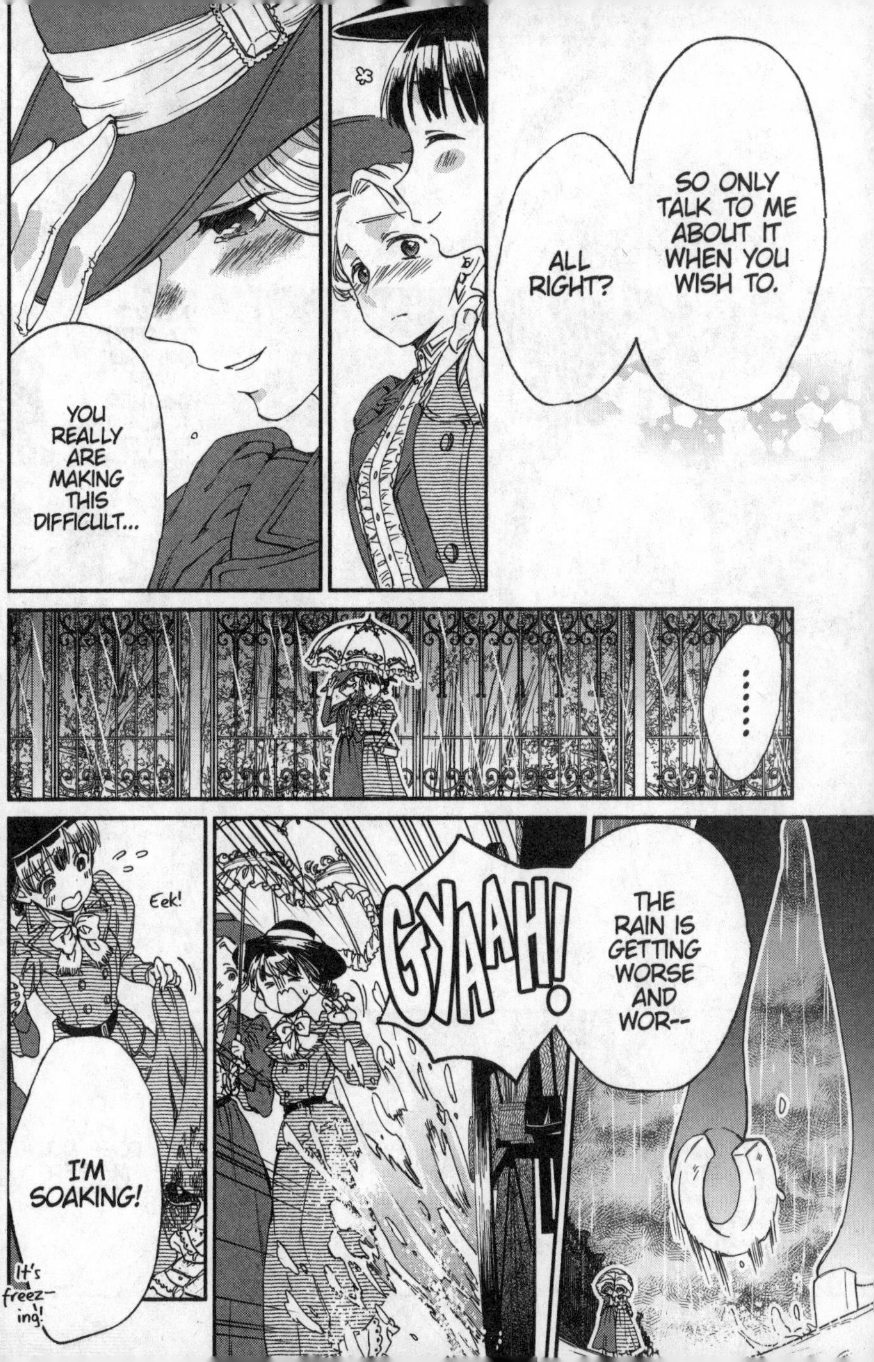
SO ONLY TALK TO ME ABOUT IT WHEN YOU WISH TO.
ALL RIGHT?
YOU REALLY ARE MAKING THIS DIFFICULT...
......
THE RAIN IS GETTING WORSE AND WOR--
GYAAH!
Eek!
I'M SOAKING!
It's freez-ing!

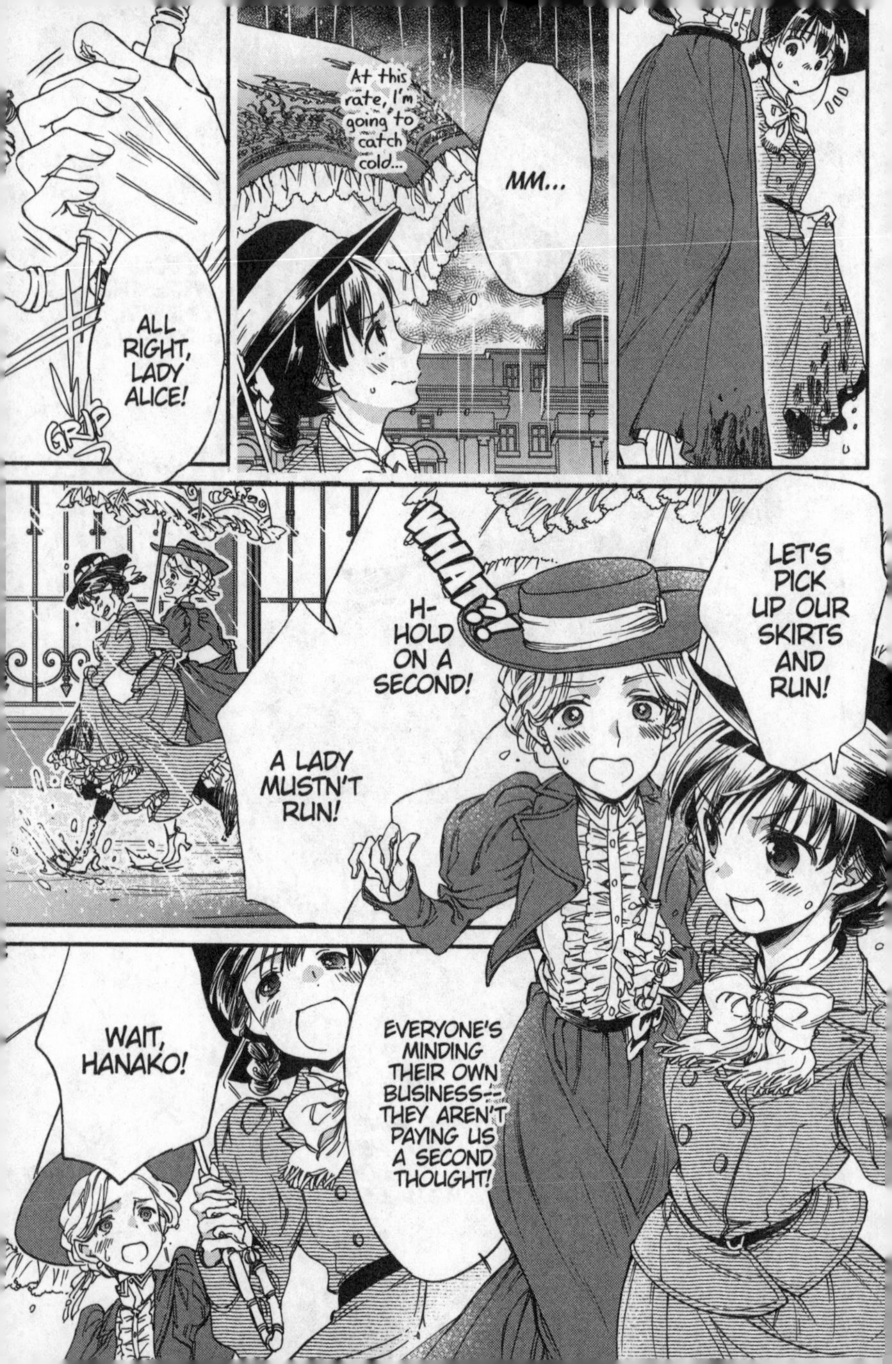
MM...
At this rate, I'm going to catch cold...
ALL RIGHT, LADY ALICE!
GRIP
LET'S PICK UP OUR SKIRTS AND RUN!
WHAT?!
H-HOLD ON A SECOND!
A LADY MUSTN'T RUN!
EVERYONE'S MINDING THEIR OWN BUSINESS-- THEY AREN'T PAYING US A SECOND THOUGHT!
WAIT, HANAKO!

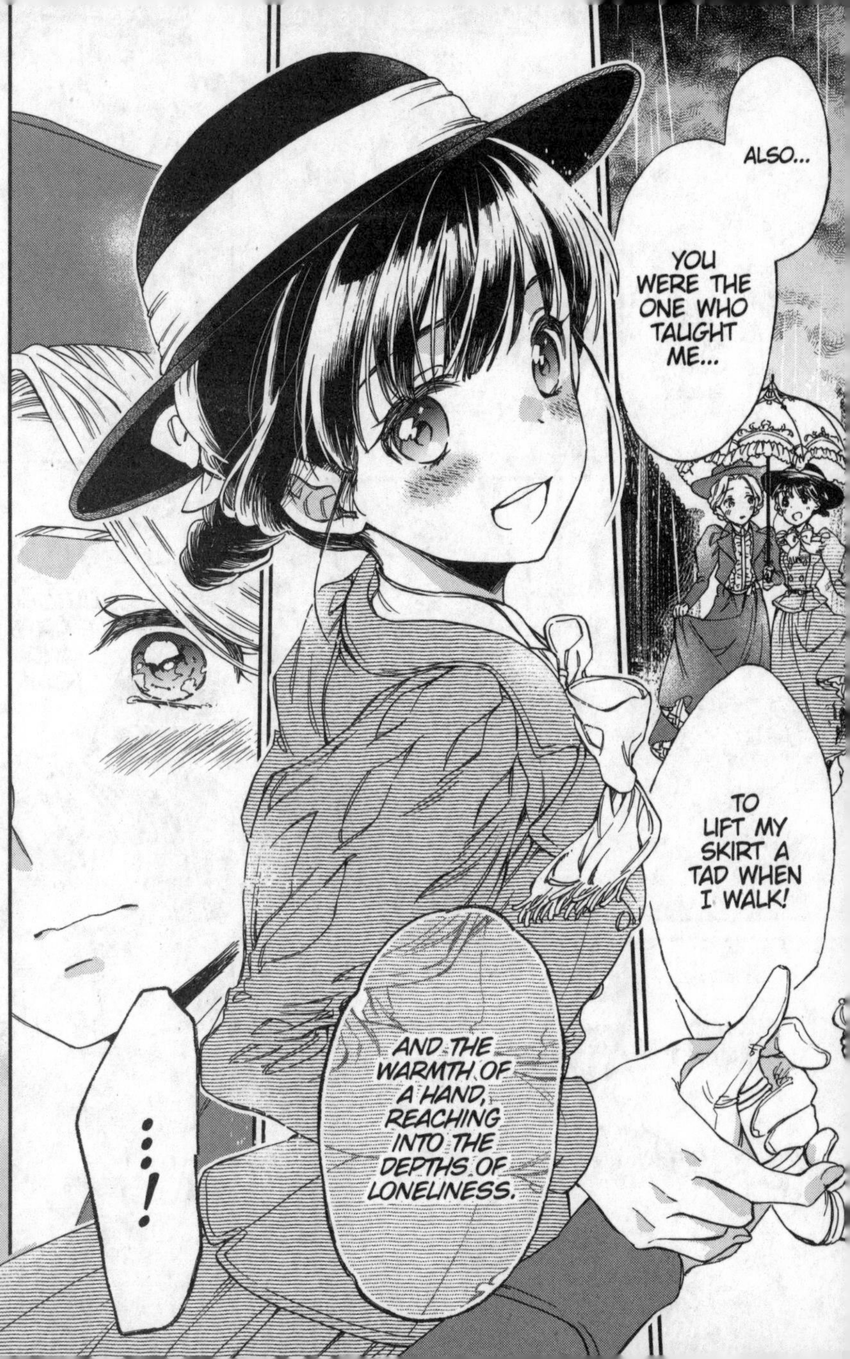
ALSO...
YOU WERE THE ONE WHO TAUGHT ME...
TO LIFT MY SKIRT A TAD WHEN I WALK!
AND THE WARMTH OF A HAND, REACHING INTO THE DEPTHS OF LONELINESS.
...!

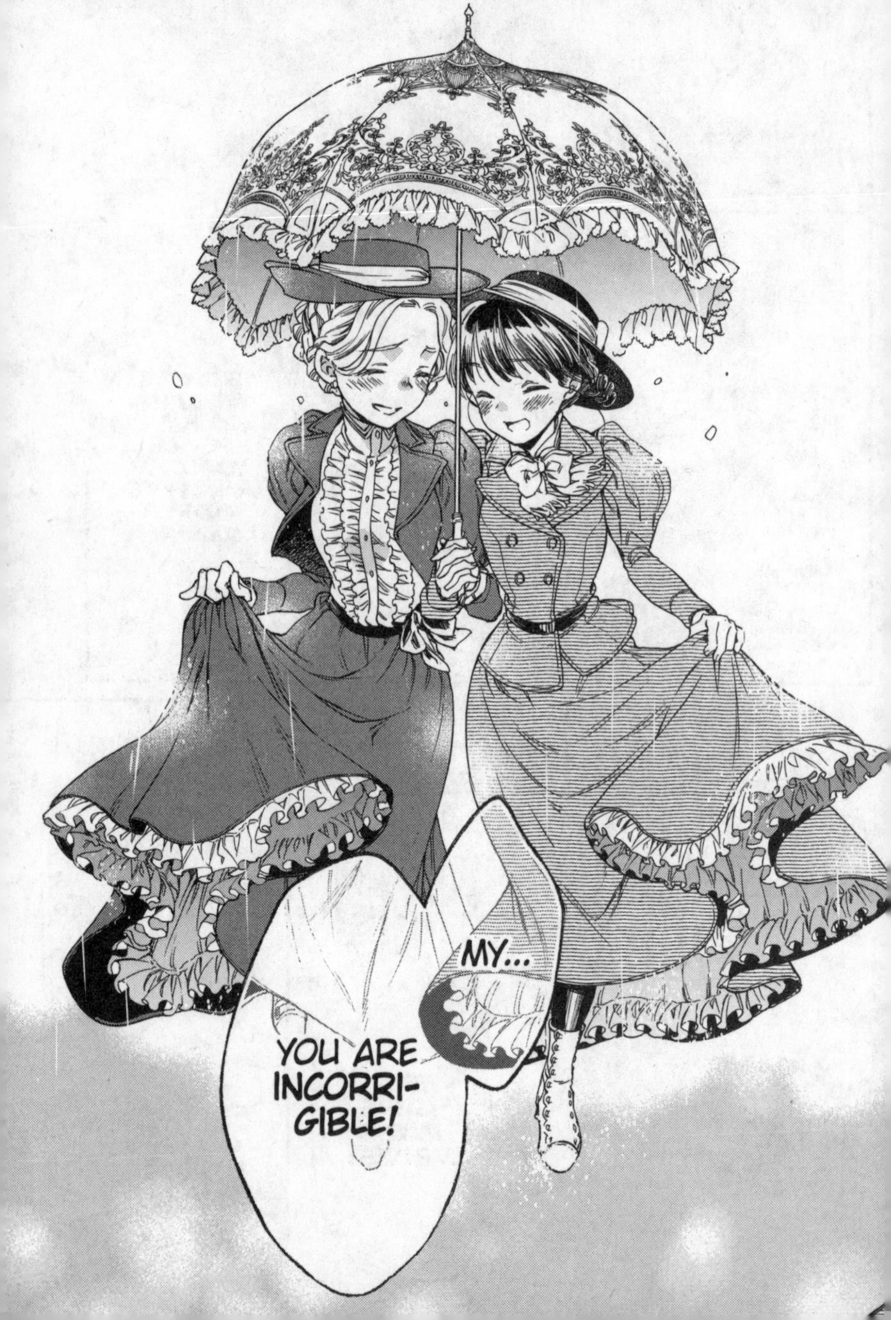
MY...
YOU ARE INCORRI-GIBLE!

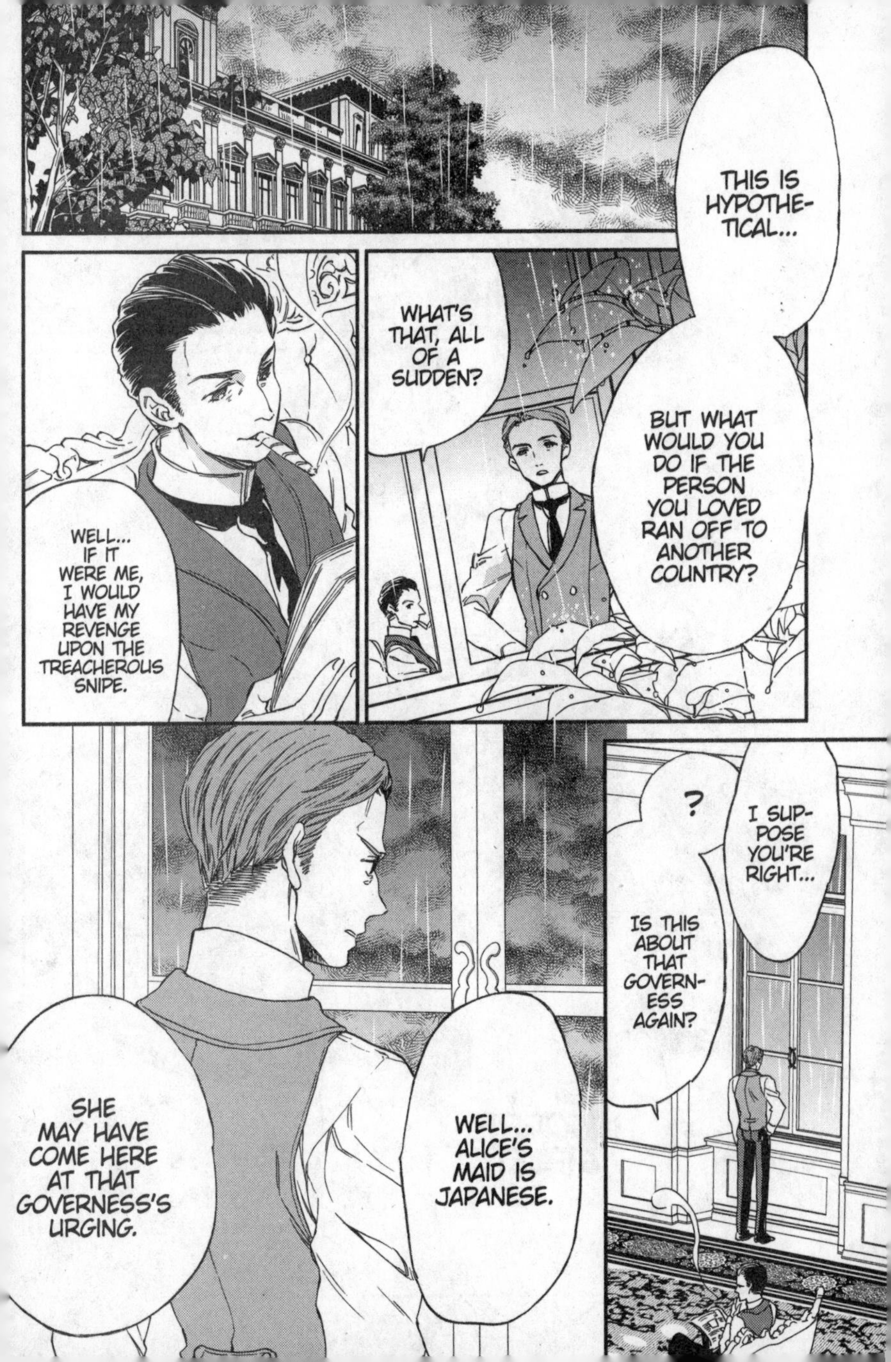
THIS IS HYPOTHETICAL...
BUT WHAT WOULD YOU DO IF THE PERSON YOU LOVED RAN OFF TO ANOTHER COUNTRY?
WHAT'S THAT, ALL OF A SUDDEN?
WELL... IF IT WERE ME, I WOULD HAVE MY REVENGE UPON THE TREACHEROUS SNIPE.
I SUPPOSE YOU'RE RIGHT...
?
IS THIS ABOUT THAT GOVERNESS AGAIN?
WELL... ALICE'S MAID IS JAPANESE.
SHE MAY HAVE COME HERE AT THAT GOVERNESS'S URGING.

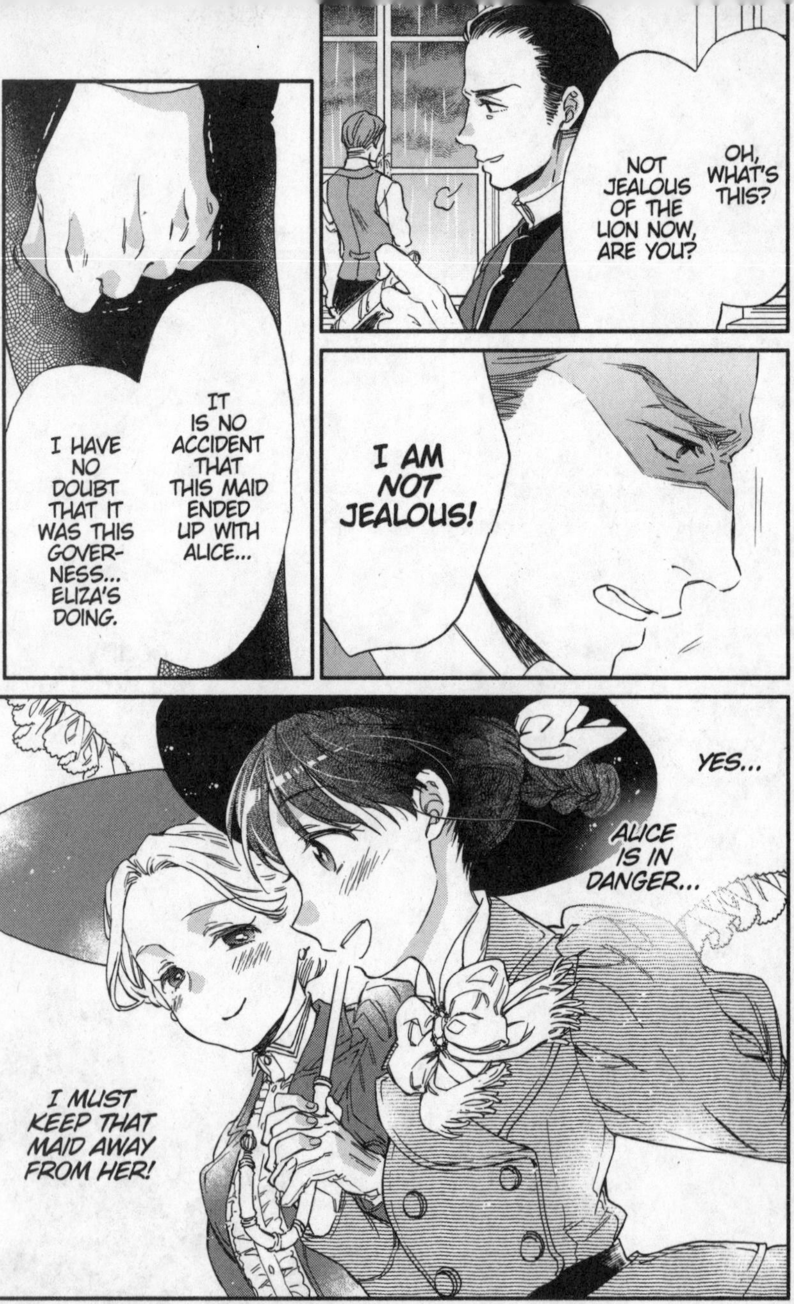
OH, WHAT'S THIS?
NOT JEALOUS OF THE LION NOW, ARE YOU?
I AM NOT JEALOUS!
IT IS NO ACCIDENT THAT THIS MAID ENDED UP WITH ALICE...
I HAVE NO DOUBT THAT IT WAS THIS GOVERNESS... ELIZA'S DOING.
YES...
ALICE IS IN DANGER...
I MUST KEEP THAT MAID AWAY FROM HER!

Goodbye, My Rose Garden **1** End

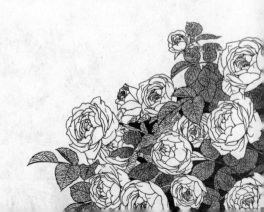

Goodbye,
my Rose Garden

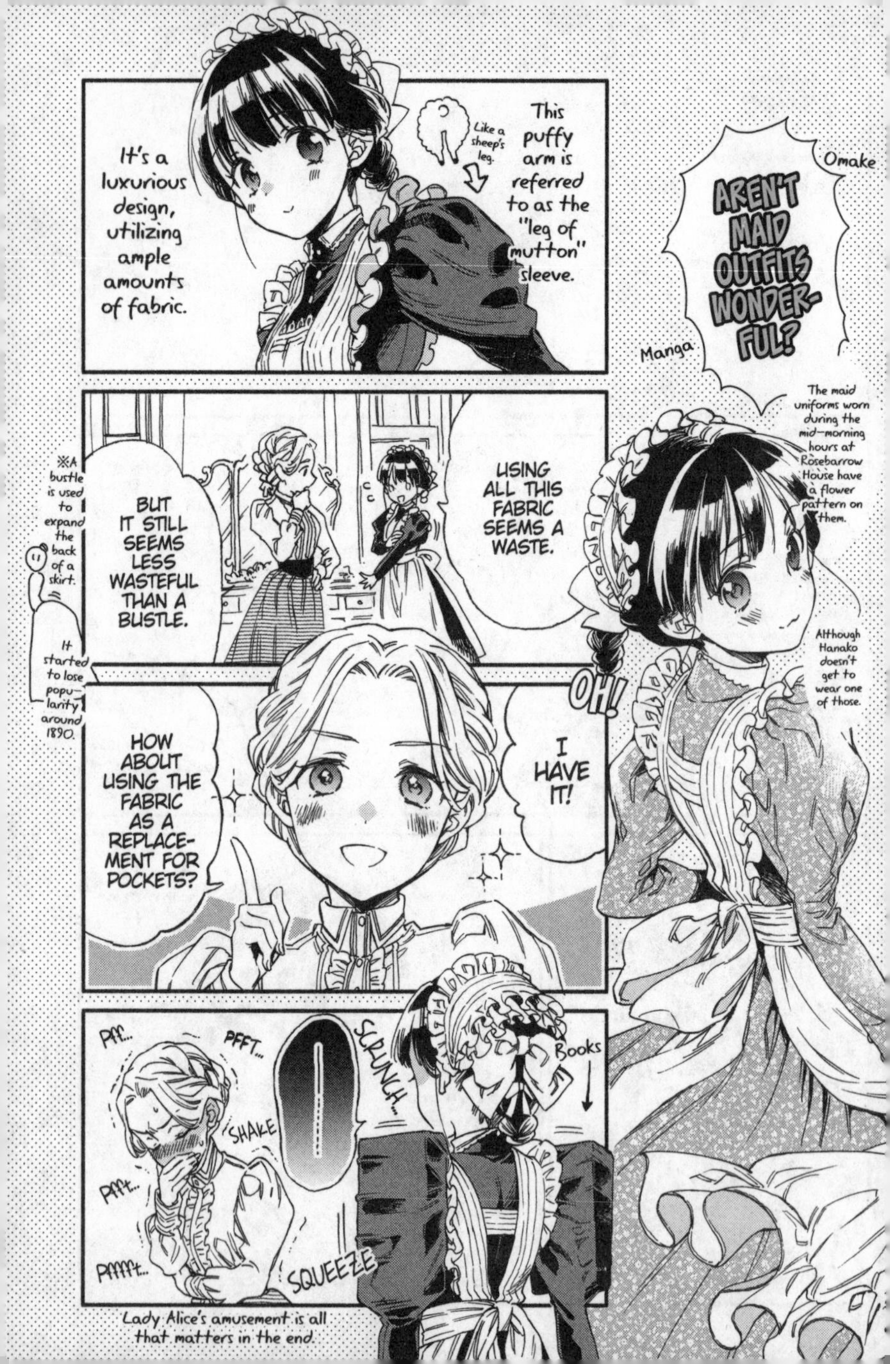
Omake
AREN'T MAID OUTFITS WONDERFUL?
Manga
The maid uniforms worn during the mid-morning hours at Rosebarrow House have a flower pattern on them.
Although Hanako doesn't get to wear one of those.
This puffy arm is referred to as the "leg of mutton" sleeve.
Like a sheep's leg.
It's a luxurious design, utilizing ample amounts of fabric.
USING ALL THIS FABRIC SEEMS A WASTE.
BUT IT STILL SEEMS LESS WASTEFUL THAN A BUSTLE.
※A bustle is used to expand the back of a skirt.
It started to lose popu-larity around 1890.
OH!
I HAVE IT!
HOW ABOUT USING THE FABRIC AS A REPLACE-MENT FOR POCKETS?
Books
SCRUNCH...
SQUEEZE
PFFT...
Pff...
SHAKE
Pfft...
Pffft...
Lady Alice's amusement is all that matters in the end.

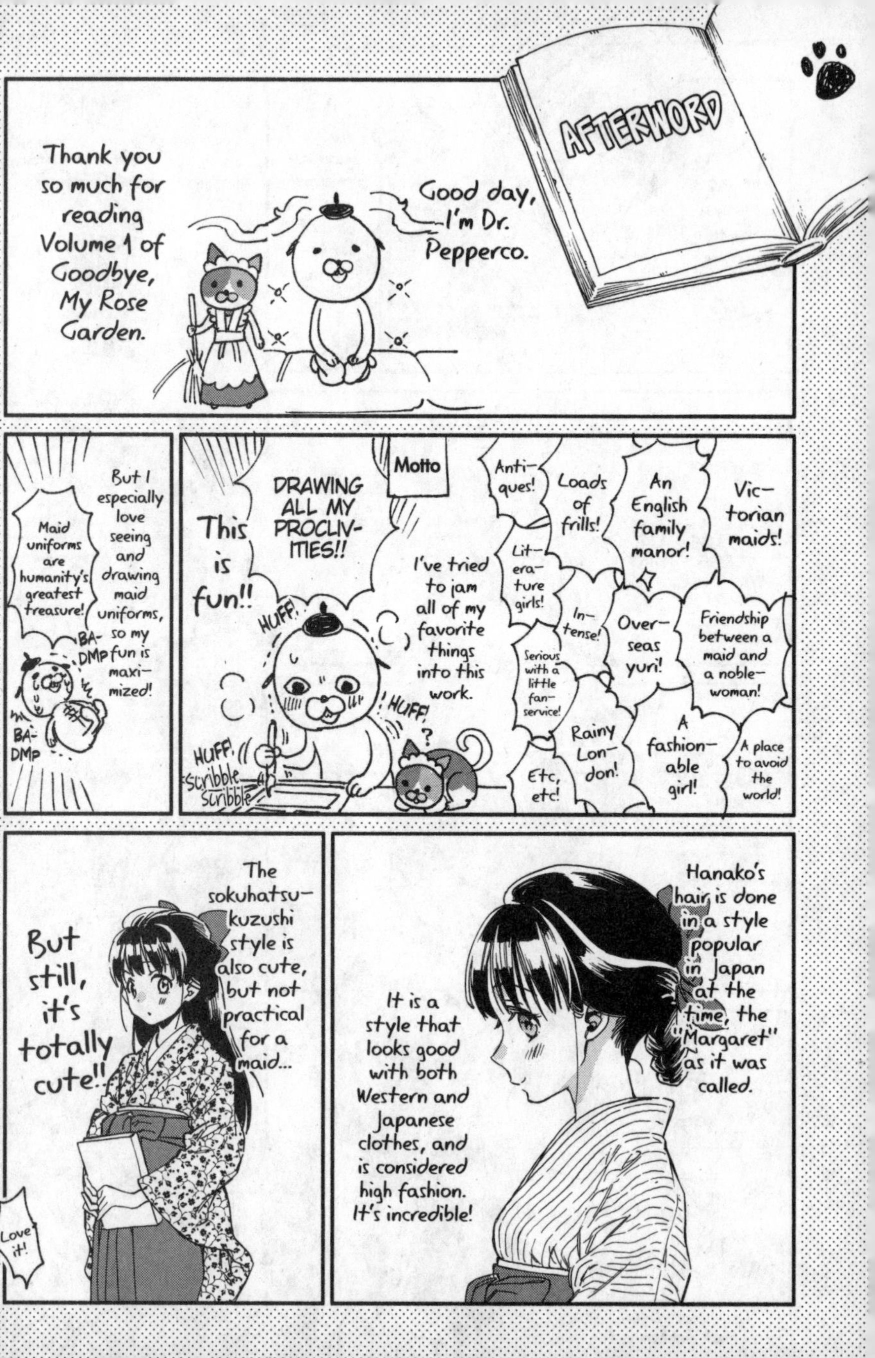
AFTERWORD
Good day, I'm Dr. Pepperco.
Thank you so much for reading Volume 1 of Goodbye, My Rose Garden.
Motto
Vic-torian maids!
An English family manor!
Loads of frills!
Anti-ques!
Friendship between a maid and a noble-woman!
Over-seas yuri!
In-tense!
Lit-era-ture girls!
Serious with a little fan-service!
A place to avoid the world!
A fashion-able girl!
Rainy Lon-don!
Etc, etc!
I've tried to jam all of my favorite things into this work.
DRAWING ALL MY PROCLIV-ITIES!!
This is fun!!
HUFF!
HUFF!
HUFF!
?
Scribble Scribble
But I especially love seeing and drawing maid uniforms, so my fun is maxi-mized!
Maid uniforms are humanity's greatest treasure!
BA-DMP
BA-DMP
Hanako's hair is done in a style popular in Japan at the time, the "Margaret" as it was called.
It is a style that looks good with both Western and Japanese clothes, and is considered high fashion. It's incredible!
The sokuhatsu-kuzushi style is also cute, but not practical for a maid...
But still, it's totally cute!!
Love it!

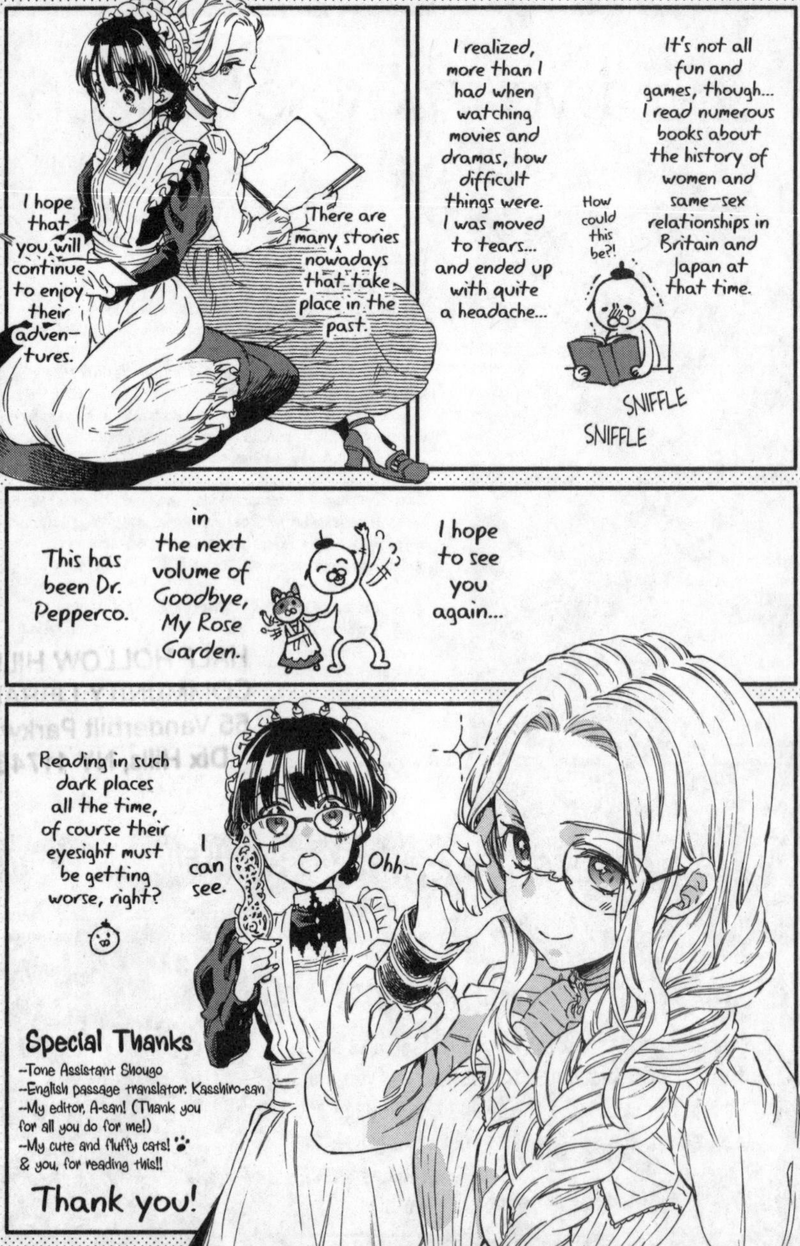
It's not all fun and games, though... I read numerous books about the history of women and same-sex relationships in Britain and Japan at that time.
How could this be?!
I realized, more than I had when watching movies and dramas, how difficult things were. I was moved to tears... and ended up with quite a headache...
SNIFFLE
SNIFFLE
There are many stories nowadays that take place in the past.
I hope that you will continue to enjoy their adven-tures.
I hope to see you again...
in the next volume of Goodbye, My Rose Garden.
This has been Dr. Pepperco.
Ohh-
I can see.
Reading in such dark places all the time, of course their eyesight must be getting worse, right?
Special Thanks
--Tone Assistant Shougo
--English passage translator: Kasshiro-san
--My editor, A-san! (Thank you for all you do for me!)
--My cute and fluffy cats!
& you, for reading this!!
Thank you!

SEVEN SEAS ENTERTAINMENT

 P9-DIG-642

Goodbye, *my* Rose Garden

story and art by DR. PEPPERCO

VOLUME 1

TRANSLATION
Amber Tamosaitis

ADAPTATION
Cae Hawksmoor

LETTERING AND RETOUCH
Kaitlyn Wiley

COVER DESIGN
Nicky Lim
(LOGO) **George Panella**

PROOFREADER
Danielle King

EDITOR
Jenn Grunigen

PREPRESS TECHNICIAN
Rhiannon Rasmussen-Silverstein

PRODUCTION MANAGER
Lissa Pattillo

MANAGING EDITOR
Julie Davis

ASSOCIATE PUBLISHER
Adam Arnold

PUBLISHER
Jason DeAngelis

GOODBYE, MY ROSE GARDEN VOL. 1
© Dr. Pepperco 2019
Originally published in Japan in 2019 by MAG Garden Corporation, Tokyo.
English translation rights arranged through TOHAN CORPORATION, Tokyo.

Seven Seas press and purchase enquiries can be sent to Marketing Manager Lianne Sentar at press@gomanga.com. Information regarding the distribution and purchase of digital editions is available from Digital Manager CK Russell at digital@gomanga.com.

Seven Seas and the Seven Seas logo are trademarks of Seven Seas Entertainment. All rights reserved.

ISBN: 978-1-64505-291-3

Printed in Canada

First Printing: April 2020

10 9 8 7 6 5 4 3 2 1

FOLLOW US ONLINE: *www.sevenseasentertainment.com*

READING DIRECTIONS

This book reads from *right to left*, Japanese style. If this is your first time reading manga, you start reading from the top right panel on each page and take it from there. If you get lost, just follow the numbered diagram here. It may seem backwards at first, but you'll get the hang of it! Have fun!!

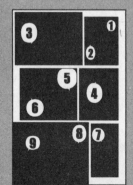

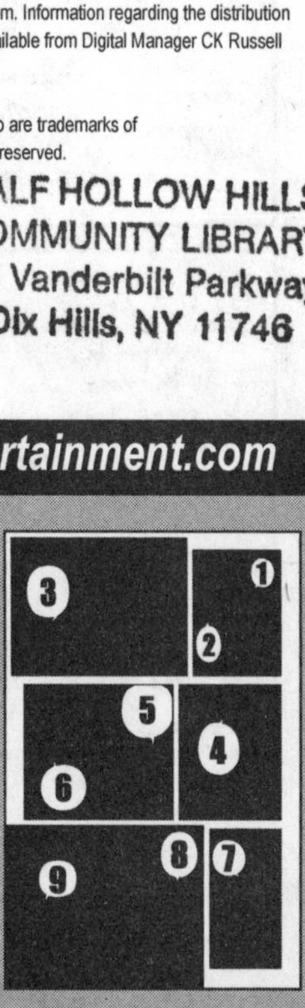